SO-BEF-885

Trademark Acknowledgments

Wrox has endeavored to correctly render trademarks for all the companies and products mentioned in this book with the appropriate use of capitals. However, Wrox is unable to guarantee the accuracy of this information.

Credits

Authors
Chris Knowles
Stephen Mohr
J Michael Palermo IV
Pieter Siegers
Darshan Singh

Commissioning Editor
Ian Blackham

Technical Editors
Richard Deeson
Jon Hill
Gerard Maguire

Managing Editor
Louay Fatoohi

Project Manager
Christianne Bailey

Author Agent
Cilmara Lion

Technical Reviewers
Kapil Apshankar
Danny Ayers
Daniel Cazzulino
Stuart Conway
Cristian Darie
Craig McQueen
Chad Osgood

Production Project Coordinator
Neil Lote

Illustrations
Neil Lote

Cover Design
Natalie O'Donnell

Proof Reader
Chris Smith

Index
Andrew Criddle

About the Authors

Chris Knowles

Chris started in IT in the late eighties as a mainframe programmer. Contracting took him throughout the UK, on to Dallas, Texas, and then Australia for a short twelve-month contract. Six years later he is still in Australia but, much to the relief of his parent's address book, has finally settled down just outside Canberra, the national capital. He lives there with his Australian wife, Louise, their two fantastic young kids, Katie and Matty, Banjo the dog, Bourbon the horse, Monty the pony – and a whole host of creepy-crawlies that could only come from Oz.

Canberra also provided Chris with the opportunity to switch from mainframe to Internet development, and he has spent much of the last four years immersing himself in the new and ever-changing technologies of the Web. He now splits his time, with varying degrees of success, between working for the small consultancy company run by him and his wife, being Katie and Matty's dad, and removing aforementioned creepy-crawlies from the corners of the house.

Chris always wanted to be an author, although he says this is not quite what he had in mind. He can be contacted at chris@pommiegranit.com. Chris wrote Chapter 8 and the case study.

> *I would like to thank the Wrox Press team for their infinite patience, Katie and Matty for keeping my feet firmly on the ground, and most of all, Louise, for just being there.*

Stephen Mohr

Stephen Mohr is a senior software systems architect with Omicron Consulting and XMLabs in Philadelphia, USA. He has over twelve years' experience developing software and systems for various platforms. Currently focusing on XML and related technologies as they apply to web applications, he has research interests in distributed computing and artificial intelligence. Stephen holds BS and MS degrees in computer science from Rensselaer Polytechnic Institute.

Stephen wrote Chapters 2 and 3, and contributed to Chapter 1.

J Michael Palermo IV

J. Michael Palermo IV is currently the Director of Development Technologies at Interface Technical Training – the technical training leader in the state of Arizona. His passions for technology encompass XML, SQL Server, and .NET. He is an MCT, MCSE, MCDBA, and MCSD. Michael also owns his own consulting firm (Palermo 4, LLC), which offers services to organizations across the United States regarding enterprise-level applications. In his spare time, Michael enjoys spending time with his family and maintaining coral reef aquariums.

Michael is currently building his web site at www.Palermo4.com, and can be reached at J.Michael@Palermo4.com. Michael's chapters are 4, 5, 6, and 7.

> *I want to first thank my wife Toshia and my two daughters for supporting me through very busy times while I was engaged in this project. I also owe Mike La Gioia with Interface Technical Training a special "thanks" for the overwhelming support he provided. Finally, I want to extend my appreciation to the Wrox team for patiently dealing with my hectic life while writing my chapters.*

Pieter Siegers

Pieter Siegers is an employee at a major Mexican Publishing Company, *Editora El Sol*, which is based in Monterrey, Mexico. This company publishes four major newspapers and has a number of smaller ones. Each of the four major newspapers has a dedicated web site, and they are constantly updated. He started building his Intranet and Internet Knowledge Base back in 1996, developing intranets for replacing internal applications. In 1999, he and a select group of developers set up the company's first public Internet web site, elnorte.com, followed by reforma.com, then mural.com, and recently palabra.com. In the meantime he continues to explore emerging web technologies, mostly XML-related, in addition to solving any performance issues that arise during implementation and support of the web sites. Today, his main job at the company is to diffuse new web technologies into a developer team of about 35 people.

He has been writing articles for Wrox's *ASPToday* (www.asptoday.com) site since 1999, and has a passion for discovering and using new technologies, always searching for improved application performance and code quality.

In his spare time, he loves to walk in the mountains that surround the city of Monterrey or ride a bicycle, with his Mexican wife and two children. Another passion is traveling, although accommodating this and the heavy workload is difficult. Originally from the Netherlands, he and his small family have lived in Mexico for the last seven years, where he tries to learn the culture and habits, and of course enjoys the delicious food and drink.

He can be reached at pieter.siegers@elnorte.com. Pieter wrote Chapters 9 and 10.

To my wife and children, for their love, their belief in me, and their great support.

Darshan Singh

Darshan Singh works as Senior Developer at InstallShield Software Corporation. He has been working with ASP.NET for more than 18 months, and has created around a dozen intranet and extranet sites based on ASP.NET and XML. His specialties include SQL Server 2000, XML, and .NET development.

Darshan Singh also manages the XML community web site at www.PerfectXML.com, and can be reached at darshan@PerfectXML.com.

Darshan contributed to Chapter 1.

I would like to dedicate my work on this book to James Robinson of Wrox Press. James, you are the best!

Table of Contents

Table of Contents

Table of Contents

Table of Contents

Table of Contents

Introduction

Ever since XML first arrived on the scene in the late 1990s, it has been the focus of a lot of fervent activity and wild speculation. Now, it is beginning to come of age, and it's steadily permeating an increasing proportion of the computing world. Based on nothing but ordinary text, it offers a means of communication between just about any two computer systems, be they new or old, on an intranet, or across the world on the other side of a company firewall.

XML, together with the XML-based standard of SOAP, forms an important part of the structure upon which Web Services are built, and this will only increase its prevalence and importance. It will become increasingly important for web developers to know how to capitalize on XML and its related technologies, so that they can efficiently extract data from XML documents, filter it, merge it, and display it in applications – especially web applications.

ASP.NET can handle XML data from a wide range of sources, from plain old XML documents on disk, to relational databases on remote servers. In this book, we'll examine how to access these sources, apply transformations to the data once we have it, and render that data for display. We'll also look at how to analyze the performance of our XML web applications, interpret the results to remove bottlenecks, and put it all together in an e-commerce case study.

Microsoft's .NET Framework makes heavy use of XML, and forms the perfect platform for creating web applications with XML functionality. In this book, we'll investigate the areas of ASP.NET that developers will need to exploit in order to create useful and efficient web applications that use XML.

Who Is This Book For?

This book is aimed at the experienced web developer who already has a grasp of ASP.NET and C#, and a basic familiarity with XML and related technologies.

Intermediate in level, this book aims to augment the skill set of those seeking to progress their .NET experience, and to discover how to apply the XML capabilities of the .NET Framework to their web applications.

What Does This Book Cover?

Chapter 1 provides a quick roadmap of the world of web development, looking at important architectures that can be applied, and taking a quick tour of XML-related specifications and standards that you may encounter when programming for the Web.

Chapter 2 discusses two fundamental classes for handling XML from web pages – XmlReader and XmlWriter – and their derived classes. These are lightweight classes that provide an efficient but forward-only way of reading and writing XML documents, and offer validation against an XML Schema or DTD if required.

Chapter 3 moves on to cover the more powerful but consequently less efficient XmlDocument class, and associated classes for manipulating XML structures. Based on the W3C Document Object Model (DOM) specification, this class supports random access to elements and attributes, and lets us filter data according to our requirements.

Chapter 4 examines the XPath standard, which underpins many technologies that surround XML, and is sometimes referred to as the SQL of XML. We see how to use its non-XML syntax to search through an XML document from ASP.NET, and extract only those elements that we want to look at further.

Chapter 5 takes a close look at ASP.NET's support for the XML language for transforming XML documents from one format to another: XSLT. We see how this technology can allow us to render data taken from XML documents or relational databases for display in an HTML browser.

Chapter 6 checks out the key features of the cornerstone of XML data access in .NET – namely, ADO.NET – and demonstrates its intrinsic capabilities for handling XML. We use a DataSet object in an ASP.NET page to read data from an XML document and a relational database, applying an XSLT stylesheet for good measure.

Chapter 7 looks at the .NET classes that are specially tailored for accessing relational data from SQL Server databases. We show how to query SQL Server to obtain results in XML format, and how to capture those results for display in our ASP.NET pages.

Chapter 8 delves into the world of XML Web Services, examining the transport protocols and structures that enable these poster children of the Internet age to interact with all manner of computers, from modern palmtops, to monolithic mainframes.

Chapter 9 introduces a web application based on the upcoming XQuery technology, using Microsoft's add-in XQuery classes, which conform to the W3C Working Draft. XQuery is an XML-based language for specifying queries to run against XML documents, and as we see here, is now sufficiently advanced to capitalize upon in web applications.

Chapter 10 examines that important topic for all web developers: application performance, concentrating on applications that use XML. We have a close look at how the Application Center Test product, included with Visual Studio .NET Enterprise Edition, can be used to highlight performance trouble spots.

We cap it all off with an in-depth **Case Study** to see how what we've learned during the course of the book can be applied to a real-world web site. We walk through the process of creating a fully functioning XML-dependent e-commerce site, with a product catalog from which items can be added to a basket, and then orders placed.

What You Need to Use This Book

To run the samples in this book, you need to have the following software installed:

- ❏   Windows 2000/XP Professional or higher, with IIS installed
- ❏   Any version of Visual Studio .NET
- ❏   SQL Server 2000, or MSDE (provided with VS.NET)

In addition, the book assumes:

- ❏   An intermediate knowledge of the C# language
- ❏   A basic understanding of SQL Server and its query syntax
- ❏   Some familiarity with XML

Conventions

We've used a range of different styles of text and layout in this book to help differentiate between the different kinds of information. This section contains examples of the styles used, together with explanations of what they mean.

Code has several styles. If we're talking about code in the text – for example, if we're discussing a `for` loop – it's in `this font`. If it's a block of code that can be typed as a program and run, then it will appear separate from the main text, within a gray box:

```
<?xml version 1.0?>
```

Sometimes, code is presented in a mixture of styles, like this:

```
<?xml version 1.0?>
<invoice>
  <part>
    <name>Widget</name>
    <price>$10.00</price>
  </part>
</invoice>
```

In this case, the code with a white background is code we have already seen, while lines highlighted in gray represent new code to be added to the program.

Advice, hints, and background information come in this type of font.

Important pieces of information appear in boxes like this.

Bullet points appear indented, and marked as follows:

❑ **Important words** use a bold type font.

❑ Words that appear on the screen, or in menus like Open or Close options, are in a similar sans-serif font to the one you might see on a Windows desktop.

❑ Words that represent keys to press on the keyboard are shown in italics, like *Ctrl* and *Enter*.

Customer Support

We always value hearing from our readers, and we want to know what you think about this book: what you liked, what you didn't like, and what you think we can do better next time. You can send us your comments, either by returning the reply card in the back of the book, or by e-mail to feedback@wrox.com. Please be sure to mention the book title in your message.

How to Download the Sample Code for the Book

When you visit the Wrox web site, www.wrox.com, locate the title through our Search facility or by using one of the title lists. Click Download Code on the book's detail page, or on the Download item in the Code column for title lists.

The files that are available for download from our site have been archived using WinZip. When you've saved the archives to a folder on your hard drive, you need to extract the files using a decompression program such as WinZip or PKUnzip. When you extract the files, the code will be extracted into separate folders for each chapter of this book, so ensure your extraction utility is set to use folder names.

Errata

We've made every effort to make sure that there are no errors in the text or in the code. However, no one is perfect and mistakes do occur. If you find an error in one of our books, such as a spelling mistake or a faulty piece of code, we would be very grateful to hear about it. By sending in errata you may save another reader hours of frustration, and of course, you will be helping us to provide even higher quality information. Simply e-mail the information to support@wrox.com – your information will be checked and if correct, posted to the errata page for that title, and used in reprints of the book.

To find errata on the web site, go to www.wrox.com, and simply locate the title through our Advanced Search or title list. Click the Book Errata link below the cover graphic on the book's detail page.

E-Mail Support

If you wish to query a problem in the book with an expert who knows the book in detail, then e-mail support@wrox.com with the title of the book and the last four numbers of the ISBN in the subject field of the e-mail. A typical e-mail should include the following things:

❑　The **title of the book**, the **last four digits of the ISBN** (7248), and the **page number** of the problem.

❑　Your **name**, **contact information**, and the **problem** in the body of the message.

We need the above details to save your time and ours – we *never* send unsolicited junk mail. When you send an e-mail message, it will go through the following chain of support:

❑　Customer Support – Your message is delivered to our customer support staff, who are the first people to read it. They have files on most frequently asked questions and will answer anything general about the book or the web site immediately.

❑　Editorial – Deeper queries are forwarded to the technical editor responsible for that book. They have experience with the programming language or particular product, and are able to answer detailed technical questions on the subject.

❑　The Authors – Finally, in the unlikely event that the editor cannot answer your problem, they will forward the request to the author. All Wrox authors are glad to help support their books. They will e-mail the customer and the editor with their response, and again all readers should benefit.

The Wrox support process can only offer support for issues that are directly pertinent to the content of our published title. Support for questions that fall outside the scope of normal book support is provided via the community lists of our http://p2p.wrox.com/ forum.

p2p.wrox.com

For author and peer discussion, join the P2P mailing lists. Our unique system provides **programmer to programmer**™ contact on mailing lists, forums, and newsgroups, all in addition to our one-to-one e-mail support system. If you post a query to P2P, you can be confident that the many Wrox authors and other industry experts who are present on our mailing lists are examining it. At p2p.wrox.com, you will find a number of different lists that will help you not only while you read this book, but also as you develop your own applications. Particularly appropriate to this book are the aspx and the aspx_professional lists.

To subscribe to a mailing list, just follow these steps:

1. Go to http://p2p.wrox.com/.

2. Choose the appropriate category from the left menu bar.

3. Click on the mailing list you wish to join.

4. Follow the instructions to subscribe, and fill in your e-mail address and password.

5. Reply to the confirmation e-mail you receive.

6. Use the subscription manager to join more lists and set your e-mail preferences.

Why this System Offers the Best Support

You can choose to join the mailing lists, or you can receive them as a weekly digest. If you don't have the time (or the facility) to receive the mailing lists, then you can search our online archives. Junk and spam mails are deleted, and your own e-mail address is protected by the Lyris system. Queries about joining or leaving lists, and any other general queries about lists, should be sent to listsupport@p2p.wrox.com.

Introduction to XML Technologies

In this chapter, we'll look at current and upcoming Extensible Markup Language (XML). We'll begin by describing what XML is and then talk about where it can help us, some related standards, and focus on some important design considerations when writing an XML application.

More specifically, this chapter follows this route map:

- ❑ An Introduction to XML
- ❑ The Appeal of XML
- ❑ XML in Vertical Industries
- ❑ Web Architecture Overview
- ❑ ASP.NET Web Development
- ❑ XML 1.0 Syntax
- ❑ Processing XML
- ❑ XML Data Binding and XML Serialization
- ❑ Validating XML
- ❑ Navigating, Transforming, and Formatting XML
- ❑ Other Standards in the XML Family
- ❑ XML Security Standards
- ❑ XML Messaging

By the end of this chapter, you'll have a good understanding of the key XML standards, what they do, where they fit, and how they relate to each other.

An Introduction to XML

The success of XML can be gauged by the fact that since its release in February 1998, there are now more than 450 other standards based on XML or directly relating to XML in some way. A day seldom goes by without our encountering XML somewhere, either in a press release, or white paper, or online/print article. Almost all new (mostly Web) application development jobs post XML experience as a preferred skill to have. Microsoft's .NET Framework represents a paradigm shift to a platform that uses and supports XML extensively. Every database and application vendor is adding some kind of support for XML to their products. The success of XML cannot be overemphasized. No matter which platform, which language you are working with, knowledge of this technology will serve you well.

What is XML?

In its simplest form, the XML specification is a set of guidelines, defined by the World Wide Web Consortium (W3C), for describing structured data in plain text. Like HTML, XML is a markup language based on tags within angled brackets, and is also a subset of SGML (Standard Generalized Markup Language). As with HTML, the textual nature of XML makes the data highly portable and broadly deployable. In addition, XML documents can be created and edited in any standard text editor.

But unlike HTML, XML does not have a fixed set of tags; rather it is a meta-language that allows creation of other markup languages. It is this ability to define new tags that makes XML a truly extensible language. Another difference from HTML, which focuses on presentation, is XML's focus on data and its structure. For these reasons, XML is much stricter in its rules of syntax, or "well-formedness", which require all tags to have a corresponding closing tag, not to overlap, and more. For instance, in XML you may define a tag, or more strictly the start of an **element**, like this, `<invoice>`, and it could contain the attribute `customer="1234"` like so: `<invoice customer="1234">`. This element would have to be completed by a corresponding closing tag `</invoice>` for the XML to be well-formed and useable.

The W3C

The W3C is an independent standards body consisting of about 500 members, formed in 1994 under the direction of Tim Berners-Lee. Its primary purpose is to publish standards for technologies directly related to the Web, such as HTML and XML.

However, the syntax and usage that the W3C devises do not have governmental backing, and are thus not officially 'standards' as such, hence the W3C's terminology of 'Recommendation'. However, these Recommendations are de facto standards in many industries, due to the impartial nature of the W3C itself.

Once a standard has achieved Recommendation status, it will not be modified or added to any further. Before reaching that status, standards are first classed as Working Draft, which is still subject to change, and finally a Last Call Working Draft, where no significant changes are envisaged.

XML Design Goals

There were ten broad goals that the designers of the XML 1.0 specification (http://www.w3.org/TR/REC-xml) set out to achieve:

1. XML must be readily usable over the Internet.

2. XML must support a wide variety of applications.

3. XML must be compatible with SGML.

4. It must be easy to write programs that process XML documents.

5. The number of optional features in XML is to be kept to the absolute minimum, ideally zero.

6. XML documents should be human-readable and reasonably clear.

7. The XML specification should be ready quickly.

8. The principles of the specification must be formal and concise.

9. XML documents must be easy to create.

10. Terseness in XML markup is of minimal importance.

Overall, the team did a pretty good job of meeting these aims. As plain text, like HTML, XML side-steps many platform-specific issues and is well suited to travel over the Internet. In addition, the support for Unicode makes XML a universal solution for data representation (Design Goal 1).

It is a common misconception that XML is useful only for Web applications. However, in reality, the application of XML is not restricted to the Web. As XML is architecture-neutral it can easily be incorporated in any application design (Design Goal 2). In this chapter we'll see how and where XML is being used today.

XML is in effect simplified SGML, and if desired can be used with SGML tools for publishing (Design Goal 3). For more information on the additional restrictions that XML places on documents beyond those of SGML, see http://www.w3.org/TR/NOTE-sgml-xml-971215.

Apart from the textual nature of XML, another reason for XML's success is the tools (such as parsers) and the surrounding standards (such as XPath, XSLT), which help in creating and processing XML documents (Design Goal 4).

The notion behind XML was to create a simple, yet extensible, meta markup language, and this was achieved by keeping the optional features to the minimum, and making XML syntax strict (at least, in comparison to HTML) (Design Goal 5).

Prior to XML, various binary formats existed to store data, which required special tools to view and read that data. The textual (if verbose) nature of XML makes it human readable. An XML document can be opened in any text editor and analyzed if required (Design Goal 6).

11

The simplicity of XML, the high availability of tools and related standards, the separation of the semantics of a document from its presentation, and XML's extensibility all result from meeting Design Goals 7 through 10.

Before looking at XML syntax and XML-related standards, let's first review some of the applications of XML.

The Appeal of XML

The second design goal of the XML specification was that XML's usefulness should not be restricted to the Web, and that it should support a wide variety of applications. Looking at the current situation, there's no doubt that this goal has been very well met.

The Universal Data Exchange Format

When Microsoft announced OLE DB as part of the Windows DNA initiative, everybody started talking about what it was promising, namely Universal Data Access. The underlying concept is that, as long as we have the proper OLE DB provider for the backend, we can access the data using either low-level OLE DB interfaces or by using the high-level ADO object model. The idea of Universal Data Access was very well received on the Microsoft platform, and is still a very successful model for accessing data from any unspecified data store. However, the missing piece was the data *exchange*. There was no straightforward way to send data from one data-store to the other, over the Internet, or across platforms.

Today, if there is need to transfer data from one platform to the other, the first thing that comes to mind is XML, for the reasons already discussed. If we compare XML as a means of data transfer against the traditional Electronic Data Interchange (EDI), XML wins hands down because of its openness, simplicity, extensibility, and lower implementation cost. This lower cost stems mainly from XML's use of the Internet for data exchange, which is not easily achieved (if not impossible) with EDI, which relies on private networks.

Let's take an example of how XML enables universal data exchange. Consider a company, ABC Corp., that has outsourced some of its technical support to another company, XYZ Corp. Let's assume that there is a need to send support requests from ABC Corp to XYZ Corp, and vice versa, everyday. To add to the soup, the companies are located in different countries, and do not share a network. In addition, ABC Corp. runs SQL Server 2000 on Windows 2000 Advanced Server, while XYZ Corp. runs Oracle 8 on Sun Solaris. As both SQL Server and Oracle support XML, and there are many tools and APIs available to import and export XML, and as XML data can be very easily accessed over HTTP or FTP, the clear choice here would be to exchange the support requests in XML format. The two companies can establish a **Schema** to define the basic structure of their XML documents, which they then adhere to when sending XML data to each other. We'll discuss Schemas later in the chapter.

Business transactions over the Internet require interoperability while exchanging messages, and integrating applications. XML acts like the glue that allows different systems to work together. It is helping to standardize the business processes and transaction messages (invoices, purchase orders, catalogs, etc.), and also the method by which these messages are transmitted. E-business initiatives such as ebXML, BizTalk, xCBL, and RosettaNet make use of XML and facilitate e-business, supply chain and business-to-business (B2B) integration. XML mainly helps in streamlining the data exchange format.

XML – Industrial Glue

XML is not just well suited for data exchange between companies. Many programming tasks today are all about application integration: web applications integrate multiple Web Services, e-commerce sites integrate legacy inventory and pricing systems, intranet applications integrate existing business applications.

All these applications can be held together by the exchange of XML documents. XML is often an ideal choice, not because someone at Microsoft (or Sun or IBM) likes XML, but because XML, as a text format, can be used with many different communications protocols. Since text has always been ubiquitous in computing, standard representations are well established, and are supported by many different platforms. Thus, XML can be the language that allows your Windows web application to communicate easily with your inventory system running on Linux because both support Internet protocols and both support text. What is more, through the .NET classes for Windows and various Java class libraries for Linux, both support XML.

Data Structures for Business

We're all used to data structures in programs. In theory, these structures model the business objects – the "things" we deal with in our programs – which describe a business and its activities. A retail business may have structures to represent customers; or in manufacturing, structures might model the products that the company makes.

Ideally, these data structures would be idealized representations of the business entities that they model, and their meaning would be independent of the program for which they were originally designed. In practice however, data structures don't faithfully replicate their real-world counterparts, as, through pressures of time or technical limitations, programmers generally employ shortcuts and workarounds in order to make the application work. To deal with a particular problem, programmers all too often opt for the quick and easy solution, adding a little flag here or a small string there. Such quick fixes are commonly found in working systems, which can become encrusted with so many such adornments that they can no longer usefully be exchanged with other programs. They are far removed from the faithful representations of real-world entities that they should be, and they serve merely to keep a specific application going and no more.

This specialization impedes reuse, hindering application-to-application integration. If you have five different representations of a customer throughout your organization, the web site that talks to your legacy applications will have to include a lot of hard-to-maintain code to translate from one object to another. It's important to create structures that promote integration as we go forward.

Making XML vocabularies that represent the core structures of a business is an excellent way to go about this. We can develop a vocabulary for each major object or concept in the business detailed enough for programs to manipulate objects of that type using that vocabulary alone. For example, if we are describing a person outside our organization, we could stop at the name and telephone number. This might serve our current needs, but could cause problems when we develop further applications. It is worth the initial effort to establish a more comprehensive, 'future-proof' representation, such as that represented by the following XML document:

```xml
<ExternalPerson>
  <Person id="jack-fastwind">
    <Name first="Jack" last="Happy" prefix="Mr."/>
    <EContact>
```

```
            <Telephone>2095551212</Telephone>
            <EMail>jack@fastwind.com</EMail>
        </EContact>
        <Title>Engineering Manager</Title>
    </Person>
    <loc:Address xmlns:loc="urn:xmlabs-com-schemas:location">
        <loc:Street1>180 Pershing Blvd</loc:Street1>
        <loc:City>Cheyenne</loc:City>
        <loc:PoliticalDivision>WY</loc:PoliticalDivision>
        <loc:PostalCode>82009</loc:PostalCode>
    </loc:Address>
    <Organization id="proto01">
        <OrgName>Fast Wind Prototypes, Inc.</OrgName>
        <Classification id="x12345"/>
    </Organization>
</ExternalPerson>
```

This brief document is enough to identify the person, communicate with them, and locate them. There are probably other details we could add, depending on the needs of our business.

On a related note, when creating these schemas, it's unwise to do so within the context of a single project team. Get the buy-in of a variety of stakeholders. Preferably, developing the schemas for a business is performed separately to any single programming task. Otherwise, the risk is that the vocabulary will get specialized to a particular application (just as binary formats did), or the schema will lack the support of other groups and the vocabulary will never get adopted. If you are lucky, a standards body associated with your particular market may have already developed schemas suitable for your business, in which case all that development work has already been done for you, not to mention the other potential benefits of adopting an industry standard.

The effort of devising a schema divorces data from application logic, a separation that becomes all the easier to maintain in applications. If the vocabulary is well designed, it will facilitate the creation of database schemas to hold the data, and code components to operate on them, and the code and database schemas will be useful throughout the business. When the time comes to integrate two applications built on one of these schemas, the applications already have a suitable communications medium as both use XML documents conforming to the same schemas.

A word of caution is in order, however. XML is not especially compact and efficient as a storage medium, and you certainly don't want to model every data structure in XML, nor do you necessarily want to use XML documents as your primary data structures in applications. Still, for modeling a large-scale, widely-used business concept, the advantages of XML make it hard to beat.

Merging Data

Integrating data with application logic is simple when there is a single database technology in use. Things get harder when several databases – say Oracle and SQL Server – or a mix of relational and non-relational data are employed. If all the data for a given concept resides in a single data store, life is still simple. It is when the data for a concept is spread across various storage media that there is some integration to perform. For example, employee information might be stored in a relational database in Human Relations and an LDAP directory (an hierarchical store) for the IT department. Putting together an employee's address (from HR) with their e-mail URL (from IT) would require dealing with two disparate structures. Both formats are binary, but one is relational, with a flat sequence of rows. The other is hierarchical, so may contain similar information in a nested format.

If, however, the primary concepts are modeled in XML, integration like this becomes a lot easier. Technologies like XPath and XSLT can be used to splice, insert, or otherwise manipulate data from multiple sources to get the final, integrated result required.

Consider the employee information example again where we need some information from the HR database, while other information must be drawn from the IT directory. We have to merge the two subsets to get the final structure relevant to our needs. If we are dealing with native binary formats, we'll end up writing a lot of special-purpose code. On the other hand, if we convert the results from each source into XML before performing the merge, we can use XPath to retrieve the data for each employee, and the Document Object Model or some other XML-related technology to perform the merging. Better still, many data stores are becoming equipped with native support for XML, so the data store may be able to output the data directly in XML, as depicted in the following figure. Performing initial conversions like this can open up the possibility of using off-the-shelf XML tools to work on the data, greatly reducing the code we have to write.

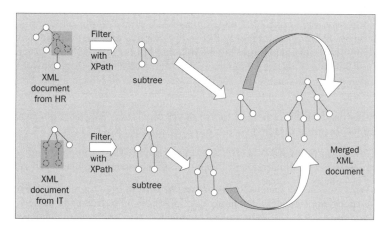

Separation of Content and Presentation

With HTML, the actual data and its presentation logic are interleaved. HTML tags do not add any semantic meaning to the data content, but just describe the presentation details. This approach makes it hard to manipulate just the data or just the way it is presented. The Cascading Style Sheets (CSS) initiative made an effort to separate data from the presentation, but still many Web pages squirrel data away inside presentation tags.

As XML makes no assumption about how tags might be rendered on the display device (browser, wireless cell phone, PDA, or whatever), but simply provides a means to structure data with tags we define ourselves, it is quite natural to use the same XML data document and present it differently on different devices. This separation of data from presentation also facilitates easy access to the data.

Increasing numbers of HTML Web sites now offer an XML interface. For example, Amazon offers an XML interface that allows its associates to build targeted, customized Amazon placements (http://associates.amazon.com/). Google exposes its search engine via a SOAP-based XML interface (http://www.google.com/apis/). Microsoft's MapPoint .NET initiative allows us to integrate maps, driving directions, distance calculations, and proximity searches into our applications. Separating data from presentation is the key allowing developers to build new and innovative applications.

Other W3C standards, such as Extensible Stylesheet Language Formatting Objects (XSL-FO) and Transformations (XSLT), can be used for the formatting and presentation of XML data.

XML-based Languages

Already, many new markup languages based on XML syntax have been created to meet the needs of specific application domains. The most well known of these have general utility, and include:

❑ **MathML** (http://www.w3.org/TR/MathML2) enables mathematical equations to be served, received, and processed on the Web.

❑ **SMIL** (Synchronized Multimedia Integration Language, http://www.w3.org/TR/smil20) is an XML-based language for writing interactive multimedia presentations. Using the XML syntax, it allows the mixing of many types of media, text, video, graphics, audio, and vector animations together, synchronizing them to a timeline, for delivery as a presentation over the Web.

❑ **SOAP** (http://www.w3c.org/2002/ws) applies XML syntax to messaging, and is at the core of Web Services. SOAP enables highly distributed applications that can run over the Internet without any firewall issues. Extra layers are being built on top of SOAP to make it more secure and reliable. These layers include WS-Security, WS-Routing, WS-License, and so on, which form part of Microsoft and IBM's Global XML Web Services (GXA) Specification, discussed later in this chapter.

❑ **SVG** (Scalable Vector Graphics, http://www.w3.org/TR/SVG) is a language for describing two-dimensional vector and mixed vector/raster graphics in XML.

❑ **VoiceXML** (http://www.w3.org/TR/voicexml20) is an XML-based language for the definition of voice interfaces and dialogs, and it can be used in v-commerce and call centers.

❑ **WML** (Wireless Markup Language, http://www.wapforum.org) is a markup language based on XML for specifying content and defining user interfaces for narrowband devices, including cellular phones and pagers. It has been optimized for small screens and limited memory capacity.

❑ **XML-RPC** (XML-based Remote Procedure Calling protocol, http://www.xmlrpc.com) uses XML as the encoding, HTTP as the transport, and facilitates cross-platform remote procedure calls over the Internet.

❑ **XForms** (http://www.w3.org/TR/xforms) is an embryonic XML standard aimed at creating a platform-independent way of defining forms for the Web. An XForm is divided into the data model, instance data, and the user interface – allowing separation of presentation and content. This facilitates reuse, provides strong typing, and reduces the number of round-trips to the server, as well as promising device independence and a reduced need for scripting. Take a look at Chapter 9 for a working example based on XForms.

Content Management and Document Publishing

Using XML to store content enables a more advanced approach to personalization, as it allows for manipulation at the content level (opposed to the document level). That is, individual XML elements can be selected based on the user preferences. We could store preferences with client-side cookies, which we access to filter our XML content for each individual user. This filtering can be performed with the XML style sheet languages (XSL-FO and XSLT), allowing us to use a single source file, and manipulate it to create the appropriate content for each user, and even for multiple devices (cell phones, Web browsers, Adobe PDF, and so on).

Using XML for content management, instead of proprietary file formats, readily enables integrating that content with other applications, and facilitates searching for specific information.

WebDAV, the web-based Distributed Authoring and Versioning protocol from the IETF (http://www.webdav.org), provides an XML vocabulary for examining and maintaining web content. It can be used to create and manage content on remote servers, as if they were local servers in a distributed environment. WebDAV features include locking, metadata properties, namespace support, versioning, and access control. XML is used to define various WebDAV methods and properties.

Other standards related to XML metadata and content management include RDF (Resource Description Framework), PRISM (Publishing Requirements for Industry Standard Metadata), and ICE (Information and Content Exchange), whose description is beyond the scope of this chapter.

XML and Instant Messaging

Jabber (http://www.jabber.org/) is an example of how XML can be used for Instant Messaging. It is a set of XML-based protocols for real-time messaging and presence notification.

XML as a File Format

Many applications now use XML as a file format. For instance, .NET web application configuration data saved in `.config` files is written using XML syntax. Many other applications use XML files to store user preferences and other application data, such as Sun Microsystems's StarOffice XML file format (http://xml.openoffice.org/).

The qualities that make XML a good file format include its intrinsic hierarchical structure, coupled with its textual and extensible nature, and the large number of off-the-shelf tools available to process such documents.

XML in Vertical Industries

XML's simplicity and extensibility is attracting many individuals and industries, who are increasingly coming together to define a "community vocabulary" in XML, so that they can interoperate and build integrated systems more easily.

These community vocabularies include XML dialects already being used by a wide range of industries, such as finance (XBRL, for business reporting, and IFX for financial transactions), media and publishing (NewsML), insurance (ACORD), health (HL7), and shipping (TranXML), to name but a few. There are many more that also are rapidly gaining popularity.

Distributed Architecture

Now that we've set the scene a little, and have seen some of the areas in business applications where XML can be useful, let's move on to look at some architectural issues.

The extremely brief history of web applications is a natural progression of developments in distributed architectures. The relative simplicity of HTTP-based web servers has allowed people who would never have tried to build a distributed application with prior technologies such as DCOM and CORBA to throw together simple distributed applications. At first, there was little emphasis on architecture of web apps, the priority being to get something up and running. Over time though, people asked their web servers to perform more and more advanced techniques. Developers began to rediscover distributed computing models in the attempt to improve performance and make their web applications reliable in the real world.

There are many models for distributed applications, just as there are many people who confuse scribbles on a cocktail napkin for revealed wisdom. To bring some order to the confusion, we'll look at a brief history of the growth of the Web, looking at how the models change to overcome problems encountered with what went before. The three models we will examine are:

❑   Client-server

❑   3-tier

❑   n-tier

Although each of these models applies to any sort of distributed application, we're going to focus on web applications, where the client is a web browser displaying pages with only limited processing power of its own. This 'thin-client' model is not always the case, but it seems to be where web development is headed. The lack of significant uptake for either Java applets or ActiveX controls on the client, in conjunction with divergent browsers on multiple platforms, has led to a tendency to favor processing on the server.

In the Beginning: Client-Server

The Web, of course, is inherently distributed. There is no such thing as a standalone web application. A client makes requests, which are answered by the server, and everything in the application except presentation is carried out by the server. While there are dynamic HTML applications relying heavily on client-side script as exceptions to this, general practice has been to keep functionality on the server in order to avoid the issue of varying browser capabilities. Logic and data are found there, leaving the client with nothing to do except make requests and display the answers. The model is very simple as this figure shows:

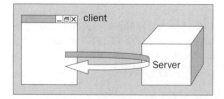

The client-server model offers a big advantage over standalone programming. The key processing in an application is confined to a single machine under the control of the application's owners. Once installation and configuration is out of the way, administrators keep watch over the server on an ongoing basis. This gives the application's owners a great deal of control, yet users all over the network – indeed, all over the world in the case of the Internet – can access the application. Life is good for the administrator.

The advent of the 'mass-market' Web came in the late 1980s and early 1990s, at a time when relational databases using the client-server model were rapidly gaining acceptance. Networks were becoming commonplace, and administrators and users were accustomed to a machine called a server living somewhere off in the ether serving up answers to queries. The fact that web servers sent their application data as HTML documents instead of binary-format recordsets meant little to the average user, protected by their browser from the intricacies of what was going on.

Programmers, however, were not satisfied with this model. From the programming viewpoint, such applications are almost as bad as standalone applications. Data and logic are tangled up in one great big mess, other applications cannot use the same data very easily, and the business rules in the server-side code must be duplicated when other programs need the same features. The only bright spot is that programmers can forget about presentation logic, leaving the task of displaying HTML tags to the browser.

The client-server model was perfect when web applications were simple static HTML pages. Even the very earliest ASP applications could fit with this model. As users clamored for more dynamic information, however, developers had to go back to the drawing board.

Architecture Reaches the Web: 3-Tier

3-tier architecture takes its name from the division of processing into three categories, or **tiers**:

❑ Client

❑ Application logic

❑ Data

The client handles request generation and user interface tasks as it did in the client-server model. The application logic tier, sometimes referred to simply as the middle tier, contains all the business rules and computation that make up the features of the application. The data tier holds all of the data in the application and enforces data integrity. Typically, the data tier consists of a relational database management system. The sequence of processing is as follows:

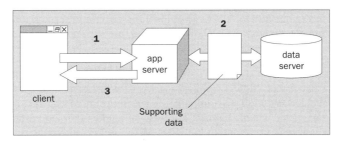

1. The client generates a service request and transmits it to the application server.

2. The application server produces a query corresponding to the client's request, and sends it to the data server.

3. The application logic server applies business logic to the data as relevant, and returns the final answer to the client where it is displayed for the user.

19

By separating the user interface (client), the logic (middle tier), and the data (data tier), we achieve a nice, clean separation of function. We can easily apply integrity checks to the database, and require any application or application tier running against it to pass these checks, thus preserving data integrity. Similarly, the business rules of the application are all located together, in the application tier. The application tier has to know how to query the data tier, but it doesn't need to know anything about maintaining and managing the data. Likewise, it doesn't concern itself with details of the user interface.

The different tiers become more useful because, having been separated and provided with some sort of API, they can be readily used by other applications. For example, when customer data is centralized in a relational database, any application tier that needs customer information can access that database, often without needing any changes to the API. Similarly, once there is a single server that queries the customer database, any client that requires such information can simply go to that server. This aspect of 3-tier programming is generally less important than the integrity and software engineering benefits we just described, but it can nonetheless be valuable.

Note that the different tiers are logical abstractions and need not be separated in any physical sense. Many small web applications run their database on the web server due to a lack of resources, although this is bad practice from a security standpoint. Since the web server must by nature be available to the outside world, it is the most exposed link in the application. It is the most prone to attack, and if it should be compromised when the database resides on the same machine, the database will also be compromised. Generally speaking, though, the acceptance of the relational database prior to the advent of public web applications drove web architects to 3-tier systems fairly rapidly. It just makes sense to have the relational database kept distinct from the code that runs on the web server.

In practice, the distinction between the application logic and data tiers is often blurred. As an extreme example, there are applications that run almost entirely by stored procedures in an RDBMS. Such applications have effectively merged the two tiers, leaving us back in the realm of the client-server model. The stored procedures are physically resident on the data tier, but they implement a good deal of the business rules and application logic of the system. It is tricky to draw a clear line between the two tiers, and frequently it comes down to an arguable judgment call. When developing a good architecture, the effort of deciding where to draw the line, especially if you have to defend it to your peers, is more valuable than attempting to apply some magic formula good for all cases. A general-purpose rule can never apply equally to all possible applications, so you should take architectural rules simply as guidelines, which inform your design effort and guide your thought processes. An honest effort will shake out problems in your design. Slavish adherence to a rule with no thought to the current problem risks leaving many faults in the design.

At the other end, separating presentation – the function of the client – from application logic is harder than it might appear, particularly in web applications. Any ASP.NET code that creates HTML on the server is presentation code, yet you have undoubtedly written some of that as few browsers are ready to handle XML and XSLT on the client (Internet Explorer being the notable exception). Here, we explicitly decide to keep some presentation functions on the server, where the middle tier is hosted, but we strive to keep it distinct from application logic. In this way, we are observing the 3-tier architecture in spirit, if not fully realizing it in practice. An example of maintaining this split would be having application code that generates XML as its final product, then feeding that to code that generates HTML for presentation to the client. The XML code remains presentation-neutral and can be reused; the presentation code can be eliminated if we get better client-side support. In fact, XML-emitting application code is an important enabler for the next, and current, architecture: n-tier design.

Today: n-Tier

Applications developed for a particular platform or architecture can benefit greatly from sharing useful sections of code. This not only saves time writing the code, but can also drastically reduce the effort required to fully test the application, compared to one developed from all-new source. If the developers have done things properly, this might take the form of function libraries or DLLs that can easily be used from a variety of applications. If they've been less meticulous, this may require the copying and pasting of source code for reuse.

Something similar holds true for web applications. It is a short step from writing static pages to incorporating simple scripts for a more dynamic experience, and that's pretty much how web applications got started. Likewise, it is a short step from linking to someone else's content to actually using their web code in your own site (while observing due legal requirements, of course). Google, for example, offers an HTTP interface to its service for adding web search capability to a site without its visual interface (see http://www.google.com/services/ for more information on Google's array of free and premium search solutions). Weather information is available from a number of sources and is frequently included dynamically on portal pages.

In short, we need some mechanism that supports and encourages reuse in web applications, a mechanism that conforms to the HTTP and text based architecture of the web.

Exchanging XML documents is one mechanism that meets these requirements, as many people have realized independently. *Designing Distributed Applications* (Wrox Press, 1999, ISBN 1-86100-227-0) examines this technique at length. The idea, in short, is to provide services through pairs of XML request/response documents. When a document written in the request vocabulary arrives over HTTP, it is assumed to be a request for service that is answered by returning a document written in the response vocabulary. The linkage is implicit, and is inferred by the code at either end through their knowledge of the XML vocabularies in use. Visual Studio .NET provides a similar service in the Web Service wizard, which generates code that exchanges XML documents as a means of communicating requests and responses.

This concept leads to a distributed architecture that is gaining popularity among developers of large-scale applications, particularly corporate intranet sites. In this architecture, we still segregate presentation, application logic, and data, but we are no longer confined to just three tiers. We may have multiple implementations of logic and data, and we may even have an additional tier for combining application logic results before sending them on for presentation. The number of tiers isn't important (at least for theoretical purposes; practical performance will constrain you); the separation of logic and data, as well as the encapsulation of functions into discrete services, is what characterizes n-tier architecture. Consider the illustration below:

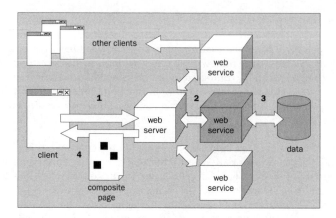

1. A client sends a request to a web server. The server uses several Web Services, bits of application logic, to provide partial answers, which, taken together, result in the answer the client requested. A portal page is a great example: it might include news, weather, and stock prices, each of which could come from a different provider.

2. The web server, then, breaks the client request into a series of HTTP requests to the Web Services needed to get the required information.

3. The Web Services, in turn, may make data requests to obtain raw information. They could also, in theory, make request of their own to other Web Services, leading to many, many tiers of logic.

4. The web server receives the responses from the Web Services, and combines them into a composite page that it eventually returns to the client as the response to the client's original request.

The client has no idea that the result is a composite of the efforts of multiple services, nor does it need to have this information. Future changes in Web Services, code deployment, or functional implementation will not affect the client. Of further benefit is the fact that the Web Services are not tied to the web server or the client. Multiple applications can call on any Web Service. In fact, application logic can call Web Services and use their results without any presentation to a user.

This architecture is very compatible with the web platform. HTTP requests are used for communication, XML, a textual format, conveys data in an open and platform-neutral manner, and all components are interconnected with HTTP links. The use of proprietary XML vocabularies that implicitly denote either requests or responses is a weak point of the architecture, though, as it precludes the development of general purpose software for connecting Web Services to applications.

One way to solve this is would be to create an open standard for Web Service communication. At the moment, the best effort is SOAP, which provides an XML envelope for conveying XML documents that can represent function calls with their required parameters. Web Services created with Visual Studio .NET's Web Service template support SOAP. SOAP is a de facto standard, and so general purpose toolkits for creating and consuming SOAP messages can be produced. Such toolkits can pop the parameters out of the request document and present them to your application code as actual function or method parameters.

SOAP implementations generally adhere to the SOAP 1.1 version, though version 1.2 is in draft form (http://www.w3.org/TR/soap12-part0 and http://www.w3.org/TR/soap12-part1/) and implementations are migrating to it. SOAP was originally an ad hoc effort of several software vendors, but has now been handed over to the W3C, where further development is under way in the form of XML Protocol (http://www.w3.org/TR/xmlp-am/).

Another way to resolve this would be with the aid of integration servers. These are proprietary server software products offered by a variety of vendors that act as middleware between applications for the purpose of integrating them. They handle issues of protocol and format translation. A message could come in as an XML document on SMTP and be sent back out as a different XML document (differing in form, but with the same data content) over HTTP, for example. Some also add business process semantics, to ensure that a series of messages adheres to the established business process. Some of these products adhere to standards advanced by various consortia such as RosettaNet (http://www.rosettanet.org), while others, such as Microsoft BizTalk Server (http://www.microsoft.com/biztalk) are open to your own business processes. In addition to Microsoft, established vendors include Ariba (http://www.ariba.com) and CommerceOne (http://www.commerceone.com).

Sample Architectures

So now we've had a close look at three generic architectures, finishing up with the n-tier model, the likely future of web applications. We've seen how XML can fulfill many internal needs of these architectures. Now we'll examine two common web applications that benefit from a 3- or n-tier architecture with XML. These applications are:

❑ Content sites – high volume web sites with changing content consisting primarily of HTML pages rather than interactive code, for example, a news site

❑ Intranet applications – medium volume sites providing application access on an intranet

Content Site

A site with a great deal of content, such as an online newspaper or magazine, might not seem to be an application at all. The site framework seldom changes, though new documents are frequently added and old ones removed. There is rarely much in the way of interactivity, aside from a search feature for the site. But XML offers some advantages for maintaining the site and facilitating searching.

One issue with such sites is that they periodically undergo style changes. Hand written HTML is therefore out of the question as you would scarcely want to redo all the pages just to change style and layout. The use of cascading style sheets addresses many of the styling issues, but they lack the ability to truly transform and rearrange pages if so desired. The word "transform" there might provide a clue as to what I'm getting at: XSLT. If we store the content in XML, we can manipulate it to produce the visual effects we desire through an XSLT style sheet. When a site redesign is warranted, we just change the style sheet. We can even update links to reflect hosting changes with XSLT, a feat that is impossible in CSS. You should not, however, use XSLT dynamically for a high volume site. The performance overhead from even a fast XSLT processor is something a high-volume site cannot afford. Instead, use XSLT to perform a batch conversion of your XML documents when you redesign, then serve up the resultant HTML as static pages between site designs. New documents are transformed once, as they are added to the site. This gives the site all the speed of static HTML while still maintaining the ability to automate site redesign.

You might ask why you would want to use XML instead of a database for the information content of the site. Well, firstly, this is not necessarily an either-or proposition. Increasingly, databases can store XML documents, or access relational data using XML documents, thereby giving you the best of both worlds. Secondly, we can use XPath to enhance our search capability. Once information is marked up as XML, we can search by specific elements, such as, title, summary, author byline, or body. Furthermore, we can selectively publish fragments with another XSLT style sheet. For example, we might select title and summary only for people browsing with PDAs or customers who have subscribed to a clipping service. Similarly, we might mark some content as premium content, whether it be by whole page or by subsections of individual pages.

Intranet Application

A substantially different architecture is required for intranet applications. These sites provide access to sophisticated corporate functions such as personnel management applications or retirement fund selections. If we are writing entirely new functions using the latest technology and platforms, there isn't a problem. We can just write our applications using ASP.NET. XML is optional. The problem for intranet applications arises because we often have to provide access to legacy systems, or at least exchange information with them.

The easiest way to deal with this is to wrap the legacy code in a Web Service. This only works when the legacy applications offer an API that we can call from .NET. COM components work quite well, but older interfaces can pose a problem. This is where Web Services can help, by isolating the rest of the system from the legacy, XML-illiterate code. Everything beyond the Web Service is XML, limiting the spread of legacy data structures. The situation is depicted below:

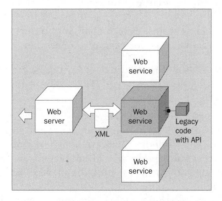

A bigger problem arises when the code cannot be directly called by .NET or when scalability concerns preclude the use of synchronous SOAP calls. If we require our system to achieve close to 100% uptime, we cannot afford to drop requests as is the case when traffic to a synchronous service like SOAP spikes beyond supported levels. The buffering offered by a queued solution is needed, and in such cases, we need the help of an integration server, such as BizTalk Server. We can communicate with the integration server, and leave it to pass the message on in a protocol that is supported by the legacy application. This might at first seem to leave out many existing applications, until we realize that most integration servers support exchanges via disk files. The server monitors a particular directory for the appearance of a file, or it writes a file to the directory that is monitored by the legacy application. This is a very common, least-common-denominator approach. Now consider the web application architecture depicted opposite:

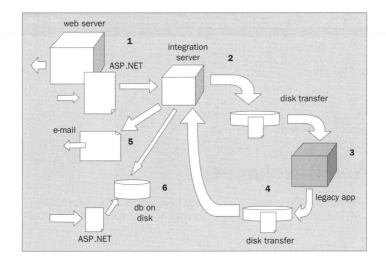

1. Request arrives from the client tier through an ASP.NET application, which writes an XML message to the integration server

2. Integration server sends a message to the legacy application, in this case via disk-based file transfer. Format translation occurs en route.

3. Legacy application receives the message and produces output

4. Output message is exchanged with the integration server via the supported protocol

5. Integration server sends message to client via e-mail, possibly as XSLT styled XML

or, alternatively

6. Upon receiving notification via e-mail, client returns via ASP.NET and retrieves a result written to a database by the integration server

The asynchronous communication of this design makes it inherently scalable. The client gets an immediate response via the initial web application indicating that the request has been submitted. The communications protocol with the legacy application should provide a buffer – typically through some sort of messaging middleware like MSMQ or through files accumulating on disk. If the protocol is synchronous, you probably could have wrapped it with a SOAP Web Service.

> *There are long term plans for asynchronous Web Services using SOAP, but present implementations use synchronous calls via HTTP.*

This design is also clearly n-tier. The ASP.NET applications provide the application logic, as does the legacy application. The integration server may be considered application logic or part of the infrastructure. Any database used by the legacy application is data, as is the database used by the alternative Step 6, above.

Although we've used the example of an intranet application, this architecture can apply to e-commerce sites as well. In that case, the client tier is located outside the corporate firewall, but order fulfillment and billing systems are internal, possibly legacy, applications. In such a case, the Web Service would typically be deployed in a demilitarized zone, or DMZ, between two firewalls. The first firewall protects the web server hosting the service and provides minimal protection. The web server takes steps to authenticate requests before passing them through the second, more stringent firewall protecting the internal network from the Internet. The second architecture, using an integration server, is preferred as it scales better, but you can use the less costly Web Services architecture if volume is moderate or the Web Services do not involve much processing.

ASP.NET Web Development

So far we have seen what XML is and some of its general applications. Let's now look at how XML fits in with the ASP.NET world and its role in the development of ASP.NET web applications.

Welcome to ASP.NET

ASP.NET represents the next generation of web development on the Windows platform. It is an evolutionary and revolutionary improvement on traditional ASP 3.0, and many things have changed. It is a totally new platform (although there's a fair amount of backward compatibility) designed to support high-performance scalable web applications.

Traditional ASP code is generally written using either JavaScript or VBScript, and because of the design model that it employs, developers are generally obliged to mix the presentation with the logic, causing code to become less maintainable and harder to understand. Traditional ASP does not *natively* support XML. MSXML can be used from within ASP pages to process the XML documents. In addition, every time the ASP page is called, the engine *interprets* the page.

ASP.NET changes all this. It runs in a compiled environment, such that the first time an `aspx` page is called after the source code has changed, the .NET Framework compiles and builds the code, and caches it in a binary format. Each subsequent request does not then need to parse the source, and can use the cached binary version to process the request, giving a substantial performance boost.

The second important change from the developer's perspective is that we are no longer restricted just JavaScript and VBScript for server-side programming. As a first class member of the .NET Framework, ASP.NET allows any Framework language to be used for web development, be it Visual Basic .NET or C# .NET or JScript .NET. ASP.NET makes web programming very similar to standard Windows application development in .NET.

In ASP.NET, the separation of presentation from the program logic is achieved via the concept of **code-behind files**, where the main ASPX page has a corresponding language file *behind* it. For instance, `default.aspx` would contain the presentation code (HTML and client-side scripts), while an associated file, such as `default.aspx.cs`, would contain the C# code for that page. This allows us to keep code nicely separated from its presentation details.

ASP.NET includes many other new features related to Web Forms, such as deployment, state management, caching, configuration, debugging, data access, as well as Web Services. It is however beyond the scope of this chapter to provide a complete discussion of all these topics. Try *Professional ASP.NET 1.0, Special Edition* (Wrox Press, 1-86100-703-5) if that is what you need. Here, we'll focus on the XML and Web Services features of ASP.NET.

The Role of XML in ASP.NET

The .NET Framework itself makes use of XML internally in many situations, and thus it allows XML to be easily used from our applications. In short, XML pervades the entire .NET Framework, and ASP.NET's XML integration can be used to build highly extensible web sites and Web Services. In this section, we'll briefly look at the XML integration in the .NET Framework, specifically in ASP.NET.

The System.Xml Namespace

This is the core namespace that contains classes which can:

❑ Create and process XML documents using a pull-based streaming API (Chapter 2) or the Document Object Model (DOM, Chapter 3)

❑ Query XML documents (using XPath, Chapter 4)

❑ Transform XML documents (using XSLT, Chapter 5)

❑ Validate XML documents (using a DTD, or an XDR or XSD schema, Chapter 2)

❑ Manipulate relational or XML data from a database using the DOM (XmlDataDocument class, Chapter 6)

Almost all applications that use XML in any way will refer to the System.Xml namespace in order to use one or more of the classes that it contains.

Chapters 2 through 4 focus on the System.Xml namespace and discuss how these classes can be used in ASP.NET web applications.

Web Services

As well as web sites, .NET web applications can represent Web Services, which can be defined in a sentence thus:

> **ASP.NET Web Services are programmable logic that can be accessed from anywhere on the Internet, using HTTP (GET/POST/SOAP) and XML.**

We'll talk about this a little more in the section *XML Messaging* towards the end of this chapter, and in detail in Chapter 8.

SQLXML Managed Classes

Although not part of the core .NET Framework, the SQLXML managed classes are available as a separate download from http://www.microsoft.com/sql/techinfo/xml/default.asp. These classes form part of the Microsoft.Data.SqlXml namespace and allow access to SQL Server 2000's native and extended XML features. SQLXML managed classes can be used in our ASP.NET applications to build scalable and extensible web applications, and they are discussed in detail in Chapter 7.

The ADO.NET DataSet Class

Probably the most fundamental design change in the data access model in the .NET Framework is the differentiation of the objects that provide *connected* database access from those that provide *disconnected* access. In regular ADO, we use the same objects and interfaces for both connected and disconnected data access, causing lot of confusion. The improved ADO.NET data access API in .NET provides stream-based classes that implement the connected layer, and a new class called `DataSet` that implements the disconnected layer.

The `DataSet` can be thought of as an in-memory representation of data records. It can easily be serialized as XML, and conversely it can be populated using data from an XML document. The .NET data access classes are present in the `System.Data` namespace and its sub-namespaces.

Another marked improvement in ADO.NET is the ability to *easily bind* the data to graphical controls. We'll talk more about the role of ADO.NET and the `DataSet` when dealing with XML in Chapter 6.

The .config Files

With ASP.NET, Microsoft has introduced the concept of XCopy deployment, which means that the deployment of an application does not require any registry changes or even stopping the web server. The name comes from the fact that applications can be deployed by just copying the files onto the server with the DOS XCopy command.

Prior to .NET, all web application configuration data was stored in the IIS metabase. The .NET Framework changes this with the notion of XML-based extensible configuration files to store many configuration details. These files have the `.config` extension – and play an important role in XCopy deployment. As these files are plain text XML files, configuration data can be edited using any text editor, rather than a specialized tool such as the IIS admin console. The `.config` files are divided into three main categories, containing application, machine, and security settings.

C# Code Documentation

Another interesting new feature is found in C# (or strictly speaking, C# .NET), and extends the syntax for comments beyond the standard `//` and `/*...*/`, to create a new type that begins with three slashes (`///`). Within these, we can place XML tags and descriptive text to document the source code and its methods. The C# complier is then able to extract this information and automatically generate XML documentation files. It can also generate HTML documentation directly from these comments.

Currently, this feature is only available in C#, and none of the other .NET languages support it.

XML 1.0 Syntax

The XML 1.0 (Second Edition) W3C recommendation (http://www.w3.org/TR/REC-xml) defines the basic XML syntax. As we know, XML documents are text documents that structure data, and bear some similarity to HTML documents. However as noted earlier, tags in XML, unlike tags in HTML, are completely user-definable: there are virtually no 'reserved' tags. Also unlike HTML, XML is case-sensitive.

An XML document (or data object) has one and only one root element – that is, top level element – which may contain any number of **child elements** within it. All elements must be delimited by start- and end-tags, and be properly nested without overlap. Any element may contain attributes, child elements, and character data. The XML 1.0 specification allows most of the characters defined by 16-bit Unicode 2.0 (which includes UTF-8, UTF-16, and many other encodings), hence making XML truly a global standard.

The XML specification identifies five characters (<, >, &, ', and ") that have a special meaning and hence if any of these characters is required, the alternative *entity references* (<, >, &, ', and ") must be used in their place.

In addition to elements and attributes, an XML document may contain other special purpose tags such as comments (<!-- ... -->), processing instructions (<? ... ?>), and CDATA (<![CDATA[...]]>) sections.

All documents that conform to the XML 1.0 rules are known as **well-formed** XML documents. If a well-formed document also meets further validity constraints (defined by a DTD or schema), it is known as a **valid** XML document. We'll discuss XML validity later in this chapter.

It is a good practice, although not a strict requirement, to begin an XML document with the **XML declaration**. If present, it should be the very first line in the document. The XML declaration identifies the XML version to which the document syntax adheres (a required attribute), the document encoding scheme (optional), and if the document has any external dependencies (again optional).

Another extension to the XML 1.0 specification is XML Base, where an xml:base attribute may be included on an element to define a base URI for that element and all descendent elements. This base URI allows relative links in a similar manner to the HTML <base> element.

Special Attributes

The XML specification defines two special attributes that can be used within any element in an XML document. The first, **xml:space**, is used to control whitespace handling and the second, **xml:lang**, is used to identify the language contained within a particular element. The xml:lang attribute allows internationalized versions of information to be presented, and makes it easier for an application to know the language used for the data in the element.

Whitespace Handling

An XML document may contain whitespace (space characters, tabs, carriage returns, or line feeds) at various places. Sometimes whitespace is added to indent the XML document for better readability, and when an application is processing this document, the whitespace can be ignored. At other times however, the spaces are significant, and should be preserved. We can use the xml:space attribute on the element to indicate whether the parser should preserve whitespace or use its default whitespace handling. The xml:space attribute can have one of two values: preserve or default.

According to the W3C XML specification, if the whitespace is found within the mixed element content (elements containing character data and optionally child elements) or inside the scope of an xml:space='preserve' attribute, the whitespace must be preserved and passed without modification to the application. Any other whitespace can be ignored.

With MSXML 4.0 and the .NET XML classes in the `System.Xml` namespace, we can use the `PreserveWhitespace` property in the code to indicate if the whitespace should be preserved or not. In other words, if we would like to preserve the whitespace for an XML document, we can either use the `xml:space` attribute with the elements in the XML document or set the `PreserveWhitespace` property in the code to `true` (default is `false`).

Let's look at an example of this. Consider the following XML document, saved as `c:\test.xml`:

```
<Root>     <Child>Data</Child>     </Root>
```

Note that there are five space characters before and after the `<Child>` element.

We could create a simple C# console application containing the following code in the `Class1.cs` file, and when we ran it, we'd see that the whitespace has not been preserved in the XML displayed on screen, and in fact carriage return characters have been added (you might want to place a breakpoint on the closing brace of the `Main` method):

```csharp
using System;
using System.IO;
using System.Xml;

namespace ConsoleApplication1
{
    class Class1
    {
        [STAThread]
        static void Main(string[] args)
        {
            XmlDocument xmlDOMDoc = new XmlDocument();
            xmlDOMDoc.Load("c:\\test.xml");
            xmlDOMDoc.Save(Console.Out);
        }
    }
}
```

There are two ways we could preserve the whitespace. The first is to add the `xml:space` attribute to the XML document. Change the `c:\test.xml` file as shown below:

```
<Root xml:space='preserve'>     <Child>Data</Child>     </Root>
```

Run the above code again and this time, the whitespace is preserved and the document will appear exactly as it does in the file.

The other way is to set the `PreserveWhitespace` property to `true` in the code. Add the following line to the `Main` method:

```csharp
XmlDocument xmlDOMDoc = new XmlDocument();
xmlDOMDoc.PreserveWhitespace = true;
xmlDOMDoc.Load("c:\\test.xml");
```

Now whitespace will be preserved, even without the `xml:space` attribute in the XML file.

Likely Changes in XML 1.1

On April 25, 2002, the W3C announced the last call working draft of XML 1.1 (codenamed Blueberry), at http://www.w3.org/TR/xml11/. The XML 1.1 draft outlines two changes of note, although they are unlikely to have a major impact on most web developers. These changes allow a broader range of Unicode characters, and improve the handling of the line-end character.

In XML 1.0, characters not present in Unicode 2.0 (and some forbidden names) cannot be used as names; XML 1.1 changes this so that any Unicode character can be used for names (with the exception of a few forbidden names). This change was made to make sure that as the Unicode standard evolves (the current version is 3.2), there won't be a consequent need to explicitly change the XML standard.

The other important change relates to how the end-of-line characters are treated. Microsoft uses CR-LF (hex #xD #xA) to represent end-of-line characters, while Unix (and GNU/Linux) use LF (#xA), and MacOS uses CR (#xD). XML 1.0 currently requires processors to normalize all these newline characters into #xA. The XML 1.1 working draft adds the IBM mainframe newline characters and requires XML processors to normalize mainframe-specific newline characters (#xD #x85, #x85, and #x2028) to #xA.

Well-Formedness

Well-formed XML documents *must* meet the following requirements:

- ❑ All tags must be closed
- ❑ Tags are case sensitive
- ❑ The XML document must have a *single* root element
- ❑ Elements must be nested properly without overlap
- ❑ No element may have two attributes with the same name
- ❑ Attribute values must be enclosed in quotes (using either ' or ")

Without further delay, let's look at an example of the following well-formed XML document, called MyEvents.xml:

```xml
<?xml version="1.0" encoding="UTF-8" standalone="yes"?>
<MyEvents xmlns='uuid:06F699FA-C945-459a-BFCE-CFED4A4C7D51' >

  <!-- Live Webinars -->
  <Webinar type='live' ID='1'>
    <Title>ProductA Kick-Start Webinar</Title>
    <Date>20020504</Date>
    <Time zone='CST' AMorPM='PM'>3:00</Time>
    <Desc>
      <![CDATA[&copy; 2002 ABC &amp; PQR Corp.]]>
    </Desc>
    <URL>http://www.company.com/events/events.asp?ID=1</URL>
  </Webinar>
```

```
<Webinar type='live' ID='2'>
  <Title>ProductB In-depth Webinar</Title>
  <Date>20020507</Date>
  <Time zone='CST' AMorPM='AM'>10:00</Time>
  <Desc>
    <![CDATA[&copy; 2002 ABC &amp; PQR Corp.]]>
  </Desc>
  <URL>http://www.company.com/events/events.asp?ID=2</URL>
</Webinar>

<!-- Recorded Webinars -->
<!-- *** None *** -->

<!-- Trade shows -->
<TradeShow ID="91">
  <Title>ABC Magazine Live!</Title>
  <Address>
    <Location>MGM Grand Hotel and Casino</Location>
    <City>Las Vegas</City>
    <State>Nevada</State>
    <Country>USA</Country>
  </Address>
  <Dates>
    <From>20020607</From>
    <To>20020610</To>
  </Dates>
  <URL>http://www.ABCMagazineLive2002.com</URL>
</TradeShow>
</MyEvents>
```

The above XML document illustrates various points that we have discussed so far. It begins with an XML declaration statement indicating that the syntax follows the XML 1.0 specification, the document encoding is UTF-8, and the `standalone="yes"` attribute indicates that this document does not depend on any other external resource (such as a DTD, schema, or style sheet). The above document contains a single root element (`<MyEvents>`), which in turn contains various child elements (two `<Webinar>` elements, a `<TradeShow>` element, and several comments). Do not worry about the `xmlns` attribute yet, as we discuss this in the next section. Note also the attributes, comments, and CDATA sections in the above document.

Namespaces in XML

Wherever they may be found, namespaces generally serve two basic purposes:

1. To group related information under one umbrella

2. To avoid name collision between different groups

XML namespaces also serve these two purposes, and are defined as an extension to the XML 1.0 specification.

In the above sample XML document, we have various element names (such as `MyEvents`, `Webinar`, `TradeShow`, and so on). It is possible that somebody else might also use the same names in their XML documents, but for something not quite the same as we did. So how can the processing application associate elements with their correct meanings? The solution is provided by XML namespaces.

While writing XML documents, it is good practice to use namespaces, to avoid the potential for name clashes. All elements or attributes belonging to a given namespace can be prefixed with the name of the namespace, thus making a unique identifier. Hence, namespace names are required to be unique (in the above XML, `uuid:06F699FA-C945-459a-BFCE-CFED4A4C7D51` is the namespace name), and it is for this reason that URLs are often chosen for the purpose. For instance, if our company has its own URL, we can be fairly sure that no-one else will use that URL in their namespaces. For instance, Wrox Press might choose namespace names for its XML documents such as `http://www.Wrox.com/Accounting`, `http://www.Wrox.com/Marketing`, and so on; while another company, say Friends of ED, might use `http://www.friendsofED.com/Accounting`, `http://www.friendsofED.com/Marketing`, and so on.

Notice that we don't actually prefix any of the element names with a namespace name in the above example XML document. This is because we have a **default namespace** declaration on the root element (`xmlns='uuid:06F699FA-C945-459a-BFCE-CFED4A4C7D51'`), which binds that element and all contained elements to this URI. By using the `xmlns` syntax, *all* the elements in the document now belong to the `uuid:06F699FA-C945-459a-BFCE-CFED4A4C7D51` namespace (more precisely, all descendent elements of the element defining the namespace). Note that the default namespace declaration has no effect upon attribute names, and so in the above XML document, the attributes do not explicitly belong to any namespace.

It is quite possible for an XML document to contain multiple namespaces for various elements and attributes, and although we could prefix any element or attribute with the full namespace name, it would be very cumbersome in practice. A better solution in XML namespaces is to define short **prefixes**, which we can then use instead of the long namespace names. An element or attribute name without a prefix is referred as the *local name* of the element, and with the prefix it is known as the **qualified name** or **QName**.

Consider the following example:

```
<evts:MyEvents xmlns:evts='uuid:06F699FA-C945-459a-BFCE-CFED4A4C7D51'
               xmlns:ol='uuid:465CE3B3-A2E9-40ca-8BE1-65B68421F191' >

  <evts:Webinar evts:type='live' evts:ID='1' ol:vcsItemID="DER-ER" />

  .
  .
  .

</evts:MyEvents>
```

The above XML document declares two namespace names with the prefixes `evts` and `ol` assigned. These short prefixes save our writing the full namespace names over and over. All elements and attributes above belong to the `evts` namespace, except `vcsItemID`, which belongs to the `ol` namespace. Note how the attributes are namespace prefixed. The name `evts:Webinar` is an example of a qualified name (or QName) for this document, while `Webinar` is the corresponding local name.

XML Information Set

The XML Information Set (InfoSet) is a W3C specification that tries to help make sure that as new XML languages are drawn up, they exploit consistent definitions and terminology, and that the dialects used do not create any confusion.

The current XML InfoSet W3C recommendation (http://www.w3.org/TR/xml-infoset/) defines an abstract data set for well-formed XML data that also complies with the XML Namespaces naming rules. There is no requirement for an XML document to be valid in order to have an information set.

Processing XML

Today, there are many tools available to create, read, parse, and process XML documents from our programs. The primary goal of these tools is to efficiently extract the data stored in between tags, without having to text-parse the document. Almost all of these tools are based on two standard abstract APIs – the Document Object Model (DOM) or the Simple API for XML (SAX). We'll have a look at these two now.

Document Object Model (DOM)

The DOM is an abstract API defined by the W3C (http://www.w3.org/DOM) to process XML documents. It is a language- and platform-independent abstract API that any *parser* can implement, and it allows applications to create, read, and modify XML documents.

Using the DOM, the parser loads the entire XML document into the memory at once as a tree, providing random access to it for searching and modifying any element in the document.

Microsoft XML Core Services (MSXML) version 4.0 (http://msdn.microsoft.com/xml) supports the DOM. Other freely available DOM implementations include JAXP from Sun Microsystems (http://java.sun.com/xml/) and Xerces from the Apache XML foundation (http://xml.apache.org).

> *Most of the current DOM implementations (including that in .NET) support DOM Level 1 Core (http://www.w3.org/TR/DOM-Level-1) and DOM Level 2 Core (http://www.w3.org/TR/DOM-Level-2-Core). W3C recently announced the DOM Level 3 Core Working Draft (http://www.w3.org/TR/DOM-Level-3-Core).*

Simple API for XML (SAX)

SAX, like DOM, defines a set of abstract interfaces for processing XML. It differs from the DOM in that, instead of loading the entire document into memory, SAX follows a streaming model, reading an XML document character by character as a stream, and generating events as each element or attribute is encountered. The SAX-based parser passes these events up to the application through various notification interfaces.

> *As DOM loads the entire document in the memory, the DOM parser checks the well-formedness (and optionally validity) of documents on opening them; whereas since SAX reads the XML document as a character-by-character stream, without caching the document in the memory, it is not able to check for well-formedness of the document.*

SAX is an excellent lightweight alternative to DOM for processing XML documents. Unlike DOM, SAX is not a product of the W3C, and was created by the XML-DEV mailing list members, led by David Megginson.

Note that SAX is a stream-based API that uses the **push** model, where XML documents are read as a continuous stream, and the SAX engine fires events for each item as it is encountered. SAX allows very simple parser logic, although the application logic required to use it is consequently more complex. The .NET Framework contains a class (called XmlReader) which also processes XML as a stream, but using the **pull** model, where the parser advances from item to item in an XML document when instructed to do so by the application. This can simplify application logic, while providing the same benefits as SAX. The XmlReader class provides the best of both worlds: streaming high-performance parsing (as in SAX), and simplicity of usage (as in the DOM). Neither SAX nor XmlReader maintains state, and so we must provide our own means of preserving information from XML items that have been read if needed. We'll look at XMLReader much more closely in Chapter 2.

By not fully loading XML documents into memory, SAX requires less system resources and proves to be a very efficient API for parsing large XML documents. However, programming SAX is not as simple as the DOM, firstly because we must implement notification interfaces and maintain state, and also because SAX does not allow random access to the document or provide editing functionality as does the DOM.

Most of the current SAX implementations, including MSXML 4.0, JAXP, and Xerces, support SAX 2.0. The .NET Framework does not support true SAX, but an alternative (and simpler to work with) pull-model stream-based parsing API (the XmlReader classes in the System.Xml namespace). As we shall see in Chapter 2, we can however use XmlReader to read a document according to a push model should we wish.

XML Data Binding and XML Serialization

XML data binding refers to the mapping of XML elements and attributes onto a programmatic data model, in order to use the XML data directly as components of an application, and vice versa. In .NET, data binding allows us to link data within an XML file directly to a DataSet, which we can then display in a DataGrid. Any changes to the XML data will appear immediately in the DataGrid, and conversely, any changes made to the values in the DataGrid will be reflected immediately in the XML file.

XML serialization is the name given to the rendering of programmatic data as XML for transmission between computers or storage on some external system. An obvious analogy would be packaging eggs in a carton for transport and storage, which can be unpackaged intact (deserialized) when they are to be used. In .NET, an object can be marshaled (or serialized) as a XML stream, and at the other end, an XML stream can be un-marshaled (or deserialized) back to an object. This allows programmers to work naturally in the native code of the programming language, while at the same time preserving the logical structure and the meaning of the original data, and can be readily used instead of using the low-level DOM/SAX API to manipulate the XML data structural components.

The .NET Framework namespace System.Xml.Serialization contains the classes that serialize objects into XML streams, and deserialize them back again.

Validating XML

One of the primary goals of XML is to enable the free exchange of structured data between organizations and applications. To do this, the XML document format that will be used for the exchange of information must first be defined and agreed upon. It's fairly elementary to ensure that any XML document is well-formed, but we also need to ensure that it is *valid*: in other words that it strictly follows the agreed structure, business logic, and rules. We can do this by defining a schema that we can then use to validate any XML document.

The initial solution for defining XML document structure was the existing Document Type Definition (DTD) syntax. However, it was soon realized that DTDs are very restrictive; they do not support strong data typing, are not extensible, and can perform only limited validation with regards to the sequence and frequency of elements.

The XML Schema Definition (XSD) language was introduced by the W3C as a replacement for DTDs. XML Schemas (http://www.w3.org/XML/Schema) overcome all the shortcomings of DTDs, and they provide a very flexible and extensible mechanism for defining the structure of XML. As with so many other XML-related specifications from the W3C stables, XML Schemas are themselves constructed from XML syntax, with the many advantages that brings.

> *XML Schemas can be used for much more than merely validating an XML document. Visual Studio .NET, for instance, uses schemas to determine possibilities for the IDE's IntelliSense feature, allowing it to auto-complete partially typed keywords. In addition, XML Schemas are also used in database and object technologies.*

In May 2001, XML Schema 1.0 reached W3C Recommendation status, meaning that that version of the specification will not be modified further. The Recommendation is divided into three parts:

❑ XML Schema Part 0: Primer (http://www.w3.org/TR/xmlschema-0) – This document introduces some of the key concepts and is a good place to get started with XML Schemas.

❑ XML Schema Part 1: Structures (http://www.w3.org/TR/xmlschema-1) – This part describes how to constrain the structure of XML documents.

❑ XML Schema Part 2: Datatypes (http://www.w3.org/TR/xmlschema-2) – This part defines a set of built-in datatypes and the means for deriving of new datatypes.

While the W3C was finalizing XSD, Microsoft created XDR (XML-Data Reduced) so that it could start using XML Schemas as soon as possible. Various Microsoft products (such as MSXML 3, SQL Server 2000, and BizTalk Server 2000) still support and use XDR.

The current release of the MSXML parser and the .NET Framework both fully support the XML Schema (XSD) W3C Recommendation. XDR is still supported in .NET – but not recommended. Microsoft recommends, as do I, XSD for all schema-related purposes.

The W3C is currently working on the XML Schema 1.1 standard (http://www.w3.org/XML/Schema).

Navigating, Transforming, and Formatting XML

Among complementary standards created by the W3C are some that further help process XML documents. In this section, we'll discuss three such standards: XPath, XSLT, and XSL-FO.

XPath

Right now there is only one widely supported technology for searching through XML documents and retrieving specific components, and it is the XML Path Language, or XPath. Once we have structured data available in XML format, we can easily find the information we require with XPath, a W3C specification that enables the querying, locating, and filtering of elements or attributes within an XML document.

XPath is based on the notion that all XML documents can be visualized as a hierarchical tree; it is a language for expressing paths through such trees from one leaf, or **node**, of the tree to another. It enables us to retrieve all elements or attributes satisfying a given set of criteria. Most XPath implementations provide very fast random-access retrieval of XML content when we know something about the structure of a document.

XPath provides a declarative notation, known as an **expression** or a **pattern**, to specify a particular set of nodes from the source XML document. An XPath expression describes a path up through the XML 'tree' using a slash-separated list of discrete steps. XPath provides basic facilities for manipulation of strings, numbers and Booleans that can be applied within these steps.

Let's look at an example XPath expression to select data from the `MyEvents.xml` document:

```
/MyEvents/Webinar[@ID=2]/Title
```

This expression selects the `<Title>` child element of the `<Webinar>` element that has an attribute called `ID` with the value 2. XPath expressions are namespace aware, and thus we would need to specify the namespace of the elements in a real-world expression. I'll leave this, and the complete explanation of XPath syntax, for Chapter 4.

XPath .NET classes are found in the `System.Xml.XPath` namespace (also discussed in Chapter 4), and include the `XPathDocument` class to load an XML document, and the `XPathNavigator` class for executing complex expressions.

XPath 1.0 (http://www.w3.org/TR/xpath) was published as a W3C Recommendation on December 20th 2001, and XPath 2.0 is currently at working draft stage (http://www.w3.org/TR/xpath20/). XPath is used by other standards such as XSLT, XPointer, and XQuery. The current releases of MSXML and the .NET Framework implement XPath 1.0.

XSLT

XSL, the Extensible Stylesheet Language, is an XML-based language to create *style sheets*. XSL covers two technologies under its umbrella:

1. **XSL Transformations (XSLT)** is a declarative language used to transform XML documents from one format to another.

2. **XSL-Formatting Objects (XSL-FO)** is a page-formatting language with major focus on very precisely specifying the visual presentation of XML.

In this section, we'll talk about XSLT, and discuss XSL-FO in the next section.

Earlier in the chapter we learned about XML's role in separating data from its presentation. XSLT has a lot to offer here. A single source XML document can be *transformed* to various output formats (HTML, WML, XHTML, and so on) using an appropriate XSLT *stylesheet*.

We've also learned that XML acts as glue for integrating e-business and B2B applications. XSLT is the key player as it can transform one XML dialect to any another.

There are many other potential uses for XSLT, such as performing client-side transformation of raw XML in a web application, thus reducing the load on the server. This would require a browser with XSLT support of course, but your web server can detect the user agent type to determine this.

Let's look at an example XSLT stylesheet, called `renderHTML.xsl`:

```
<xsl:stylesheet version="1.0" exclude-result-prefixes="xsl src"
            xmlns:xsl="http://www.w3.org/1999/XSL/Transform"
            xmlns:src="uuid:06F699FA-C945-459a-BFCE-CFED4A4C7D51" >

    <xsl:output method="html" />

    <xsl:template match="/">
        <b>Webinars</b><br/>
        <xsl:for-each select="//src:Webinar">
            <a href="{src:URL}"><xsl:value-of select="src:Title" /></a>
            <br/><br/>
        </xsl:for-each>
    </xsl:template>

</xsl:stylesheet>
```

This style sheet provides a good demonstration of the value of namespaces in XML. Note the two prefixes declared at the top of this style sheet: one is `xsl` and denotes elements related to XSLT, and the other is `src`, for elements from the source XML file. This prevents any ambiguity, should our own XML dialect also define `<template>` elements, say. The `<stylesheet>` element also specifies the `exclude-result-prefixes` attribute with `"xsl src"` as its value, thus preventing elements bound to these prefixes from appearing in the result tree.

When the above style sheet is applied on our sample `MyEvents.xml` XML document discussed earlier, it produces the following HTML output:

```
<b>Webinars</b><br/><a
href="http://www.company.com/events/events.asp?ID=1">ProductA Kick-Start
Webinar</a><br/><br/><a
href="http://www.company.com/events/events.asp?ID=2">ProductB In-depth
Webinar</a><br/><br/>
```

Essentially, this works by embedding XSLT elements inside HTML code, and these elements transform certain elements from the source XML (as specified by XPath expressions) to an appropriate HTML form for viewing.

The simplest method to try out the above style sheet (without writing a single line of code), is to add the following processing instruction just below the XML declaration (`<?xml ...?>`) in the XML file, and opening it in Internet Explorer:

```
<?xml-stylesheet type="text/xsl" href="renderHTML.xsl" ?>
```

> *As `renderHTML.xsl` uses the final release XSLT namespace*
> *(`http://www.w3.org/1999/XSL/Transform`) you'll need to run the above example with*
> *Internet Explorer 6.0 (which installs MSXML 3.0 in replace mode) or with Internet Explorer 5.0+*
> *and make sure it is using MSXML 3.0.*

The current release of MSXML and the .NET Framework support XSLT 1.0 (a W3C Recommendation at http://www.w3.org/TR/xslt).

Note that the W3C Working Draft of XSLT 1.1 (http://www.w3.org/TR/xslt11/) was frozen, not to be continued, on release of the XSLT 2.0 Working Draft (http://www.w3.org/TR/xslt20req), so refer to XSL 2.0 to track the progress of the XSLT standard.

XSL-FO

XSL-FO, now also simply called XSL, is a W3C Recommendation (http://www.w3.org/TR/xsl) designed to help in publishing XML documents (both printing and displaying electronically), and it mainly focuses on the document layout and structure (such as output document dimensions, margins, headers, footers, positioning, font, color, and the like).

Currently, MSXML and the .NET Framework do not support XSL-FO.

Other Standards in the XML Family

In addition to XPath and XSLT, W3C is working on various other standards related to XML. Even though there isn't as yet a great deal of support for these standards, it is nonetheless useful to be aware of them. In this section, we'll briefly discuss these standards and see where they are as far as the W3C standardization process is concerned.

XLink and XPointer

Resembling an HTML-type linking mechanism for XML documents is the XML Linking Language, XLink. XLink is a W3C Recommendation that describes elements that can be inserted into XML documents to create and describe links between resources. This specification not only allows simple one-way links between two resources, but also supports more sophisticated bi-directional links, 'multi-choice' links, and also links between resources that don't normally have the ability to contain links, such as image files.

XLink v1.0 is now a W3C Recommendation at http://www.w3.org/TR/xlink/.

XLink can be used to create a link in one document pointing to another XML document. To point to just a part of another XML document, we use the XML Pointer Language (XPointer). XPointer, currently in candidate recommendation status, is a W3C specification based on XPath, and allows referring to some portion (a sub-tree, attributes, text characters, etc.) of another XML document.

The specification lives at http://www.w3.org/TR/xptr.

XQuery

The W3C XML Query Working Group is tasked to formulate a universal XML-based query language that can be used to access XML, relational, and other data stores. XQuery is intended to provide a vendor-independent, powerful, but easy-to-use method for query and retrieval of XML and non-XML (exposed as XML by some middleware) data. XQuery can be treated as a superset to XPath 2.0.

Microsoft has created an online demo, and downloadable .NET libraries, that can be used to play about with the XQuery 1.0 Working Draft. More details on this can be found at http://131.107.228.20.

There are already many commercial products available that have implemented XQuery, such as those listed at http://www.w3.org/XML/Query#products.

XQuery 1.0 is currently in Working Draft status, and is available at http://www.w3.org/TR/xquery/.

XHTML

XHTML is nothing but HTML 4.01 written in conformance to XML rules. This means XHTML documents must be *well-formed*. The W3C tagline for XHTML specification is **"a reformulation of HTML 4 in XML 1.0"** (http://www.w3.org/TR/xhtml1).

The W3C has also designed modularized XHTML (http://www.w3.org/TR/xhtml-modularization/), which essentially splits XHTML into separate abstract modules, each of which represents some specific functionality in XHTML.

Finally, a simplified and minimal set of these modules have been defined as XHTML Basic (http://www.w3.org/TR/xhtml-basic).

All three W3C specifications – XHTML 1.0, Modularization of XHTML, and XHTML Basic – have reached Recommendation status.

XForms

Forms are an integral part of the Web. Nearly all user interaction on the Web is through forms of some sort. However, today's HTML forms blend the form's *purpose* with its *presentation*, are device and platform dependent, and do not integrate well with XML.

W3C is working on defining the next generation of forms, and calling it XForms (http://www.w3.org/MarkUp/Forms/). The biggest strength of XForms is the distillation of forms into three layers – purpose, presentation, and data.

The data layer refers to the **instance data** – an internal representation of the data mapped (using XPath) to the form controls.

The presentation layer is dependent on the client loading the XForms – this makes XForms device independent, and the same form can be rendered as HTML or WML, or sent to an audio device.

The XForms namespace defines elements such as `<input>`, `<choices>`, and `<selectOne>`; these are the basic constructs used in XForms – and define the purpose, with no reference to the presentation.

XForms 1.0 is a Last Call Working Draft, at http://www.w3.org/TR/xforms/.

XML Security Standards

When XML is used as the medium to perform business data transactions over the Internet, it becomes critical that the XML is secured: that data privacy and integration rules are met.

W3C has started three initiatives to create a robust mechanism to ensure data integrity and authentication for XML. These are XML Signature, XML Encryption, and the XML Key Management Specification (XKMS).

XML Signature

Out of the three initiatives outlined above, XML Signature is the most mature specification, and as of writing the only specification that has reached the Recommendation status. XML-Signature Syntax and Processing (http://www.w3.org/TR/xmldsig-core/) is a joint initiative between the IETF and W3C to outline the XML syntax and processing rules for creating and representing digital signatures. More details on XML Signatures can be found at http://www.w3.org/TR/xmldsig-core/.

XML Encryption

The XML Encryption Syntax and Processing specification (http://www.w3.org/TR/xmlenc-core/) reached the W3C candidate recommendation status on March 4, 2002. This specification outlines the process for encrypting data and representing the result in XML. The result of encrypting data is an XML Encryption `EncryptedData` element, which contains (via its children's content) or identifies (via a URI reference) the cipher data. More details on XML Encryption can be found at http://www.w3.org/TR/xmlenc-core/.

XML Key Management Specification (XKMS)

XML Signature specification provides no means to properly validate the signer's identity before accepting a signed message. Similarly, when the encrypted message is received, XML Encryption specification does not provide anything to retrieve the encryption key. The Public-key infrastructure (PKI) can be helpful in such situations.

W3C has defined another specification, called XKMS, that specifies the protocols for distributing and registering public keys, suitable for use in conjunction with the XML Signature and XML Encryption standards. More details can be found at http://www.w3.org/TR/xkms/.

Visit http://www.xml.org/xml/resources_focus_security.shtml to get more information on XML Security standards.

XML Messaging

Before delving deep into this section, let's consider a few facts:

❑   XML is plain text. It is license free. It is platform and language independent

❑   XML is a standard, and is widely implemented

❑   XML allows encapsulating structured data, and metadata

❑   XML is extensible

❑   HTTP is also widely accepted, very well implemented, and a standard protocol

❑   Most firewalls readily work with HTTP and have port 80 open

❑   HTTP is based on request-response model

❑   By adding 'S' to the end of HTTP, we make HTTP communication secure (using SSL)

❑   It is very difficult (if not impossible) to write distributed applications that can run over the Internet and across different platforms using proprietary technologies and messaging formats (DCOM, CORBA, RMI, etc.).

Considering all the above facts, we can surely say that the combination of XML with HTTP (to begin with) makes a very interesting platform from which to build distributed applications that can run over the Internet and across platforms.

XML-RPC

Dave Winer of UserLand Software, Inc. (www.userland.com) initiated talks with other industry experts (from DevelopMentor and Microsoft) about *"remote procedure calls over the Internet"*. Not getting the expected response from Microsoft, Dave Winer went ahead and announced XML-RPC. The bottom line is that the XML-RPC specification allows software running on disparate systems to make procedure calls over the Internet, using HTTP as the transport and XML as the message encoding scheme. More details on XML-RPC can be found at http://www.xmlrpc.com.

SOAP

The result of discussion between UserLand, DevelopMentor, Microsoft, and a few other organizations on the topic of building a platform-independent distributed systems architecture using XML and HTTP, SOAP was submitted for a W3C Note under the name of SOAP (for Simple Object Access Protocol), at http://www.w3.org/TR/SOAP/. Note that from SOAP 1.2, the term SOAP is no longer officially an acronym, although it originally stood for Simple Object Access Protocol.

The original name pretty much indicates SOAP's prime aims, namely to provide a simple and lightweight mechanism for exposing the functionality of objects in a decentralized, distributed environment. It is built on XML.

SOAP forms one of the foundation stones of XML Web Services. XML Web Services can be defined as loosely coupled software components that interact with one another dynamically via standard Internet technologies.

The SOAP specification uses the XML syntax to define the request and response message structure, known as the *Envelope*. With HTTP, the client *POST*s the request envelope to the server, and in result gets a response envelop back.

Let's see an example of a SOAP request envelope to illustrate:

```
<?xml version="1.0" encoding="utf-8"?>
<soap:Envelope xmlns:xsi="http://www.w3.org/2001/XMLSchema-instance"
               xmlns:xsd="http://www.w3.org/2001/XMLSchema"
               xmlns:soap="http://schemas.xmlsoap.org/soap/envelope/">
  <soap:Body>
    <GetAmazonPrice xmlns=
     "http://www.PerfectXML.com/NETWebSvcs/BookService">
      <ISBN>186100589X</ISBN>
    </GetAmazonPrice>
  </soap:Body>
</soap:Envelope>
```

The above SOAP request envelope calls a method called `GetAmazonPrice` passing an ISBN as the parameter. When the above SOAP envelope is posted to the Web Service endpoint, the following response envelope is received in reply:

```
<?xml version="1.0" encoding="utf-8"?>
<soap:Envelope xmlns:xsi="http://www.w3.org/2001/XMLSchema-instance"
               xmlns:xsd="http://www.w3.org/2001/XMLSchema"
               xmlns:soap="http://schemas.xmlsoap.org/soap/envelope/">
  <soap:Body>
    <GetAmazonPriceResponse xmlns=
     "http://www.PerfectXML.com/NETWebSvcs/BookService">
      <GetAmazonPriceResult>$34.99</GetAmazonPriceResult>
    </GetAmazonPriceResponse>
  </soap:Body>
</soap:Envelope>
```

There are many toolkits available today that simplify SOAP development. Microsoft's SOAP Toolkit, at http://msdn.microsoft.com/soap, allows writing SOAP clients and servers, and in addition, allows COM components to be easily converted into SOAP servers that can then be used as Web Services.

The .NET Framework supports XML Web Services very well, and Web Services and clients can be created very easily in ASP.NET. In addition to the SOAP interface, Web Services created with .NET also support the regular HTTP GET and POST interfaces. Thus SOAP is not required to access the Web Service, and a regular HTTP GET or POST request can access the Web Service and retrieve the results as XML. We'll have a look at ASP.NET XML Web Services in a B2B context in Chapter 8.

The SOAP Toolkit and the .NET Framework implement SOAP 1.1. The current working draft of SOAP 1.2 is divided into three parts:

1. **SOAP 1.2 Part 0: Primer** (http://www.w3.org/TR/soap12-part0/) is an easily readable tutorial on the features of SOAP version 1.2.

2. **SOAP 1.2 Part 1: Messaging Framework** (http://www.w3.org/TR/soap12-part1/) describes the SOAP envelope and SOAP transport binding framework.

3. **SOAP 1.2 Part 2: Adjuncts** (http://www.w3.org/TR/soap12-part2/) describes the RPC convention and encoding rules along with a concrete HTTP binding specification.

WSDL

The Web Services Description Language (WSDL) is another important pillar in the XML Web Services architecture. It is an XML based format describing the complete set of interfaces exposed by a Web Service. As the component technologies (such as COM) make use of an IDL file to define the component interfaces, the XML Web Services make use of the WSDL file to define the set of operations and messages that can be sent to and received from a given Web Service. A WSDL document (.wsdl file) serves as a **contract** between clients and the server.

WSDL 1.1 is currently a W3C Note described at http://www.w3.org/TR/wsdl.

When an ASP.NET Web Service project is created using Visual Studio .NET, it automatically creates a WSDL file, and updates it automatically as Web Service methods are added or removed. A Web Service client can then access this .wsdl file (by selecting Project | Add Web Reference in Visual Studio .NET or by running wsdl.exe), and create a proxy class from it which allows them to access the Web Service's exposed methods (**web methods**). The WSDL documents created by Visual Studio .NET describe HTTP GET and POST based operations in addition to SOAP. This allows a client to access web methods by HTTP GET or POST request (application/x-www-form-urlencoded), instead of posting a SOAP request envelope. In addition to SOAP and HTTP GET/POST, the WSDL specification also permits a MIME binding.

The WSDL document can be divided into two main sections:

❑ Abstract Definitions: Defines the SOAP messages without references to the site that processes them. Abstract definitions sections contain three sections, <types>, <messages>, and <portType>.

❑ Concrete Descriptions: Contains site-specific information, such as transport and encoding method. The Concrete Descriptions comprise two sections, <binding> and <service>

The <types> section contains the type definitions that may be used in the exchanged messages. The <messages> section represents an abstract definition of the data being transmitted. It contains one <message> element for each request and response message. Each <message> element in turn contains <part> elements describing argument and return values, and their types. The input and output <message> are clubbed together under an <operation> element, and all <operation> elements are placed under the <portType> element, which identifies the messages exposed by the Web Service.

To map the above abstract definitions to physical concrete descriptions, we use the `<binding>` and `<service>` sections. The `<binding>` section specifies the physical bindings of each operation in the `<portType>` section. Web Services WSDL documents created with Visual Studio .NET contain three `<binding>` sections, for SOAP, HTTP GET, and HTTP POST. Finally, the `<service>` section is used to specify the port address (URL) for each binding. WSDL is described in detail in Chapter 8.

UDDI

Universal Description, Discovery, and Integration (UDDI) offers three main operations: *publish*, *find*, and *bind*. The notion behind UDDI is that it should be possible to dynamically locate businesses and businesses' Web Services, and bind to them so that they may be used in an application. The UDDI initiative outlines the specification and defines an API to perform these operations.

The UDDI registry is in public domain, and privately developed Web Services can be registered with the *registrars*. The links to version 1.0 of the IBM and Microsoft registry, and version 2.0 of the Hewlett-Packard, IBM, Microsoft, and SAP registries can be found at http://www.uddi.org/register.html.

Microsoft has released a UDDI SDK for the .NET Framework under the Software Development Kits hive at http://msdn.microsoft.com/downloads/. In addition, Microsoft .NET Server comes with UDDI Enterprise Server, which can be used to publish and find Web Services in an enterprise environment.

DIME

Direct Internet Message Encapsulation (DIME) is a specification submitted by Microsoft to the Internet Engineering Taskforce (IETF – see http://search.ietf.org/internet-drafts/draft-nielsen-dime-01.txt), and it defines a lightweight, binary message format that can be used to encapsulate one or more application-defined payloads of arbitrary type and size into a single message construct.

In other words, DIME can be used to send binary data with SOAP messaging, and it represents a very efficient means for transmitting multiple data objects (including binary) within a single SOAP message.

> *PocketSOAP (http://www.pocketsoap.com/) is one of the first SOAP Toolkits to support DIME. You can discuss DIME at http://discuss.develop.com/dime.html.*

GXA

In October 2001, Microsoft announced the Global XML Web Services Architecture (GXA) set of specifications to add static and dynamic message routing support, and security facilities to XML Web Services. These are technically SOAP extensions under the following four categories:

- ❑ **WS-Routing** (http://msdn.microsoft.com/library/en-us/dnglobspec/html/ws-routing.asp) defines how SOAP messages are routed from one node to the other.

- ❑ **WS-Referral** (http://msdn.microsoft.com/library/en-us/dnglobspec/html/ws-referral.asp) provides the mechanisms needed to enable SOAP applications to insert, delete, and query routing entries in a SOAP router through the exchange of referral information.

❑ **WS-Security** (http://msdn.microsoft.com/library/en-us/dnglobspec/html/ws-security.asp) describes SOAP extensions to ensure the message integrity, message confidentiality, and single message authentication.

❑ **WS-Inspection** (http://msdn.microsoft.com/library/default.asp?url=/library/en-us/dnglobspec/html/wsinspecspecindex.asp) supports querying the point of offering to retrieve a list of services offered. It is expected to replace .NET's Disco (for Discovery) interface.

WS-I

In February 2002, Microsoft and IBM announced a joint initiative to promote Web Services interoperability, in the form of the Web Services Interpretability Organization (http://www.ws-i.org/).

At the time of writing, WS-I membership has grown to more than 100. The two primary goals of the organization are to promote Web Services interoperability across platforms, operating systems, and programming languages; and to provide guidance, best practices, tools, and resources for developing Web Services solutions, with the aim of accelerating the adoption of Web Services.

REST

Representational State Transfer (or REST) is based on Roy Fielding's PhD dissertation (http://www.ebuilt.com/fielding/pubs/dissertation/top.htm), and is an architectural style that models system behavior for network-based applications. The idea behind REST is to describe the characteristics of the Web, with the aim of providing a model that can be exploited by developers

With this model, the traditional HTTP GET/POST URI-based model is used to create and access XML Web Services instead of SOAP. For instance, instead of posting a SOAP envelope request, we'll simply send a GET request containing method parameters in the querystring appended to the URL. We recieve the XML result without any SOAP packaging overhead. There is currently a little debate about what exactly SOAP adds, and if it isn't just a lot simpler to use existing web facilities (HTTP, GET, POST) for XML Web Services.

To keep abreast with REST, join the mailing list at http://groups.yahoo.com/group/rest-discuss/.

Summary

Hopefully this chapter has provided a good grounding in XML and its surrounding standards. We have talked about almost all key XML standards, current and future. We've seen that XML is much more than just a format for representing data, and there is a wealth of supporting technologies for common tasks with XML documents. As these technologies mature, third-party implementations arise to support them. If your core data is in XML, you may well be able to find an implementation that will let you do what you want in far fewer lines of code.

If you need to navigate a document, add to it, or change it in simple ways, there are at least two ways: the Document Object Model (DOM), a W3C Recommendation widely supported in code, and SAX, a de facto model also enjoying wide support. The .NET XML classes introduce yet another way to do the same thing, as we shall see in the next chapter.

XPath currently allows querying of an XML document. In the future XQuery will arrive, although software implementations are currently lacking. Visual rendering? Use XSLT to convert the XML into appropriate HTML and feed it to a web browser. Better still, there are a number of XML vocabularies for which native rendering code is available. In vector graphics, the SVG vocabulary is well supported by a free component from Adobe (http://www.adobe.com/svg). If you need mathematical formulae in text, you can encode your data in MathML and use one of several renderers for it (for example, Design Science's MathPlayer, http://www.dessci.com/webmath/mathplayer/). SMIL encodes multimedia, while VoiceXML covers voice response applications. ChemML is useful for visualizing chemical structures, and a viewer already exists for it. The list increases daily.

You can use the same technique, XSLT, to translate from one XML vocabulary to another. You can refer to one bit of XML from another using XPointer, XLink, or XInclude. Security issues are being addressed through XML signatures (http://www.w3.org/TR/xmldsig-core/) and XML encryption (http://www.w3.org/TR/xmlenc-core/). SOAP, as noted earlier, is an XML vocabulary, and all of the integration servers support XML as one of their primary formats. Messaging with Microsoft Message Queuing supports XML very well using features of the XML and MSMQ COM classes. Communications, therefore, should be easy.

Once you have your native data in XML form, you are, to borrow a phrase, "halfway to anywhere". XML is such a useful format and enjoys such market penetration that software support is widely available for any commonly used XML technology. The W3C, among others, has extended XML in so many useful ways that you will find that many common and useful tasks can be readily performed using one of these technologies. The .NET classes provide built-in support for many of them. If you use XML, you will find that you can leverage this base of existing code and programming tools when building your web applications.

For a more in-depth discussion of XML and its related standards, take a look at *Professional XML 2nd edition* (Wrox Press, ISBN 1-86100-505-9).

2

XmlReader and XmlWriter

Having read through the previous chapter, you're probably eager to start applying some of your XML know-how to XML documents in ASP.NET. In order to do that, you need to understand how to move documents back and forth, how to read them, how to parse them, and how to create them programmatically. In this chapter, we're going to see a series of .NET Framework classes that provide all these abilities, observing the rules of well-formed XML markup as they go. Specifically, this chapter will cover:

- The nature of stream-based document processing
- The object model of the portion of the `System.Xml` namespace that deals with stream-based XML document processing
- Parsing documents with `XmlTextReader`
- Validating documents using `XmlValidatingReader`
- Writing new XML markup using `XmlTextWriter`

The most basic task in XML programming is reading an existing document, and the `XmlReader` class provides this capability. We'll take a look at it, and put two of its derived classes – `XmlTextReader` and `XmlValidatingReader` – to work in a sample application. We'll use them to read, categorize, and validate XML documents posted to a server using a web form. While we're at it, we'll also explore a caching mechanism for XML validation that will make your ASP.NET applications more efficient.

Once you're confident reading XML documents, you'll want to start creating and writing your own XML documents from ASP.NET. `XmlWriter` (and its derived class, `XmlTextWriter`) is the class for that. We'll return to our sample application, and modify it to write XML log files on the server.

Reading XML: XmlReader

The best way to get to grips with XML in ASP.NET is through the XmlReader class, which is found in the System.Xml namespace. However, no ASP.NET application, no matter how rudimentary, will use XmlReader directly – it's an abstract class. Instead, you must instantiate one of the three classes derived from it, or derive one of your own. We'll shortly consider two of the derived classes that will usually be sufficient for ASP.NET applications. If, having seen the abilities of these classes, you find that you need specialized processing for your particular application, you can derive your own class from XmlReader.

Inevitably, all of the classes derived from XmlReader are closely related, and we can take an overview of how they work before diving into the detail of actually using them in an application.

Processing Concept

XmlReader is **stream-oriented**, which means that it regards an XML document as an incoming stream of text data. Unlike some other processing models, stream-oriented interfaces work on the document as it flows through the reader; nothing is captured for you in a data structure. If you want to hang on to some piece of information, you must record it yourself. This is what gives XmlReader its low overhead and superior efficiency. Without any need for an in-memory data structure to contain the document as a whole, XmlReader consumes only as much memory as it needs to look at the current chunk of the document. Since it performs only minimal checking on the document, classes derived from XmlReader are fast – of the three built-in ones (XmlTextReader, XmlNodeReader, and XmlValidatingReader), only the third even performs XML validation, and is slower than the other two as a consequence.

So how does the stream look to an instance of a class derived from XmlReader? The first thing to make clear is that XmlReader does *not* expose the stream to an application on a character-by-character basis – if it did, you might as well implement your own parser! Rather, XmlReader returns **nodes** of information, where each node is meaningful in the context of XML: elements, comments, attributes, and CDATA sections are all just nodes to XmlReader.

XmlReader classes work on a stream by reading it one *node* at a time. The Read method is called iteratively to process a single node from the stream. Consider the following illustration:

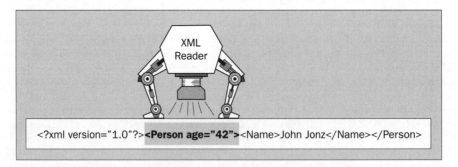

This shows how the XmlReader class processes XML documents one element at a time. Be aware that XmlReader uses a **pull model** for stream processing. Pull models require that the program using the class must take some action to move the data stream through the processor.

*The alternative to pull models is the **push model**, as used (for example) by the popular SAX processor. Here, once document processing is initiated, the stream moves through the processor continuously. The processor fires events, and the application responds to those events.*

In the figure, Read has been called twice: once to get to the XML declaration, and once to reach the <Person> element's opening tag. Since XmlReader steps through meaningful units of information, we are able to interrogate the reader and determine that the current node is an element and that its name is Person, as well as other pertinent information. As soon as we move to the <Person> element, the XML declaration is gone, drifting off downstream beyond our reach. The <Name> element, on the other hand, is upstream, and equally inaccessible to us until we make another call to the Read method.

The streaming nature of XmlReader does create some restrictions. <Person> includes <Name> as a child element, and <Name> has a child text node, but although the reader is currently at the <Person> element, it doesn't have any knowledge about the elements within it, and we won't find out about them without further calls to Read. XmlReader, like all other stream-oriented readers, compromises accessibility in the name of speediness by simply reading opening or closing tags as they are encountered in the document. Given that no elements have previously been encountered in the stream in the above example, our reader knows that it is processing the start of an element.

There is one final nuance to consider. Attributes are wholly contained in the opening tag of an element, and so they *are* read along with the tag. As we shall see shortly, getting at attributes requires that we call specialized methods on reaching the start of an element, to iterate through the attributes set for it.

Derived Classes

As we've mentioned a couple of times already, XmlReader is an abstract class, so we need to use one of the derived classes that inherits the features of XmlReader. The following diagram shows the classes available; the box in the lower right-hand corner represents a variety of supporting classes that work with the main classes to provide features that are not provided by the basic XmlReader interface. The very existence of these classes should serve to remind you that XmlReader is a lean implementation that requires a little effort to perform more advanced operations. Happily, we can usually just add the class or classes that are needed for the task at hand, thereby keeping system resource consumption to a minimum.

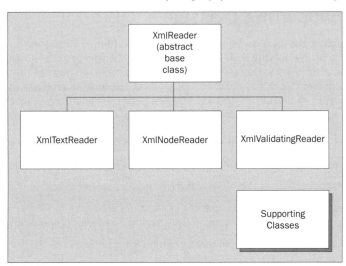

The .NET System.Xml namespace includes three classes derived from XmlReader:

❑ XmlTextReader: a high performance reader that processes XML documents as streams of text without caching, entity resolution, or validation. It does, however, enforce XML rules for well-formedness.

❑ XmlValidatingReader: an implementation of XmlReader that's similar to XmlTextReader, but also performs validation against a DTD, a Microsoft XDR Schema, or a W3C XML Schema (XSD format).

❑ XmlNodeReader: a variation on XmlReader that processes XML from an instance of XmlNode.

In this chapter, we'll use the first two of these three classes. XmlTextReader represents the fastest, leanest way to process XML documents in .NET, and it's most useful when you're working with documents that are either known to be valid, or do not conform to an explicit schema and therefore only need to be well-formed. The former case can arise when validation occurs in some other part of the application (as a result of an authoring or pre-processing step, for example). The latter frequently occurs in web applications, where programmers often create 'implicit' schemas when using XML internally. There is no formal schema (or DTD), and the XML need only be good enough for the application. This certainly isn't the best way to program with XML, but it happens a lot and benefits from the simplicity and speed offered by XmlTextReader.

If, however, you are a careful programmer, you are likely to need to validate a document at some point, and XmlValidatingReader provides one way to do that. It is very closely related to XmlTextReader – in fact, you generally construct an instance of this class by passing it an instance of XmlTextReader! We'll do just that in a later section of this chapter.

XmlNodeReader is something of a hybrid that's constructed by passing in an instance of XmlNode, and can be used to navigate through a tree of such nodes that have been placed in memory (say, a DOM tree) using some other technique, or a different family of XML-processing classes. We'll be giving no further coverage to XmlNodeReader in this chapter, but it's treated well in the MSDN documentation.

XmlReader Supporting Classes

As we described above, the XmlReader model uses some additional classes for dealing with tasks such as handling schema or to resolving XML entities. The act of 'factoring out' such functionality further streamlines XmlReader, leaving the reader itself lean and compact. As you require additional services, you instantiate the helper classes you need, and assign those instances to properties of the reader. This is a nice model, because if you don't need the help, you don't incur the overhead. The main classes provided to support XmlReader are also drawn from the System.Xml namespace, and they're listed below:

❑ XmlNameTable: a lookup table implementation for the storage of repeating names (see below)

❑ XmlConvert: type conversions between CLR and schema types

❑ XmlNamespaceManager: resolves and stores namespace information

❑ XmlParserContext: maintains parsing context (for example: namespaces, document encoding, public or system IDs, xml:lang, and xml:scope information)

❑ XmlUrlResolver: external resource resolution from URIs

A reader object will create an instance of `XmlNametable` (or rather, of the derived class, `NameTable` – `XmlNameTable` is abstract) to record the names it encounters while parsing a document. This allows it to record a repeated element name (say, `TaxablePrice`), assign it a token, and use that (much shorter) token wherever the name appears. The other classes listed above, like `XmlParserContext`, are set up by the application programmer and passed to the reader to help it make sense of an incoming document. In general, you'll find that either the Framework will take care of things for us behind the scenes, or the need for a helper will be clear from the context.

Besides the classes that provide additional features, the `System.Xml` namespace contains enumerations that describe various aspects of XML processing. These enumerations, which you will encounter frequently in this chapter, are:

❑   `XmlNodeType`: the type of an XML node (element or attribute, for example)

❑   `WhitespaceHandling`: XML options for processing whitespace and exposing it to an application

❑   `ValidationType`: the type of document validation to perform

❑   `XmlSpace`: the type of whitespace (that is, whether it's significant)

❑   `ReadState`: the internal processing state of the XML processor

At this stage, we've covered enough groundwork to be ready for a look at the leanest class in the `XmlReader` family: `XmlTextReader`.

XmlTextReader

If you want to read an XML document with the best performance possible, but you don't require validation, then the workhorse `XmlTextReader` class is the one to use. It provides the means to open and parse documents, and it contains hooks for resolving external entities and DTDs with the help of the supporting classes we mentioned earlier. This class will let us get into XML processing with minimal effort, and it will serve to explain some key `XmlReader` concepts in depth.

Constructors

As usual, the first thing we need to do to use this class is create an instance of it, using one of the many overloaded constructors that `XmlTextReader` provides for this purpose. The multiplicity of constructors is due to the fact that the constructor can also open the XML document you want to process, and how you open a document depends on how you locate it. Here are your options:

Constructor	Use
`XmlTextReader()`	Protected constructor that initializes an empty reader. If, for example, you were deriving a class that stuffed information into a database as the document is processed, you might use this constructor to initialize a database connection.
`XmlTextReader(Stream)`	Creates a new reader poised to begin reading the XML document contained in the stream passed in.

Table continued on following page

Constructor	Use
`XmlTextReader(String)`	Creates a new reader poised to read the XML document whose URL is passed as the input parameter.
`XmlTextReader(TextReader)`	Initializes a new `XmlTextReader` given an XML document in a `TextReader` instance. `TextReader` is a simple text-file reading class.
`XmlTextReader(Stream, XmlNameTable)`	Initializes the reader object with a document in the stream parameter, using the names in the `XmlNameTable` parameter. `XmlNameTable` allows some economy of representation by providing a lookup table of names.
`XmlTextReader(String, Stream)`	The value of the base URI (namespace qualification) for the XML document in the stream parameter is contained in the string parameter.
`XmlTextReader(String, TextReader)`	As above, except that the input document is contained in a `TextReader` object.
`XmlTextReader(String, XmlNameTable)`	Initializes a reader with a document pointed to by the URL in the string parameter; the `XmlNameTable` parameter contains commonly used names for the document.
`XmlTextReader(Stream, XmlNodeType, XmlParserContext)`	The stream parameter contains an XML fragment; the `XmlNodeType` parameter is an enumeration indicating what sort of fragment (element, attribute, document, etc.) is being passed, and the parser context identifies a collection of information that includes encoding type, name table, and language.
`XmlTextReader(String, Stream, XmlNameTable)`	The string contains the base URI of the document contained in the stream parameter, while the `XmlNameTable` parameter provides commonly used names for use when parsing the document.
`XmlTextReader(String, TextReader, XmlNameTable)`	As immediately above, except that the document is contained in a `TextReader` object.
`XmlTextReader(String, XmlNodeType, XmlParserContext)`	As `XmlTextReader(Stream, XmlNodeType, XmlParserContext)`, except the document is referred to by the URL in the string parameter.

There is also a protected constructor of the form XmlTextReader(XmlNameTable), but this is intended for use by code in the Framework, and cannot be used by applications.

Properties

Once you've initialized a reader object, you have to start parsing the document by pulling nodes from the stream using its Read method, which we'll discuss in the next section. For now, assume that you have a markup node. The properties of XMLTextReader provide information about that node (or the document as a whole), as detailed in the following table:

Property	Meaning
AttributeCount *(read-only)*	Integer count of attributes belonging to the current node (only used for nodes of type Element, DocumentType, and XmlDeclaration).
BaseURI *(read-only)*	String containing the URI of the document's namespace.
CanResolveEntity *(read-only)*	Boolean returning true only when the reader supports DTD information and can resolve XML entities in a document. It therefore returns false for XMLTextReader.
Depth *(read-only)*	Integer indicating the level of the current node in the document hierarchy. The document element has depth zero.
Encoding *(read-only)*	(Object) property describing the character encoding of the document.
EOF *(read-only)*	Boolean value that is true when the end of the document is reached.
HasAttributes *(read-only)*	Boolean property that's true only when the current node has attributes.
HasValue *(read-only)*	Boolean value that's true when the current node has a value. Will always be true for Attribute, CDATA, Comment, DocumentType, Text, ProcessingInstruction, Whitespace, SignificantWhitespace, and XmlDeclaration node types.
IsDefault *(read-only)*	Boolean property that always returns false in XmlTextReader, as this class does not expand default attributes.
IsEmptyElement *(read-only)*	Boolean that's true when the current node is an empty element.
Item *(read-only)*	Overloaded indexer property. Given the zero-based ordinal index (integer) or string name of an attribute, this property returns a string containing the contents of that attribute.
LineNumber *(read-only)*	Integer indicating the line number of the current node in the XML document.

Table continued on following page

Property	Meaning
LinePosition *(read-only)*	Integer indicating the (one-based) position within the line of the current node in the XML document.
LocalName *(read-only)*	Unqualified string name of the current node.
Name *(read-only)*	Qualified string name of the current node.
Namespaces *(read-write)*	Boolean set to `true` when namespace support is to be used, or `false` otherwise.
NamespaceURI *(read-only)*	String containing the URI of the current node's namespace.
NameTable *(read-only)*	Property returning the `XmlNameTable` object that contains a lookup table of repeated names in the document.
NodeType *(read-only)*	Enumerated type denoting the type of the current node (`Element`, `Attribute`, etc.)
Normalization *(read/write)*	Property that controls whitespace and attribute normalization. This is `true` when normalization is on, but it may be changed between calls to `Read`. When `true`, non-significant whitespace is normalized to a single space character, and character entities are resolved to the referenced characters.
Prefix *(read-only)*	String containing the namespace prefix of the current node.
QuoteChar *(read-only)*	A character value containing the character used to enclose attribute values.
ReadState *(read-only)*	Enumeration indicating the state of processing of the reader. Possible values are: `Closed` – the reader's `Close` method has been called `EndOfFile` – the end of the document has been reached `Error` – an error that prevents further processing has occurred `Initial` – the reader has been initialized but the `Read` method has yet not been called `Interactive` – the reader is processing a document (`Read` has been called at least once)
Value *(read-only)*	String value of the current node; see `HasValue` for relevant nodes.

Property	Meaning
`WhitespaceHandling` *(read/write)*	Enumerated value that controls what happens when the reader passes whitespace to the application. Possible values are:
	`All` – returns all whitespace and significant whitespace nodes
	`None` – does not return whitespace nodes of any type
	`Significant` – returns only significant whitespace nodes.
`XmlLang` *(read-only)*	String indicating the `xml:lang` scope of the current node ("en-us", for example).
`XmlResolver` *(write-only)*	Property for setting an instance of `XmlResolver` for use in retrieving DTDs and schemas, as well as schema include and import items (see later).
`XmlSpace` *(read-only)*	Enumerated value describing the `xml:space` attribute of the document. Possible values are:
	`Default` – default whitespace handling
	`None` – no `xml:space` scope
	`Preserve` – `xml:space` has the value `preserve`
	Controls how whitespace is handled in certain contexts (within elements, for example). Processors usually normalize non-significant whitespace, but document authors can use `xml:space` to prevent this. Note, however, that the value of the `xml:space` attribute (or the value of this property) is strictly advisory, and many processors other than these classes do not respect it.

Although they belong to the document reader as a whole, many of these properties detail specifics of the node that's currently 'in view'. As the stream is pulled through the reader, the reader's properties reflect the nature of the node currently being read.

Methods

While the properties of `XmlTextReader` can tell us things about the current node, the methods of the class perform the stream-based mechanics of navigating through the document. Since the `XmlReader` interface is a pull model, the sequence in which you call these methods completely controls the flow of the stream through the reader. The only thing you cannot control, however, is the direction: the flow is *always* forward only. If we wish to retain information about elements after the stream has moved on, we must create and use our own data structures.

> *For brevity in this table, we'll omit the methods inherited from `System.Object`. Since we haven't discussed the base class `XmlReader` in depth, we'll note which methods are overloaded or inherited from that class in this table, but then omit them when we discuss the `XmlValidatingReader` class.*

Method	Parameters and Purpose
Close	Ends processing and releases resources used by the processor. If the reader was constructed with a `Stream` object, the stream is closed. No parameters.
GetAttribute	Overloaded method that takes either an integer ordinal index or a string name, and returns the attribute referenced by the passed parameter.
GetRemainder	Takes no parameters and returns a `TextReader` object containing the unread, buffered remainder of the XML document. After this method is called, the `EOF` property is set to `true`.
IsName	Inherited from `XmlReader`, this method takes a string containing a name and returns `true` if the string value is a valid XML name.
IsNameToken	As with `IsName`, except that the reader is testing whether the parameter is a valid XML name token.
IsStartElement	Takes no parameters and returns `true` if the current node is the opening tag of an element.
LookupNamespace	Takes a string namespace prefix and returns the URI of the namespace associated with that prefix.
MoveToAttribute	This method is overloaded and takes either an integer (zero-based) or a string name and moves the current node to the desired attribute.
MoveToContent	Inherited. Moves to the next content node (non-whitespace text, `CDATA`, `Element`, `EndElement`, `EntityReference`, or `EndEntity`) if the current node is not itself a content node. No parameters.
MoveToElement	Overridden. Checks to see if the current node is an attribute. If not, it returns `false`. If it is, it moves the current node back to the element containing the attribute and returns `true`. No parameters.
MoveToFirstAttribute	Overridden. Takes no parameters and moves the current node to the first attribute of the current node (if the current node has an attribute). Returns `true` if successful, `false` otherwise.
MoveToNextAttribute	Overridden. Returns `true` and moves the current node to the next attribute (if any), or `false` otherwise. No parameters.
Read	Overridden. This key method takes no parameters and advances the reader to the next node. Returns `true` if the reader advances, `false` if there are no more nodes.

Method	Parameters and Purpose
ReadAttributeValue	Overridden. Used to process attributes containing entity values, this method takes no parameters and advances the current node to the next Text, EndEntity, or EntityReference value in the attribute. Returns false if the end of the attribute value has been reached, or the reader's current node is not positioned on an attribute when the method is called.
ReadBase64	Reads a node containing base-64 encoded content, decodes it, and writes the equivalent text into an array. Its parameters are: Array – an array of bytes to receive text Offset – integer offset from the start of the array denoting where to begin writing text Len – integer length of bytes to write
ReadBinHex	Same parameters and meaning as ReadBase64, except that the encoding is binary hexadecimal.
ReadChars	Same parameters as ReadBase64, except that the array is typed as char[]. This method reads text content into a character array. The purpose is to grant applications control over how much text is read from a potentially lengthy source in any given read operation.
ReadElementString	Inherited. Used to read text-only element values, this method has three overloaded forms: The first takes no parameters and returns the text node of the element. The second takes a string representation of an element name and returns the text node if and only if the name matches the element name. The third form takes two string parameters – localname and URI – and returns the text node if the qualified element name matches these parameters.
ReadEndElement	Inherited. This method advances the reader to the next node. If the current node is not an element end tag, an XmlException instance is thrown.

Table continued on following page

Method	Parameters and Purpose
ReadInnerXml	No parameters. Reads the child markup of the current node when the current node is an element or an attribute, and returns that markup as a string. If the current node is some other type, or the current node has no content, it returns an empty string.
	If the current node is an element, the current position is advanced past the end tag; if an attribute, the current node pointer remains on the attribute. If the current node is an element with no further child content, the result is the same as a call to Read.
ReadOuterXml	As with ReadInnerXml, except that the containing node is returned with the child markup.
ReadStartElement	Checks that the current node is an element, and moves the current node pointer to the next node. No return value. There are three overloaded forms:
	The first takes no parameters.
	The second takes a string and moves the pointer only if the current node is an element with that name.
	The final form takes two strings – name and namespaceURI – and ensures that the current node is an element with the qualified name indicated by the parameters.
ReadString	Reads, concatenates, and returns all text, whitespace, and CDATA sections of the current node. It stops when any markup is encountered (mixed content models). If the current node is an attribute, the returned string is the content of the element possessing the attribute.
ResolveEntity	Inherited from XmlReader, this method is simply overridden to throw an InvalidOperation exception in all cases. XmlTextReader sacrifices the ability to resolve XML entities in favor of performance and a minimal footprint.
Skip	Advances the current node pointer to the next sibling node – that is, the next peer element. Takes no parameters and returns no value.

Typically, we use Read to iterate through nodes, and we'll have an example of that shortly. As an alternative, however, the MoveToContent method is ideal when we're processing a document in which we only have interest in the textual content. MoveToContent skips over nodes that cannot contain textual content (processing instructions, for example), and it skips over whitespace. We might want to use this in an application that uses XML to organize data within text nodes. In such structures, we seldom use attributes, and the content model of the document is relatively flat, using the text nodes (the bottommost leaves of the document tree) as slots for content.

XMLCategorizer Example: Web Forms and Reading XML

We'll illustrate the XmlTextReader class with an example that's useful for exploring stream-based processing models. The idea is to load a document and extract information such as the count of its elements and attributes. This has the interesting side effect of demonstrating the nested nature of XML structure. When processing a nested document, the sample will show:

- ❏ Element names
- ❏ Count of attributes on each element processed
- ❏ Attribute names
- ❏ Attribute values
- ❏ Comment text
- ❏ Textual content
- ❏ Global counts for elements, attributes, CDATA sections, comments, and processing instructions

Additionally, we'll note the document type declaration, if any, as it goes by.

Web Form Interface

The application takes the form of an ASP.NET Web Application project; so create a new one called XMLCategorizer now. Delete the default web form, and create a new one called selector.aspx. The visual elements of the user interface will be defined in this file, backed up by the processing code in the code-behind page selector.aspx.cs.

In the Design view for selector.aspx, open the HTML tab of the Toolbox, and drag out the following controls:

Control Type	(id) Property
Label	*blank*
File Field	fileSelector
Button	analyzeBtn
Text Area	resultsArea

Lay out these controls on the form, as shown below:

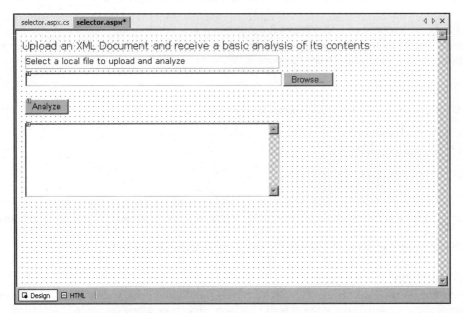

Notice that when the **File Field** input control is added, the **Browse** button is automatically placed alongside it. Notice also that you enter text for the HTML label by clicking it once to select it, and then clicking again (not double-clicking) to enter text. You can create the top label, which reads, **Upload an XML document and receive a basic analysis of its contents**, by switching to the HTML view and typing it in immediately after the `<body>` tag.

We're now ready to start thinking about how we'll code the page. When the user has selected a local file using the `fileSelector` control, we want to submit it to the server when they click the **Analyze** button. At this point, the contents of the selected file are picked up on the server, where the code-behind page will perform the processing we require. The code will output to the text area at the bottom of the page, and then the finished page can be returned to the user as the response to the form being posted.

The complete project can be found in the code download for this chapter, in the `XmlCategorizer` project folder.

Setting up the Web Form

We need to do two things to make the user interface work. First, we have to ensure that the selected file's contents will be posted to the server. Switch to the HTML view, and set the `enctype` attribute of the HTML `<form>` element to `multipart/form-data`:

```
<form id="selector" method="post" enctype="multipart/form-data" runat="server">
```

This `enctype` value ensures that the *contents* of the file are posted, rather than just the fully qualified path. (The path would be useless to the server, as it pertains to the client's local file system.) Now return to the Design view, and right-click and check **Run as Server Control** for the file field control, the **Analyze** button, and the text area.

Parsing an XML Document

The event handler for the button being clicked will be invoked by the .NET Framework whenever the web form is posted to the server. At this point, our code will have the contents of the posted file available, and because our form elements are configured as server controls, we can manipulate them in code too. This lets us get hold of the file (as a `Stream` object), and output information into the text area control so that it can be returned to the client as HTML text.

Double-click the **Analyze** button in the Designer to create an event handler where we can put our XML processing code. This is how the event handler starts:

```
private void analyzeBtn_ServerClick(object sender, System.EventArgs e)
{
    XmlTextReader xmlDoc = null;

    int nElements = 0;
    int gnAttributes = 0;
    int nComments = 0;
    int nPIs = 0;
    int nCDATAs = 0;

    string sWorkingText = "";
    resultsArea.InnerText = "";
```

So far, all we've done is to declare and initialize a bunch of variables – mainly integers – that we'll use to categorize the documents we read. The only variables that directly relate to a control or to XML processing are `xmlDoc`, which will be used to hold our `XmlTextReader` instance, and `resultsArea`, which is the name of the text area control.

The `XmlTextReader` class handles any problems with XML documents by throwing an exception of type `XmlException`. This makes it easy to respond to errors when the document is not a text document, or when an XML document is not well formed. We write code that we expect to work, and wrap it in a `try..catch` block:

```
try
{
    xmlDoc = new XmlTextReader(fileSelector.PostedFile.InputStream);
    xmlDoc.WhitespaceHandling = WhitespaceHandling.None;
```

The first line after the `try` statement feeds the document posted from the client web form into the `XmlTextReader` class constructor that takes a `Stream` object. We get the posted file by using the `fileSelector` variable, which represents the file field control. Since this is a server-side control, the .NET Framework will have created an object for it, named after the `id` of the control, which will contain the information passed in the HTTP POST. The `PostedFile` property of this object refers to that file; had we not set the `enctype` of the form as we did, it would only have contained the fully qualified filename.

So, the `PostedFile` property is an object whose `InputStream` property holds the contents of the file in the form of a stream, but the .NET Framework is doing a considerable amount of work behind the scenes to make things easy for us. The process is that the client opens a file, reads it, and passes it over HTTP to ASP.NET, which receives the stream and exposes it to us as the property of a class. Our code passes it to the constructor, and we are ready to work with the document. We set the reader's `WhitespaceHandling` property to the enumerated value `WhitespaceHandling.None` because we're not interested in whitespace in the document for this application.

Now that we've got the file as a stream in `xmlDoc`, we can step through it, reading one element at a time. The reader starts off positioned at the very beginning of the stream, and doesn't actually read anything until the first call to `Read`. Because `Read` returns `false` when the end of the document is reached, it's quite simple to run through the document an element at a time with a `while` loop:

```
while(xmlDoc.Read())
{
```

In the body of the loop, we're simply going to check what type of node we're currently at, and increment the appropriate counter variable. We check the type of the current node by examining the `NodeType` property of the reader in a `switch` statement:

```
switch(xmlDoc.NodeType)
{
```

The heart of our application lies in the body of this `switch` statement. The most important case is when element content is found:

```
case XmlNodeType.Element:
    nElements++;
    resultsArea.InnerText += "Element: " + xmlDoc.Name + " has " +
                        xmlDoc.AttributeCount +
                            " attributes" + Environment.NewLine;
    gnAttributes += xmlDoc.AttributeCount;
```

> *The `Environment.NewLine` property generates the character defined in the current operating environment as the newline character, allowing us to output information on individual lines. We can also indent a line by inserting the escaped literal character `\t`.*

The first and most obvious thing to do is to increment the global count of elements in the document, `nElements`. Then we insert a line of information into the text area (`resultsArea.InnerText`). The `Name` property gives us the element name, while `AttributeCount` conveniently tells us how many attributes are defined on the element. We reuse the last property in the next line, when we add it to the global count of attributes, `gnAttributes`.

Now we have to iterate through the attributes that have been specified for this element. To do this, we must explicitly iterate through the element's attributes while the reader's current node is the start element tag:

```
while(xmlDoc.MoveToNextAttribute())
{
    resultsArea.InnerText += "\t" + xmlDoc.Name + " = " +
```

```
                                xmlDoc.Value + Environment.NewLine;
            }
        break;
```

Notice how the `Name` property is again used here. As we move from the start of the element into the collection of attributes, the current node 'becomes' each attribute in turn, and `Name` takes on the value of the attribute name. Attributes are nodes that can have a value, so the `Value` property of the reader can be used to output those values, rounding out our element node processing.

Now we have the code to handle text nodes. We want to output a line of information that includes the text node's value. We're not going to maintain a count of text nodes, so the output line is the whole of our processing for this node type:

```
        case XmlNodeType.Text:
            sWorkingText = "Text: " + xmlDoc.Value + Environment.NewLine;
            resultsArea.InnerText += sWorkingText;
            break;
```

A well-formed XML document can have at most one document type declaration. If there is more than one, an exception will be thrown. Consequently, if we encounter this type of node, we simply want to generate a line noting the presence of the declaration:

```
        case XmlNodeType.DocumentType:
            resultsArea.InnerText += "Document has a DOCTYPE" +
                                    Environment.NewLine;
            break;
```

Comment handling is similar to text node processing, except that we also keep track of the number of comments in the document in the `nComments` variable:

```
        case XmlNodeType.Comment:
            nComments++;
            resultsArea.InnerText += "Comment: " + xmlDoc.Value +
                                    Environment.NewLine;
            break;
```

XML processing instructions are application-specific by nature. Since we're only interested in broadly characterizing a document, we simply increment the counter `nPIs`. We do the same thing for CDATA sections:

```
        case XmlNodeType.ProcessingInstruction:
            nPIs++;
            break;
        case XmlNodeType.CDATA:
            nCDATAs++;
            break;
    }
}
```

After we emerge from the `switch` statement, we hit the end of the `while` loop and move the reader's current node pointer to the next node. When we drop out of the `while` loop, it's because `Read` returned `false` on reaching the end of the document. Our counters will then contain global statistics to append to our results:

```
        sWorkingText = Environment.NewLine + "Total number of elements: " +
                    nElements + Environment.NewLine;
        sWorkingText += "Total number of attributes in document: " +
                    gnAttributes + Environment.NewLine;
        sWorkingText += "Total comments: " + nComments + Environment.NewLine;
        sWorkingText += "Total PIs: " + nPIs + Environment.NewLine;
        sWorkingText += "Total CDATA sections: " + nCDATAs;
        resultsArea.InnerText += sWorkingText;
    }
```

That completes the `try` section of the `try..catch` block, which will be executed as long as everything works as it should. Now let's code what happens when an exception is thrown:

```
    catch(XmlException exc)
    {
        sWorkingText = "Exception while parsing:" + Environment.NewLine;
        sWorkingText += "Line number: " + exc.LineNumber + Environment.NewLine;
        sWorkingText += "Line position: " + exc.LinePosition +
                    Environment.NewLine;
        sWorkingText += "Message: " + exc.Message +
                    Environment.NewLine + Environment.NewLine;
        sWorkingText += "Stack Trace:" + Environment.NewLine + exc.StackTrace;
        resultsArea.InnerText = sWorkingText;
    }
```

The `LineNumber` and `LinePosition` properties of the `XmlException` class locate the spot where parsing failed. `Message` is a human-readable statement of the problem. Just to round out the error handling (and overload the unsuspecting user), we toss in the contents of the `StackTrace` property. This is a list of the Framework classes that were executing at the time the reader failed parsing.

There's one more part of a `try..catch` block in .NET, and that's the `finally` statement. The code in this section will be executed whether or not exceptions were caught. We use it to clean up by closing the reader stream:

```
    finally
    {
        if(xmlDoc != null)
            xmlDoc.Close();
    }
```

Our code is now complete, and we're ready to run the project by hitting *F5*. Click the **Browse** button, and select one of the sample XML files that were provided with the code download (such as `sample_event.xml`). When you now click **Analyze**, the text area will show some results a little like this:

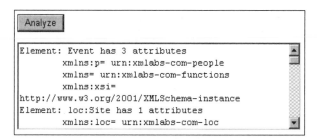

If you scroll down to the bottom of the text area, you will see the global statistics for the document. Experiment using different source XML files, and verify that the results are as expected. To test the exception handling, you might also like to try loading up an XML document that is not well formed, such as the `malformed_sample_event.xml` file:

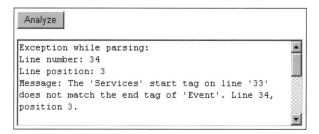

This code illustrates the basics of XML parsing with `XmlTextReader`, giving us the ability to read and analyze a well-formed document. What we lack is the ability to generate *new* markup, or to change anything at all. We'll come to these points later in the chapter, but for now let's address the other thing that `XmlTextReader` lacks: the ability to perform XML validation.

XmlValidatingReader

Although the classes in the `XmlReader` family are intended for lightweight and efficient XML processing, there are times when you have to validate an XML document against a formal specification of the document's XML vocabulary – when you're receiving a document from an external source, for example. The `XmlValidatingReader` class permits you to do this, while retaining many of the virtues of the `XmlReader` class. It works with DTDs, with Microsoft's XDR schemas, and with XSD-format schemas that conform to the W3C schema recommendation.

Architecture

`XmlValidatingReader` derives from `XmlReader`. It implements the basic stream-reading interface, and adds a layer of methods and properties for XML validation. As a result, it consumes more system resources than `XmlTextReader`.

What do you get for the extra money? Well, `XmlValidatingReader` resolves XML entities. It also manages namespace and metadata (DTD and schema) information. But even though these features require memory during the validation process, `XmlValidatingReader` is still a very efficient class in comparision to processing models that hold entire documents in memory, such as the Document Object Model (DOM). The DOM is the W3C's contribution to in-memory XML document processing, and is the topic of the next chapter.

While `XmlValidatingReader` implements the `XmlReader` class, we don't always start with an XML document and associate a validating reader with it. More commonly, we already have an `XmlTextReader` attached to an XML file (as in the preceding example), and *then* attach it to a validating reader to perform validation functions. This reflects the fact that `XmlValidatingReader` is a layer of validation functionality over and above the core, stream-based model, and allows us to write programs in which *we* decide whether to validate at run time, conserving system resources.

Constructors

The layered approach is brought home by the three constructors available for building validating readers:

Constructor	Usage
`XmlValidatingReader(XmlReader)`	Accepts an `XmlReader` instance (only `XmlTextReader` is supported in the current version of the Framework) and reads from it during validation. Throws an `ArgumentException` if the passed parameter is not an instance of `XmlTextReader`. This is used when you want to layer validation on top of an existing reader.
`XmlValidatingReader(Stream, XmlNodeType, XmlParserContext)`	Takes a stream containing a markup fragment, an enumerated type denoting the type of the fragment (only `Node`, `Document`, and `Attribute` are supported), and a parser context object. This is used when you have an existing parser context, typically when you have gone to the trouble of declaring a number of namespaces and want to reuse the information.
`XmlValidatingReader(string, XmlNodeType, XmlParserContext)`	As with the previous constructor, except that the markup fragment is contained in the string parameter.

The first constructor is the one most commonly used to validate complete documents. In concert with the `XmlTextReader` on which it is based, it provides the ability to open and process a document file (either locally, or from a remote source via a URL).

The other two constructors are for validating document fragments. If you were building a document over the course of several input forms, for example, you could use `XmlValidatingReader` to perform input field checking by validating partial documents as they are constructed. Alternatively, if you have a large document, you can extract a sub-tree that's of interest to your application, and validate it on its own.

Before we can work a validating reader, we need to know about the run-time interface it exposes. We'll begin with its properties.

Properties

Most of the properties of `XmlValidatingReader` are inherited from or overrides of the properties in `XmlReader`. In this table, we've omitted those properties that are simply inherited from `XmlReader`. A few properties, which are noted explicitly, are introduced by this class and serve to support validation:

Property	Meaning
AttributeCount *(read-only)*	Returns an integer count of the number of attributes on the current node. Applies to element, document type, and XML declaration nodes. Since metadata is now available, this count includes default attribute values. This permits application developers to use default values in their applications.
BaseURI *(read-only)*	As for XMLTextReader.
CanResolveEntity *(read-only)*	Returns a Boolean value of `true` if the reader can resolve entities. This class's implementation always returns `true`.
Depth *(read-only)*	As for XMLTextReader.
Encoding *(read-only)*	Duplicates a property of `XmlTextReader`, but does not inherit this from `XmlReader`. Returns an `Encoding` instance denoting the character encoding of the document. If none is provided in the document, UTF-8 is returned.
EntityHandling *(read/write)*	This property is introduced by the `XmlValidatingReader` class and describes how XML entities are processed. The property is typed as an instance of the public enumeration `EntityHandling`. If the value is `ExpandCharEntities`, character entities are expanded and returned as nodes; the `ResolveEntity` method must then be called to see the results of expansion. If the value is `ExpandEntities` (the default), entities are expanded and the expanded form is returned in lieu of the entity reference.
EOF *(read-only)*	As for XMLTextReader.
HasValue *(read-only)*	Returns the Boolean value `true` when the current node is of a type that can have values. See the equivalent entry in `XmlTextReader` for the node types that support values.
IsDefault *(read-only)*	Returns Boolean `true` when the current node is an attribute and the value is a default provided by the DTD or schema. Although `XmlReader` declares this property, `XmlValidatingReader` is the first class to implement the ability to detect this information, and therefore the only derived class that can return `true` as well as `false`.
IsEmptyElement *(read-only)*	As for XMLTextReader.

Table continued on following page

Property	Meaning
Item *(read-only)*	Indexer for the class. Three overloaded versions are provided. One takes a zero-based integer index and returns the referenced attribute of the current node. The other two take strings representing the attribute's name and return the attribute's value. One takes a single string providing the name, while the other takes a string representing the attribute's base URI and a second string providing the base name of the attribute.
LocalName *(read-only)*	As for XMLTextReader.
Name *(read-only)*	As for XMLTextReader.
Namespaces *(read/write)*	Although XmlTextReader has a similar property, this Boolean property is not inherited from XmlReader. When true, namespaces are supported. When false, namespaces are ignored. The default value is true.
NamespaceURI *(read-only)*	As for XMLTextReader.
NameTable *(read-only)*	The value of this property of type XmlNameTable is an atomized table of node names used in the document.
NodeType *(read-only)*	A NodeType enumeration indicating the XML type of the current node. This property won't return values for Document, DocumentFragment, Entity, or Notation nodes.
Prefix *(read-only)*	As for XMLTextReader.
QuoteChar *(read-only)*	As for XMLTextReader.
Reader *(read-only)*	XmlReader value containing the reader instance used to process the document. Introduced by XmlValidatingReader.
ReadState *(read-only)*	As for XMLTextReader.
Schemas *(read-only)*	Property returning an instance of XmlSchemaCollection. Used to cache schema files and associate them with their URIs (see later). New with XmlValidatingReader.
SchemaType *(read-only)*	New with this class, this Object property returns the type of the reader's current node, as declared in the schema. The value will be an XmlSchemaDatatype object if the node is declared as one of the built-in types defined in W3C XSD schemas, an XmlSchemaSimpleType if the node is an XSD simpleType, and an XmlSchemaComplexType if the node is declared as an XSD complexType. The property is null if the current node is not typed in the schema.

Property	Meaning
ValidationType *(read-write)*	Introduced with this class, this property has one of the ValidationType values to describe what sort of validation is to be performed. The values are:
	Auto – validation occurs based on a reference to DTD or schema information in the document
	DTD – XML 1.0 DTD validation
	None – XML 1.0-compliant non-validating processing
	Schema – W3C XSD format schema validation
	XDR – XML-DR validation
	The default is Auto.
Value *(read-only)*	As for XMLTextReader.
XmlLang *(read-only)*	As for XMLTextReader.
XmlResolver *(write-only)*	As for XMLTextReader.
XmlSpace *(read-only)*	As for XMLTextReader.

Methods

Most of the public methods of XmlValidatingReader have the same names as and behave identically to those of XmlTextReader, so we need not duplicate their descriptions here. The two entries in this table are peculiar to this class; add them to the list in the earlier table, noting as you do so that ReadBase64, ReadBinHex, and ReadChars are exclusive to XmlTextReader, and therefore absent from this class.

Method	Parameters and Purpose
ReadTypedValue	Introduced by this class, this method returns an object based on the type of the node as declared in the schema. Types returned are the CLR equivalent of XSD types. You may check the type with GetType, and then cast the value.
ResolveEntity	Overridden. Returns void. This method, inherited from XmlReader and given a non-trivial implementation in this class, is used to resolve XML entities. The current node must be an EntityReference node, or an InvalidOperationException will be thrown. If the entity is within an attribute, calling ReadAttributeValue returns the entity replacement text. For other nodes, calling Read causes the replacement text to be parsed.

Catching ValidationEvents

Validation warnings and errors are exposed to the application by validating readers in the form of `ValidationEventHandler` events, which are caught by an event handler assigned by the application. As with all events, we can catch them with a function with the required functional signature. Once we've set up a callback as the handler for this event type, the .NET Framework calls that function when the event is fired. Here's the required signature for the validation event handler:

```
public void funcname(object sender, ValidationEventArgs args);
```

The name of the function, *funcname*, can be anything you like. The `sender` parameter is the object originating the event (in this case, your instance of `XmlValidatingReader`). `ValidationEventArgs` inherits from `EventArgs`, but may not be further subclassed. It has three properties:

❑ `Exception` – an instance of `XmlSchemaException` that, like most exceptions, provides a stack trace as well as line number and line position information regarding the location of the validation error in the XML document. There are also members that point back to the schema object that was used for validation.

❑ `Message` – read-only string property describing the validation problem.

❑ `Severity` – read-only property of type `XmlSeverityType` indicating whether this is merely a warning, or a fatal error.

You construct an instance of a `ValidationEventHandler` by passing the constructor the address of your callback. When you have a new instance, you assign the callback function to the `ValidationEventHandler` with the += operator. Thereafter, any call to `Read` that results in a validation problem will invoke your callback.

> *Note that with many .NET events, particularly the ones for visual controls, the process of assigning the event handler is performed automatically by Visual Studio .NET. For instance, when we double-click on a button in the Designer, VS.NET not only creates the appropriate signature in the code-behind page, but also adds the correct code to assign it as the event handler within the `InitializeComponent` method in the Designer-generated code region.*

Extending the Categorizer with Validation

Let's put this theory into practice by extending our previous sample to include validation. In fact, we'll create two iterations of the application: one that acts on any validation information it finds in an incoming document, and a second that builds on that to manage a collection of schemas actively. Our parsing, output, and visual interface will be as before, but we'll inject any warnings or errors detected into the output.

Rather than lose the existing `selector.aspx` web page, copy and paste it, and rename it as `vselector.aspx`. Open up the code-behind file, and change the name of the class from `selector` to `vselector`.

Inherent Validation

Any validating XML processor that's compliant with XML 1.0 or the XML Schemas recommendation has to be able to detect XML metadata or metadata references (that is, schema or DTD information) in the documents it processes, to retrieve that metadata, and to act on it. A document specified by a DTD uses a DOCTYPE declaration with either an inline DTD, or a URI identifying an external DTD. For XSD format schemas, the schemaLocation attribute locates the schema file. I call this **inherent validation**: the processor reacts to such declarations, and does not manage metadata until it encounters a DTD or schema reference in the document. Enabling this in XmlValidatingReader is relatively straightforward. The first thing we must do is to import another .NET namespace, to give access to the supporting classes and enumerations:

```
using System.Xml.Schema;
```

Next, we have to create an instance of XmlValidatingReader. Since that class is layered on top of XmlTextReader, this is a two-step process. At the top of the click handler for the **Analyze** button, change the identifier for the XmlTextReader, and add a declaration for an XmlValidatingReader:

```
XmlTextReader XmlReader = null;
XmlValidatingReader xmlDoc = null;

int nElements = 0;
```

As before, we instantiate the XmlTextReader object, associating it with the document posted from the client side (don't forget to change the identifier!). When we've got that, we pass it to the XmlValidatingReader constructor, which returns a validating reader for that document:

```
try
{
    XmlReader = new XmlTextReader(fileSelector.PostedFile.InputStream);
    XmlReader.WhitespaceHandling = WhitespaceHandling.None;
    xmlDoc = new XmlValidatingReader(XmlReader);
```

The ValidationType property of XmlValidatingReader defaults to ValidationType.Auto. This tells the reader to act on any of the three types of metadata documents (DTD, XML-DR, or XSD), which is precisely what we want to happen in this case. (We *could* specify one of the schema or DTD types, to restrict validation to a specific metadata format.) Although the default suffices, we'll include it explicitly for clarity in our code, and to help any maintenance programmers who may come after us.

Also, the ValidationEventHandler property of XmlValidatingReader should be set with an instance of the eponymous delegate. The constructor for that takes the name of the callback function, which will be called ValidationEvtCallback, as a parameter:

```
    xmlDoc.ValidationType = ValidationType.Auto;
    xmlDoc.ValidationEventHandler +=
                    new ValidationEventHandler(this.ValidationEvtCallback);

    while(xmlDoc.Read())
    {
```

This technique lets us write custom error processing code for validation errors without having to subclass `ValidationEventHandler`. Now we have to code the validation callback function itself:

```
public void ValidationEvtCallback(object sender, ValidationEventArgs args)
{
   if(args.Severity == XmlSeverityType.Warning)
      resultsArea.InnerText += "Validation warning: " +
                                 args.Message + Environment.NewLine;
   else
      resultsArea.InnerText += "Validation error: " +
                                 args.Message + Environment.NewLine;
}
```

All we do here is inject a line of text, including the value of `Message`, into our text control. We use the `Severity` property to distinguish between warnings and errors. Unlike compiler errors, a validation error does not necessarily terminate processing.

Set `vselector.aspx` as the start page, and build and run the revised project by pressing *F5*. If you now post a document with an inline DTD, validation will occur as expected. If, however, you post a document with an external DTD or schema, the code will throw an exception. Once again, a helper class is needed.

> *You can test the application as it stands with the files* `good_inline.xml` *and* `bad_inline.xml`*. If you're using the source code download from our site, be sure to comment out the line in which* `XmlResolver` *is set. There's a comment in the code to help you find the correct line.*

XmlUrlResolver

The problem here is that we have a URL, but `XmlValidatingReader` doesn't know how to resolve this into a DTD or a schema file. The aptly named `XmlUrlResolver` class exists for this very task. Attaching one of these objects is as simple as calling its constructor, and assigning the returned object to a property of our `XmlValidatingReader`:

```
xmlDoc.ValidationType = ValidationType.Auto;
xmlDoc.XmlResolver = new XmlUrlResolver();
```

> *`XmlUrlResolver` will usually be sufficient, but if you need application-specific logic for resolving URLs – perhaps to refer to a local cache, rather than making a round trip to a heavily trafficked public site – you can subclass its abstract base class,* `XmlResolver`*.*

It really is as easy as creating the resolver object and 'snapping' it onto the reader object. The Framework takes care of the rest. Whenever a URL is encountered and the resource it locates is needed, `XmlValidatingReader` will invoke the resolver object to go and get it.

As we will see when we start managing schema caches, there are validation scenarios that do not require URL resolution. By delegating this task to a helper class, `XmlValidatingReader` is able to conserve system resources in such cases, as it uses the extra memory only when a resolver is actually needed. You, as the programmer, determine this necessity in advance and supply a resolver object to the reader as required.

The code download includes several sample schemas and XML documents. If you use them with `vselector.aspx`, *you can see what happens when errors occur during processing. Documents with deliberate errors in them are* `bad_sample_person.xml` *and* `bad_urn_sample_person.xml`. *The latter document, however, will not be useful to you until we implement schema caching in the next section.*

Schema Caching

As written, `vselector.aspx` will do a fine job of validating documents (as long as they use one of the recognized methods for identifying their metadata), and provide an accessible URL to the schema or DTD. Sometimes, however, this is inconvenient. If you're using a public schema, it might be situated on an underpowered, overwhelmed server somewhere, and unavailable just when you need it. Better to keep a local copy – but then we have to change the URL in any documents to match. One way around this would be to provide a URN that uniquely identifies a particular XML vocabulary, rather than a URL, and then use some local cache to resolve that into a physical schema document or DTD.

In other situations, such as a newspaper site in which the content consists of XML documents that use the site's own schemas, an application will specialize in documents written according to a limited number of schemas. In such a case, for performance reasons it is much better to cache the schemas in memory, regardless of whether the documents provide a URL or URN.

In the .NET Framework, the `System.Xml.Schema` namespace provides the `XmlSchemaCollection` class for precisely this purpose, and `XmlValidatingReader` can use it as a helper class. The `Schemas` property of `XmlValidatingReader` is designed to hold an instance of the collection class.

When our application initializes, we can take advantage of this provision and load any schemas that we'll require into a cache. When a document comes in that contains a reference to a schema, we'll make the reader check the URI against those in the cache. If a match is found, the associated schema is used. If not, and the URI is a URL, the resolver is invoked to load the schema, just as it did in the previous example.

Imagine, for example, that we have a vocabulary for scheduling social functions and their attendant support services (sound systems, catering, and the like). This vocabulary is modularized. We have a schema and a namespace for defining physical locations (the event venue), people (event contacts), and a social functions schema that makes use of the other two. The document below conforms to this vocabulary; the specific details important here, but notice how the three schemas are intermingled, and how each is identified by URN:

```xml
<?xml version = "1.0" encoding = "UTF-8"?>
<Event xmlns = "urn:xmlabs-com-functions"
       xmlns:p = "urn:xmlabs-com-people"
       xmlns:xsi = "http://www.w3.org/2001/XMLSchema-instance">
   <loc:Site xmlns:loc = "urn:xmlabs-com-loc">
      <loc:Address>
         <loc:Company>Omicron</loc:Company>
         <loc:Building>World Headquarters</loc:Building>
         <loc:City>Philadelphia</loc:City>
         <loc:State>PA</loc:State>
         <loc:ZipCode>19102</loc:ZipCode>
      </loc:Address>
      <loc:Room>Fishbowl Conference Room</loc:Room>
   </loc:Site>
   <p:Contact>
```

```
        <p:First>Doan</p:First>
        <p:Last>Needme</p:Last>
        <p:EContact preferred = "phone">
            <p:Telephone>215-555-1212</p:Telephone>
            <p:EMail>goway@omicron.com</p:EMail>
        </p:EContact>
    </p:Contact>
    <Scheduled attendance = "100" start = "2001-11-13T08:00:00"
               end = "2001-11-13T16:00:00"
               prepStart = "2001-11-13T07:00:00"
               postEnd = "2001-11-13T17:00:00" />
    <Services>
        <Catering menuCode = "mstry-101A"
                  vendor = "Meat Eaters" workOrder = "EZS-123"/>
        <AudioVisual workOrder = "01101100" vendor = "Computing Droids, Inc."/>
        <AudioVisual workOrder = "OU812" vendor = "Sound Guys"/>
    </Services>
</Event>
```

Back in our `XMLCategorizer` example, we'll leave the other validation code intact (so that other documents are still handled correctly), but we want to provide for validation of documents such as this one in a scalable and efficient manner. The first step is to set up the cache of our three schema documents (provided in the code download), which we can do in the `Page_Load` event handler for our web form. If you host them on another server, or you're using a virtual directory other than `XMLCategorizer`, be sure to change the URLs given here.

```
private void Page_Load(object sender, System.EventArgs e)
{
    if(Application["cache"] == null)
    {
        XmlSchemaCollection cache = new XmlSchemaCollection();
        cache.Add("urn:xmlabs-com-people",
                  "http://localhost/XMLCategorizer/People.xsd");
        cache.Add("urn:xmlabs-com-loc",
                  "http://localhost/XMLCategorizer/Location.xsd");
        cache.Add("urn:xmlabs-com-functions",
                  "http://localhost/XMLCategorizer/SocialFunctions.xsd");
        Application["cache"] = cache;
    }
}
```

When the page loads, we first check the `Application` object to see if a cache exists. If it doesn't, we create a new schema collection object, load the schema files, and store the object in the `Application`.

The `Add` method of `XmlSchemaCollection` is overloaded and comes in four varieties. The one shown here takes two strings, the first of which is the schema's URI, and the second of which is the URL locating the schema. If a `null` URI is provided and the schema is in XSD format, the `targetNamespace` value in the schema is used. The other forms of `Add` accept an `XmlSchemaCollection` instance (as we will see next), an instance of `XmlSchema`, and lastly a string URI and an `XmlReader` instance containing the schema.

Next, add the following line to the `try` block of our click event handler:

```
xmlDoc = new XmlValidatingReader(XmlReader);
xmlDoc.ValidationType = ValidationType.Auto;
xmlDoc.Schemas.Add((XmlSchemaCollection)Application["cache"]);
```

This code retrieves the cached schema collection and snaps it onto the validating reader as we set it up. Now when a document comes in bearing one of the URNs in the collection, the copy of the schema in memory will be used rather than the disk copy. At the cost of checking a URN against a collection and retaining these schemas in memory, we save a file or HTTP roundtrip, a disk read, and the overhead of parsing a schema file.

Compile and run the project now, and test it out it by posting any of the sample documents (`urn_sample_person.xml`, `bad_urn_sample_person.xml`, or `sample_event.xml`) to our ASPX page.

Writing XML: XmlWriter

As far as reading XML documents goes, we've done about as much as we can. Our XML-handling know-how is a little lacking, however, until we've got the ability to write XML documents as well as read them. Beyond the realm of validators and categorizers, we need to be able to create entirely new documents, and write them out for some other program or user.

`XmlReader` has a complementary, stream-based writer class that meets this need. Predictably, it's called `XmlWriter`. Like `XmlReader`, `XmlWriter` offers a lean-and-mean technique for the efficient writing of documents using a stream model. It also shares the problems inherent in that model – chiefly, the lack of random access, the absence of enduring context, and no intrinsic mechanism to contain the document in memory.

XmlTextWriter

`XmlWriter` is an abstract class with, at present, one predefined derived class: `XmlTextWriter`. Despite its name, this class can write to more than just text files. It is named as it is because it writes text, but that text can be sent to any sort of stream, as will become apparent when we examine the class constructors. Since this is the only implementation of `XmlWriter` that can be instantiated in the current release of the .NET Framework, the two classes are very close in terms of their interfaces. We'll be practical, then, and discuss XML writers by exploring the details of `XmlTextWriter`.

Eventually, we'll use `XmlTextWriter` to extend our `XMLCategorizer` example with server-side log files. Before we can do that, though, we'll take a formal look at the public interface of this class. The first task in working with a writer is of course to create an instance of it, so the first stop on the tour of `XmlTextWriter` must examine its constructors.

Constructors

The XmlTextWriter class provides three public constructors that allow you to write XML documents to a variety of media. All of the constructors associate a file or a stream with the writer.

Constructor	Usage
XmlTextWriter(TextWriter)	Builds a writer on top of an existing TextWriter object. The encoding used is taken from the TextWriter object.
XmlTextWriter(Stream, Encoding)	Builds a writer on a given stream for writing, with the given encoding. It fails, throwing ArgumentException, if the stream cannot be written to or the encoding is not supported.
XmlTextWriter(String, Encoding)	Takes a string filename and an Encoding object, and opens the named file for writing with the given encoding. If the file exists, it is overwritten. If it does not exist, one is created. On failure, a number of exceptions are possible: ArgumentException – encoding is not supported; filename string is empty; filename string contains only whitespace, or contains one or more invalid characters. UnauthorizedAccessException – file access is denied. ArgumentNullException – the filename parameter is null. DirectoryNotFoundException – the directory named in the filename string is not found. IOException – the filename string has invalid syntax for the fully qualified file path. SecurityException – the caller lacks sufficient privileges to write to the specified file.

The first constructor – the one built on an existing TextWriter object – is more useful than it might at first appear. The most obvious use is when we already have a file open for writing, and later decide that it's necessary to write XML into the file. A more subtle use is for writing XML to forms that we cannot address directly by using one of the other constructors. TextWriter is an abstract class, so the object passed to the XmlTextWriter constructor will actually be an instance of IndentedTextWriter, StreamWriter, StringWriter, HttpWriter, or HtmlTextWriter.

The second form in this table is really useful, since it lets us write to a variety of objects that present a stream interface. This includes the intrinsic ASP.NET Response object, memory streams, network streams, and cryptographic streams. For sheer ease of use, though, the third form cannot be beat. If you provide a fully qualified path, .NET will take care of the ugly little details of opening, creating, or overwriting files.

Properties

`XmlTextWriter` has a small number of properties, as listed in the following table:

Property	Meaning
BaseStream *(read-only)*	The underlying stream on which the writer is writing. If the writer was constructed with a `TextWriter` that does not derive from `StreamWriter`, the property is `null`. If the specific subclass of `TextWriter` inherits from `StreamWriter`, the property is equivalent to `StreamWriter.BaseStream`. If the writer was constructed with any other stream, the property is that stream.
Formatting *(read/write)*	A `Formatting` enumeration controlling what formatting the writer will observe. Possible values of that enumeration are: `Indented` – element content will be indented using the values of `Indentation` and `IndentChar` `None` – no formatting (default)
Indentation *(read/write)*	Integer property indicating how many `IndentChar` characters are repeated for each level of indentation. The default value is two.
IndentChar *(read/write)*	The character (type char) used for indenting. Although you may set any value in `XmlTextWriter`, any value other than a valid XML whitespace character (0x9, 0x10, 0x13, 0x20) will result in invalid XML.
Namespaces *(read/write)*	Boolean value controlling whether namespace support is to be provided. The default is `true` (meaning that namespaces *are* supported).
QuoteChar *(read/write)*	Controls which character (type char) is used to delimit attribute values. Throws an `ArgumentException` for any character other than a single or double quote. Defaults to double quote.
WriteState *(read-only)*	`WriteState` enumerated value indicating the internal state of the writer. Possible values are: `Attribute` – an attribute is being written `Closed` – the writer has been closed `Content` – element content is being written `Element` – an element start tag is being written `Prolog` – the XML document prolog is being written `Start` – writing has not begun

Table continued on following page

Property	Meaning
XmlLang *(read-only)*	String value indicating the current xml:lang scope, or null if no such scope is current.
XmlSpace *(read-only)*	String value indicating the current xml:space scope. Possible values are: None – no scope exists Default – xml:space="default" Preserve – xml:space="preserve"

In contrast with XmlReader, the properties of this class *control the details* of writing, rather than containing information about the element currently under construction.

Methods

XmlTextWriter has public methods that offer an easy means of writing any of the items defined in XML 1.0: elements, attributes, and so on. Additionally, it takes advantage of the fact that it's 'just' writing to a stream to provide some low-level writing capability through the WriteBase64 and WriteBinHex methods. The public methods of this class are as follows:

Method	Parameters and Usage
Close	Closes the stream for writing. No parameters.
Flush	Clears the internal buffer by writing it to the stream, then flushes the stream. The stream remains open for writing. No parameters, returns void.
LookupPrefix	Takes one parameter (a string URI representation), checks it against the namespace table, and returns the closest namespace prefix as a string.
WriteAttributes	Writes all attributes found at the current node of a given XmlReader. Returns void. Takes two parameters: Reader – an open XmlReader instance from which to copy WriteDef – a Boolean indicating whether to write default attributes (true) or to omit them (false) Fails and throws ArgumentException if Reader is null, or XmlException if the current node of the reader is not an element, attribute, or XML declaration.

Method	Parameters and Usage

WriteAttributeString	Writes an attribute with the specified name and value, plus namespace if supplied. There are three overloaded forms, all taking string parameters exclusively:
	
	`localname, value`
	
	`localname, namespaceURI, value`
	
	`prefix, localname, namespaceURI, value`
	
	Fails and throws `InvalidOperationException` if the writer is closed or the writer is not writing an element, and throws `ArgumentException` if the `xml:space` or `xml:lang` attribute is invalid.

WriteBase64	Takes bytes from `buffer`, encodes them as base 64, and writes them. Takes three parameters: `Byte[] buffer` – byte array that is the source to write `int index` – index into buffer denoting the start of the bytes to write `int count` – number of bytes to write Fails and throws `ArgumentNullException` if `buffer` is `null`; `ArgumentException` if `index` leaves fewer bytes in the array than `count`; `ArgumentOutOfRangeException` if `index` or `count` is less than zero.
WriteBinHex	Same parameters and usage as `WriteBase64`, except that the bytes drawn from `buffer` are encoded as binary hexadecimal.
WriteCData	Takes a string parameter and writes it as a CDATA section. Returns `void`. Fails and throws `ArgumentException` if the parameter would, if written, not result in a well-formed XML document. However, if the parameter is `null` or `String.Empty`, an empty CDATA section is written.
WriteCharEntity	Takes a Unicode character as the input parameter, and writes it as a hexadecimal character entity reference. Returns `void`. Fails and throws `ArgumentException` if the character is in the surrogate pair range ($0xd800 - 0xdfff$) or well-formedness would be violated by writing the reference.

Table continued on following page

Method	Parameters and Usage
WriteChars	Writes a series of characters from a buffer in a single operation. void method taking the following parameters: char[] buffer – character buffer source int index – offset into buffer denoting the start of the characters to write int count – number of characters to write Fails and throws ArgumentNullException if buffer is null; ArgumentException if index leaves fewer chars in the array than count; ArgumentOutOfRangeException if index or count is less than zero.
WriteComment	Takes a string parameter, returns void, and writes an XML comment with the parameter as its content.
WriteDocType	void method that writes a DOCTYPE declaration. Takes the following parameters: string name – name of the DOCTYPE string pubid – Public ID of the DOCTYPE if non-null string sysid – System ID of the DOCTYPE if non-null string inline – contents of an inline DTD Throws InvalidOperationException if the writer is outside the prolog (that is, it's called following the document element), or ArgumentException if name would, if written, not result in a well-formed document.
WriteElementString	void method for writing an element with a specified text node. Two overloaded forms with string parameters: localname, value localname, namespaceURI, value Throws InvalidOperationException if the operation would not result in a well-formed document, or ArgumentException if localname is null or String.Empty.
WriteEndAttribute	void method, taking no parameters, that completes an attribute.
WriteEndDocument	void method that closes any open elements or attributes, and closes the document. The writer state reverts to Start. Fails and throws XmlException if the operation would result in a document that is not well formed. No parameters.

Method	Parameters and Usage
WriteEndElement	void method that closes an element. No parameters. If the element is empty, the shorthand form is written, otherwise a full end tag is written.
WriteEntityRef	void method with one string parameter – name – that writes the entity reference &name;. Fails and throws ArgumentException if the operation doesn't result in a well-formed document, or name is null or String.Empty.
WriteFullEndElement	void method with no parameters that closes an element. A full end tag is always written.
WriteName	void method with one string parameter – name – that's written if it's a valid XML name. Throws ArgumentException if name is not a valid XML name, null, or String.Empty.
WriteNmToken	Like WriteName except the parameter is written if it is a valid XML NmToken type.
WriteNode	Writes the current node from reader to the stream, and advances the reader's node pointer to the next node. Takes two parameters: XmlReader reader – reader providing the source node bool defattr – if true, default attributes are written Throws ArgumentException if reader is null.
WriteProcessingInstruction	void method that writes a processing instruction. Takes two parameters: string name – name of the processing instruction string text – text of the PI Throws ArgumentException if text violates well-formedness, if name is null or String.Empty, or if the method is being used to create an XML declaration after WriteStartDocument has been used to create one.
WriteQualifiedName	void method that writes a qualified name. The current prefix for the URI parameter provided is determined from the namespace table. Takes two parameters: string name – base name string uri – namespace URI Throws ArgumentException if name is null, String.Empty, or not a valid XML name.

Table continued on following page

Method	Parameters and Usage
WriteRaw	`void` method that writes raw XML markup to the stream. Two overloaded forms are provided:
	`string markup` – writes the markup provided
	`char[] buffer, int index, int count` – writes markup from `buffer`, starting at `index` and continuing for `count` characters
	The second form fails and throws `ArgumentNullException` if `buffer` is `null`, `ArgumentException` if `index` does not leave `count` characters in `buffer`, or `ArgumentOutOfRangeException` if `index` or `count` is less than zero.
WriteStartAttribute	`void` method that starts an attribute. Two overloaded forms are provided:
	`string localname, string namespaceURI`
	`string prefix, string localname, string namespaceURI`
	Throws `ArgumentException` if `localname` is `null` or `String.Empty`.
WriteStartDocument	method that begins a document with an XML declaration. The version attribute is always written with the value `1.0`. Two forms are provided: the first takes no parameters, while the second takes a Boolean that's written as the value of the `void` XML `standalone` attribute.
WriteStartElement	`void` method that opens an element. Three overloaded forms are provided:
	`string prefix, string localname, string namespaceURI`
	`string localname`
	`string localname, string namespaceURI`
	All three forms fail and throw an `InvalidOperationException` if the writer is closed.
WriteString	`void` method that writes the text node provided. Takes one string parameter providing the content. Throws `ArgumentException` if the parameter contains an invalid surrogate pair. The characters &, <, and > are replaced with their entity references. Characters in the range `0x00` – `0x1f`, excluding whitespace characters, are replaced with numeric entity references. If called while writing an attribute value, any single or double quotes in the parameter are replaced with " or ' respectively.
	Surrogate characters are a Unicode mechanism for accommodating new characters. The mechanism consists of two 1K blocks of unassigned characters. By taking one character from each block (a low and a high character), you get over a million potential new characters.

Method	Parameters and Usage
WriteSurrogateCharEntity	void method that generates and writes a surrogate character entity from the two given parameters:
	char low – low surrogate char (range 0xDC00 – 0xDFFF)
	char high – high surrogate char (range 0xD800 – 0xDBFF)
	Throws ArgumentException if the surrogate pair is invalid.
WriteWhitespace	void method that takes a single string parameter consisting exclusively of whitespace, and writes it. Throws ArgumentException if the parameter contains non-whitespace characters.

You may have noticed that a number of the methods subject to namespace considerations include overloaded forms that take a namespace URI, but no prefix. XmlTextWriter will generate a prefix if needed, and it keeps track of prefixes and attempts to reuse them as required.

XMLCategorizer with Log File

To illustrate the use of the XmlTextWriter class, let's return to our original text reader web form and modify it to write an XML-format log file that summarizes the results of categorizing the document submitted to the server. This example will illustrate the following:

- ❑ Writing to a file stream
- ❑ Creating a new document
- ❑ Writing XML declarations, elements, and attributes
- ❑ Namespace support

You can start by copying and pasting selector.aspx in the Solution Explorer, and renaming it write_selector.aspx. Also change the class name appropriately, and make the new page your start page.

Log File Format and Location

The idea behind this exercise is to keep a collection of XML log files on the server containing summary results for each submitted document.

Our document element will be <DocumentCategorization>, from the urn:xmlabs-com-cat namespace. It will have two child elements, the first being the document element drawn from the submitted document. We'll maintain the namespace on that element. The other element in our namespace will be <GlobalCount>, which will have a series of attributes giving the global count of XML constructs found in the original document. That element, in turn, will have a <ClientPath> element whose textual content is the fully qualified filename of the submitted document.

Here's a sample log file that puts all of the above into context:

```
<?xml version="1.0" encoding="utf-8"?>
<DocumentCategorization xmlns="urn:xmlabs-com-cat">
   <TestCase xmlns="urn:foo" />
   <GlobalCount attributes="1" elements="2" comments="0" pi="0" cdatas="0">
      <ClientPath>C:\temp\junk.xml</ClientPath>
   </GlobalCount>
</DocumentCategorization>
```

Incidentally, the indented formatting you see above was *not* added by hand. `XmlTextWriter` permits control over certain aspects of formatting, which can be a welcome addition if you're debugging an application that generates XML.

Creating the Log File

The first thing to do is to create a text writer by passing the filename to the constructor. We can't use the filename passed in `fileSelector.PostedFile.Filename`, however, as that path will be local to the submitting client. We must extract the unqualified filename from that string, and provide a path to a directory on our server.

In addition, we'll prefix the filename on the server with the client session ID, so that different submissions may be distinguished. (The intrinsic ASP.NET `Session` object has a property called `SessionID` that returns a unique string for the client session.) The code uses the `c:\temp` directory to store log files, but you can change this easily enough by modifying the first line of the code below. Add this code immediately after the variable declarations in the **Analyze** button's click handler:

```
resultsArea.InnerText = "";

string sLogFileName = "c:\\temp\\" + Session.SessionID;
string sFile = fileSelector.PostedFile.FileName;
sLogFileName += Path.GetFileName(sFile);
```

Now that we've got a suitable filename, we can call the `XmlTextWriter` constructor. We've chosen UTF-8 encoding, which will be picked up when we write an XML declaration in the next section. While we're at it, we tell the writer that we want indented output using the `Formatting` property, and set the indentation to three characters:

```
try
{
    xmlDoc = new XmlTextReader(fileSelector.PostedFile.InputStream);
    xmlDoc.WhitespaceHandling = WhitespaceHandling.None;

    xmlLog = new XmlTextWriter(sLogFileName, System.Text.Encoding.UTF8);
    xmlLog.Formatting = Formatting.Indented;
    xmlLog.Indentation = 3;
```

Using a file stream as we have here (the Framework will create one for us) introduces the possibility of a number of file-related errors, and as a result the constructor we used is capable of throwing an impressive range of exceptions. Our code should include catch *blocks for* ArgumentException, UnauthorizedAccessException, IOException, DirectoryNotFoundException, *and* SecurityException. *We omit only* ArgumentNullException *for the very good reason that, having just created a filename, we know that the argument is not* null. *Bad, perhaps, but not* null. *This code requires the addition of using statements for the* System.IO *and* System.Security *namespaces.*

Starting the Document

The XML recommendation encourages (but does not require) the use of the XML declaration in every XML document. Since we strive to be conscientious XML programmers, we will start off our document by creating one, using WriteStartDocument. This method also writes the version attribute with the value 1.0. XmlTextWriter also picks up the encoding we've set in the constructor, and writes the appropriate attribute in the declaration:

```
xmlLog.Formatting = Formatting.Indented;
xmlLog.Indentation = 3;
xmlLog.WriteStartDocument();
xmlLog.WriteStartElement("DocumentCategorization",
                         "urn:xmlabs-com-cat");
```

Having started the document, we immediately write the <DocumentCategorization> document element, using the version of WriteStartElement that allows us to declare a URI for the element's namespace. The writer takes care of writing the xmlns attribute for us. Note that the method is called WriteStartElement rather than WriteElement because anything we now write, prior to calling WriteEndElement for this element, will be a descendent of it.

Writing the Original Namespace

The next task is to extract the document element from the original document and write it to the log file while preserving its original namespace. We place the code to do this in the part of the switch statement that handles elements. Since XmlReader is stream based, we have to worry about which element is the document element. Fortunately, the Depth property of XmlTextReader comes to our rescue, as it will have the value zero when the current node is the document element. Here's the code now:

```
case XmlNodeType.Element:
   if(xmlDoc.Depth == 0)
   {
      xmlLog.WriteStartElement(xmlDoc.Name,
                               xmlDoc.GetAttribute("xmlns"));
      xmlLog.WriteEndElement();
   }
```

First, notice the position of this code. As you may recall from our first example, this case also processes the attributes of the element. If we waited to write the element to the log file until *after* this – perhaps out of a desire to segregate the log file code from the reader code – we would find that the current node was no longer the document element. This may appear obvious now, but it's an easy mistake to make in practice. When you are using a stream-based model and you have something you need to manipulate, don't delay! Do the manipulation while you have the proper context.

What happens if the original document doesn't declare a namespace? As it is written,
`GetAttribute` *returns* `String.Empty`, *and* `WriteStartElement` *is smart enough not to*
write an `xmlns` *attribute. Strictly speaking, failing to declare a namespace puts the document*
element into the `null` *namespace, according to the Namespaces recommendation*
(http://www.w3.org/TR/REC-xml-names/). However, if we don't write such an attribute in our
log file after creating a default namespace on our document element, the original document element
will be erroneously placed in the `urn:xmlabs-com-cat` *namespace, which is not what we*
want. In practice, most programmers who fail to declare a namespace simply do not care about
namespaces – particularly if validation is not an issue. To be perfectly correct, we should break
`GetAttribute` *out onto a line of its own, test for* `String.Empty`, *and generate* `xmlns=""`.
This is a fairly pedantic point, however, and reduces the clarity of the sample code.

Finally, we round out our response to element nodes by closing the element with a call to
`WriteEndElement`. Since no intervening content has been written, the output will take the compact
form of an empty element: `<name xmlns="..." />`.

Writing Summary Information

After all of the `XmlTextReader` processing is complete, and we emerge from the `Read` loop, we want
to write the count of various XML items into the log file as attributes. One option might be to write
them as attributes of the document element, but a problem that's a direct result of the stream-processing
model prevents this. Since we have now written other content – the original document element – the
writer has moved on from the document element. Even though the intervening element has been closed,
the writing context cannot return to the document element's opening tag – the stream has moved on.
Conversely, we cannot write the attributes when we create the document element, because we don't
have the totals yet.

This is why our XML dialect has the `<GlobalCount>` element. Using this separate element also
provides a good opportunity to reinforce the concept of nesting elements when we write the fully
qualified filename. Add this call to `WriteStartElement`, passing in the element name `GlobalCount`,
immediately after the totals have been written to the text area following the loop:

```
sWorkingText += "Total CDATA sections: " + nCDATAs;
resultsArea.InnerText += sWorkingText;

xmlLog.WriteStartElement("GlobalCount");
```

We don't need to specify a namespace URI. Since the namespace of the original document's document
element is scoped to that element, the namespace scope in our document reverts to the default scope we
established in the log file's document element. Now we want to write a series of attributes using
`WriteAttributeString`:

```
xmlLog.WriteAttributeString("attributes", gnAttributes.ToString());
xmlLog.WriteAttributeString("elements", nElements.ToString());
xmlLog.WriteAttributeString("comments", nComments.ToString());
xmlLog.WriteAttributeString("pi", nPIs.ToString());
xmlLog.WriteAttributeString("cdatas", nCDATAs.ToString());
```

The only novelty to remember here is to call the `ToString` method on our integers to ensure that our
parameters are of the proper type for `WriteAttributeString`.

Now it's time to write the element that contains the fully qualified pathname of the original document. Since we haven't yet called `WriteEndElement`, `<GlobalCount>` remains open. Writing another element at this point makes it the second child of `<GlobalCount>`:

```
xmlLog.WriteStartElement("ClientPath");
```

The local variable `sFile` contains the pathname we want, and we pass it to the `WriteString` method to insert it as a text node in our XML log file:

```
xmlLog.WriteString(sFile);
xmlLog.WriteEndElement();
xmlLog.WriteEndElement();
```

The last two lines here close our nested XML in a similar way to the closing brackets in a programming language – when you're finished, there are often several elements to close in succession. Keep careful track of element depth when writing such code, and make sure that all `WriteStartElement` calls are balanced appropriately and in the correct place. At best, an error will lead to misplaced elements; at worst, you will attempt to write markup that's not well formed and `XmlTextWriter` will throw an exception.

Finishing the Document

Finally, we need to clean up resources. Since we built our writer on top of a file stream, we have an open file handle somewhere in the operating system. To clean up our resources immediately, we expand the `finally` block so that the log file gets closed:

```
finally
{
    if(xmlDoc != null)
        xmlDoc.Close();
    if(xmlLog != null)
        xmlLog.Close();
}
```

Here's what a finished summary document looks like:

```
<?xml version="1.0" encoding="utf-8"?>
<DocumentCategorization xmlns="urn:xmlabs-com-cat">
   <Event xmlns="urn:xmlabs-com-functions" />
   <GlobalCount attributes="18" elements="25" comments="0" pi="0" cdatas="0">
      <ClientPath>C:\Inetpub\wwwroot\XMLCategorizer\sample_event.xml
      </ClientPath>
   </GlobalCount>
</DocumentCategorization>
```

Summary

In this chapter, we brought XML onto the ASP.NET platform with an exploration of XmlReader and XmlWriter. These have proved to be lean, efficient classes for processing XML, due to the use of a stream-based model. The benefits of these classes stem directly from certain tradeoffs, namely the loss of global document context and the inability to move in both directions through a document. This means we have to act on things as we read them, and we must be sure to write items in the order in which they are to appear in the document. To preserve the content of a document we have to provide data structures to do so ourselves. Nevertheless, these classes are a good place to start. They stick to the essentials of XML 1.0 and XML namespaces, making them relatively easy to learn.

Readers and writers are closely tied to a particular document, and are somewhat disposable. We attach a document to a reader or writer when we call the constructor, and when we are finished with that document, we cannot reuse the object – so we just call Close and dispose of it.

Both XmlReader and XmlWriter are abstract classes, and we've seen that the capabilities of these classes broaden considerably when used in their derived classes. XmlTextReader can take documents from a variety of sources, depending on which constructor is used to create the reader. Additional capabilities can be added as required by attaching helper objects to properties of the reader. This means that we can control an application's resource usage by selecting only those capabilities the application requires.

We can write some very powerful applications using these classes alone. If we require access to some of the other technologies related to XML, however, we need to explore some classes that use a processing model that is not stream-based. This is the topic of the next chapter, when we take up the Document Object Model, an in-memory tree representation of complete documents.

3

XmlDocument

In the last chapter, we introduced stream-based processing of XML documents. In this chapter, we'll look at the in-memory, tree-based model for creating and manipulating XML documents known as the Document Object Model (DOM). In some cases, the .NET implementation of the DOM uses the classes we saw in the last chapter, but there are also a number of additional classes that exist solely to support DOM manipulation.

The DOM offers a powerful processing model for the XML programmer that provides random access to all elements in the current document. There is no need to maintain any data structures of our own to store information, as the entire document is persisted in memory. The tradeoff of the DOM over the stream-based model is that the tree model requires significantly greater system resources, chiefly memory. This is no lean and efficient set of classes, so it's unlikely that we'd want to use them to process documents many megabytes in size.

In this chapter, we will examine:

- ❑ The class hierarchy supporting the DOM in the .NET Framework
- ❑ The seven key DOM classes, and their use in the .NET Framework
- ❑ How to load and save XML documents using DOM methods
- ❑ How to traverse and manipulate XML documents in the DOM
- ❑ How to obtain information on XML items in a document using DOM methods and properties
- ❑ How to create new documents programmatically using the DOM

At the end of the chapter, we will put all of this information into action as we create an ASP.NET application that generates speaker schedules for each of several days of a conference. We will read and traverse an existing XML document in ASP.NET, and create a new document from it for return to the client, with all XML processing taking place on the server.

Document Object Model

The Document Object Model (DOM) is endorsed by a formal, vendor-neutral body: the World Wide Web Consortium (W3C). The DOM is an API, not an implementation, so it's language-neutral too. Since the W3C is not, strictly speaking, a standards body – it lacks legal authority – its final, formal specifications are called **recommendations**, not standards.

The DOM is now at its second version. In the nomenclature of the DOM Working Group, these versions are called **levels**. Level 2 is the latest version to achieve full recommendation status, though preliminary work is in progress for level 3. The bulk of commercially available XML processors supporting the DOM are at level 1 and quickly migrating to level 2. The .NET classes we will discuss in this chapter implement level 2 of the DOM.

> *The specification for DOM Level 1, dated 1 October 1998, may be found on the W3C web site at http://www.w3.org/TR/REC-DOM-Level-1. DOM Level 2, also a recommendation, is more complicated and is split across five documents. The core is specified in a document dated 13 November 2000, which can be found at http://www.w3.org/TR/DOM-Level-2-Core.*

Where stream-based models create inherently transient structures, the DOM's fundamental construct is a completely parsed document that resides in memory, in the form of a tree. Every XML document has a single element that contains all other elements in the document. This element is known as the **document element**, and is the root of the DOM tree. Every XML item beneath the document element forms a node in the tree. Note that a DOM tree may have one or more **prolog nodes** that represent special items such as processing instructions and the XML declaration. In XML 1.0, prolog nodes are those that precede the document element.

Beyond this point, the DOM has two distinct structures: one for containing elements, comments, processing instructions, and the like; and the other for containing attributes. Anything other than an attribute is represented as a node of the tree, which will be a 'child' of some higher node. The document element has children, which may have children of their own, and so forth until the bottom of the tree is reached. As we'll see later in the chapter, the traditional methods of tree traversal taught in computing courses (depth first, breadth-first, etc.) work well with the DOM.

Attributes, on the other hand (and although they are also nodes, as we saw in the last chapter), exist as a flat collection attached to their owning element. Thus, if you want to inspect all the attributes in a DOM tree, you must find each element and separately iterate through its attributes. The following diagram depicts the logical structure of a DOM tree for an XML document in memory:

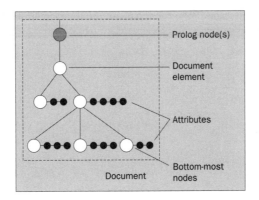

Because we have the entire document in memory, we're consuming far more resources than a stream-based processor would require. On the other hand, we have everything in the document available to us at all times. You are free to move up, down, and sideways in the tree to get to the data you require. The DOM's structure inherently preserves the state of the document for us, so we can frequently get away with very few, if any, major data structures of our own. The DOM tree itself becomes our data structure.

That's the theory, and in fact the practical aspects of working with the DOM in ASP.NET aren't much more complicated. With that in mind, let's turn our attention to the .NET Framework classes that support this style of processing. Microsoft has supported the DOM for years, first with its COM-based XML processor component, and now with the .NET classes that represent Microsoft's implementation of the latest DOM recommendation. There are more DOM-related classes than you might at first expect, and the key to getting a handle on them is to understand the class hierarchy.

.NET Class Hierarchy for the DOM

Every major .NET class for processing XML documents with the DOM belongs to the System.Xml namespace, and the Framework makes extensive use of inheritance to add extra features as and when they're needed. Below is a depiction of the classes you will use, and how they inherit from base classes:

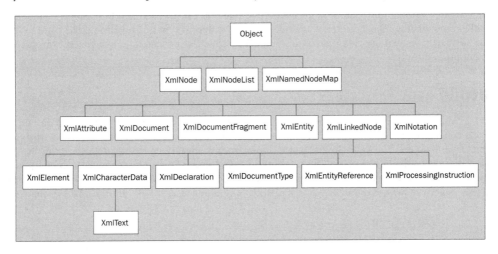

In this chapter, we'll be concentrating on the most commonly used classes. In particular, we will provide reference material for the following:

- ❑ XmlNode
- ❑ XmlNamedNodeMap
- ❑ XmlNodeList
- ❑ XmlAttribute
- ❑ XmlDocument
- ❑ XmlDocumentFragment
- ❑ XmlElement

A quick look at that diagram will let you know that the .NET Framework gets a lot of mileage out of XmlNode, and the diversity of the classes beneath it might make you wonder just how object-oriented this solution is. However, having a base class that ties everything below the document element together lets the .NET DOM get away with far fewer methods and properties than it would need if every sort of node was independent from every other one. The derived classes add capabilities when it makes sense, but XmlNode does the lion's share of the work.

Core Classes

As you can see from the class hierarchy above, there are three core classes that derive directly from System.Object:

- ❑ System.Xml.XmlNode
- ❑ System.Xml.XmlNamedNodeMap
- ❑ System.Xml.XmlNodeList

Of these, XmlNode is absolutely key. Consider the general case of an element – as its 'child' content, it could have any number of other elements, character data, entity references, or processing instructions. When we access the child content of an element – a key task in traversing a document – we don't usually know what we'll encounter. But since all these different types of possible child content derive from XmlNode, we can use this class at first, and specialize our processing once we've examined the content more closely.

XmlNode

Having built XmlNode up in the last few paragraphs, let me knock it down just a little. You will seldom, if ever, create an XmlNode instance. Rather, you'll create instances of its derived classes: attributes, elements, and so on. The value in XmlNode comes from the interface that it provides to all the other classes that derive from it. Even so, we're going to spend more time on this one class than any other, because all of the classes that derive from it either inherit or overload the properties and methods it exposes. Once we have a sound grasp of XmlNode, the other classes will fall into place quite easily.

In the sections for the derived classes, we will only list properties or methods that overload those of XmlNode in significant ways. Thus, if a property or method discussed here is not mentioned specifically for a deriving class, the implication is that it works as described for XmlNode. Also note that we are exclusively dealing with the public methods and interfaces of the DOM-related classes. There are some protected methods and properties, but knowing about these is not a common requirement for ASP.NET programming.

As you read the following sections, notice the lack of a public constructor for this class, meaning that we *never* create an instance of XmlNode using the new keyword. Nodes are always created using one of the methods of XmlDocument, and nodes always belong to the document that created them. If you wish to transfer a node from one document to another, you must use the Import method of XmlDocument. This point is particularly relevant for programmers moving to .NET from MSXML, as that component was somewhat forgiving of careless node transfer. The .NET classes are much stricter in this regard.

Properties

The XmlNode class has the following public properties:

Property	Meaning
Attributes *(read-only)*	If the node is of type XmlNodeType.Element, this returns an XmlAttributeCollection (derived from XmlNamedNodeMap) containing the attributes of the element. Otherwise it returns null.
BaseURI *(read-only)*	Returns a string whose value is the URI from which the node was loaded. In most cases, this will be the URI of the XML document. However, when one of the XML inclusion mechanisms is used, the value of this attribute will reflect the URI of the external resource. Returns String.Empty if the document was not loaded using a URI.
ChildNodes *(read-only)*	Returns an XmlNodeList of all the child nodes of this node. If the node has no children, an empty list is returned.
FirstChild *(read-only)*	Returns an XmlNode representing the first child of the current node. If there are no child nodes, a null reference is returned.
HasChildNodes *(read-only)*	Returns a Boolean value indicating whether the node has children. true is returned if there is child content, false otherwise.
InnerText *(read/write)*	A string whose value is the concatenated textual content of the current node and all its children. Changing this value replaces all child nodes of the current node with the character data provided. If the current node is a leaf node (that is, it has no children other than a text node), this property is equivalent in function to Value.
InnerXml *(read/write)*	Returns or sets the child content markup of the current node as a string.

Table continued on following page

97

Property	Meaning
IsReadOnly *(read-only)*	Returns a Boolean value: `true` if the node is read-only, `false` otherwise. For example, entity nodes are always read-only.
Item *(read-only)*	Used to get an `XmlElement` instance representing the desired element. Available in two overloaded implementations. The first takes a single string whose value is the qualified name of the desired element. The second takes two strings: one for the local name of the desired element, and the second for the namespace URI of the element. In C#, this property is the indexer for `XmlNode`.
LastChild *(read-only)*	Returns an `XmlNode` instance representing the last child node of the current node, or a null reference if no such node exists.
LocalName *(read-only)*	Returns a string providing the local name of the node. The behavior of this property depends on which derived class it is called upon (that is, on what type of node is being checked). For elements, attributes, entities, entity references, and notations, the local name of the item is returned. For DOCTYPE nodes, the document type name is returned. For a processing instruction, the PI's target is returned. For all other types, a string literal denoting the type of the node (`#xml-declaration`, `#text`, `#document`, etc.) is returned.
Name *(read-only)*	Returns the qualified name of the node as a string. As with `LocalName`, the behavior of this property depends on the implementing derived class. Behavior for the different node types is the same as for `LocalName`, except that the qualified name is returned instead of the local name.
NamespaceURI *(read-only)*	String property returning the URI of the node's namespace. If none exists, `String.Empty` is returned.
NextSibling *(read-only)*	Property returning the `XmlNode` instance representing the next peer item to (that is, with the same depth as) the current node in document order. If no such node exists, a null reference is returned.
NodeType *(read-only)*	Returns one of the `XmlNodeType` values denoting the XML type of the node. `XmlNodeType` is an enumeration of the types provided in the XML 1.0 W3C recommendation, along with such useful things as `EndEntity` and `EndElement`. This property, however, will never return the enumerated values `EndElement`, `EndEntity`, or `None`.
OuterXml *(read-only)*	String property returning the XML markup of the current node and all its children, recursively.
OwnerDocument *(read-only)*	Property returning the `XmlDocument` instance to which this node belongs. If the node is itself a document, this property is `null`.

Property	Meaning
ParentNode *(read-only)*	Returns the XmlNode that serves as the parent of this node. If the node is newly created or detached from a document, this property is null. Some XML types (attributes, documents, document fragments, entities, and notations) do not have parents, and for these, this property is also null.
Prefix *(read/write)*	String property whose value is the namespace prefix of the node. Fails and throws ArgumentException for a read-only node, or XmlException if the prefix is malformed, contains an illegal character, or is xml for a namespace other than the one defined by the XML 1.0 recommendation. Note that setting this property does not change the namespace of the node. If no prefix is defined, getting this property results in a String.Empty value.
PreviousSibling *(read-only)*	Returns the preceding XmlNode at the same depth as the current node, or null if none exists.
Value *(read/write)*	String property whose value is the value of the node. The exact value depends on the type of the node. Nodes directly containing textual content (CDATA sections and attributes) return the values you would expect. A PI node returns everything except the target, while an XML declaration returns everything excluding the <?xml and ?> markup. Node types that do not directly contain text (DOCTYPE, for example) return a null reference. Note that an element node will return a null value. If an element has textual content, that content is a child node of the element.

The first thing to notice is that there is one collection for Attributes, and another for child content (ChildNodes). It cannot be stressed too strongly that attributes, while they belong to elements, are *not* child content. You must iterate through attributes separately from child nodes.

Another important point here is that there are several means available for traversing DOM trees using this interface. When we discuss XmlNamedNodeMap and XmlNodeList, we will see that these collections have their own properties and methods for iterating over the node collection they represent. But the XmlNode class also provides FirstChild, LastChild, PreviousSibling, and NextSibling, as well as some other ways to move through a DOM tree.

> *Microsoft's COM-based DOM implementation, MSXML, offers significantly improved performance using the First- and Next- methods for iteration when compared with index-based iteration. It remains to be seen whether this holds true for the .NET implementations.*

A final point to bear in mind is that we can use NodeType to distinguish between instances of different derived classes. This is important when we use the Value property, as it returns different things depending on what sort of XML type we're currently working on.

Methods

The methods for populating an XML document programmatically to create a particular structure are all to be found in the XmlNode class. The only thing that XmlNode *doesn't* contribute to the problem of building documents is creating the nodes in the first place – that function, together with loading and saving documents, is reserved for XmlDocument. Here, then, are the public methods of the XmlNode class, and they are the most commonly used methods in the entire DOM:

Method	Usage
AppendChild	Takes a single parameter of type XmlNode (or one of its derivatives) and adds it to the end of the list of child nodes for the current node. The return value is the node added.
Clone	Makes a **deep copy** of the node (that is, including all descendent nodes and attributes). Takes no parameters, and returns the XmlNode copy. Equivalent to CloneNode(true). This method is a proprietary Microsoft extension to the DOM.
CloneNode	Abstract method. Copies the current node. Takes a single Boolean parameter indicating whether to make a deep copy (true) of the node. Returns XmlNode. The cloned node has no parent. Fails and throws InvalidOperationException for node type Notation, which cannot be cloned.
CreateNavigator	Creates an XPathNavigator object positioned on the node for use with XPath selection. No parameters. This is a proprietary Microsoft extension to the DOM.
GetEnumerator	Returns an IEnumerator instance to enable for each-style iteration over the children of the node. No parameters. This is a proprietary extension to the DOM.
GetNamespaceOfPrefix	Takes a string parameter containing a namespace prefix and returns the closest matching namespace URI that's in scope for the node. This is a proprietary extension to the DOM.
GetPrefixOfNamespace	Takes a string parameter containing the namespace URI and returns the prefix as a string. This is a proprietary extension to the DOM.

Method	Usage
InsertAfter	Inserts a node immediately after a given reference node in the list of children for this node. Takes two parameters of type XmlNode: the child node to add and the reference node, in that order. If the reference node is null, the new node is added at the beginning of the list. The return value is the XmlNode being added.
	Fails with InvalidOperationException if the node cannot accept children of the type provided, or if the node to add is in fact an ancestor of this node. It fails with ArgumentException if the new node belongs to another document, if the reference node is not a child of this node, or if the node is read-only. This is a proprietary extension to the DOM.
InsertBefore	Exactly like InsertAfter, except that the new node is inserted immediately *before* the reference node (unless the reference node is null, when the node is added at the end of the list of children).
Normalize	Normalizes whitespace in the sub-tree that's anchored by the current node by ensuring that only markup separates text nodes. Takes no parameters, returns void. Used to ensure a consistent tree structure between saves when tree comparisons must be made that would be rendered invalid if whitespace appeared. Processors are free to discard non-significant whitespace during loads and saves, so this method is used to eliminate this potential source of change in the tree structure.
PrependChild	Adds a node to the beginning of the child node list for this node. Takes a single parameter of type XmlNode, and returns that node if it is successfully added. If the new node is already a child of this node, it is removed and re-added. If the given node is a document fragment, the entire fragment is inserted.
	Throws InvalidOperationException if the calling node does not permit children of the exact type passed as a parameter, or if the node to add is an ancestor of the calling node. Throws ArgumentException if the node to add belongs to a different document, or the calling node is read-only.
RemoveAll	Removes all children and/or attributes of the calling node. If the node is an element known to have default attributes, these attributes immediately reappear with their default values. No parameters, void return. This is a proprietary extension to the DOM.

Table continued on following page

Method	Usage
RemoveChild	Removes the specified child node. Takes a single parameter of XmlNode type, and returns that node if successful. Throws ArgumentException if the parameter is a node belonging to another document, or the calling node is read-only.
ReplaceChild	Replaces one child node with a new node, returning the old (replaced) child. Takes two parameters, new and old, of type XmlNode. Fails and throws InvalidOperationException if new is not a type permitted as a child of the calling node or if new is an ancestor of that node. Throws ArgumentException if new was created by another document, if old is not a child of the calling node, if or the calling node is read-only. If new is already a child, it is removed and reinserted.
SelectNodes	Returns an XmlNodeList of nodes that match a given XPath expression, when that expression is applied in the context of the calling node. Two overloaded forms are provided. The first takes a string containing the XPath expression and assumes that the document belongs in the empty namespace. If the expression contains a prefix, an exception of type XPathException will be thrown.
	The second form supports namespaces and takes two parameters:
	expr – a string containing the XPath expression
	nsMgr – an XmlNamespaceManager for resolving prefixes in expr
	This form throws XPathExpression if any prefix in expr cannot be resolved using nsMgr.
SelectSingleNode	Selects the first node matching an XPath expression. Provides two overloaded forms whose parameters and behavior are as noted in SelectNodes. The return type of both forms is the XmlNode matching the expression, or null.
Supports	Tests for the presence of support for a particular feature in the DOM implementation. Takes two string parameters, feature and version, and returns a Boolean (true if supported). The feature parameter is the XML package name of the feature to check, and version is a string denoting the XML version. feature must always be XML in this implementation, while version may be 1.0, 2.0, or null. If null, all versions are checked.
WriteContentTo	This method is abstract in XmlNode, but implemented in derived classes. It writes the children of the calling node to the XmlWriter instance passed as the sole parameter of this method. Returns void. This is a proprietary extension to the DOM.
WriteTo	Abstract in XmlNode, this method writes the node *and* all its children to the XmlWriter passed as the sole parameter of this method. Returns void.

The various Append-, Insert-, and Remove- methods let us assemble and disassemble DOM trees one layer at a time. Clone and CloneNode provide easy shortcuts for assembling repeated content, as we'll see when we get to our code sample. The technique is to assemble the basic structure once, and whenever we need a new section with the same structure, we set the element and attribute values to reflect the new section, and then clone the root of the sub-tree that represents the repeated section. After that, we insert the copy into the proper position. No matter how we assemble a sub-tree, we will have to set the values, but this technique allows us to avoid repeating the node creation and insertion steps.

Before we leave the topic of the XmlNode class, remember that XmlDocument derives from it. This may seem to be circular in nature, but it is not. Each document is represented in its entirety by a document node. The document element is then attached to that node. The nice thing about deriving XmlDocument from XmlNode is that we can perform all the same operations on the document itself as we can on the nodes that make it up. For example, the property in XmlDocument that accesses the document element is read-only. We can create a new document from nothing, however, by instantiating an XmlDocument instance, using the appropriate method to create an element, then use AppendChild or one of the Insert- methods to attach that node, which promptly becomes the document element. Once we have a document and some nodes, XmlNode methods are then all we need to build up the document.

XmlNamedNodeMap

This is a utility class used chiefly to collect the attributes of an element. (As we saw in the last section, it's used to implement an XmlElement's Attributes property.) Now, attributes must have names that are unique in any particular element's attribute collection (though of course they can be used on other elements elsewhere in the document), so it's natural to access attributes by those names. That's where the "Named" part of this class's name comes from.

Like so many other classes in the DOM hierarchy, XmlNamedNodeMap has no public constructor. We get an instance of it through a property of some other class, such as the Attributes property of XmlNode, which is the most common source. Once we have such a collection, it's fairly straightforward to work with it – there are a small number of methods, and only one property. All we're doing is getting at the contents of a collection, inserting or removing members, but never changing them.

Properties

The single property of this class is called Count. It's a read-only integer property that indicates how many nodes belong to the map.

Methods

The public methods of XmlNamedNodeMap are as listed in the following table:

Method	Usage
GetEnumerator	Provides an IEnumerator instance for supporting for each-style enumeration over the contents of the map.
GetNamedItem	Returns the named XmlNode from the map. There are two overloaded forms. The first takes a string whose value is the qualified name of the node to match. The second takes two strings, localname and nsURI, which are the local name and the namespace URI of the node to match. If no match is found, null is returned.

Table continued on following page

Method	Usage
Item	Takes a zero-based integer index and returns the XmlNode at that position in the map. If the index is less than zero or greater than Count, null is returned.
RemoveNamedItem	Removes the specified node from the map. Two overloaded forms are provided that match the two different versions of GetNamedItem.
SetNamedItem	Inserts a provided instance of XmlNode into the map. If the passed node is already in the map (as when you're changing the content of a node), the old (replaced) node is returned. If the node is new, null is returned.

GetNamedItem and RemoveNamedItem let you access and remove existing members of the collection. SetNamedItem lets you replace an existing attribute with one of the same name (essentially changing the value in place), or add an attribute that was not previously in the collection.

While the primary method of accessing items in the collection is by name, there are always going to be times when you'd like to access the members of the collection by their ordinal position instead, and that is the role fulfilled by the Item method.

Enumerating Attributes

Let's take a closer look at these two access techniques – names and ordinal indexes – and contrast them. GetNamedItem lets us directly access any attribute when we know its name, but it gives no way of iterating through the collection exhaustively. The following line is an example of GetNamedItem's usage:

```
String s = myNode.Attributes.GetNamedItem("age");
```

This requires that you know the name of the attribute. If you don't know all the names of the attributes for a particular element, the best you can do without recourse to Item is to use a foreach statement (or a For Each..Next statement in Visual Basic) that calls GetEnumerator behind the scenes and inspects the names of the returned attributes. Thus, for some XmlElement called elt:

```
foreach(XmlAttribute attr in elt.Attributes)
    String s = attr.Name;
```

On the other hand, exhaustive enumeration is a key feature of the Item property:

```
for(int i = 0; i < elt.Attributes.Count; i++)
    String s = elt.Attributes.Item(i).Name;
```

These two code snippets are outwardly the same. The point is that while GetNamedItem enables access by name, Item only offers an ordinal index. Now, in XML 1.0, attribute order is not only not guaranteed, but it's insignificant. In other words, we shouldn't write code that relies on calling Item with an index that we 'know' points to a particular attribute. Sooner or later, such code will fail when you're least expecting it. If we know the name of the attribute we're after, we should just use GetNamedItem. If we have to plow through the entire collection (if we're writing general-purpose code to handle multiple XML vocabularies, for instance), that's when we should use Item explicitly (or GetEnumerator implicitly), and inspect the attribute returned in each iteration, rather than make assumptions.

XmlNodeList

In our discussion of the DOM, we noted that items are assembled in two distinct ways: attributes are attached to an element in a flat collection, while all other XML items are attached to one another in a nested tree structure. As we've seen, XmlNamedNodeMap provides the means for dealing with attributes. XmlNodeList is the collection class for accessing nested content.

Unlike attributes, elements are poor candidates for named access – a <Library> element could have dozens of child elements, each named <Book>. Worse, nested content can include other XML types, such as text nodes, that don't have names at all. XmlNodeList deals with content by position rather than by name.

As with XmlNamedNodeMap, there is no public constructor, and we do not create and destroy instances of the XmlNodeList class. The most common way to obtain an instance of XmlNodeList is by reference to the ChildNodes property of XmlNode.

Properties

The XmlNodeList class has two public properties:

Property	Meaning
Count (read-only)	Integer property denoting the total number of nodes in the list.
ItemOf (write-only)	Takes an integer index (zero-based) and returns the XmlNode at that position in the list. Returns null if the index is outside the bounds of the list. In C#, this property is the class indexer.

Count, of course, is what lets us write loops to iterate through a level of the DOM tree, like this:

```
for(int i = 0; i < node.ChildNodes.Count; i++)
{
  // some action here
}
```

To do something useful inside such a loop, we have to delve into the methods of this class.

Methods

XmlNodeList has a pair of public methods:

Method	Usage
GetEnumerator	Takes no parameters and returns an IEnumerator instance supporting for each-style iteration over the list.
Item	Takes a zero-based integer index and returns the XmlNode at that position in the list. Returns null if the index is out of bounds for the list.

Let's revisit the loop we presented in our discussion of the properties:

```
for(int i = 0; i < node.ChildNodes.Count; i++)
{
    DoSomething(node.ChildNodes.Item(i));
}
```

It doesn't really matter what the DoSomething routine actually does; Item lets us pass it each child node in turn. In fact, we can write recursive routines that traverse the entire tree with very few lines of code, as we'll see next.

Traversing the Tree

The most common way to traverse a DOM tree is through the ChildNodes collection of XmlNode. A recursive algorithm for visiting every non-attribute node of an XML document using this collection might look something like this:

```
// Somewhere in the code...
XmlDocument doc = new XmlDocument();
doc.Load("http://mysite//mydoc.xml");
Descend(doc.DocumentElement);

...

protected void Descend(XmlNode node)
{
    if(node.NodeType == XmlNodeType.Element)
    {
        for(int i = 0; i < node.ChildNodes.Count; i++)
        {
            // Do something with the node here, if you wish

            // Iterate through attributes too, if you need to

            // Recursively call Descend on any child nodes
            Descend(node.ChildNodes.Item(i));
        }
    }
    else
        // Process non-element nodes here
}
```

This algorithm will progress *depth* first. That is, it will go as far down the tree as it can, popping a level of recursion off the stack when it reaches a leaf node. When that happens, it moves to the next node at the previous level of the tree, and traverses its sub-tree.

An alternative is to use a *breadth*-first approach with the NextSibling property of the XmlNode class. We can traverse a given level of the tree like this:

```
XmlNode node = parentNode.FirstChild;
while(node != null)
{
```

```
    // Do something here

    // Move onto next element at this level in the tree
    node = node.NextSibling;
}
```

This is most useful for driving across a single level of the tree. If you don't mind depth-first traversal, though, you can use sibling navigation to re-implement the first algorithm above, accomplishing the same effect as in the previous sample but using a sibling linked list (NextSibling) instead of a collection:

```
protected void Traverse(XmlNode node)
{
    XmlNode child;

    // Do something here

    child = node.FirstChild;
    while(child != null)
    {
        Traverse(child);
        child = child.NextSibling;
    }
}
```

Numerous tree traversal algorithms are presented in Algorithms in C++ *by Robert Sedgewick (Addison-Wesley, 1992, ISBN 0-201-51059-6). There are similar volumes by the same author presenting the algorithms in Pascal and Java.*

Derived Classes

So far, we've looked at DOM nodes and two collection classes. Let's round up our review of DOM classes by considering the document class and the specialized classes that derive immediately from XmlNode: XmlDocument, XmlAttribute, and XmlDocumentFragment. There is another, XmlEntity, but entities are usually used as shorthand to avoid repeating keystrokes, and they're seldom found in ASP.NET programming (or in any other programmatic approach to XML, for that matter). Later on, a swift examination of XmlLinkedNode will lead us to the next level of the class hierarchy, but we'll set that aside for a moment. We're about to have our hands full with XmlDocument.

XmlDocument

The XmlDocument class brings us to the big picture. Not only does it implement the interface of the all-encompassing construct that is the DOM model, but also it's the class that lets you create new nodes. We'll use this feature to build and modify documents in our sample application later in the chapter.

Constructors

Unlike nodes and the various collection classes, you *will* be creating documents out of thin air using new. Here, then, are the public constructors for XmlDocument:

Constructor	Usage
`public XmlDocument()`	Initializes a new, empty instance of an XML DOM document.
`public XmlDocument(XmlNameTable)`	Initializes a new instance with the provided name table. Provides name initialization with public scope.

In practice, we almost always use the first form. However, the second form can be very useful too. The `XmlNameTable` argument is not a list of namespaces, but a list of the unique names of all the XML items (elements, attributes, etc.) along with a set of atomized tokens that it uses internally to replace the names whenever they appear. We can use this constructor when we've gone to a lot of trouble to establish a set of names for XML items and wish to reuse them in a new document. Doing so can give a small performance edge when parsing a new document that comes from the same vocabulary as an earlier one.

Properties

The following table lists the public properties of the `XmlDocument` class that add to those inherited from `XmlNode`:

Property	Meaning
DocumentElement *(read-only)*	Returns the `XmlElement` that forms the root of the DOM tree.
DocumentType *(read-only)*	Returns the `DOCTYPE` declaration, if any, as an `XmlDocumentType` object.
Implementation *(read-only)*	Returns the `XmlImplementation` object for the document.
InnerXml *(read/write)*	String comprising the child markup of the document.
IsReadOnly *(read-only)*	Always returns `false` for this class, as documents always have some children that can be changed.
LocalName *(read-only)*	Returns the string #document.
Name *(read-only)*	Returns #document.
NameTable *(read-only)*	Returns an `XmlNameTable` of atomized strings for the document. The names contained therein are single entries for every unique name used in the document.
NodeType *(read-only)*	Returns `XmlNodeType.Document`.
OwnerDocument *(read-only)*	Returns `null`.
PreserveWhitespace *(read/write)*	Boolean property controlling whether whitespace is preserved during `Load`, `LoadXml`, and `Save`. If true before one of these operations, whitespace is preserved.
XmlResolver *(read/write)*	Property getting or setting the `XmlUrlResolver` instance used to resolve external references. Throws `XmlException` if this value is `null` and an external DTD or entity is encountered.

The two properties you'll use most often are `DocumentElement` and `PreserveWhitespace`. The first is used in virtually every DOM-based application to supply the root of the tree, while `PreserveWhitespace` controls the appearance of documents that are intended for viewing by users (or, more likely, by us during debugging). `InnerXml` is also useful for debugging; it provides a quick look at the structure of a document we've parsed or are building.

Methods

The next table lists the public methods of `XmlDocument`, including those essential ones that create new nodes. Remember that the methods of `XmlNode` are also available from this class.

Method	Usage
CloneNode	Copies the node. Takes a Boolean parameter, which, when `true`, causes the method to make a deep copy. When `false`, only the node itself is copied. Returns the `XmlDocument` node.
CreateAttribute	Creates an `XmlAttribute` node with a given name. The new attribute is not attached to any element. Three overloaded forms are provided: `string name` – qualified attribute name `string qname, string nsURI` – qualified attribute name, namespace URI `string prefix, string localname, string nsURI` – namespace prefix, local attribute name, namespace URI This method is a proprietary Microsoft extension to the DOM.
CreateCDataSection	Creates a `CDATA` section (`XmlCDataSection`). Takes a string parameter representing the content for the `CDATA` section.
CreateComment	Creates an `XmlComment` node from the string parameter passed in.
CreateDocumentFragment	Creates a new document fragment (`XmlDocumentFragment`). Takes no parameters.

CreateDocumentType	Creates a new `DOCTYPE` declaration given the following parameters:
	
	`string name` – `DOCTYPE` name
	
	`string pubID` – public `DOCTYPE` identifier or `null`
	
	`string sysID` – system `DOCTYPE` identifier or `null`
	
	`string internalsubset` – internal DTD subset
	
	Returns an `XmlDocumentType` object.

Table continued on following page

Method	Usage
CreateElement	Creates an XmlElement node. Three overloaded forms are provided:
	string qname – qualified element name
	string qname, string nsURI – qualified element name and namespace URI
	string prefix, string localname, string nsURI – namespace prefix, local name of element, URI identifying the namespace of the new element
CreateEntityReference	Creates and returns an instance of XmlEntityReference, given a string parameter containing the name of the entity reference. Fails and throws ArgumentException if the name parameter has an invalid character prohibited by XML naming rules.
CreateNode	Creates and returns an XmlNode, given a type, name, and namespace information. Three overloaded forms are provided:
	string type, string name, string nsURI – string denoting the type, qualified name of the node, namespace URI
	XmlNodeType type, string name, string nsURI – type of the node, qualified name of the node, namespace URI of the node
	XmlNodeType type, string prefix, string name, string nsURI – node type, namespace prefix, local name, and namespace URI of the node
	These all throw ArgumentException instances if a name is required and one is not provided. In addition, such an exception is thrown if the string type parameter of the first form is not one of the permitted values. These values are simple, lowercase representations of the XML node types ("attribute", "element", "entity reference", etc.).
CreateProcessingInstruction	Creates an XmlProcessingInstruction instance from the following parameters:
	String target, string data – PI target (first part) and data (rest of PI)
CreateSignificantWhitespace	Creates an XmlSignificantWhitespace node for use in formatting a document. Takes a single string parameter composed entirely of whitespace characters (that is, &#20;,
, , or 	).

Method	Usage
CreateTextNode	Creates and returns an XmlText node, given a string containing the textual content of the new node.
CreateWhitespace	Creates and returns an XmlWhitespace node, given a string of whitespace characters (&#20;,
, , 	).
CreateXmlDeclaration	Creates an XmlDeclaration node, given the following parameters: string version, string encoding, string standalone – XML version, character encoding, and either "yes" or "no" to indicate whether this document is standalone. The version parameter must be "1.0". Fails and throws ArgumentException if version is any other value, or if standalone differs from the two permitted values.
GetElementById	Returns an XmlElement matching the given string ID parameter. ID attributes must be declared with an associated DTD (schemas cannot be used to declare IDs for use with this method in this version). If no such element is found, null is returned.
GetElementsByTagName	Returns an XmlNodeList composed of all child elements whose name matches the given name. Two overloaded forms are provided: string qname – qualified element name string localname, string nsURI – local element name and namespace URI The wildcard character * matches all elements.
ImportNode	Imports a node from another document into this one. Takes two parameters – XmlNode node, bool deep – which are the node to import and a flag indicating whether a deep copy (true) should be imported, or only the node itself (false). Namespace information is imported even if a shallow copy is made. Fails and throws InvalidArgumentException if the node is a type that cannot be imported (document, entity, notation).

Table continued on following page

Method	Usage
Load	Loads an XML document and parses it. Four overloaded forms are provided: `stream input` – stream containing the document `string docURL` – URL of the document to load `TextReader reader` – reader object used to bring the document in `XmlReader reader` – reader object used to load the document Significant whitespace is always preserved. (Setting `PreserveWhitespace` only applies to non-significant whitespace) This method fails and throws an `XmlException` if an error occurs during parsing. Validation is not performed; if you want validation, you must use one of the latter two forms and provide an `XmlValidatingReader` and its supporting objects, as discussed in Chapter 2. This method is a proprietary extension to the DOM.
LoadXml	Loads an XML document from a string. The single string parameter is composed of the document markup. No whitespace is preserved. Validation is not provided. This is a proprietary extension to the DOM.
ReadNode	Creates and returns an `XmlNode` (or `null`), given an `XmlReader` parameter. The node is built based on the current position of the reader. If the reader is positioned on a node that does not translate into a DOM type (`EndElement` or `EndEntity`, for example), the method fails and an `InvalidOperationException` is thrown. The reader is advanced to the next node. If the current node is an element, the entire child sub-tree is copied.
Save	Writes the XML document to a given location. Four overloaded forms are provided: `stream out` – stream to which to write the document `string filename` – disk-based file location to which to write `TextWriter out` – text writer object to which to write. The `Encoding` of the object controls the encoding of the written document. `XmlWriter out` – XML writer object to which to write. Again, the `Encoding` property of this object controls the encoding of the written document. All forms fail and throw an `XmlException` if this method would result in an XML document that is not well formed. This method is a proprietary extension to the DOM.
WriteContentTo	Saves the children of the document node to the single `XmlWriter` parameter. The `Encoding` property of the `XmlDeclaration` node, if any, controls the encoding of the document written (UTF-8 is the default). This method is a proprietary extension to the DOM.

Method	Usage
WriteTo	Writes the document node and all children to the XmlWriter provided as the single parameter. Encoding of the written document is as for WriteContentTo.
	This method is a proprietary extension to the DOM.

As you can see from the table, there are two methods for creating any type of XML node: the general CreateNode, and the specific CreateX method, where X represents the type of node being created. Which form you choose really depends on the requirements of your application. In general, CreateX is easier and more convenient when building a well-known, specific structure, while CreateNode is better when building general-purpose code, as it allows you to perform conditional initialization of the parameters, based on the circumstances of your application.

A crucial method that it would be easy to overlook here is ImportNode. If we have two XmlDocument instances and we wish to transfer a node between them, we *must* use ImportNode. Exceptions result if we attempt to insert nodes created in another document into the current document by any other means.

Two other methods worthy of note are GetElementById and GetElementsByTagName. While XML is inherently hierarchical (as is the DOM), it does offer relational constructs through the ID, IDREF, and IDREFS attribute types. If we have a formal specification such as a DTD or an XML schema, we can use GetElementById and exploit this referential mechanism: an attribute of one element can act as a pointer to another related element, because they share the same value. Obviously, a formal declaration is needed to identify these types, but it is just as well to have one so that we can validate instance documents. This lets us catch problems like ID values that are not unique, or IDREF or IDREFS values that have no corresponding ID value in the document.

> *A far better approach, XPath, is presented in the next chapter. It is more sophisticated than GetElementById, yet does not require a formal metadata document. Also note that the current (May 2002) XmlDocument implementation only supports DTDs for use with GetElementById.*

GetElementsByTagName, on the other hand, is a brute force approach to retrieval. If we know the tag name of an element, we can retrieve it using this method. Unfortunately, we will also get every other element with the same name. This might be what we want, or we may find it useful to get the collection and iterate through it if we know that the collection will be small. This method does not require that metadata in the form of a DTD or schema should be available.

Events

With all the things that can be done in a DOM tree, it stands to reason that one of the DOM classes should support events. You might, for example, want to know when a new node is inserted, so that you can update a user interface or do some application-specific constraint checking. That honor falls to XmlDocument in its capacity as the principal, unifying structure of the DOM. Anything that happens in a document is visible from this object, so it makes sense to add events to this class.

Event	Meaning
NodeChanged	Fired after the Value property of a node has changed
NodeChanging	Fired just before the Value property of a node is changed
NodeInserted	Fired after a node has been inserted into the 'child nodes' list of another node
NodeInserting	Fired just before a node is to be inserted into the child list of another node
NodeRemoved	Fired after a node has been removed from another node's child list
NodeRemoving	Fired just before a node is removed from another node's child list

Each event passes an instance of XmlNodeChangedEventArgs to the event handler. This class has four properties that may be of interest to you:

- ❑ Action – an instance of the XmlNodeChangedAction enumeration (Insert, Remove, Change) denoting the type of event

- ❑ NewParent – an instance of XmlNode that is the value of the node's ParentNode property after the operation completes

- ❑ Node – XmlNode instance to which the operation is occurring (that is, the node being added, changed, or removed)

- ❑ OldParent – XmlNode instance that is the value of Node's ParentNode property before the operation

Action lets us discriminate between the three types of events, but doesn't differentiate between the before (-ing) and after (-ed) versions of the events. If we need this information, we must use separate event handlers, rather than employing a single, multi-purpose one.

Note once again that node-related events are part of XmlDocument, and *not* XmlNode and its derivatives. This makes sense, because the document has the scope that includes the parent-child relationship. Moreover, it gives us one place to put all event handling. We can watch nodes from the point at which a newly created node is placed into the document, through changes, and through removal. Putting events on XmlNode would result in more code, and would not give us such a global view.

Creating Document Components

XmlDocument is the generator of nodes that are used to make up XML documents through DOM trees. It is not enough, however, simply to call one of the creation methods and receive a node. Until a node is inserted into a document, it is owned by the document, but it's not part of the tree. We can call, say, CreateElement a dozen times, but until we call InsertAfter, AppendChild, or InsertBefore, all we have is an unattached cloud of a dozen element nodes.

If we're starting with an empty document, we take advantage of the fact that XmlDocument derives from XmlNode to call one of the latter class's insertion methods on the XmlDocument instance. This results in the assignment of this pioneer node to the DocumentElement property of the document. Once we have that, we can call the various insertion methods on the document element to create a second level of elements, and so on to whatever level of nesting we need. We can add attribute nodes to an element at any time by calling the SetAttribute method on XmlNamedNodeMap with an attribute that previously did not appear in the collection.

> *Calling SetAttribute with an attribute whose name – respecting namespaces – is already found in the collection results in the replacement of the existing attribute node with the new one.*

One final shortcut for document creation should be noted. It is not necessary to create every single node through calls to XmlDocument. It is frequently the case that some nodes, particularly elements, appear many times in a single document instance, albeit with different values. We can use a shortcut and create the first instance, then clone it as needed and set the values of the new nodes.

XmlDocumentFragment

XmlDocumentFragment is a helpful utility class for creating fragments of documents – think of a clipboard for nodes that preserves structure. Note, that these are *fragments*, not subtrees – XmlDocumentFragment derives from XmlNode, not XmlDocument. It has no document element, and it is entirely possible to have a document fragment consisting entirely of peer nodes – that is, a list of elements at the same level. The fragment object itself is considered the parent of these nodes; calling ChildNodes on an instance of this class permits access to the first tier of nodes.

Properties

In addition to the properties of XmlNode, XmlDocumentFragment has the following public properties in its interface:

Property	Meaning
InnerXml *(read/write)*	String property consisting of the markup for the children of the document fragment node. Setting the property replaces the previous fragment.
LocalName *(read-only)*	Returns a string consisting of #document-fragment.
Name *(read-only)*	Returns a string consisting of #document-fragment.
NodeType *(read-only)*	XmlNodeType property with the value XmlNodeType.DocumentFragement.
OwnerDocument *(read-only)*	Returns the XmlDocument instance to which the document fragment belongs.
ParentNode *(read-only)*	XmlNode property having the constant value null for this class.

Since this class derives from XmlNode, it must provide some implementation for all of its properties, but LocalName, Name, and ParentNode will always have fixed values. Although a document fragment must *belong* to a document (as all XML constructs below the document level must do), it is not *part* of a document. This is like a node that has been created but not yet inserted into the DOM tree. It also explains why ParentNode is always null.

Methods

The following public methods may be called from XmlDocumentFragment, in addition to the other methods of XmlNode:

Method	Usage
CloneNode	Copies the document fragment. Takes a single Boolean parameter, which when true instructs the method to make a deep copy of the document fragment. If the parameter value is false, only the document fragment node is copied. Returns the copy as an XmlNode.
WriteContentTo	Writes the children of the fragment to an XmlWriter instance passed as the sole parameter of this method. Returns void. This is a proprietary extension to the DOM.
WriteTo	Like WriteContentTo, except that the document fragment node is written as well. This is a proprietary extension to the DOM.

Each of these methods appears in the public interface of XmlNode, but they've been included here because they are overloaded. The implementations in XmlDocumentFragment account for the fact that the document fragment object serves as the owning 'root node' of the fragment. They ensure that only actual XML nodes are copied or written.

XmlAttribute

After XmlDocument and XmlElement (which we'll see shortly), XmlAttribute is the most frequently used DOM class in the System.Xml namespace. It derives from XmlNode, and adds properties and methods that make it uniquely suited to representing XML attributes.

Properties

In addition to the properties of the XmlNode base class, XmlAttribute offers the following public properties for your use:

Property	Meaning
BaseURI *(read-only)*	Returns the base URI of the attribute as a string, or `String.Empty` if none exists. In contrast to `NamespaceURI`, below, an attribute can inherit this property from the element to which it belongs. This URI will be the URL from which the document was loaded (if the owning document was loaded).
InnerText *(read/write)*	Equivalent to `Value` for this class. Textual value of the attribute as a string.
InnerXml *(read/write)*	String value of the attribute as markup.
LocalName *(read-only)*	Returns the local name of the attribute as a string.
Name *(read-only)*	Returns the qualified name of the attribute as a string.
NamespaceURI *(read-only)*	Namespace URI of the attribute (if one has been explicitly declared) as a string. `String.Empty` if the attribute belongs to the null namespace.
NodeType *(read-only)*	An `XmlNodeType` enumeration with the value `XmlNodeType.Attribute`.
OwnerDocument *(read-only)*	Returns the `XmlDocument` to which this attribute belongs.
OwnerElement *(read-only)*	Returns the `XmlElement` bearing this attribute, or `null` if the attribute has not yet been attached to an element.
ParentNode *(read-only)*	Always `null` for this class, typed as `XmlNode`.
Prefix *(read/write)*	Namespace prefix of this attribute, or `String.Empty` if none exists. String type.
Specified *(read-only)*	Returns `true` if the attribute was explicitly given a value in the document, or `false` if it implicitly appears with a default value due to a DTD declaration.
Value *(read/write)*	Textual string value of the attribute. Throws `ArgumentException` if you attempt to set this property on a node that is inherently read-only because of its type.

In this class, `InnerText`, `InnerXml`, and `Value` are essentially the same thing. This is one of the perils of inheritance: sometimes, you end up with too much of a good thing! Of note, however, are `Specified` and `OwnerElement`. `Specified` is unique, and reflects the fact that a DTD or schema can specify default values. In a document, an attribute declared with such a default is automatically created with the default value, if the document does not explicitly define that attribute on the element for which it is declared. When working with an attribute node at run time, the only way to determine whether an attribute actually appears in the original document on disk is to check the value of the `Specified` property.

Given what we've presented on tree traversal so far, you might think that `OwnerElement` is unnecessary – the designers of the DOM must have been paid by the property! Generally speaking, the tools of this chapter only permit us to traverse the DOM tree from the document element down – but if we need the element that bears the attribute, why not just grab it when it went by in the traversal?

However, this property can come in handy when we use XPath, which we'll discuss in the next chapter. That technology lets us access nodes randomly, by supplying the path to them without explicitly traversing the nodes between the start point and the desired node(s). Having `OwnerElement` lets us jump back to the element from the retrieved attribute. From there, we can navigate anywhere else. This property is a way of ensuring that we can drop into a document at any point, and still inspect the immediate neighborhood when we get there.

Methods

The following new public methods are available on `XmlAttribute`:

Method	Usage
CloneNode	Copies the attribute and returns the copy as an `XmlNode`. Takes a single Boolean value denoting a deep (`true`) or shallow (`false`) copy. A clone of an attribute whose `Specified` property is `false` will have `true` for its `Specified` property.
WriteContentTo	Equivalent to `InnerXml`, this method writes the value of the attribute to the `XmlWriter` instance passed as its sole parameter.
	This method is a proprietary extension to the DOM.
WriteTo	Writes the entire attribute (that is, the attribute and its value) to the provided `XmlWriter` instance.
	This method is a proprietary extension to the DOM.

As with `XmlDocumentFragment`, these methods, which are overloads of `XmlNode` methods, appear here because the class requires special handling.

A Word about XmlLinkedNode

If you refer back to the inheritance hierarchy we presented at the beginning of this chapter, you'll find a number of classes derived from `XmlLinkedNode`. They include classes for all of the XML constructs other than attributes, entities, and notations. What's significant about `XmlLinkedNode` classes is that they represent the XML types for which node order is important. In consequence, `XmlLinkedNode` overloads those properties of `XmlNode` that are important to ordered traversal, namely `NextSibling` and `PreviousSibling`.

`XmlLinkedNode` is an abstract class, so we never instantiate it explicitly. Therefore, we'll skip over its properties and methods in favor of moving directly to `XmlElement`, one of the classes derived from it. `XmlElement` is a very important class; you will deal with it in every DOM application you write in .NET.

XmlElement

Elements are the heart of XML documents. You can write a document without attributes, but you must always have at least one element. This is, therefore, the last class we need to study before getting down to the practical business of programming with the .NET DOM classes.

Properties

The following table lists the public methods added or overloaded by this class:

Property	Meaning
Attributes *(read-only)*	Returns an `XmlAttributeCollection` containing all of the attributes of this element.
HasAttributes *(read-only)*	Returns `true` if the element has attributes, or `false` otherwise. This property is an extension to the DOM.
InnerText *(read/write)*	Gets or sets the concatenated text nodes of the element and any children. If set, the children of this element are replaced with the provided string. This property is a proprietary extension to the DOM.
InnerXml *(read/write)*	Gets or sets the markup comprising the children of this element.
IsEmpty *(read/write)*	Boolean. When `true`, the element is empty and written in the abbreviated form `<name/>`. If the element has child content or is written in long form `<name></name>`, this returns `false`. If this property is *set* to `true`, any child content will be deleted, as you are indicating that the element should be empty. This property is a proprietary extension to the DOM.
LocalName *(read-only)*	Returns the local name of the element as a string.
Name *(read-only)*	Returns the qualified name of the element as a string.
NamespaceURI *(read-only)*	Returns the namespace URI for the element as a string. If none exists (that is, the element belongs to the null namespace), it returns `String.Empty`.
NextSibling *(read-only)*	Returns the `XmlNode` immediately succeeding this element or `null` if no such node exists.
NodeType *(read-only)*	Returns `XmlNodeType.Element`.
OwnerDocument *(read-only)*	Returns the `XmlDocument` to which the element belongs.
Prefix *(read/write)*	Returns the namespace prefix of the element as a string, or `String.Empty` if no such prefix exists.

The most significant entries in this table are `Attributes` and `HasAttributes`. The `Attributes` collection provides access to any attributes of an element, while `HasAttributes` determines whether it is worthwhile checking that collection. `IsEmpty` is another interesting property – if it has the value `true`, we know not to expect any information other than attributes. Careful use of `HasAttributes` and `IsEmpty` can cut out significant amounts of processing in our applications.

Methods

`XmlElement` adds the following public methods (or inherits them from `XmlNode` and overloads them in its implementation):

Method	Usage
CloneNode	Copies the element and returns the copy as an `XmlNode` instance. Takes a Boolean parameter (`true` to recursively copy child content for a deep copy, `false` to copy only the element).
GetAttribute	Returns the value of the named attribute as a string. Has two overloaded forms:
	`string name` – qualified name of the attribute for which to search
	`string localname, string nsURI` – local name and namespace URI
	An empty string is returned if no match is found.
GetAttributeNode	Like `GetAttribute` (including both overloaded parameter lists), except that the return type is `XmlAttribute` if a match is found, and `null` if one is not.
GetElementsByTagName	Returns an `XmlNodeList` composed of all descendent elements matching the tag name provided. Two overloaded forms are available:
	`string qname` – qualified element name for which to search
	`string localname, string nsURI` – local name and namespace URI of the element for which to search
	If the `name` parameter is an asterisk (*), all elements match.
HasAttribute	Boolean. Returns `true` if the element has the specified attribute, `false` otherwise. Two overloaded forms are provided:
	`string qname` – qualified name of the attribute
	`string localname, string nsURI` – local name and namespace URI of the attribute
RemoveAll	Removes all child nodes and specified attributes of the element. No parameters, `void` return. Unspecified attributes (that is, attributes that exist because of a default value declaration in an associated DTD) are not removed.

Method	Usage
RemoveAllAttributes	Removes all specified attributes of the element. Default attributes remain. No parameters, void return.
	This method is a proprietary extension to the DOM.
RemoveAttribute	Removes the specified attribute, if any, from the Attributes collection. If you attempt to remove a default-valued attribute, it is immediately and automatically replaced. Two overloaded forms are provided:
	string qname – qualified attribute name
	string lname, nsURI – local attribute name and namespace URI
RemoveAttributeAt	Removes the attribute at the specified index in the Attributes collection. Takes a single integer parameter for the zero-based index. If the attribute is unspecified (it's a default value), it is immediately replaced. Fails and throws ArgumentException if the node is read-only.
	This method is a proprietary Microsoft extension to the DOM.
RemoveAttributeNode	Removes and returns an XmlAttribute from the element. If the removed attribute is a default value, it is immediately replaced. Two overloaded forms are provided:
	string lname, string nsURI – local attribute name and namespace URI
	XmlAttribute attr – object to remove
SetAttribute	Sets the value of the specified attribute. Two overloaded forms are provided:
	string qname, string value – qualified attribute name and value to set
	string lname, string nsURI, string value – local attribute name, attribute namespace URI, and attribute value to set
	The first form throws XmlException if the name contains an invalid character, and ArgumentException if the node is read-only.

Table continued on following page

Method	Usage
SetAttributeNode	Adds a new `XmlAttribute` node to the `Attributes` collection. Two overloaded forms are provided, both returning the `XmlAttribute` you added:
	`XmlAttribute attr` – node to add. This form throws `ArgumentException` if `attr` was created by a different document or the element is read-only, and `InvalidOperationException` if `attr` currently belongs to another element. You must clone attribute nodes to reuse them.
	`string lname, string nsURI` – local attribute name and namespace URI.
WriteContentTo	Writes the element's child content to an `XmlWriter`. Takes one parameter – the `XmlWriter` instance – and returns `void`.
	This method is a proprietary extension to the DOM.
WriteTo	Writes the element and its child content to an `XmlWriter`. Same parameter and return type as `WriteContentTo`.
	This method is a proprietary extension to the DOM.

Notice the variety of methods for attribute checking and management. The main tasks we perform with elements are either management of nested content (chiefly, though certainly not exclusively, more elements), or management of attributes. The former is handled through the methods of the `XmlNodeList` contained in the `ChildNodes` property, while the latter – a key differentiator of elements – is handled with such methods as `SetAttribute` and `RemoveAllAttributes`.

Conference Schedule Sample Application

Imagine that you're attending a conference, and you want to know the schedule for a day. You've lost the brochure that details the schedule, or perhaps you're worried about changes. Maybe you had entirely too much fun last night, and you simply can't *remember* today's schedule? What you need is an ASP.NET application that produces the schedule when you supply it with the day you're interested in. In this section, we'll write a schedule sample that's based on XML documents.

The sample will demonstrate the following DOM features:

❑   Loading documents using `Load` and a URL

❑   Navigating a document

❑   Retrieving elements with `GetElementById`

❑   Constructing XML documents using `XmlDocumentFragment` and `XmlDocument`

❑   Using shortcuts for document construction

If you want to run the sample, copy the download files to a virtual directory on your IIS server. If your directory has a URL other than http://localhost/Agenda, be sure to modify the URL in the DOCTYPE *declaration for* master_schedule.xml.

User Interface and Application Lifecycle

To get the information you need, you access the conference intranet (you did bring your laptop, didn't you?) and navigate to a page where you select one of the days of the conference to see the schedule. The client side of the application relies solely on basic HTML, and will not perform script processing or XML manipulation in the browser. The server side of the application consists of a single ASP.NET page that uses Web Forms. The HTML elements of the user interface can be found in GetSchedule.aspx, while the DOM code is located in GetSchedule.aspx.cs.

If you'd rather start from scratch, select an ASP.NET Web Application from the New Project Wizard in Visual Studio .NET, and enter Agenda for the project name. Delete the default WebForm1.aspx, and add a new one called GetSchedule.aspx. Switch to the HTML view for the new form, and enter the following within the <body> element:

```
<body MS_POSITIONING="GridLayout">
  <strong>
    <font face="Verdana" size="4">Obtain A Daily Schedule</font>
  </strong>
  <form method="post" runat="server">
    <table height="49" cellSpacing="1" cellPadding="2"
           border="0" width="161" bgcolor="silver">
      <tr>
        <td>Day:</td>
        <td>
          <select id="daySelect" name="daySelect" runat="server">
            <option selected>1</option>
            <option>2</option>
            <option>3</option>
          </select>
        </td>
      </tr>
      <tr>
        <td colspan="2" align="middle">
          <input id="Submit1" type="submit" value="Submit"
                 name="Submit1" runat="server" />
        </td>
      </tr>
    </table>
  </form>
  <h3><font face="Verdana">Schedule</font></h3>
</body>
```

If you wish, you can also do this through the Visual Studio .NET IDE by inserting a form element into the page (through the Insert *menu on the Design view), and then dragging a listbox and a* Submit *button onto the form from the HTML tab of the Toolbox. Right-click on both controls, and check* Run as Server Control. *Be sure to set the* id *properties of the controls as shown in the HTML source shown above.*

The top portion of the page, where the user will specify the information they're after, uses a standard HTML form with runat attributes with the value "server" added to the <form> and <select> elements, so that we can work with these controls in server-side code.

When you switch back to the Design view, you should see this:

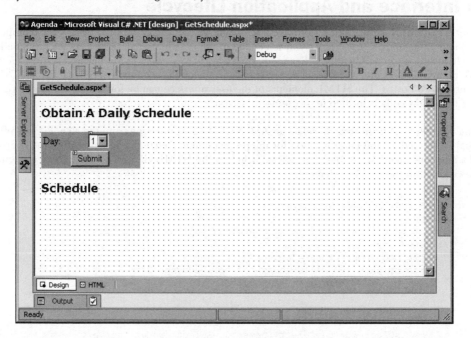

Since there is no action attribute on the form element, the Web Form will hit GetSchedule.aspx whenever the Submit button is clicked. (If present, the action attribute would have a URL for its value, and would POST the form to the page specified by that URL.) The server will then retrieve the schedule in XML format, using DOM code. To enable construction of the schedule in a human-friendly format, we use an XSLT stylesheet to convert the XML schedule document into HTML that will be embedded in the page after the form.

To aid with the final task mentioned in the previous paragraph, drag an XML control from the Toolbox's Web Forms tab onto the page. This is a utility control that's going to take the XML document we generate and convert it into the HTML that's streamed to the client. It will do this by applying an XSLT stylesheet that we will specify. Here's what Visual Studio .NET inserts into the page's HTML code in order to create the control and set it as a server-side form element:

```
<asp:Xml id="Xml1" runat="server"></asp:Xml>
```

When DOM processing completes, we'll assign the output document to the XML control's Document property, and assign an XSLT stylesheet to the Transform property of that control. The control then takes over, performing the transformation and returning the resulting HTML in the page's Response stream without further intervention from us. The result is that a pure HTML page is returned to the browser: no XML appears on the client at any time.

Data Documents

When we come to putting our data on the server, things become a little contrived. In a real application, we would likely use a relational database for the conference schedule. We might use XML and XSLT to simplify the user interface, but there isn't any compelling reason to use XML for the raw schedule data.

The aim of this example, however, is to demonstrate DOM processing, so we'll store the conference schedule as an XML file. The output document – the day's schedule – is extracted from the master document. Just to make things interesting, we'll give the output document a different vocabulary from the one used in the master document. This will give us the opportunity to work with DOM tree traversal and node inspection in the master document, and to create the document programmatically as we build a document for the daily extract.

Here is the master schedule document for our application. (Some elements have been elided for brevity.) In short, a <Conference> element consists of a series of <Day> elements, followed by a <Speakers> element and a <Topics> element:

```
<?xml version = "1.0" encoding = "utf-8"?>
<!DOCTYPE Conference SYSTEM "http://localhost/Agenda/conference.dtd">
<Conference>
  <Day>
    <Event speaker = "A2" room = "Main" topic="keynote" time = "8:00"/>
    <Event speaker = "A1" room = "Greenhouse" topic="Data1" time = "09:00"/>
    <Event speaker = "B1" room = "Corsican" topic="Theory1" time = "10:00"/>
    <Event speaker = "A1" room = "Versailles" topic="Web1" time ="11:00"/>
    <Event speaker = "A2" room = "Greenhouse" topic="Web2" time ="13:00"/>
    <Event speaker = "B2" room = "Corsican" topic="Data2" time = "14:00"/>
  </Day>

  ...

  <Speakers>
    <Speaker id = "A2">
      <Name>Bill Gates</Name>
    </Speaker>

    ...

  </Speakers>

  <Topics>
    <Topic id = "Data1">
      <Title>Making SQL Server Jump Through Hoops</Title>
      <Abstract>SQL Statements are boring. Let's jazz things up with
                a confluence of .NET, XML, and portable devices.
      </Abstract>
    </Topic>

    ...

  </Topics>
</Conference>
```

Each day consists of one or more <Event> elements, and each <Event> represents a single presentation of a topic that might be given several times during the conference. The document uses ID – IDREF relationships to model the 1:1:1 relationship between <Event> elements, conference speakers, and topics. This is a structure that would work well as the XML representation of some relational query.

So, each <Event> element refers to a <Speaker> element. In our document, each <Speaker> contains nothing more than the speaker's name, but you might easily include additional information such as a job title and some biographical text. <Event> also refers to a <Topic> element. These elements contain the presentation title and an abstract describing the presentation. <Event> elements also provide the name of the room in which the presentation will be given, and the starting time. Note that <Event> elements are empty, relying solely on attributes to convey the relevant information.

> *We've used a DTD, rather than an XML schema, to describe our vocabulary. This is because the* GetElementById *method only supports resolution of the* ID – IDREF *relationship via DTD-format metadata.*

The application would be a good deal simpler if the output looked like the master schedule. In fact, given our use of XSLT for the output, we could write the entire application in an XSLT stylesheet! Our application is being deliberately awkward, therefore, by making us specify a different XML dialect for the output document. This form, which is not formally declared in a DTD or a schema, follows the hierarchical form for XML. Here's a sample of the XML document our application will create:

```
<AGENDA>
  <SESSION>
    <TOPIC>Define the Universe, Give Two Examples</TOPIC>
    <SPEAKER>Galileo Galilei</SPEAKER>
    <ABSTRACT>Dr. G talks post-modern nonsense.</ABSTRACT>
    <ROOM>Venice Room</ROOM>
    <TIME>12:00</TIME>
  </SESSION>

  ...

</AGENDA>
```

Server-Side Processing

When the Submit button on our ASP.NET Web Form is clicked, the page makes an HTTP POST that's handled by the code in GetSchedule.aspx.cs. All activity necessary to retrieve scheduling information and format the response occurs in that handler, or in the protected methods it calls. Various optimizations are possible, such as caching the master schedule document and the XSLT stylesheet, but we've kept the code in one place for clarity in this prototype.

Top-Level Processing

The general flow for the server-side processing is as follows:

1. Get the index of the 'day selection' drop-down box from the posted data

2. Create an XmlDocument instance and load the master schedule document

3. Create a skeleton response document

4. Create a document fragment for a <SESSION> element and its children

5. Recover the appropriate <Day> element through DOM traversal

6. Iterate through the <Event> child elements of <Day>, creating and appending new <SESSION> elements to the output document

7. Create an XslTransform instance and load the XSLT stylesheet

8. Configure the XML server-side control

Since the Submit button was adorned with the runat attribute, we have access to server-side code for this button. The event handler method, Submit1_ServerClick, captures the general processing tasks. Here's how that method starts:

```
private void Submit1_ServerClick(object sender, System.EventArgs e)
{
    int i = daySelect.SelectedIndex;
    XmlDocument data = new XmlDocument();
    data.Load(Server.MapPath("master_schedule.xml"));
```

The drop-down box was also marked as running on the server, and given the ID daySelect, so there will be an object with that name to represent it on the server. This conveniently allows us to retrieve the zero-based index of the selected option. The <Day> elements are listed sequentially, but ChildNodes is a zero-based collection, so this index will allow us to locate the correct <Day> element in that collection. We *could* retrieve the option text itself from the intrinsic Request object, but that would be a string. This index comes as an integer, which is what we'll need shortly.

Loading the master schedule document, data, is easy: we use the simplest constructor for XmlDocument, and then invoke Load. Note the use of Server.MapPath to get a file URL for this document on the server. Now we can turn our attention to the response document, doc:

```
    XmlDocument doc = new XmlDocument();
    MakeDoc(data, doc, i);
```

These two lines encompass a lot of tasks from the above list. MakeDoc, which we'll write shortly, takes an initialized master schedule document (data, which we just created), an empty XmlDocument instance for the response document (doc), and a zero-based day index. It is in MakeDoc that all retrieval and construction tasks take place. When it returns, doc holds a complete DOM tree representing the schedule document we want to return to the client.

Before we dive into the details, let's wrap up the top-level processing by looking at how the XSLT stylesheet gets loaded and assigned to the XML control:

```
    XslTransform styler = new XslTransform();
    styler.Load(Server.MapPath("agenda.xslt"));
    Xml1.Document = doc;
    Xml1.Transform = styler;
}
```

127

The constructor for XslTransform is as simple as the one we used in XmlDocument (in fact, the former derives from the latter). That means that loading the stylesheet, itself an XML document, has the same form as the load of the master schedule. The last two lines above invoke the transformation simply by assigning our response document to the XML control's Document property, and our stylesheet document to the Transform property. The XML control then executes the transformation and streams the output – an HTML fragment – to the intrinsic ASP.NET Response object.

Building a Response Document

MakeDoc receives data, an empty document object, and an index indicating which day's data to retrieve from the master document. The first thing to do is to set up the response document with the document element it requires, <AGENDA>:

```
protected void MakeDoc(XmlDocument src, XmlDocument tgt, int day)
{
  try
  {
    XmlElement root = tgt.CreateElement("AGENDA");
    tgt.InsertAfter(root, null);
```

The first line creates root as a rootless element node. The document is empty at this point, and the DocumentElement property is read-only. Happily, XmlDocument derives from XmlNode, so InsertAfter is available to us. We pass null as the second parameter, and the value of root becomes the new document element. We have a well-formed XML document!

It's a very short document, though, so now we need data with which to feed it. The first task is finding the day in which the user is interested. We know from the structure of the master schedule vocabulary that <Day> elements are immediate children of the document element, and that they are arranged in order at the beginning of the ChildNodes collection. The day index passed in is the zero-based index of the day we want, so we can reach directly into the ChildNodes collection:

```
    XmlNode Day = src.DocumentElement.ChildNodes.Item(day);
```

It's still too early to start grabbing <Speaker> and <Topic> elements; that must wait until we iterate through the <Event> elements of the master schedule. We do know, however, that we're going to need a series of <SESSION> elements, and to this end we'll use the shortcut introduced in the discussion of creating documents: using XMLDocumentFragment and cloning nodes. We create a fragment for a single <SESSION> element, but we don't bother filling in any of the text nodes, as we have to change them for every session according to the values obtained from the <Event> (and related) elements.

```
    XmlDocumentFragment sessionFrag = tgt.CreateDocumentFragment();

    XmlNode session = tgt.CreateElement("SESSION");
    sessionFrag.InsertAfter(session, null);
```

So far, this is just the same as creating a document. The document fragment and the node are created within the context of the document that will receive the cloned <SESSION> element sub-trees – that way, we can bypass importing the nodes into the document. There is a distinction between this and document creation, however: sessionFrag, being an instance of XmlDocumentFragment, has no document element. If you called sessionFrag.ChildNodes.Item(0), you'd receive root. This might *look* like a document element, but we could add additional elements using InsertAfter, and they'd all end up as *siblings* of root.

Now we create all the children of `<SESSION>`, and attach them to that element:

```
XmlNode topic = tgt.CreateElement("TOPIC");
XmlNode speaker = tgt.CreateElement("SPEAKER");
XmlNode abs = tgt.CreateElement("ABSTRACT");
XmlNode room = tgt.CreateElement("ROOM");
XmlNode time = tgt.CreateElement("TIME");

session.AppendChild(topic);
session.AppendChild(speaker);
session.AppendChild(abs);
session.AppendChild(room);
session.AppendChild(time);
```

The preliminaries are at last out of the way. We can now iterate through the `<Event>` elements that are children of `<Day>` elements, and start retrieving the data to which their attributes point:

```
    for(int i = 0; i < Day.ChildNodes.Count; i++)
    {
      tgt.DocumentElement.AppendChild(
        MakeSession(sessionFrag, (XmlElement)Day.ChildNodes.Item(i), src));
    }
  }
  catch(XmlException e)
  {
    Response.Write("Error: XML Exception");
  }
}
```

We've crammed a lot into one line here, but the key to unraveling it all is to know what `MakeSession` does. As the name suggests, it creates a `<SESSION>` element. More specifically, it will set the values of our document fragment and clone it, but that isn't important right now. Its parameters comprise a document fragment, `sessionFrag`, an `<Event>` element, and the master schedule. Getting the `<Event>` element is easy – it is an immediate child of `<Day>`, and we have an index in the loop variable `i`.

Since we're iterating through the `<Event>` elements sequentially, we need to add the `<SESSION>` elements (and their dependent sub-trees) in the same order. They will be attached to the document element, `<AGENDA>`, so calling `AppendChild` on the document element is ideal.

Configuring a Session

We've peeled away another layer of processing and arrived at the lowest, most detailed level of our algorithm. This is perhaps the most interesting part, as it is where we stitch together the relationship between `<Event>`, `<Speaker>`, and `<Topic>` elements.

```
protected XmlNode MakeSession(
    XmlDocumentFragment frag, XmlElement evtElt, XmlDocument resource)
{
  try
  {
    XmlAttribute speakerID =
```

```
            (XmlAttribute)evtElt.Attributes.GetNamedItem("speaker");
    XmlElement speakerElt = resource.GetElementById(speakerID.Value);

    XmlAttribute topicID =
        (XmlAttribute)evtElt.Attributes.GetNamedItem("topic");
    XmlElement topicElt = resource.GetElementById(topicID.Value);
```

We follow the same pattern in each case: we get the IDREF value, and then pass it to GetElementById on the master schedule document. In each case, we get the attribute as a named item from the Attributes collection of the <Event> element. The Value property of the returned node is the value we need for the parameter of GetElementById in the next line. The result is a pair of nodes representing the <Speaker> and <Topic> elements referred to by the <Event> element we are processing.

We're now ready to set the text node values of our document fragment, but the last two items – the room name and the start time – are kept in attributes of <Event> itself. We know the order of the child elements of <SESSION>, so we're going to do this using ChildNodes and ordinal access. We're using the proprietary Microsoft extension InnerText as shorthand; the equivalent procedure using strict DOM method calls would involve creating text nodes using CreateTextNode, attaching them to the children of <SESSION>, and *then* setting their value here. Microsoft's shortcut lets us skip the first two steps:

```
    XmlElement sessionNode = (XmlElement)frag.ChildNodes.Item(0);

    // Topic title
    sessionNode.ChildNodes.Item(0).InnerText =
                        topicElt.ChildNodes.Item(0).InnerText;
    // Speaker name
    sessionNode.ChildNodes.Item(1).InnerText =
                        speakerElt.ChildNodes.Item(0).InnerText;
    // Abstract
    sessionNode.ChildNodes.Item(2).InnerText =
                        topicElt.ChildNodes.Item(1).InnerText;
    // Room name
    sessionNode.ChildNodes.Item(3).InnerText =
                        evtElt.Attributes.GetNamedItem("room").InnerText;
    // Start time
    sessionNode.ChildNodes.Item(4).InnerText =
                        evtElt.Attributes.GetNamedItem("time").InnerText;
```

The last two values come from attributes of the Event element, so we use the now familiar GetNamedItem method of XmlNamedNodeMap. The final step is to clone the document fragment and return it from the method, so that MakeDoc can append the new <SESSION> element to the response document:

```
      return (XmlElement)sessionNode.CloneNode(true);
    }
    catch(XmlException e)
    {
      return null;
    }
  }
```

XSLT Transformation

Although we're going to look at XSLT in depth in the next chapter, we'll get a taste of it here to transform the response document into HTML. The Framework's XML server-side control handles all of the tasks involved in executing a transformation, and it only requires a small knowledge of XSLT syntax to understand what is going on.

Basically, we turn each displayed element of our output XML document into an HTML DIV element with fixed style characteristics. The results of the transformation are inserted into the shell of the HTML document returned to the client, so we don't need to generate that in the stylesheet:

```
<?xml version="1.0"?>
<xsl:stylesheet version="1.0"
                xmlns:xsl="http://www.w3.org/1999/XSL/Transform">
  <xsl:output method="html"/>

  <xsl:template match="/">
    <xsl:apply-templates />
  </xsl:template>

  <xsl:template match="SESSION">
    <xsl:apply-templates/>
  </xsl:template>

  <xsl:template match="TOPIC">
    <div style="color:black;font-family:Verdana;font-size:18pt;
                font-weight:700">
      <xsl:value-of select="."/>
    </div>
  </xsl:template>

  <xsl:template match="SPEAKER">
    <div style="font-family:Verdana;font-size:14pt;color:white;
                background-color:teal;">
      <xsl:value-of select="."/>
    </div>
  </xsl:template>

  <xsl:template match="ABSTRACT">
    <div style="color:black;font-family:'Times New Roman';font-size:12pt;">
      <xsl:value-of select="."/>
    </div>
  </xsl:template>

  <xsl:template match="ROOM">
    <div style="color:gray;font-family:Verdana;fint-size:12pt;
                font-style:italic;font-weight:400;">
      <xsl:value-of select="."/>
    </div>
  </xsl:template>
```

```
<xsl:template match="TIME">
  <span style="color:gray;font-family:Verdana;font-size:12pt;
               font-style:italic;font-weight:400;">
    <xsl:value-of select="."/>
  </span>
</xsl:template>
</xsl:stylesheet>
```

Save the above as agenda.xslt in the directory containing your ASP.NET project code, and compile and run the project with *F5*. Here's what the application looks like when showing the first day's schedule:

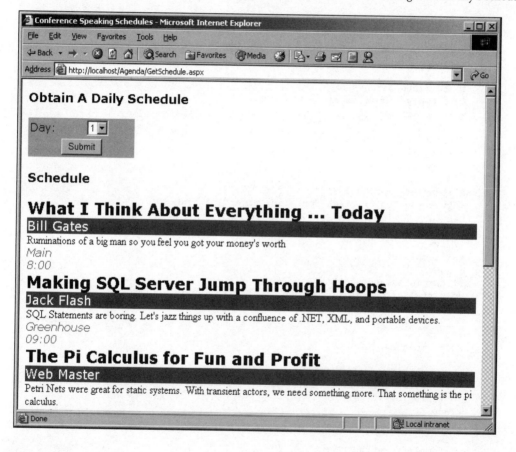

Summary

We've now introduced the classes that ASP.NET uses to implement the Document Object Model. The DOM is a product of the W3C's standardization process, and enjoys wide support from vendors. The DOM trades away the simplicity and efficiency of stream-based processing, but in return gets a robust, tree-structured model that maintains a comprehensive view of the document in memory at all times. We've looked at the following concepts:

❏   DOM class hierarchy in terms of the .NET Framework classes

❏   Document traversal

❏   The difference between named and ordinal collection class access

❏   Document and node creation

❏   Use of document fragments as a shortcut for creating repeated content

The DOM is a very powerful model and forms an essential part of every professional XML programmer's toolkit. It is well supported in ASP.NET – In fact, the Framework classes represent Microsoft's most advanced implementation of the DOM yet. For programmers of XML applications in ASP.NET, the Framework offers a broad array of weaponry for dealing with XML documents.

4

XPath

Try to imagine a large data source such as those that SQL Server can support, but without a SELECT statement to retrieve that data. Imagine for a moment that the only way to see your data was to retrieve the entire table at once! Without the filtering capabilities of SQL statements, life would get pretty difficult when dealing with a table consisting of thousands of rows.

An XML document can represent a data source, and thousands of XML nodes are possible, so where is the SELECT statement to retrieve and filter nodes to a manageable level? The established way to query data in an XML document is through XPath. We look at an alternative, XQuery, in Chapter 9.

We will be using XPath extensively throughout the rest of the book, and this chapter aims to cover the following essential points:

- ❑ Introduction to XPath
- ❑ Understanding node types in the XPath node tree
- ❑ Location paths – absolute and relative
- ❑ Location steps – axis, node-test, and predicate
- ❑ Using XPath with XmlNode methods
- ❑ XPath operators and functions
- ❑ Using XPathNavigator

We will also create two Web Forms: one to exploit the XmlNode methods that execute XPath expressions, and the other to demonstrate the features of the XPathNavigator object.

Why XPath?

Put simply, XPath is a standard language for retrieving data in an XML document. XPath 1.0 became a W3C Recommendation on November 16, 1999, and the specification is available for review at http://www.w3c.org/TR/xpath. We will be focusing on this version in this book, as this is the version used in the .NET Framework. XPath 2.0 is currently at working draft level, and more information on it can be found at http://www.w3.org/TR/2001/WD-xpath20-20011220.

XPath is a standard expression language for identifying, selecting, or manipulating nodes (a node is a generic term for any part of an XML document – elements, attributes and so on) and is used by several technologies today. We'll take a look at these now, starting with where XPath is found in the .NET world.

XPath and .NET

The .NET Framework contains classes that support XPath queries, including:

❑ `System.Xml.XmlNode` and all of its derivatives such as `XmlDocument` – XPath expressions are generally passed into one of two methods, `SelectSingleNode` and `SelectNodes`, according to whether a single matching `XMLNode` is to be returned, or a set of nodes. (Alternatively, we can execute the XPath statement from an `XPathNavigator` object returned by the `CreateNavigator` method. See last bullet point.)

❑ `System.Xml.XPath.XPathDocument` – This is an optimized, read-only cache of the underlying XML. XPath statements are executed by retrieving the `XPathNavigator` object using the `CreateNavigator` method. See next bullet point.

❑ `System.Xml.XPath.XPathNavigator` – Both `XmlNode` (and its descendants) and `XPathDocument` contain a method called `CreateNavigator`, which returns an instance of this object. With this object, we can compile an XPath expression, and determine its validity and even the return type. We cover this later, in the section *Using XPathNavigator*.

This chapter will extensively explore the use of XPath in these methods.

XPath and XSLT Style Sheets

XSLT style sheets also use XPath expressions to select nodes from an XML source document that will be transformed according to a series of template rules. Each template rule defines how the selected nodes should be transformed in the resulting output.

Chapter 5 contains more information on XSLT style sheets.

XPath and SQL Server 2000

Microsoft SQL Server 2000 is rich with XML support. Not only does SQL Server 2000 allow data to be returned as XML, it also enables developers to query the database using XPath expressions. This is accomplished by creating an annotated XML Schema (which serves as an XML view to the underlying tables). The XPath expression is performed against the XML view, which generates an XML response.

For more information about retrieving XML using XPath in SQL Server 2000, see Chapter 7.

XPath and Other XML Technologies

Knowledge of XPath comes in handy for various other XML technologies as well. Below is a list of those XML technologies followed by the role that XPath can play:

- ❑ XPointer – Links one document to nodes in another
- ❑ XML Schemas – Enable referential constraints; Schemas can use XPath to enforce uniqueness and establish relationships
- ❑ XML Signature – Enable node-set filtering and transformation support

Clearly, learning how to use XPath will sharpen our XML skills in all these differing technologies.

Let's now move on to examine exactly how we can access node information using XPath.

Accessing Node Information

What information do we as developers have access to in the source XML document? How do we differentiate between elements, attributes, or comments within such a document? When invoked, what does an XPath expression return? To answer these questions, let's take a look under the hood to see how it all works.

Understanding the XPath Tree

How XPath "sees" an XML document is the starting point to understanding how XPath works. With this in mind, let's take a look at an XML file named shopping-cart.xml, which is a simplified version of a file that I once used in a production environment. Don't worry too much about the custom-error processing instruction at the beginning, its meaning is processor specific, and has been included just for illustrative purposes.

> **The following XML document will be referenced in many examples this chapter, and is included in the code download for the book.**

```xml
<?xml version="1.0" encoding="UTF-8" ?>
<?custom-error code="0" message="OK" ?>
<!--Shopping Cart Example-->
<shopping-cart xmlns="urn:wrox-asp.net-xml-xpath">
  <header>
    <customer id="P4LLC" billingId="001" shippingId="001" >
      <contact>Toshia Palermo</contact>
    </customer>
    <order-type>Regular</order-type>
  </header>
  <items>
    <item id="ITM-1001" productLine="1">
      <quantity>1</quantity>
       <list-price>123.45</list-price>
        <description>Gadget XYZ</description>
```

```
      </item>
      <item id="ITM-1002" productLine="1">
        <quantity>3</quantity>
         <list-price>4.00</list-price>
         <description>XYZ Accessory</description>
      </item>
      <item id="ITM-1003" productLine="2">
         <quantity>1</quantity>
         <list-price>15.00</list-price>
         <description>Gizmo Part</description>
      </item>
      <item id="ITM-1004" productLine="3">
         <quantity>1</quantity>
         <list-price>44.00</list-price>
         <description>Widget X</description>
      </item>
    </items>
  </shopping-cart>
```

The question to ask now is – how does XPath interpret the preceding XML document? The underlying principle is that it, as any other XML document, is viewed as a hierarchical *tree* of nodes. Each node in the tree is classed as a specific node type. Let's quickly look at what these node types are.

Node Types

As a reference, the table below identifies and describes the seven node types recognized in the XPath tree:

Node Type	Description
Root	Every XML document begins with an implicit root node, which lies at the top of the XPath tree, and therefore never has a parent. This is not to be confused with the document node, which is an explicit element, and in the above sample XML file is the `<shopping-cart>` element. The root node is the implicit node that is the parent of this node.
Processing Instruction	Processing instructions are distinguished by the `<?` and `?>` delimiters. One of the most commonly-used processing instructions links the XML file to an XSLT style sheet like so: `<?xml-stylesheet type="text/xsl" href="name.xsl"?>` **Note:** Although XML declarations share the `<?` and `?>` delimiter syntax, they are not considered processing instructions, and are not represented in the XPath tree.
Comment	Comments are distinguished by the `<!--` and `-->` delimiters. It is not required for an XML parser to pass comments to a higher application, but Microsoft's parser does so, as do most.
Element	Every element in an XML document maps to a distinct element node in the corresponding XPath tree. Every well-formed XML document consists of a single document element, which contains any number of descendent elements.

Node Type	Description
Attribute	Every attribute in an XML document maps to a distinct attribute node in the corresponding XPath tree. The parent of an attribute is the element in which it is contained, although attribute nodes are *not* considered children of element.
	If an attribute is not explicitly set in an XML document, but has a default value specified in the corresponding DTD or XML Schema, it will be represented in the XPath tree.
Namespace	Each distinct namespace node is associated with the element in which it was declared. Although the namespace node in many ways resembles an attribute node of an element (for instance, the parent of a namespace node is the element associated with it, yet the namespace node is not considered a child of that element), it is considered a special case, and is distinguished by the following syntax:
	`xmlns:prefix="URI"`
	where `prefix` indicates a string which precedes any element belonging to that namespace in the document. Note that it is not required to specify a prefix:
	`xmlns="URI"`
	in which case the namespace is said to be the default namespace, and any unprefixed descendent elements are taken to be members of it.
	Namespace nodes are not shared. If an element defines a namespace, that namespace will cascade down to all child elements, but each child element will have its own distinct namespace node in the XPath tree.
Text	The content of an element is considered a separate text node. Text separated by markup is normalized to form one single text node. A text node contains at least one character. The parent of a text node is the element which contains it, likewise, the text node is a child of the element.

Now let's take a look at the following illustration which shows the top of the XPath tree for the `shopping-cart.xml` document:

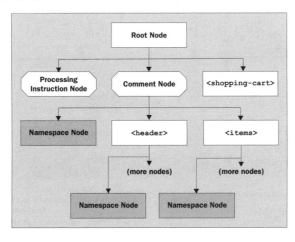

As the illustration indicates, there are more nodes under the `<header>` and `<items>` nodes. Before we look at those though, let's just consider the top of this tree. As we have seen, there are seven node types recognized by XPath. The very first node is the implicit **root node**, of which there is only ever one. Consider the root node as the "starting point" for the entire XML document.

In this case, the first node we come to after the root node is a **processing instruction node**. It represents an instruction for the XML parser, and its exact meaning is not important. Notice though the XML declaration given right before it:

```
<?xml version="1.0" encoding="UTF-8"?>
```

which, although outwardly appearing much like a processing node, is *not* represented in the XPath tree, in accordance with the XPath specification.

Hence there are just two other nodes under the root node in our example – a **comment node** containing the string "Shopping Cart Example", and the single document element of `<shopping-cart>`, which has a node type of **element node**.

Under `<shopping-cart>` we find three nodes, two of which are also element node types – `<header>` and `<items>`, and the third being a **namespace node**. Remember that although it is under `<shopping-cart>`, it is not considered a child of the element – even though the element `<shopping-cart>` is considered a parent of the namespace node. If this seems a little nuts right now, it does simplify things when selecting the children of elements, where we usually do not wish to include namespace nodes.

In our example, the namespace node contains the value:

```
urn:wrox-asp.net-xml-xpath
```

As no prefix was given, this specifies the *default* namespace for descendent elements. Notice however that it is not shared with `<header>` or `<items>`, as each element now is given its own distinct namespace node – although they will all contain the same value.

Underneath the `<header>` element, the tree view can be represented like this:

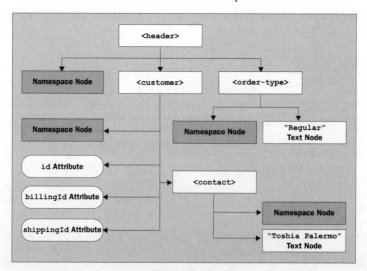

Once again, each element descendant of the document element has its own namespace node. Under the <customer> element, we see three attribute nodes named id, billingId, and shippingId. These are **attribute node** types. Like namespace nodes – and for the same reason – XPath does not consider an attribute node to be a child of the element that contains it, although the element containing the attribute is considered its parent. It might help to think of attributes as 'properties' of the element they belong to, while other child elements have their own tree structures and 'properties' (attributes) of their own.

Finally, the <contact> and <order-type> elements also each have a distinct namespace node. Plus, the characters found between the opening and closing tags of the elements are considered as a separate **text node**. In our example, the value of the text node child of <order-type> is "Regular", while the value of the text node child of <contact> is "Toshia Palermo".

Since we have seen an example of each node type, we don't need to go into the details of how the XPath tree looks under the <items> element. Just bear in mind that each <item> element is a unique child node under the <items> element, and will appear in the tree in the same order as in the source document. Also, each descendent element under <items> will have its own namespace node.

By observing the hierarchical relationships of a typical XPath tree and looking at the various node types, I hope to have laid the ground for more detailed examination of the XPath syntax for locating any desired nodes in an XML document.

Location Paths

Location paths are XPath expressions that locate specific nodes in the XPath tree. In this section, we will look at the basic structure of a location path. There are two primary kinds of location path: absolute location paths and relative location paths. This nomenclature is borrowed from the absolute and relative paths of URLs and those used in disk file systems, and work on the same principles.

> **Unless otherwise indicated, the XPath examples from this point forward will assume the shopping-cart.xml is not declared with any namespace. Namespace support will be covered later this chapter.**

Absolute Location Paths

Absolute location paths always specify nodes starting at the root node of the XPath tree. For illustration, consider how we might change to the IIS wwwroot directory by entering the following command at a DOS prompt:

> **>cd c:\inetpub\wwwroot**

This sets the current directory to the wwwroot directory, no matter where we might be in the file system when we issue it: it is an absolute file path. In the above example, beginning the file path with the drive letter (c:\) indicates we are supplying an absolute address.

In XPath, we indicate an absolute path by the forward slash character ("/") to start us at the root node. For instance, the following XPath uses an absolute path to locate the `<header>` element node in the `shopping-cart.xml` file:

```
/shopping-cart/header
```

As in the file path example above, no matter where we are in the XPath tree, the above XPath expression will always locate the same `<header>` element under `<shopping-cart>`.

What do we mean by "no matter where we are in the XPath tree"? As this statement implies, the XPath expression is executed in the context of the node we currently have access to – called the **context node**. Understanding this concept will help us to understand the next location path type. Think of the context node as the point from which execution begins. Following the analogy of a file system directory structure, the context node is equivalent to the current directory.

Relative Location Paths

If we want to access nodes relative to the current node in the XPath tree, we use a relative location path. Let's return to the familiar file path notation for illustration. Suppose we are in the `C:\Program Files` directory at a DOS prompt. To access the `Microsoft Visual Studio .NET` folder immediately under the `Program Files` directory, we could type the following:

>cd "Microsoft Visual Studio .NET"

As this file path does not begin with a drive letter, the path search is in the context of the directory where we are currently located. If we executed this statement from any other folder, we would either get a message indicating that the system could not find the path specified, or, less likely, end up in a different `Microsoft Visual Studio .NET` folder to the one we intended.

In XPath, relative location paths work in a very similar manner. Any XPath expression that does not begin with the forward slash character ("/") is executed in the context of the current node. For example, if the context node is the `<header>` element, the following XPath expression would return the `<contact>` element node:

```
customer/contact
```

Now if this were executed from any other node in the XPath tree, no nodes would be returned (resulting in null). We look at how and when the context node is changed later.

Structure of a Location Path

A location path consists of one or more "location steps", and is read left to right. The result of each step within the location path is a node-set, which provides the input for the next location step to the right. Ultimately, the location path returns a node-set of many, one, or zero nodes (in other words, a null node-set).

The generic format of an absolute path is thus something like:

```
/Step/Step/Step...
```

Whereas the format of a relative path begins *without* the forward slash character ("/"):

Step/Step/Step...

Each location step in an expression is separated with the forward slash character. Now we will examine in detail what a location step consists of.

Location Step

A location step consists of three parts: an axis, a node-test, and optionally a predicate. The syntax of a location step follows this pattern:

axis::node-test [*predicate*]

Let's consider each part of the location step.

Axis

The axis specifies the direction in which to move in order to locate the node(s) we are searching for. XPath defines a total of 13 axes, described in the following table. If a match is not found, a null value is returned.

XPath Axis	Description
ancestor	The ancestor axis of a node includes its parent node, the parent of that node, and so on all the way up to the root node. The node-set denoted by this axis will be ordered in the way that the nodes appear in the XPath tree. Therefore, the root node is always the first in the node-set.
ancestor-or-self	Same as ancestor, but the resulting node-set also includes the node itself.
attribute	When the context node is an element, this is returns a node-set of all its attributes.
child	Returns the child nodes of the context node. Attribute and namespace nodes will never be included in the resulting node-set.
descendant	Returns the child nodes of the context node, and their children, their children's children, and so on. As with the child axis, attribute and namespace nodes will never be included in the resulting node-set.
descendant-or-self	Same as descendant, but the resulting node-set also includes the context node.
following	Returns all nodes (except attribute and namespace nodes) that appear after the closing tag of the context node. Therefore, descendants of the context node are **not** included in the resulting node-set.

Table continued on following page

XPath Axis	Description
following-sibling	Returns all siblings (that is, elements at the same level in the XML hierarchy) that come after the context node in the current document. If the context node is either an attribute node or a namespace node, the node-set will return null.
namespace	Returns any namespace nodes of the context node if it is an element.
parent	Returns the parent of the context node.
preceding	Returns all nodes (except attribute nodes and namespace nodes) that appear before the opening tag of the context element. Ancestors of the context node will **not** be included in the resulting node-set.
preceding-sibling	Returns all siblings that precede the context node. If the context node is either an attribute node or a namespace node, the node-set will return empty.
self	Returns the context node.

Of these 13 axes, five allow **abbreviated syntax**. The following table has examples of how to use each axis in its abbreviated form:

XPath Axis	Unabbreviated Example	Abbreviated Example
child	child::customer	customer (in effect, child is the default axis)
attribute	attribute::id	@id
descendant-or-self	/descendant-or-self::item	//item
parent	parent::node()	..
self	self::node()	.

Note particularly that the absence of an axis implies child. node(), appearing in the above examples, returns true for all nodes at the current location, and we'll cover it further in the section headed *The Node-Test*, once we've looked at some examples of these five axes used with our sample XML file.

Using the Child Axis

The following expression retrieves the <customer> element using an absolute location path:

```
/child::shopping-cart/child::header/child::customer
```

The more readable abbreviated form would be:

```
/shopping-cart/header/customer
```

Using the Attribute Axis

If the context node is at the <items> element, we can specify the productLine attribute of the <item> element using the following relative location path:

```
child::item/attribute::productLine
```

It could also be written like so:

```
item/@productLine
```

Using the Descendant-or-Self Axis

An absolute location path to return all <description> elements that are descendants of the <items> element would be:

```
/child::shopping-cart/child::items/descendant-or-self::description
```

Using abbreviated syntax, it becomes:

```
/shopping-cart/items//description
```

To get hold of all <item> elements *anywhere* in the XPath tree, we could use:

```
/descendant-or-self::item
```

This is the same as:

```
//item
```

Note that the technical name of the // operator is the **recursive descent operator**.

Using the Parent Axis

To find the parent of the <contact> element, if <contact> is the context node:

```
parent::node()
```

This can be abbreviated to:

```
..
```

Similarly, we can retrieve the element that contains the billingId attribute, if the billingId attribute is the context node, with this expression:

```
parent::node()
```

This can also be rewritten as:

```
..
```

The latter demonstrates that the element containing a particular an attribute node is considered its parent, even though the attribute is not considered a child element.

Using the Self Axis

To search for all <quantity> elements that are descendants of the context node, we can use:

```
self::node()/descendant-or-self::quantity
```

We could use the abbreviated form equally well:

```
.//quantity
```

These examples give a good general idea of how the axes function. Now let's consider the next part of the location step – the node-test.

The Node-Test

Once we know the axis, we must next specify which node(s) we want from that axis, which we do using the node-test in one of two ways:

- ❑ Locate the node(s) by name
- ❑ Locate the node(s) by type

Locating Nodes by Name

We have several options available when referencing nodes by name. When locating nodes by name, we have the option to:

- ❑ Search for a specific name
- ❑ Search for all nodes (the asterisk "*" may be used for wildcard searches)
- ❑ Search for a specific namespace and name
- ❑ Search for all nodes in a specific namespace

We have already seen how to locate a node with a specific name. For instance, the following example demonstrates how to find any attribute called id in the XPath tree:

```
//@id
```

But what if we wanted a node-set of *all* attributes in the document? We use the wildcard "*" like this:

```
//@*
```

The same applies for elements. For example, the following XPath expression returns all elements found under the <header> element:

```
/shopping-cart/header/*
```

In our sample XML file, this would return the <customer> and <order-type> elements.

Most of the examples we have seen so far have assumed that no namespace has been declared. If we had set a namespace, and allocated it the prefix of wrx, say, our XPath expressions would require the prefix in the node-test. For example, the following XPath expression would return the <items> element:

```
/wrx:shopping-cart/wrx:items
```

The use of namespaces in XML documents is quite prevalent, and we will see more examples of namespace support throughout the chapter.

Locating Nodes by Type

We can also search for nodes by type. The following table describes the four node-tests which locate a node by its type:

Node-Test	Result
node()	True for all nodes.
text()	True for all text nodes.
comment()	True for all comment nodes.
processing-instruction() or processing-instruction(target)	True for all processing instruction nodes. Optionally, we can specify a literal target. For example, the processing instruction in our sample file: `processing-instruction("custom-error")`

In earlier examples, we saw the node() test in action for the self and parent axes. This is useful when we do not want to use (or we don't know) the actual name of the node in our location step. When we want to find specific node types, we can use the node-tests in this table as a guide, as in the following examples.

The following expression would retrieve the text node of the <contact> element:

```
/shopping-cart/header/customer/contact/text()
```

The next expression retrieves all comment nodes in the document:

```
//comment()
```

This one returns any processing instruction nodes under the root node:

```
/processing-instruction()
```

Predicate

For the most part, our location steps have been comparable to a SELECT statement with no WHERE clause. We can achieve a similar sort of filtering in XPath through use of **predicates**; the third and final part of a location step. Unlike the axis or node-test, predicates are optional. The syntax for a predicate is always contained within square brackets like this:

axis::node-test [*predicate*]

There are three different ways to filter nodes in a location step:

❑ Filter by presence

❑ Filter by value

❑ Filter by position

Let's examine each in detail.

Filtering Nodes by Presence

In some cases, we may want to select nodes based on the presence of other related nodes. All that is required is to specify the location path for such related nodes as the predicate, as in the following examples.

To select all <header> elements that contain a <customer> element as a child node:

```
/shopping-cart/header[customer]
```

To return all <item> elements that have a productLine attribute:

```
//item[@productLine]
```

To return all <contact> elements only if the direct parent element is <customer>:

```
//contact[parent::customer]
```

The last example is an example of how we can filter nodes based on the presence of nodes in whatever axis location we choose. Note that location steps specified in the predicate like this must be relative paths in order to be meaningful.

Filtering Nodes by Value

A classic WHERE clause in a SELECT statement allows us to refine our search based on data in the table, and we can do the same thing with predicates in the location step. Have a look at the following examples.

We can search for the <item> element that contains an id attribute equal to "ITM-1002":

```
//item[@id="ITM-1002"]
```

Note the use of double quotes (") around the literal string in our predicate. Enclosing the value in single quotes (') is also valid. We can also search for all <item> elements where <quantity> is equal to 1:

```
//item[quantity="1"]
```

Note that this is equivalent to:

```
//item[quantity/text()="1"]
```

These are very similar, except of course that the first example refines the search based on the value of an attribute, while the second example refines the search based on the value of an element.

Filtering Nodes by Position

We can also filter nodes based on their position within the source XML document. Note that if a reverse axis (such as ancestor, ancestor-or-self, preceding, or preceding-sibling) is specified, the nodes will nonetheless be numbered in document order. Let's see some examples.

To retrieve the third <item> element:

```
/shopping-cart/items/item[3]
```

We can search for the second preceding <item> element like this, assuming the context node is an <item> element:

```
preceding-sibling::item[2]
```

Defining Multiple Predicates

We can also define multiple predicates in the same location step. In this case, the order of the predicates makes a difference. Once again, I'll illustrate with some examples.

This expression searches for all <item> elements where <quantity> is equal to 1, narrowing the search to the second <item> in the resulting node-set (remember the left-to-right rule of location paths):

```
//item[quantity="1"][2]
```

The result of this XPath expression on our sample document would be the <item> element with an id attribute of "ITM-1003". Now if we reverse the predicates like this:

```
//item[2][quantity="1"]
```

The resulting node-set would now be empty (null), because this expression is attempting to select the second <item> element *only* if it contains a <quantity> equal to 1, which is not the case in our sample document.

Using XPath with XmlNode

Now that we have built a solid foundation in XPath basics, the next step is to see how we can use it in our ASP.NET applications. So, in this section, we will design an ASP.NET page that will load an XML document using XmlDocument, from the System.Xml namespace, and allow the user to execute XPath statements against it or any of the nodes within it.

The XPath Web Project

Let's now create a web application where we can put our XPath knowledge to use.

Open Visual Studio .NET and select File | New | New Project, and create a new C# ASP.NET web application called XPath:

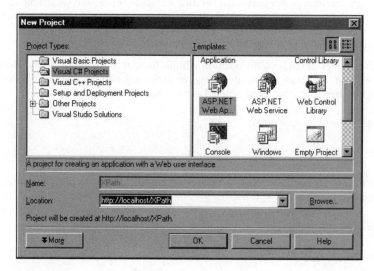

Visual Studio .NET will create a new web project and open the Web Form Designer. A blank Web Form is now available for us to design and code.

The XPath Web Form

Our objective is to design a web form that will load up an XmlDocument, capture an XPath expression from the user, and display the results on the screen. This page will serve as a utility for testing XPath expressions against the shopping-cart.xml sample file, but with minor modifications, it would not be hard to make the page a generic utility to test any specified XML document.

First, rename the default web form (WebForm1.aspx) to XPath.aspx. Then add five labels, two text boxes, and two buttons from the Web Forms tab of the Toolbox, and set their ID properties as shown in the following table:

Web Form Control	ID Property
Label	TitleLabel
Label	PrefixLabel
Label	XPathLabel
Label	MessageLabel
Label	ResultsLabel
TextBox	PrefixTextBox
TextBox	XPathTextBox
Button	SelectSingleNodeButton
Button	SelectNodesButton

Lay the controls out as in this screenshot, formatting and sizing as shown:

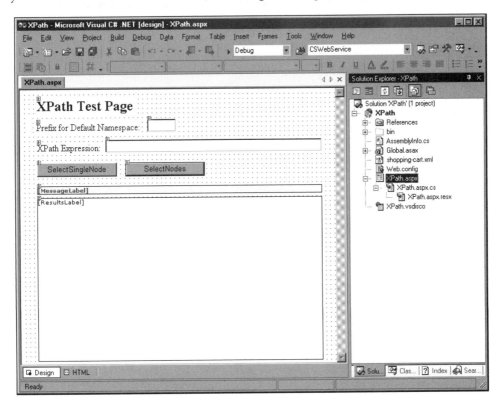

Viewing the HTML

If we click the HTML button at the bottom of the designer, we can see the Page directive right at the top of the HTML that VS.NET has generated for our web page. Note that this directive points to another file for the code behind:

```
<%@ Page language="c#"
        Codebehind="XPath.aspx.cs"
        AutoEventWireup="false"
        Inherits="XPath.WebForm1" %>
```

As we see, all the code for this Web Form will be found in the XPath.aspx.cs file, which was automatically created when we renamed the page. The Inherits attribute indicates that this page is inherited from the XPath.WebForm1 class, which is still the name of the class defined in the XPath.aspx.cs file. When we change the name of the class in the code-behind in the next section, the value of this Inherits attribute will be updated automatically to reflect the new name.

The Code-Behind for XPath.aspx

So let's now turn our attention to the code-behind file XPath.aspx.cs. Change the class name and the namespace that contains it as shown below, and add using statements for the System.Xml and System.IO .NET namespaces at the top as highlighted:

```
using System;
using System.Collections;
using System.ComponentModel;
using System.Data;
using System.Drawing;
using System.Web;
using System.Web.SessionState;
using System.Web.UI;
using System.Web.UI.WebControls;
using System.Web.UI.HtmlControls;
using System.Xml;
using System.IO;

namespace Wrox.ASPNET.Xml.XPath
{
    /// <summary>
    /// Summary description for XPath
    /// </summary>
    public class XPath : System.Web.UI.Page
    {
        protected System.Web.UI.WebControls.Label TitleLabel;
        protected System.Web.UI.WebControls.TextBox XPathTextBox;
        protected System.Web.UI.WebControls.Button SelectSingleNodeButton;
        protected System.Web.UI.WebControls.Button SelectNodesButton;
        protected System.Web.UI.WebControls.Label XPathLabel;
        protected System.Web.UI.WebControls.TextBox PrefixTextBox;
        protected System.Web.UI.WebControls.Label PrefixLabel;
        protected System.Web.UI.WebControls.Label MessageLabel;
        protected System.Web.UI.WebControls.Label ResultsLabel;
```

```
private void Page_Load(object sender, System.EventArgs e)
{
  // Put user code to initialize the page here
}// Page_Load

[Web Form Designer generated code]

  }
}
```

As we can see, the controls that were added in the designer are reflected in the code as well. The region entitled [Web Form Designer generated code] contains a block of code that is maintained by Visual Studio .NET, and contains the code to initialize the page.

Declaring Other XML Objects

Add the following object member declarations just after the last control declaration:

```
  .
  .
  .
protected System.Web.UI.WebControls.Label MessageLabel;
protected System.Web.UI.WebControls.Label ResultsLabel;

private XmlDocument _SourceXml;
private XmlNamespaceManager _NamespaceManager;
private XmlNode _SingleNode;
private XmlNodeList _Nodes;
private XmlNode _ContextNode;

private void Page_Load(object sender, System.EventArgs e)
  .
  .
  .
```

The _SourceXml object is an XmlDocument that will be used to load the shopping-cart.xml document. The _NamespaceManager object is an XmlNamespaceManager which will provide namespace support for executing our XPath expressions. The _SingleNode and _Nodes objects will be used to capture the results of our XPath query. Finally, the _ContextNode will house the current node returned so we can also execute relative location paths.

Note that the underscore "_" preceding each object name is a commonly used naming convention for private or local variable declarations. This is a matter of preference, as Microsoft does not provide any guidelines for objects at this level of scope.

Loading the XmlDocument

In the Page_Load event, let's add the following code:

```
// The try block will catch the error should the XML files not be available
try
{
  // Load the shopping-cart.xml document if not already cached
```

```
    if (Cache["SourceXml"]==null)
    {
      // shopping-cart.xml must be placed in the XPath virtual directory
      string _XmlDocPath = Server.MapPath(Request.ApplicationPath
                           + "/shopping-cart.xml" );
      _SourceXml = new XmlDocument();
      _SourceXml.Load(_XmlDocPath);

      // Save the loaded XmlDocument to the cache
      Cache["SourceXml"]=_SourceXml;
    }
    else
    {
      // Get the XmlDocument saved in the cache
      _SourceXml = (XmlDocument) Cache["SourceXml"];
    }
```

The code above attempts to load the _SourceXml object either from the shopping-cart.xml file, or from the cache. If Cache["SourceXml"] is null (meaning we have not yet stored the _SourceXml object in the cache), we get the path to the shopping-cart.xml file (assumed to be in the same directory as our Web Form), and load it. Otherwise, we can optimize performance by using the cached XmlDocument from a previous visit to the page.

The following code completes the Page_Load event handler:

```
    // Add support for namespaces
    if (PrefixTextBox.Text!="")
    {
      _NamespaceManager=new XmlNamespaceManager(_SourceXml.NameTable);
      _NamespaceManager.AddNamespace(PrefixTextBox.Text,
                                "urn:wrox-asp.net-xml-xpath");
    }

    MessageLabel.Text = "Shopping-cart.xml is loaded...";
    ResultsLabel.Text = "";
  }
  catch (Exception handledException)
  {
    MessageLabel.Text = handledException.Message;
  }
```

This code first checks to see if there is any value in the PrefixTextBox. If there is, it is mapped to the urn:wrox-asp.net-xml-xpath namespace in the source XML document with the AddNamespace method. The prefix entered by the user in this textbox will allow us to locate nodes associated with that namespace in our XPath expressions.

Preserving the Context Node for Relative Location Paths

Just as we used the Cache property to preserve the XmlDocument across round trips to the web server, we will also cache the result of our XPath queries when such return a single node, as that will be the current context node. Here is a private method we can add to our XPath class to retrieve the context node:

```
private XmlNode GetContextNode()
{
  XmlNode _ResultNode = null;
  try
  {
    _ResultNode = (XmlNode) Cache["ContextNode"];
    if (_ResultNode==null)
    {
      _ResultNode =  (XmlNode) _SourceXml;
    }
  }
  catch (Exception handledException)
  {
    MessageLabel.Text = handledException.Message;
  }

  return _ResultNode;

}
```

This function returns one of two values – either the value of the Cache["ContextNode"], or the root node of the _SourceXml if the cache is null.

Executing XPath Expressions Using SelectSingleNode

In the Design view for XPath.aspx, double-click the SelectSingleNode button to create the click event handler, and place us inside the handler in the XPath.aspx.cs code file. Add the following code, which executes an XPath statement provided by the user:

```
private void SelectSingleNodeButton_Click(object sender, System.EventArgs e)
{
  try
  {
    _ContextNode = GetContextNode();
    _SingleNode = _ContextNode.SelectSingleNode(XPathTextBox.Text,
                                                _NamespaceManager);

    if (_SingleNode==null)
    {
      MessageLabel.Text = "No matching nodes!";
    }
    else
    {
      MessageLabel.Text = "Context Node = "
                        + _SingleNode.Name
                        + ", Node Type = "
                        + _SingleNode.NodeType.ToString();
      ResultsLabel.Text=Server.HtmlEncode(_SingleNode.OuterXml);
      Cache["ContextNode"] = _SingleNode;
    }
  }
  catch (Exception handledException)
  {
    MessageLabel.Text = handledException.Message;
```

155

```
      }
    }
```

First, we call the private method we created earlier to determine the context node. We want to execute our XPath queries from this node to support relative location paths. Next we execute the XPath expression typed into the XPathTextBox by the user, and return the resulting value to _SingleNode. Notice we pass in the _NamespaceManager object (instantiated in the Page_Load event) as an argument to provide namespace support.

If _SingleNode is null, the XPath expression yielded no matching nodes, and we display a message to that effect in the MessageLabel control. If it is not null, we display the resulting node's name and node-type, as well as the markup. Note that unless we use the Server.HtmlEncode method to escape the results, the output in ResultsLabel will not appear correctly, as your browser will treat all the XML tags as invalid HTML and discard them, leaving only the content of any text nodes.

Executing XPath Expressions Using SelectNodes

Let's return to the Design view for XPath.aspx again, this time double-clicking the SelectNodes button. This generates the signature for the SelectNodes button click handler. Within this handler, add the following code:

```
private void SelectNodesButton_Click(object sender, System.EventArgs e)
{
  try
  {
    _ContextNode = GetContextNode();
    _Nodes = _ContextNode.SelectNodes(XPathTextBox.Text,
            _NamespaceManager);

    if (_Nodes.Count==0)
    {
      MessageLabel.Text = "No matching nodes!";
    }
    else
    {
      MessageLabel.Text = "Nodes found: " +
        _Nodes.Count.ToString();
      string _NodeListResults = "";

      // We could use a StringBuilder below for better performance
      foreach (XmlNode _XmlNode in _Nodes)
      {
        _NodeListResults += Server.HtmlEncode(_XmlNode.OuterXml)
                        + "<br />";
      }
      ResultsLabel.Text = _NodeListResults;
      Cache["ContextNode"] = (XmlNode) _SourceXml;
    }
  }
  catch (Exception handledException)
  {
    MessageLabel.Text = handledException.Message;
  }
}
```

This code starts much like the event handler for the `SelectSingleNode` button. After the context node is determined, the `SelectNodes` method is executed, supplying the XPath expression and namespace manager. The result of this method call returns an `XmlNodeList`, which we populate into _Nodes.

If the `Count` property is zero, no matching nodes were found. If there are matches, we iterate through each `XmlNode` in the list, and display its markup. We also inform the user how many nodes matched the search criteria. Because multiple nodes are potentially returned, we set the `Cache["ContextNode"]` to the root node of _SourceXml for the next XPath statement execution.

Testing the XPath Web Form

We're now ready to test. Press *F5* to save, build, and run the solution in your web browser. You'll see a screen similar to this one:

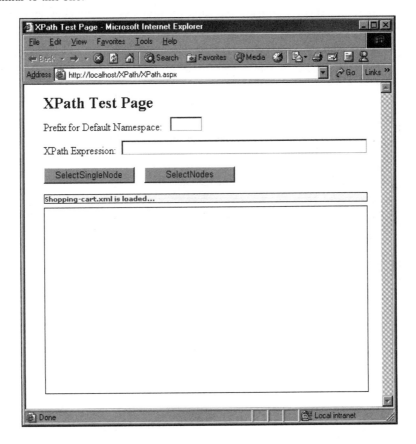

After checking that the `MessageLabel` shows that the `XmlDocument` was successfully loaded, type the following XPath expression into the `XPathTextBox`, and press **SelectNodes**:

//item

You may be a little surprised to see the message **No matching nodes!** appear in the `MessageLabel`.

So why didn't this search work? We know that there are `<item>` elements in our document, and as we know by now, this XPath should retrieve all such elements. The reason is down to namespaces: because a namespace has been declared in the XML file, we need to specify that we're looking for nodes that fall under that namespace. What we have to do is associate a prefix with the default namespace so type `wrx` in the `PrefixTextBox`. We can now use that prefix in our XPath expressions to identify nodes that belong to the default namespace.

Now change the previous XPath expression to include the prefix as shown below, and click the **SelectNodes** button:

//wrx:item

The results should look something like this:

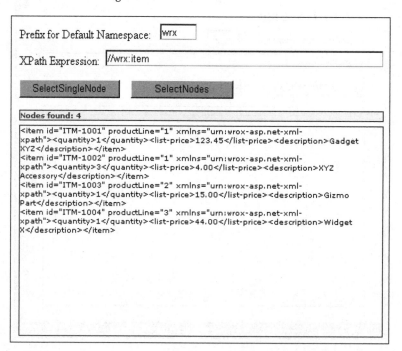

Now simply click the SelectSingleNode button, using the same XPath expression. This is the new result:

```
Prefix for Default Namespace:  wrx

XPath Expression:  //wrx:item

  [ SelectSingleNode ]      [ SelectNodes ]

Context Node = item, Node Type = Element

<item id="ITM-1001" productLine="1" xmlns="urn:wrox-asp.net-xml-
xpath"><quantity>1</quantity><list-price>123.45</list-price><description>Gadget
XYZ</description></item>
```

The MessageLabel indicates the context node is now the first `<item>` element in the document. We can see that using an XPath expression which renders multiple nodes will return only the **first** matching node when executed with SelectSingleNode.

So we've got a nice little utility to test out some basic XPath expressions. Now that the context node is `<item>`, we can explore using relative location paths. Below are some example expressions to try out.

Select the parent node:

..

Select all attributes of the current node:

@*

Select all descendants of the current node:

.//*

Using XPath Operators and Functions

Now that we have a basic understanding of what XPath expressions look like and how they behave, we can move on to some more complex syntax which allows for greater selectivity and functionality. The XPath specification provides functions and operators that enable features we are familiar with from other programming languages.

These operators and functions are grouped into the following four categories:

- ❏ Node-Set
- ❏ Boolean
- ❏ Numeric
- ❏ String

Let's look at each category separately.

Node-Set Operators and Functions

Thus far this chapter, we have been dealing with node-sets only. When we called the `SelectNodes` method of `XmlNode`, we in fact returned a node-set into an `XmlNodeList` object. For this reason, we'll start by looking at features related to node-sets as a good transition into the discussion on XPath operators and functions.

Merging Node-Sets

The **union** operator "|" is used to merge the results of multiple location paths. Below are some examples of how to use it. Note that for simplicity, I've not included the `wrx` namespace identifier, which you'll need to add to the beginning of each element name (but not attributes) if you wish to try these in our project.

Return all `<quantity>` and `<list-price>` elements:

//quantity | //list-price

Search for all `@id` attributes for either `<customer>` or `<item>` elements:

(//customer | //item)/@id

Return all elements and attributes in the document:

//* | //@*

All the above examples merge the node-sets returned by each location step into one node-set. Also note that the nodes are returned in document order, and the result contains no duplicates.

Using Node-Set Functions

Node-set functions work in various ways. The following table discusses each of them:

Node-Set Function	Description
count(*node-set*)	Returns the number of nodes in the provided node-set. Example: `count( //item )` This results in 4. We will cover expressions that return other data types later in this chapter.
Id(*unique-id*)	Returns a node-set of elements that have an ID attribute containing the *unique-id* value.
last()	Returns the number of the last node in the node-set. Example: `//item[last()]` In our document, this returns the <item> element containing an attribute id value of "ITM-1004".

local-name(*node-set*)	Returns the local part of the expanded name of the first node in the node-set. If a node-set is not passed in as the argument, the context node is used. So:
	
	`//*[local-name()="item"]`
	
	results in a node-set containing all <item> elements regardless of what namespace they are associated with.
	
	Here is another example:
	
	`local-name(/*)`
	
	In this example, the location path is passed in as the argument. This results in a string with the value of `"shopping-cart"`.

name(*node-set*)	Returns the expanded name of the first node in the node-set. If the node-set argument is not provided, the context node is used. If prefix values are used in the source XML document, these will be seen in the resulting name.
namespace-uri(node-set)	Returns the URI of the first node in the node-set. If the node-set argument is not provided, the context node is used. Example: `namespace-uri(/*)` This results in the string "urn:wrox-asp.net-xml-xpath".
position()	Returns the position of the context node. Example: `//item[position()=2]` This results with the second <item> element in document order (the one containing an attribute id value of "ITM-1002").

Boolean Operators and Functions

XPath supports a number of Boolean expressions.

Boolean Operators

The following table describes the different Boolean operators available in our XPath expressions:

Boolean Operator	Description
=	Used to evaluate equality. Example: `//item[@id = "ITM-1003"]` The equation in the predicate returns true only for the `<item>` element that contains the id attribute with the value of `"ITM-1003"`. (Remember that XML is case-sensitive.)
!=	Used to evaluate inequality. Example: `//item[@id != "ITM-1003"]` In this scenario, the resulting node-set contains all the `<item>` elements with the exception of the one containing the id attribute with the value of "ITM-1003".
>	Evaluates to true if the left side of the operator is greater than the right. Example: `//item[quantity > 1]` This results in all `<item>` elements that contain a `<quantity>` child element with a value greater than one.
>=	Evaluates to true if the left side of the operator is equal to or greater than the right. Example: `//item[quantity >= 2]` The result is the same as for the previous example.
<	Evaluates to true if the left side of the operator is less than the right.
<=	Evaluates to true if the left side of the operator is equal to or less than the right.
and	Evaluates to true if both sides of the operator evaluate to true. Example: `//item[list-price >= 10 and list-price <= 50]` This returns all `<item>` elements that contain `<list-price>` child elements with a value in the range 10 to 50 inclusive.
or	Evaluates to true if either side of the operator evaluates to true. Example: `//item[@productLine="1" or @productLine="3"]` This returns all `<item>` elements that contain a productLine attribute with a value of either "1" or "3".

Boolean Functions

The following table details the Boolean functions available and a brief description:

Boolean Function	Description
Boolean(*value*)	Converts the provided *value* into a Boolean value. If the value is a node-set, the function returns true unless the node-set is empty. If the value is numeric the result is true unless the value is zero. If the value is a string the result is true unless it is devoid of characters.
true()	This always returns true. Although it could be used in a comparison, a more practical use for it is to pass it as a parameter into an XSLT template rule. This will be covered in the next chapter.
false()	This is a static value of false. The same principal applies for this function as for true().
not(*boolean*)	Returns the inverse of the supplied Boolean expression.
lang(*string*)	Returns true if *string* (which represents a language encoding like "en") defines an xml:lang attribute starting with the same language name.

Order of Precedence

Below, the operators are listed in precedence order from highest to lowest:

1. ( )   Grouping

2. [ ]   Filters

3. /   //   Path Operators

4. < <= > >=   Comparisons

5. = !=   Comparisons

6. | Union

7. not()   Boolean NOT

8. and   Boolean AND

9. or   Boolean OR

Numeric Operators and Functions

XPath supports numeric operations, using the floating-point number type.

Numeric Operators

The following table displays the numeric operators supported in XPath syntax:

Numeric Operator	Description
+	Addition operator.
-	Subtraction operator. This is also used to invert the sign of a number. When doing so, be careful to use whitespace around the operator to avoid ambiguity with node names that contain a hyphen.
*	Multiplication operator.
div	Division operator.
mod	Modulus operator.

Numeric Functions

The following table lists the numeric functions available, and a brief description of how to use them:

Numeric Function	Description
ceiling(*number*)	Returns the smallest integer that is greater than the number argument. Example: ceiling(8.3) This returns an integer of 9.
floor(*number*)	Returns the largest integer that is less than the *number* argument. Example: floor(9.9) This returns an integer of 9.
number(*value*)	Converts the *value* argument to a numeric value. If the value is a string containing a number, the value is converted to a numeric value, otherwise the result is NaN (for 'not a number'). If *value* is a node-set, its text values are first converted to a string, and the same process follows. If the value is a Boolean, the number 1 is returned for true, 0 for false.
round(*number*)	Returns the integer that is closest to the *number* argument. Example: round(3.5) This returns an integer of 4, while: round(5.4) will return an integer of 5.

Numeric Function	Description
sum(*node-set*)	Returns the sum of all values in a node-set. If any of the values in the node-set is not numeric, the result is NaN.

String Functions

Often we are faced with the need to manipulate string values. We may need to extract subsets of a string, concatenate strings together, or determine if a value exists within a string. Among other things, we will now look at how to do just that by using the string manipulation functions of XPath.

The following table displays the string functions with a corresponding description:

String Function	Description
concat(*string*, *string**)	This returns the concatenated values of two or more strings. Example: `concat("[", //contact, "]")` This would result in a string with the value of "[Toshia Palermo]"
Contains(*string*, *string*)	This returns true or false according to whether the first string contains the second. The string comparison is case sensitive. Example: `//item[contains(description,"XYZ")]` This returns all <item> elements where the <description> element contains a text node with a value of "XYZ" anywhere in the string.
normalize-space(*string*)	This returns a string that has been stripped of any leading or trailing whitespace, and where any adjacent spaces within the string are reduced to one single space character. Example: `normalize-space(" A   B      C      ")` The resulting string is "A B C".
starts-with(*string*, *string*)	This returns true if the first string starts with the second. The string comparison is case-sensitive. Example: `//@*[starts-with(., "ITM")]` The result of this statement is to return all attribute nodes in the XML document whose value begins with "ITM".

Table continued on following page

String Function	Description
`string( value )`	Converts the *value* argument to a string. If the value is a node-set, the function converts the value of the first node to a string. If the node-set is empty, an empty string is returned. If the value is Boolean, the string "true" is returned for true; "false" for false. Numeric values are returned with an appropriate string representation.
`string-length( string )`	Returns the length of the supplied string. Empty strings return zero. Example: `string-length("ABCDEFGHIJ")` The result is 10.
`substring( string, number, number? )`	Returns a substring of the string argument starting from the position provided by the second argument. The third argument (which is optional) specifies how many characters from the position to extract. If the third argument is omitted, the remainder of the string is returned. Example: `substring(//contact, 8, 3)` The result is "Pal". By omitting the argument like this: `substring(//contact, 8)` The result is "Palermo".
`substring-after( string, string )`	Returns the remainder of the first string argument after the first occurrence of the second string argument. Example: `substring-after(//contact, " ")` The result is "Palermo".
`substring-before( string, string )`	Returns the beginning of the first string argument up to the character prior to the occurrence of the second string argument. Example: `substring-before(//contact, " ")` The result is "Toshia".

String Function	Description
translate(*string*, *string*, *string*)	Returns a manipulated version of the first string argument.
	The second string argument contains a list of characters to be searched for in the first string argument, and the search is performed character by character. Upon finding these characters, the third string argument is used for substitution.
	For example if we wanted to find all spaces in a given string, and replace them with "-" hyphens, the syntax would look something like this:
	`translate("no spaces", " ", "-")`
	The result is "no-spaces".
	To eliminate characters, provide an empty string as the last argument. For example:
	`translate("*Mike!*", "*!", "")`
	The result is "Mike".

The string functions provided by XPath enable us to perform many of the tasks required in our development environment.

Using XPathNavigator

Many of the XPath features we have just looked at return values that we cannot retrieve using our XPath.aspx page. This is because the page calls either the SelectSingleNode or the SelectNodes method of the XmlNode object, which return either an XmlNode or XmlNodeList accordingly.

So now we'll modify our example to capture the result if it is a string, Boolean, or number.

A powerful ally for XPath support is the XPathNavigator object in the System.Xml.XPath namespace. XPathNavigator offers many benefits and features, and a full rendition is unfortunately beyond the scope of this book. However, we will demonstrate how to use this class for the capture of results not of a node-set type, XmlNode or XmlNodeList.

Typed Results of an XPath Expression

An XPath expression will return one of the following types: node-set, Boolean, number, or string. With XPathNavigator, we can evaluate each of these result types.

There are two methods of `XPathNavigator` used to retrieve the results of an XPath expression:

❑ `Select` – Used to return a node-set for evaluation (much like `SelectNodes` method of `XmlNode`)

❑ `Evaluate` – Returns the typed result of the XPath expression, which is either a node-set, Boolean, number, or string.

The following table displays the XPath result type, and the corresponding type in .NET which will house the result. The .NET types are what is potentially returned with the `XPathNavigator` when using the `Evaluate` method:

XPath Data-Type	.NET Data Type	Description
Node-Set	`XPathNodeIterator`	When the result is a node-set, the nodes are placed in the `XPathNodeIterator` object for processing.
Boolean	`System.Boolean`	When the result is Boolean, it is mapped to the `bool` data type.
Number	(Any integer or floating-point value types)	When the result is numeric, we can unbox the results into any of the .NET numeric data types.
String	`System.String`	When the result is a string, the value is mapped to the `string` data type.

Determining the Result Type with XPathExpression

When we created the `XPath.aspx` page, we knew our result types. If we wanted a single node returned, we invoked the `SelectSingleNode` method which returned an `XmlNode`. If we wanted a node-set, we invoked the `SelectNodes` method which returned an `XmlNodeList`. What if we don't know what we want? (An age-old problem among developers...) Specifically, what if the result cannot be determined until run-time – how can we determine the type of the result before executing the XPath expression?

The answer is that we use the `XPathNavigator` object to 'compile' our XPath expressions into `XPathExpression` objects – which allow us to capture what *type* it returns *before* we execute it.

Let me illustrate this. Suppose we have loaded an XML document into an `XmlDocument` object named `_SourceXml`. The following code retrieves an instance of an `XPathNavigator` object by calling the `CreateNavigator` method on `_SourceXml`, and then compiles an XPath expression to an `XPathExpression` object:

```
// Get an instance of the XPathNavigator
XPathNavigator _Navigator = _SourceXml.CreateNavigator();

// Compile an XPath expression, and store into an XPathExpression object
XPathExpression _XPathExpr = _Navigator.Compile("count(//*)");
```

At this point _XPathExpr is our 'compiled' XPath expression which contains the XPath syntax count(//*). We know from earlier in the chapter that the count() function returns a number, and we can determine this programmatically by examining the ReturnType property of the _XPathExpr object.

The ReturnType property is an enumerated type called XPathResultType. Here are the enumerated values as they map to the XPath result types:

XPathResultType Member	Description
NodeSet	The result type is a node-set. When the Evaluate method of the XPathNavigator object is called, the method will return an XPathNodeIterator object containing the matching nodes.
Boolean	The result type is either true or false.
Number	The result type is numeric.
String	The result type is a string.

There are other members of XPathResultType, but the ones listed above are sufficient for our purposes. For more information on this enumeration, refer to the Framework documentation.

We now have enough information to create another Web Form to harness the various result types of our XPath expressions.

Creating the XPath2.aspx Web Form

Using the same web project we opened earlier this chapter, we will copy XPath.aspx, make some minor modifications to the presentation, and add the support for multiple return types.

Open the web project containing the XPath.aspx Web Form. In the Solution Explorer, right-click the XPath.aspx file and click Copy from the pop-up menu. Now right-click the project name, XPath, and choose Paste from the pop-up menu. A new file will appear in the list named Copy of XPath.aspx. Right-click it and select Rename, entering XPath2.aspx.

Setting Controls in Design View

Right-click XPath2.aspx in Solution Explorer, and select View Designer from the pop-up menu. Remove SelectSingleNodeButton and SelectNodesButton, and replace with a new button named ExecuteXPathButton with its Text property set to Execute XPath.

Change the TitleLabel's Text property to XPath2 Test Page, and your design view should now resemble the following screen shot:

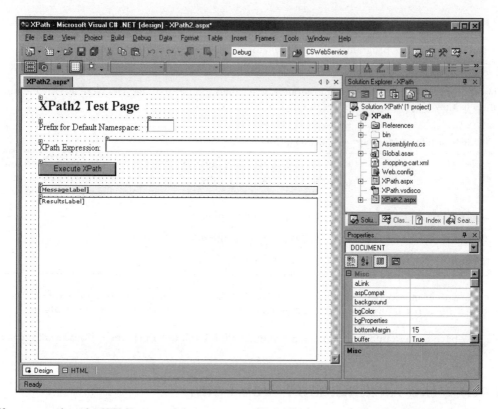

If we now select the HTML view of the page, we will see the Inherits attribute of the Page processing directive still refers to Wrox.ASPNET.Xml.XPath.XPath, but this will automatically change when we rename the class in the code-behind shortly.

Right-click anywhere on the HTML view, and select View Code from the context menu.

Modifying the Code-Behind

Feel free to scroll down and delete the event handlers for the two buttons we destroyed in the design view, although their presence won't hurt us. Then change the class name from XPath to XPath2, and add a using statement for System.Xml.XPath somewhere among the others at the top of the code file.

Next change the XML object declarations so that the _Nodes member is now declared as an XPathNodeIterator instead of an XmlNodeList:

```
private XmlDocument _SourceXml;
private XmlNamespaceManager _NamespaceManager;
private XmlNode _SingleNode;
private XPathNodeIterator _Nodes;
private XmlNode _ContextNode;
```

We don't need to make any changes to the Page_Load event handler, or the GetContextNode method.

Executing XPath Expressions using XPathNavigator

Our focus in this Web Form is to be able to evaluate any XPath expression, no matter what the result type is. As already mentioned, this is accomplished by the XPathNavigator and related objects.

Adding the Click Event Handler for ExecuteXPathButton

Switch to the Design View, and double-click the ExecuteXPathButton button. This will bring us back to the code view, at the first line of the event handler. Let's start writing some code!

Add the following lines:

```
try
{
    // Get the context node
    _ContextNode = GetContextNode();

    // Create the XPathNavigator from the context node
    XPathNavigator _Navigator = _ContextNode.CreateNavigator();

    // Compile the user's XPath expression
    XPathExpression _XPathExpr = _Navigator.Compile(XPathTextBox.Text);

    // Provide namespace support
    _XPathExpr.SetContext(_NamespaceManager);
```

At this point, we have established the context of our XPath expression and obtained a reference to the XPathNavigator object by calling the CreateNavigator method of the context XmlNode. We've also 'compiled' the user's XPath expression by the Compile method of our XPathNavigator object, resulting in an XPathExpression object. Finally we pass the _NamespaceManager object into the SetContext method of the XPathExpression object to provide namespace support.

Now we are ready to execute the XPath expression provided by the user. However, we don't know what sort of expression this is, and therefore we've no idea what the resulting data type will be. We need to check the value of the ReturnType property of our _XPathExpr object:

```
switch (_XPathExpr.ReturnType)
{
    case XPathResultType.NodeSet:
        _Nodes = (XPathNodeIterator)_Navigator.Evaluate(_XPathExpr);
        if (_Nodes.Count==0)
        {
            MessageLabel.Text="No matching nodes!";
        }
        else
        {
            MessageLabel.Text = "Nodes found: " + _Nodes.Count.ToString();
            string _NodeListResults = "";
            Cache["ContextNode"] =
                _ContextNode.SelectSingleNode(XPathTextBox.Text,
                    _NamespaceManager);
            while (_Nodes.MoveNext())
            {
```

```
         XPathNavigator _LocalNav = _Nodes.Current;
         string _NodeName = (_LocalNav.Name=="") ?
                            "(No Name)" :
                            _LocalNav.Name;
         _NodeListResults += "<b>"
                            + _NodeName + "</b>, Node-Type="
                            + _LocalNav.NodeType.ToString();

         // Does this node contain Text?
         XPathNodeIterator _TextSearch = _LocalNav.SelectChildren(
                                               XPathNodeType.Text);

         // If there is text, display the value
         if (_TextSearch.Count>0 )
         {
           _NodeListResults += ", Text=" + _LocalNav.Value;
         }
         _NodeListResults +=  "<br />";
       }
     ResultsLabel.Text = _NodeListResults;
   }
   break;
```

The first `case` of our `switch` is selected if the `XPathResultType` is a `NodeSet`. If so, we execute the XPath expression by calling the `Evaluate` method of `_Navigator`, which will return an object that we cast to an `XPathNodeIterator`. If there are no nodes in the result, we inform the user. Otherwise the rest of the code navigates each node of the result by calling the `MoveNext` method of `_Nodes`. We display the name of the node, and its type. If the node contains a child text node, we display that value as well.

The next block of code addresses the remaining `case` statements of our `switch`:

```
case XPathResultType.Boolean:
  MessageLabel.Text="XPath expression returns a boolean result";
  ResultsLabel.Text=_Navigator.Evaluate(_XPathExpr).ToString();
  break;

case XPathResultType.Number:
  MessageLabel.Text="XPath expression returns a numeric result";
  ResultsLabel.Text=
    ((double)_Navigator.Evaluate(_XPathExpr)).ToString();
  break;

case XPathResultType.String:
  MessageLabel.Text="XPath expression returns a string result";
  ResultsLabel.Text=_Navigator.Evaluate(_XPathExpr).ToString();
  break;

default:
  MessageLabel.Text="Expression returned an unknown result";
  ResultsLabel.Text="";
  break; // Don't forget the last break!
}
```

The above code continues to capture the possible result types of the compiled XPath expression. Finally, we end the method by completing the `try..catch` block:

```
    }
    catch (Exception handledException)
    {
      MessageLabel.Text=handledException.Message;
      ResultsLabel.Text="";
    }
```

Right-click `XPath2.aspx` in Solution Explorer, and choose **Set As Start Page**. Then save, build, and run the project by pressing *F5*.

Testing the XPath2.aspx Web Form

After the page loads, supply the `wrx` prefix for namespace support. Then type the following XPath expression in the textbox:

//wrx:item

The results should look similar to this:

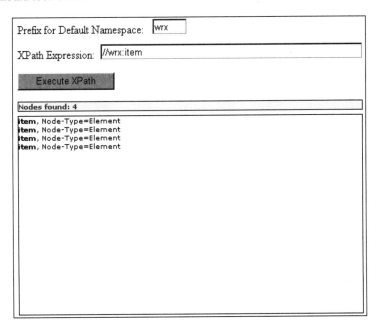

As we can see, the resulting node-set has been managed by our code. Now let's try a statement which will only return one node in the node-set:

/wrx:shopping-cart

This time just one node is found, the `shopping-cart` element, as identified in `ResultsLabel`.

Now let's try some XPath functions that do not return node-sets. For instance, let's find out how many attributes exist in the document with this XPath expression:

count(//@*)

This returns a numeric result, as seen below:

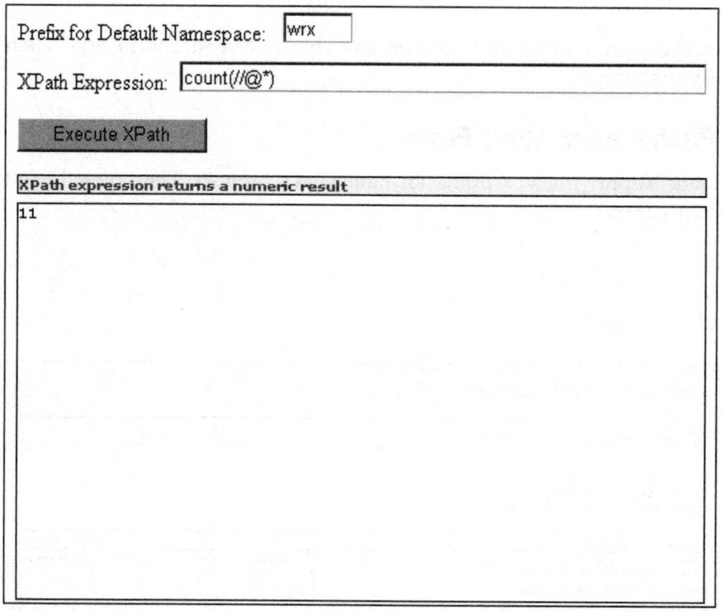

```
Prefix for Default Namespace:  wrx

XPath Expression:  count(//@*)

         Execute XPath

XPath expression returns a numeric result
11
```

Continue experimenting with other XPath functions, such as those given as examples earlier. Each expression is handled appropriately, according to its result type. Our Web Form is now ready to respond to any XPath expression we provide!

Summary

Without a doubt XPath is an invaluable language for locating and manipulating nodes within an XML document. What we've learned in this chapter is just a starting point – and one that we can apply to a wide variety of XML technologies, including .NET My Services, SOAP, XForms, and BizTalk.

Even within ASP.NET, the possibilities are amazing. We can access XML as a data source and filter out presentation data based on values we pass in our XPath expressions.

Another way to filter presentation data is by using XPath expressions in template rules in XSLT, and that is the focus of the next chapter.

5

Transformations

For the development community, one of the most useful features when working with XML is the ability to transform XML content to another format more appropriate for a given situation. To harness this power in ASP.NET, we first of all need to understand when and why we should use transformations in a web application. Once we've made that decision, we must understand the syntax necessary to create our transformation and how to execute the transformation in the managed environment of .NET.

By the end of this chapter, we will have covered the following subjects:

- ❑ What is XSLT?
- ❑ Structure of an XSLT document
- ❑ Applying XSLT Style Sheets to XML documents
- ❑ Controlling document output
- ❑ Using transformations for the presentation layer
- ❑ Using transformations for B2B

We will learn how to harness the XPath skills acquired from the previous chapter, and examine how to use transformations effectively in ASP.NET.

What is XSLT?

Extensible Stylesheet Language Transformations (XSLT) is a declarative programming language, with its origins in the early Extensible Stylesheet Language (XSL). XSLT v1.0 was endorsed by the Director of W3C as a Recommendation in November 1999, and more information can be found at http://www.w3.org/TR/xslt. We will be using version 1.0 in this chapter, as supported by the .NET Framework, although there are other versions in working draft at the time of writing.

Transforming XML Documents

XSLT is the language which instructs an XSLT processor how to convert information in an XML source document to a format of our preference – be it an XML document (including WML for example), an HTML document, or just plain text. Note that different XSLT engines will adhere to the standard to differing levels, but in this chapter, we will naturally concentrate on the behavior of .NET.

From XML to XML

There are many situations where there is a need to transform an XML document to one in a completely different XML dialect. For example, consider the following document extract:

```
<Item>
   <ID>ITM-1001</ID>
   <LineOfProduct>1</LineOfProduct>
   <ListPrice>123.45</ListPrice>
   <QTY>1</QTY>
   <Description>Gadget XYZ</Description>
</Item>
```

We may prefer to have this information in a different form, perhaps for a component we have already developed which handles data in this form:

```
<item id="ITM-1001" productLine="1">
   <quantity>1</quantity>
   <list-price>123.45</list-price>
   <description>Gadget XYZ</description>
</item>
```

Notice how the first extract is element-centric; it is devoid of any attributes. Also the first uses a different nomenclature for node names, like <QTY> vs. <quantity>, and we can't forget that XML documents are case-sensitive – thus <Description> is different from <description>.

So how can we transform one to the other? We could load the first XML document into an XmlDocument object, traverse each node and programmatically generate a second XmlDocument object. This would work, but what if we needed to make changes to the transformation? It could be quite a challenge to locate and change the code to create the new transformation. Also, the programmatic route requires recompiling the code after any such changes.

The preferred method would be to use XSLT style sheets. After all, the language is designed specifically for this purpose. Secondly, it is fairly easy to locate the template rules that perform certain aspects of a transformation (discussed later) and add, update, or delete parts to create new transformations. Finally, it is not necessary to recompile and redeploy the code which references an XSLT style sheet that has been changed.

From XML to HTML

In ASP.NET applications, it is quite common to encounter a need to present data provided as XML to the user in HTML. A typical example of this would be a symmetrical XML document that quite easily lends itself to a table format. For instance, we may be interested in taking the following XML structure:

```
<items>
  <item id="ITM-1001" productLine="1">
    <quantity>1</quantity>
     <list-price>123.45</list-price>
     <description>Gadget XYZ</description>
  </item>
  <item id="ITM-1002" productLine="1">
    <quantity>3</quantity>
     <list-price>4.00</list-price>
     <description>XYZ Accessory</description>
  </item>
  <item id="ITM-1003" productLine="2">
    <quantity>1</quantity>
     <list-price>15.00</list-price>
     <description>Gizmo Part</description>
  </item>
  <item id="ITM-1004" productLine="3">
    <quantity>1</quantity>
     <list-price>44.00</list-price>
     <description>Widget X</description>
  </item>
</items>
```

and presenting it to the user like this:

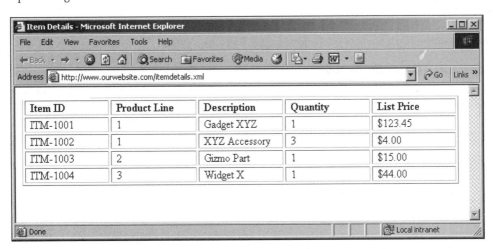

The markup to create the table above would be enclosed within an HTML `<table>` tag. By using XSLT, we can take any XML structure and convert it to HTML. We will see how to do this a little later.

From XML to Plain Text

From time to time, we may need to generate plain text. Typically, this is done to support legacy applications that consume text documents with either fixed length or comma delimited columns. Thus the `<items>` element and all of its children from the previous XML file could be transformed to a comma delimited text file like this:

```
ITM-1001,  1,  1,  123.45,  Gadget ZYZ
ITM-1002,  1,  3,  4.00,    XYZ Accessory
ITM-1003,  2,  1,  15.00,   Gizmo Part
ITM-1004,  3,  1,  44.00,   Widget X
```

Structure of an XSLT Style Sheet

Now that we have a glimpse of what XSLT style sheets can do, the next step is to examine the actual structure of a style sheet. Of course the subject of XSLT style sheets is enough to fill an entire book, so our objective in this chapter will be to provide what you need to know in order to use its features in ASP.NET applications.

XSLT is a Declarative, Rule-Based Language

Unlike procedural languages, which are executed in sequential order, XSLT is a declarative, rule-based language where the XSLT processor determines the execution sequence. Simply stated, we describe the rules (which can appear in any order), and the processor parses these rules and applies them to produce a corresponding output document.

XSLT is XML

An XSLT style sheet is an XML document. All the rules that specify the behavior of a style sheet are contained within XML elements belonging to the XSLT namespace.

The `<stylesheet>` Document Element

The document or root element of the style sheet is `<stylesheet>`. Like the XML declaration node, it contains a `version` attribute, which we will set to "1.0". Typically, the prefix `xsl` is used to reference the XSLT namespace http://www.w3.org/1999/XSL/Transform. Therefore, the declaration usually looks like this:

```
<?xml version="1.0" encoding="UTF-8"?>
<xsl:stylesheet version="1.0"
    xmlns:xsl="http://www.w3.org/1999/XSL/Transform" >

</xsl:stylesheet>
```

However, in keeping with standard XML rules, the `xsl` prefix is merely the suggested prefix for the required namespace declaration. In fact, when we create an XSLT file in Visual Studio .NET, it declares the XSLT namespace as the default.

Creating a Style Sheet in VS.NET

Open Visual Studio .NET and select File | New | File, or just press *Ctrl-N*. The following dialog box appears:

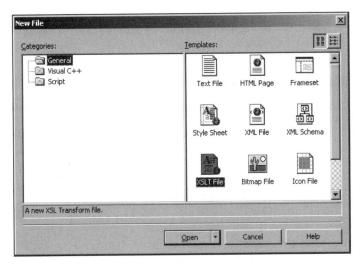

With the General folder in the Categories pane selected, select the XSLT File icon in the Templates pane. Click the Open button, and it will create an empty solution with a style sheet containing just the opening declaration as shown:

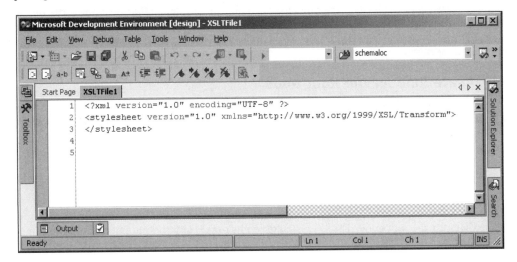

As mentioned earlier, Visual Studio .NET declares http://www.w3.org/1999/XSL/Tranform as the default namespace. Although this is the default behavior for Visual Studio .NET and won't normally cause any problems, we will use the xsl prefix in our examples this chapter. Alter the code like so:

```
<?xml version="1.0" encoding="UTF-8"?>
<xsl:stylesheet version="1.0"
                 xmlns:xsl="http://www.w3.org/1999/XSL/Transform" >
</xsl:stylesheet>
```

Now save the file by selecting File | Save XSLTFile1.xslt as... and a file dialog box will appear. When prompted, enter the name transform-one.xslt. We will add content to this style sheet shortly.

Specifying the Output Type

As stated earlier, the output of a transformation can either be XML, HTML, plain text, or qualified names (the exotic sounding qname-but-not-ncname type). By default, the output is HTML. We can specify other output types by declaring an <output> element as a child of the <stylesheet> element with the appropriate method attribute set. For example, this is how we specify XML as the output type:

```
<xsl:output method="xml" />
```

Note that as a child of the <stylesheet> document element, this element is designated as a **top-level** element of the style sheet. Top level elements are immediate children of <stylesheet>.

Other attributes of this element control behavior such as whether to omit the XML declaration in the resulting document, or which version and encoding should be specified.

Defining Template Rules

Template rules are elements that describe how the XSLT processor should transform nodes that meet certain criteria in an XML document. We declare template rules by creating a top-level element named <template>, and specifying which node(s) it contains rules for using an appropriate XPath expression in its match attribute.

The Template Rule for the Root Node

It is good practice to always declare a template rule for the root node of the source document in your XSLT style sheets, and some XSLT processors will actually fail if it is not present. Below is the syntax for a template rule matching the root node:

```
<xsl:template match="/">
  <!-- Template rules go here -->
</xsl:template>
```

Notice the XPath expression provided in the match attribute, which, as we learned in the previous chapter, identify the root node. The "/" character on its own is also the starting point for absolute location paths. Refer back to Chapter 4 if you need more information on XPath expressions and location paths.

Don't forget that <template> is a top-level element, which means it must always be an immediate child of <stylesheet>. We can define as many <template> elements as we need in a style sheet. What sets one template rule apart from another is the XPath expression in the match attribute, although we could have two templates with the same XPath expression, but differentiated by the mode attribute (covered in the *Enhancing Template Rules* section).

Specifying Template Rules for Other Nodes

The XPath expression in the `match` attribute of the `<template>` element identifies nodes in the source document that we wish to transform by applying that template. Let's illustrate this with the following XML document, which we've already seen in the previous chapter:

```
<?xml version="1.0" encoding="UTF-8" ?>
<?custom-error code="0" message="OK" ?>
<!--Shopping Cart Example-->
<shopping-cart>
  <header>
    <customer id="P4LLC" billingId="001" shippingId="001" >
      <contact>Toshia Palermo</contact>
    </customer>
    <order-type>Regular</order-type>
  </header>
  <items>
    <item id="ITM-1001" productLine="1">
      <quantity>1</quantity>
      <list-price>123.45</list-price>
      <description>Gadget XYZ</description>
    </item>
    <item id="ITM-1002" productLine="1">
      <quantity>3</quantity>
      <list-price>4.00</list-price>
      <description>XYZ Accessory</description>
    </item>
    <item id="ITM-1003" productLine="2">
      <quantity>1</quantity>
      <list-price>15.00</list-price>
      <description>Gizmo Part</description>
    </item>
    <item id="ITM-1004" productLine="3">
      <quantity>1</quantity>
      <list-price>44.00</list-price>
      <description>Widget X</description>
    </item>
  </items>
</shopping-cart>
```

This file, `shopping-cart.xml`, will be used in our examples throughout the chapter. The one difference with the file used in Chapter 4 is the absence of the namespace on the `<shopping-cart>` element, which has been removed for simplicity. The table below shows some example XPath expressions and their effect on the `shopping-cart.xml` document:

XPath Expression in **match** Attribute of **\<template>** Element	Description
`match="/shopping-cart"`	This will match the `<shopping-cart>` element – the document element of the source XML. Remember that there can only ever be one document element in well-formed XML.

Table continued on following page

XPath Expression in `match` Attribute of `<template>` Element	Description
`match="//item"`	This matches any `<item>` elements in the source XML.
`match="/*/items//@*"`	This matches any attribute nodes that are descendants of the `<items>` element, which is itself a grandchild of the root node.
`match="quantity"`	This relative expression matches any `<quantity>` children of the context node.

Once the nodes are identified, the rules inside the `<template>` element describe the transformation to perform.

Accessing Values with *<value-of>*

Within the template, we can access each node matching the XPath expression as the context node. To obtain values from the source XML, we use the `<value-of>` element. It has an obligatory `select` attribute containing another XPath expression denoting the node whose value we want. The following example demonstrates this:

```
<xsl:template match="item">
  <div>
    Item=<xsl:value-of select="@id" />,
    Quantity=<xsl:value-of select="quantity" />
  </div>
</xsl:template>
```

The template rule in the above example matches `<item>` element children of the context node. Any such `<item>` element becomes in turn the context node for XPath expressions within the template. The first `<xsl:value-of>` element has a `select` attribute with an XPath expression locating the `id` attribute of the `<item>` element. The `select` attribute of the second `<xsl:value-of>` element provides a relative location path (with abbreviated syntax) to retrieve the value of the `<quantity>` child. These values are placed within an enclosing HTML `<div>`.

Earlier we indicated that the order in which template rules are defined is irrelevant, so how did the processor get to this template rule? The starting point is the template rule that matches the root node. From there, we can explicitly apply other templates to the elements we want to transform.

Applying Templates with <apply-templates>

The `<apply-templates>` element is used to transform nodes from within other templates. To apply transformations using the template in the previous example, we could use this element within the template for the root node, like so:

```
<xsl:template match="/">
  <html>
    <head>
      <title>Transformation Example</title>
    </head>
    <body>
```

```
        <xsl:apply-templates select="//item" />
      </body>
    </html>
</xsl:template>
```

Here, we wrap the 'call' to the other template rule inside HTML markup, with the <apply-templates> element in the <body> tag. Our select attribute indicates that all of the <item> elements in the source XML document should be processed by any matching templates at this point. If we omit the select attribute, the parser would apply templates for all children of the context node.

The result of this call is similar to that produced by the SelectNodes method of the XmlNode object (or any of its descendants, such as XmlDocument). The XSLT processor builds a node-set in memory, and looks for a template rule that satisfies a match for each node. In our example, a node-list of four elements is generated, appearing in the set in the order in which they appear in the source document. The XSLT processor then processes each node one at a time by searching the style sheet for a matching template, such as this one:

```
<xsl:template match="item">
  <div>
    Item=<xsl:value-of select="@id" />,
    Quantity=<xsl:value-of select="quantity" />
  </div>
</xsl:template>
```

For the first <item> element in the document, this would produce the following output:

Item=ITM-1001, Quantity=1

The processor then moves on to the next node in the node-set, which in this case is also processed by the same template rule, and so on for each node in the node-set. The final output is this:

Item=ITM-1001, Quantity=1
Item=ITM-1002, Quantity=3
Item=ITM-1003, Quantity=1
Item=ITM-1004, Quantity=1

If we put all this together in the transform-one.xslt sheet, here is what it looks like in its entirety:

```
<?xml version="1.0" encoding="UTF-8" ?>
<xsl:stylesheet version="1.0"
            xmlns:xsl="http://www.w3.org/1999/XSL/Transform" >

  <xsl:template match="/">
    <html>
      <head>
        <title>Transformation Example</title>
      </head>
      <body>
        <xsl:apply-templates select="//item" />
      </body>
    </html>
  </xsl:template>
```

```
    <xsl:template match="item">
      <div>
      Name=<xsl:value-of select="@id" />,
      Quantity=<xsl:value-of select="quantity" />
      </div>
    </xsl:template>

  </xsl:stylesheet>
```

It is also worthy of note that we have ignored all the other nodes in the source XML document. We only need to define template rules for those nodes we need to process.

Applying an XSLT Style Sheet to an XML Document

Essentially, there are two ways to apply an XSLT style sheet to an XML document. We can either reference the style sheet in our XML document, or apply the style sheet programmatically. The first approach is considered static, while the latter is more dynamic.

Applying a Style Sheet Statically

To statically link an XSLT style sheet to an XML document, we add the `<?xml-stylesheet?>` processing directive to the start of the source XML. For instance, if the `transform-one.xslt` and the `shopping-cart.xml` files are in the same directory, we could add the following to the top of `shopping-cart.xml`:

```
<?xml version="1.0" encoding="UTF-8" ?>
<?xml-stylesheet type="text/xsl" href="transform-one.xslt" ?>
<?custom-error code="0" message="OK" ?>
<!--Shopping Cart Example-->
<shopping-cart>
  .
  .
  .
</shopping-cart>
```

The `type` attribute specifies that it is an XSLT style sheet we want to apply, as we could also specify a cascading style sheet by setting this attribute to `"text/css"`. The `href` attribute supplies the location of the style sheet. If we open the XML document in a web browser, this is what we will see:

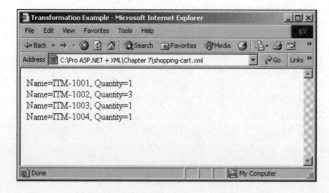

If we view the source for this page, we will see the source XML, not the XSLT output that produces the above display. In order to view the XSLT output in Internet Explorer, we can download a free plug-in from Microsoft's site at http://msdn.microsoft.com/msdn-files/027/000/543/iexmltls.exe.

Applying a Style Sheet Dynamically

To demonstrate how to apply a style sheet programmatically, let's create a new web application in Visual Studio .NET. Select File | New | Project to pull up the New Project dialog box. Create a new Visual C# ASP.NET web application project, and name it Transforms:

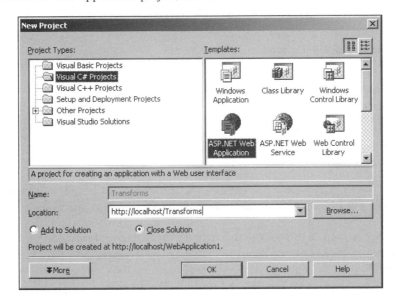

This will create the application and display the WebForm1.aspx page. Rename the WebForm1.aspx file in Solution Explorer to TransformXML.aspx.

Copy the shopping-cart.xml and transform-one.xslt files into the Transforms directory.

Now view the code-behind for the page, and change it as highlighted below:

```
using System;
using System.Collections;
using System.ComponentModel;
using System.Data;
using System.Drawing;
using System.Web;
using System.Web.SessionState;
using System.Web.UI;
using System.Web.UI.WebControls;
using System.Web.UI.HtmlControls;
using System.Xml.XPath;
using System.Xml.Xsl;
```

```
namespace Wrox.ASPNET.Transforms
{
  /// <summary>
  /// Summary description for TransformXML
  /// </summary>
  public class TransformXML : System.Web.UI.Page
  {
    private void Page_Load(object sender, System.EventArgs e)
    {
      // Put user code to initialize the page here
    }

    [ Web Form Designer generated code ]
  }
}
```

All we're doing is including the System.Xml.XPath and System.Xml.Xsl namespaces, and changing the namespace and class name.

Switch back to the TransformXML.aspx window, and view the HTML code noting how the Page processing directive has changed to reflect our changes:

```
<%@ Page language="c#" Codebehind="TransformXML.aspx.cs"
    AutoEventWireup="false" Inherits="Wrox.ASPNET.Transforms.TransformXML"%>
```

Remove *all* other markup on this page so that only the above line appears there.

Using XslTransform

Now find the Page_Load event handler, and add the following code:

```
private void Page_Load(object sender, System.EventArgs e)
{
  try
  {
    // Instantiate and Load the XPathDocument
    XPathDocument _SourceXml =
      new XPathDocument( Server.MapPath("shopping-cart.xml") );

    // Instantiate and load the XslTransform object
    XslTransform _Transform = new XslTransform();
    _Transform.Load( Server.MapPath("transform-one.xslt")) ;

    // Send result of transformation to Response.Output stream
    _Transform.Transform( _SourceXml, null, Response.Output );
  }
  catch (Exception handledException)
  {
    Response.Write(handledException.Message);
  }
}
```

First, we load the source XML into an `XpathDocument` object. This object is similar to `XmlDocument`, but is highly optimized for XSLT processing. Next, we load the `transform-one.xslt` style sheet into an `XslTransform` object. `XslTransform` implements the .NET XSLT processing engine, which is invoked when we call its `Transform` method. In the example above, we're using the overloaded `Transform` method which takes the source XML, any parameters for the style sheet (none are required, so we provide `null`), and finally where to place the results of the transformation. Our results are directed to the HTTP response stream.

Hit *F5* to compile and run the project. On the surface, the output is the same as if we applied the sheet statically. However, this time if we view the source, we see the XSLT processor output, not the source XML, because the transformation occurred on the server, not client-side in the browser. By applying the style sheet on the server, we can ensure it will be viewed correctly by a far greater range of browsers, as many do not support XSLT transformations natively.

Enhancing Template Rules

There are several situations that require special handling. In such cases, we can provide more context for our template match by providing a **mode**, or we can explicitly call a template by name, rather than by node match.

Before we investigate these topics, let's first make some changes to our `Transforms` web application. In the `TransformXML.aspx.cs` code file, make the following revisions to the `Page_Load` event handler:

```
// Put user code to initialize the page here
try
{
   string _XMLPath = Request.QueryString["xml"].ToString();
   string _XSLTPath = Request.QueryString["xslt"].ToString();

   // Instantiate and Load the XPathDocument
   XPathDocument _SourceXml = new XPathDocument( Server.MapPath(_XMLPath) );

   // Instantiate and load the XslTransorm object
   XslTransform _Transform = new XslTransform();
   _Transform.Load( Server.MapPath(_XSLTPath)) ;

   // Send result of transformation to Response.Output stream
   _Transform.Transform( _SourceXml, null, Response.Output );
}
catch (Exception handledException)
{
   Response.Write(handledException.Message);
}
```

These changes allow us to reuse the `TransformXML.aspx` page with any source document and style sheet using filenames supplied in the query string. For example, the following URL is equivalent to the previous example:

http://localhost/transforms/transformxml.aspx?xml=shopping-cart.xml&xslt=transform-one.xslt

Template Modes

Template modes are a great way to handle nodes based on a specific purpose. What if we want to perform two or more separate transformations on the same node-set? We can tailor the transformation by specifying a **mode**, in one of:

❑ the *calling* `<apply-templates>` element

❑ the *receiving* `<template>` element, containing the rules

Using our `shopping-cart.xml` file example, what if we wanted to first highlight all the quantities for each item, and also provide a separate list for each product line? Let us examine one way to accomplish this using template modes. First, create a copy of `transform-one.xslt` and name it `transform-two.xslt`.

In the template match for the root node in this new file, we will apply another template for the `<item>` nodes, placing HTML heading tags before the call to each template rule:

```
<xsl:template match="/">
  <html>
    <head>
      <title>Transformation Example</title>
    </head>
    <body>
      <h1>Item Quantities</h1>
      <xsl:apply-templates select="//item" mode="QTY" />
      <h1>Item Product Lines</h1>
      <xsl:apply-templates select="//item" mode="PL" />
    </body>
  </html>
</xsl:template>
```

The first `<apply-templates>` element for `<item>` nodes now contains an attribute named `mode` with a value of `QTY`. The second `<apply-templates>` element contains an identical XPath expression, `"//item"`, but with a `mode` attribute value of `PL`.

Now let's see the template elements that will match each of these:

```
<xsl:template match="item" mode="PL">
  <div>
  Item=<xsl:value-of select="@id" />,
  Product Line=<xsl:value-of select="@productLine" />
  </div>
</xsl:template>
```

```
<xsl:template match="item" mode="QTY">
  <div>
  Item=<xsl:value-of select="@id" />,
  Quantity=<xsl:value-of select="quantity" />
  </div>
</xsl:template>
```

Notice that we're declaring the templates in the opposite order to which they are called. We can do this because of the declarative nature of the language. Each template element has a mode attribute which corresponds to the calling <apply-templates> element. This mechanism allows us to differentiate matches on the same node, and trigger different template rules as we wish.

Now type the following URL into your browser:

http://localhost/transforms/transformxml.aspx?xml=shopping-cart.xml&xslt=transform-two.xslt

The value for xslt in the query string is now transform-two.xslt. This example also demonstrates the reusability of the TransformXML.aspx page, which we haven't had to recompile. The results appear as follows:

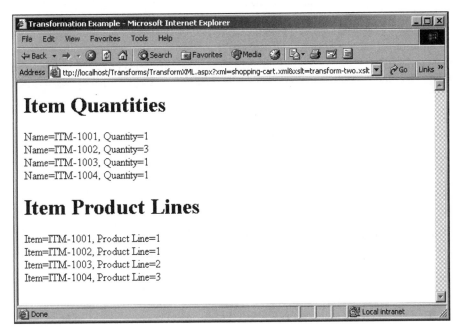

Named Templates

We also have the ability to apply a template by *name*, rather than by node match. When using this technique, the context node of the calling template becomes the context node of the named template. This allows us to call a specific template from any template in the style sheet. So, as the mirror image of the previous example, we will now apply one transformation to two separate node types.

Add the following named template to transform-two.xslt:

```
<xsl:template name="BoldRed">
  <span style="color:#FF0000;font-weight:Bold">
    <xsl:value-of select="." />
  </span>
</xsl:template>
```

Note the `name` attribute in place of the `match` attribute. As its name suggests, this template wraps the text value of the context node in a `<span>` HTML element with a `style` attribute set to make the content bold and red.

Now let's add two more templates, matching the `productLine` attribute and `quantity` element respectively:

```
<xsl:template match="@productLine">
  <xsl:call-template name="BoldRed" />
</xsl:template>

<xsl:template match="quantity">
  <xsl:call-template name="BoldRed" />
</xsl:template>
```

Both these templates call the same `"BoldRed"` template with the `<call-template>` syntax. Should we now make any changes to the `"BoldRed"` named template, they will apply to all calling templates. The final change is to apply the above two templates from the other templates, like so:

```
<xsl:template match="item" mode="PL">
  <div>
    Item=<xsl:value-of select="@id" />,
    Product Line=<xsl:apply-templates select="@productLine" />
  </div>
</xsl:template>

<xsl:template match="item" mode="QTY">
  <div>
    Item=<xsl:value-of select="@id" />,
    Quantity=<xsl:apply-templates select="quantity" />
  </div>
</xsl:template>
```

When the page is executed with these changes, the result is as follows:

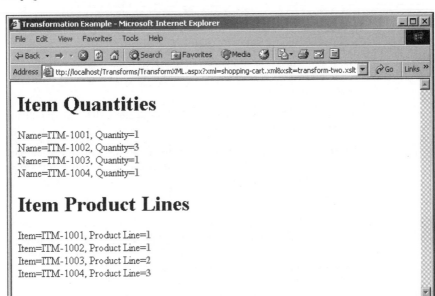

Here, the values for the `<quantity>` elements and `productLine` attributes are red and bold (trust me on this!). We can now do this for any other element, by simply calling the named template to handle the element in question.

Controlling Document Output

Now that we have a basic understanding of the purpose of template rules in a style sheet, we'll move on to investigate how to control the document output. We'll see how to sort the results of the transformation, and apply conditional logic to filter the result.

Sorting Node-Sets with `<sort>`

A common scenario when dealing with data is to provide it in a sorted order. XSLT provides the means for sorting node-sets in our style sheets with the `<sort>` element.

The `<sort>` element supports several attributes, as described in this table:

Attribute of `<sort>`	Description
select	An XPath expression using a relative location path to provide the value on which the sort is based. The default value is `"."`, which uses the context node.
lang	The language the sort is based on. If not specified, this is derived from the system environment.
data-type	Typically `"text"` or `"number"`.Sorts on `"text"` are sorted alphabetically. Sorts on `"number"` convert the node to a numeric value and then sort the node-set numerically.
order	Either `"ascending"` or `"descending"`. The default is `"ascending"`, meaning lower values appear first.
case-order	Possible values are `"upper-first"` or `"lower-first"`. This allows us to determine which comes first when a word or character begins with a different case. The default value is `"upper-first"`.

The `<sort>` element can be used in one of two ways:

❑ As a child of `<apply-templates>`

❑ As a child of `<for-each>`

We will start by exploring how to sort using `<apply-templates>`.

Using `<sort>` with `<apply-templates>`

Remember, when we call `<apply-templates>`, the node-set resulting from the XPath expression in the `select` attribute is ordered as the nodes were found in the source document. If we want to override that behavior, we can place a `<sort>` element as a child of `<apply-templates>`.

Open the `transform-two.xslt` style sheet, and locate the template match for the root node. Add two `<sort>` elements as shown:

```
<xsl:template match="/">
  <html>
    <head>
      <title>Transformation Example</title>
    </head>
    <body>
      <h1>Item Quantities</h1>
      <xsl:apply-templates select="//item" mode="QTY">
        <xsl:sort
          select="quantity"
```

```
                  data-type="number"
                  order="descending"
               />
          </xsl:apply-templates>
          <h1>Item Product Lines</h1>
          <xsl:apply-templates select="//item" mode="PL">
            <xsl:sort
               select="@id"
               data-type="text"
               order="descending"
            />
          </xsl:apply-templates>
      </body>
   </html>
</xsl:template>
```

Notice how we've changed both `<apply-templates>` elements so that they are no longer empty. Each now has a `<sort>` child element, with attributes specifying how to perform the sort. In our example, the results appear as follows:

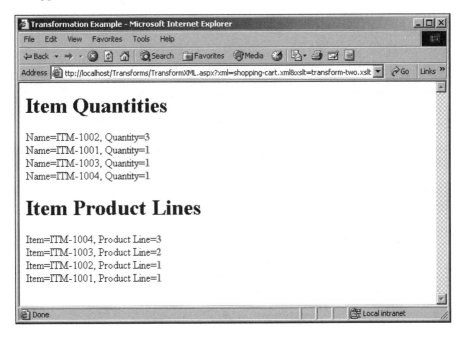

Under the Item Quantities heading, the nodes are now listed in descending order based on the value in the `<quantity>` element, whereas the nodes listed under the Item Product Lines header are listed in descending order according to the value of the id attribute on the `<item>` element.

Performing Repetition with <for-each>

When dealing with symmetrical data, we may elect to iterate through each node in a node-set. In XSLT, this is accomplished using the <for-each> element. As the name implies, it applies the same processing logic to each node in a node-set.

Creating an HTML Table

Still using the shopping-cart.xml file as our data source, let's create a new XSLT style sheet for it, named transform-three.xslt in the same directory as our Transforms project.

This all-new style sheet starts off like this:

```
<xsl:template match="/">
  <html>
    <head>
      <title>Transformation Example</title>
    </head>
    <body>
      <h2>Shopping Cart Items</h2>
      <table style="border: thick solid;">
        <tr style="background-color:#000000;color:#FFFFFF">
          <th>Line Number</th>
          <th>Item Number</th>
          <th>Description</th>
          <th align="right">Quantity</th>
          <th align="right">List Price</th>
        </tr>
```

So far, we've got some literal HTML markup in the template match for the root node to format our result. We have an opening <table> tag, followed by the column headings.

In our transformation, we want a <tr> row for each item in the document, which we will create with the <for-each> element:

```
<xsl:for-each select="//item">
  <tr>
    <td><xsl:value-of select="position()" /></td>
    <td><xsl:value-of select="@id" /></td>
    <td><xsl:value-of select="description" /></td>
    <td align="right"><xsl:value-of select="quantity" /></td>
    <td align="right"><xsl:value-of select="list-price" /></td>
  </tr>
</xsl:for-each>
```

When the XSLT processor reaches the <xsl:for-each> element above, it establishes a node-set of <item> elements in the same order as in the source XML. Inside the <xsl:for-each> element, each <item> element becomes the context node for any XPath expressions. The first <td> tag of the row represents the line number, which is generated by calling the position() XPath function to give the position of the context node in the node-set.

Finally, we close the `<table>` and other HTML tags:

```
        </table>
      </body>
    </html>
  </xsl:template>

</xsl:stylesheet>
```

We have only one template match in our style sheet. However, with the use of `<for-each>`, we were able to process each `<item>` node in the document.

Type the following URL in the browser to see the results:

http://localhost/transforms/transformxml.aspx?xml=shopping-cart.xml&xslt=transform-three.xslt

The resulting screen will be something like this:

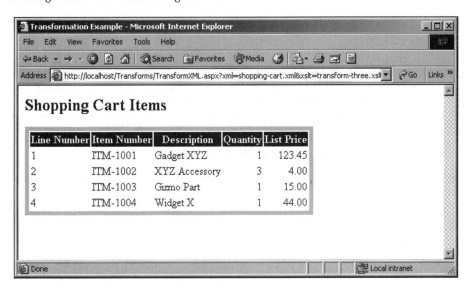

Using <sort> with <for-each>

As we mentioned earlier, we can use the XSLT `<sort>` element within a `<for-each>` element to sort the document output.

In our example, we might want the items sorted in descending order by list price. We can do this simply by adding the following element as an immediate child of our `<for-each>`:

```
<xsl:for-each select="//item">
  <xsl:sort select="list-price"
    data-type="number"
    order="descending"
  />
```

Calling the previous URL now displays this screen:

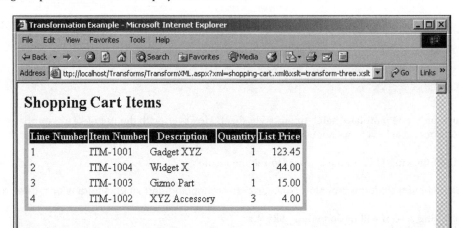

Notice that there was no change to the line number values as produced by the XPath `position()` function. This is because the sort is executed on the node-set first. Keep in mind therefore that using the `position()` function after sorting the node-set will not return the position of the node as it originally appears in the source XML document.

Using Conditional Logic in XSLT

XSLT is a programming language, and as such it has elements that provide the functionality of the `if` statement. These elements control document output according to Boolean tests, and they are:

❑ `<if>`

❑ `<choose>..<when>..<otherwise>`

The `<if>` and `<when>` elements have a `test` attribute, where we provide a Boolean expression. Since we can provide XPath expressions for this attribute, the following table shows how the results are converted to either `true` or `false`:

Expression Data-Type	Boolean Result
Boolean	The result is `true` or `false` based on the Boolean expression. For example: `5 > 8` The result of this Boolean expression is `false`.
String	If the string is empty, the result is `false`, otherwise `true`.

Expression Data-Type	Boolean Result
Numeric	If the number is zero, the result is `false`, otherwise `true`. For example: -321 This is interpreted as `true`.
Node-Set	If the node-set is empty, the result is `false`, otherwise `true`.

The expression in the `test` attribute behaves identically to the argument for the XPath `boolean()` function.

Controlling Output using <if>

Let's add a few lines to our `transform-three.xslt` style sheet to demonstrate how these elements let us easily control document output. We will add a new column to the HTML `<table>`, which will contain special information if the product line is 2:

```
<table style="border: thick solid;">
  <tr style="background-color:#000000;color:#FFFFFF">
    <th>Line Number</th>
    <th>Item Number</th>
    <th>Description</th>
    <th align="right">Quantity</th>
    <th align="right">List Price</th>
    <th>Notes</th>
  </tr>
  <xsl:for-each select="//item">
    <xsl:sort  select="list-price"
      data-type="number"
      order="descending"
    />
    <tr>
      <td><xsl:value-of select="position()" /></td>
      <td><xsl:value-of select="@id" /></td>
      <td><xsl:value-of select="description" /></td>
      <td align="right"><xsl:value-of select="quantity" /></td>
      <td align="right"><xsl:value-of select="list-price" /></td>

      <td>
        <xsl:if test="@productLine='2'" >
          Call for details!
        </xsl:if>
      </td>

    </tr>
  </xsl:for-each>

</table>
```

The test condition in the XSLT <if> element checks to see if the current item's product line is equal to the number 2. If the result is true, the message Call for details! will be output on that row. Here is how the resulting screen looks:

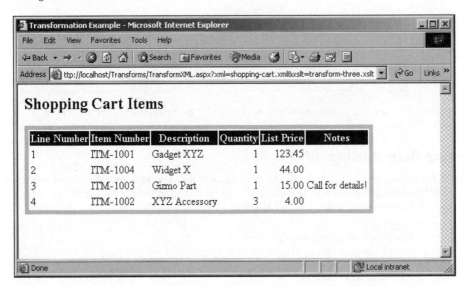

Controlling Output using <choose>..<when>..<otherwise>

Much like other languages, XSLT allows us to check for multiple conditions in one logical block. This is similar to switch..case in C# and Select..Case in VB.NET. The syntax is as follows:

```
<choose>
  <when test="Boolean expression">
    [Output 1]
  </when>
  <when test="Boolean expression">
    [Output 2]
  </when>
  <otherwise>
    [Output 3]
  </otherwise>
</choose>
```

The XSLT processor checks each <when> child of the <choose> element for an expression that returns true. If the processor finds a true result, the output is rendered and the <choose> is escaped. If no <when> test returns true, then the processor uses the output given in the <otherwise> element, if present. Thus a <choose> with only one <when> and an <otherwise> is similar to using an if..else statement.

Let's add a <choose> to our transform-three.xslt file. Our aim is to create a different background for alternating items in the table:

```
<table style="border: thick solid;">
  <tr style="background-color:#000000;color:#FFFFFF">
    <th>Line Number</th>
    <th>Item Number</th>
    <th>Description</th>
    <th>Quantity</th>
    <th>List Price</th>
    <th>Notes</th>
  </tr>
  <xsl:for-each select="//item">
    <xsl:sort  select="list-price"
      data-type="number"
      order="descending"
    />
    <xsl:element name="tr">
      <xsl:attribute name="style">
        <xsl:choose>
          <xsl:when test="position() mod 2">
            background-color:#DDDDFF;
          </xsl:when>
          <xsl:otherwise>
            background-color:#BBBBBB;
          </xsl:otherwise>
        </xsl:choose>
      </xsl:attribute>
      <td><xsl:value-of select="position()" /></td>
      <td><xsl:value-of select="@id" /></td>
      <td><xsl:value-of select="description" /></td>
      <td align="right"><xsl:value-of select="quantity" /></td>
      <td align="right"><xsl:value-of select="list-price" /></td>
      <td>
        <xsl:if test="@productLine='2'" >
          Call for details!
        </xsl:if>
      </td>
    </xsl:element>
  </xsl:for-each>
</table>
```

Now wait a minute! What is the <xsl:element> element that we just threw in there? And what is the <xsl:attribute> element? These are necessary in this example, as our XSLT here is building up the opening <tr> tag in the <table>. We will cover this more in just a moment.

For now, examine the test condition in our <when> element. It essentially checks to see whether the position of the <item> in the node-set is odd or even. If odd, the result is true, which executes the output in the <when> element. If false, the output in <otherwise> is used.

So, to come back to why we couldn't simplify the <choose> like this:

```
<xsl:choose>
  <xsl:when test="position() mod 2">
    <tr style="background-color:#DDDDFF;">
  </xsl:when>
```

```
<xsl:otherwise>
  <tr style="background-color:#BBBBBB;">
</xsl:otherwise>
</xsl:choose>
```

The issue here becomes apparent if we view the above XML fragment through the eyes of an XML parser. The parser sees two opening <tr> tags, and other elements overlapping. This is not well-formed, the parser gets upset, and our style sheet will break. That is why the earlier solution uses the XSLT <element> and <attribute> elements to accomplish the task. Note that making <attribute> a child of <element> is how we define an attribute for that element, and that the closing </element> tag inserts the corresponding </tr> tag in this case. Alternatively, we could've used <xsl:text> elements, which can produce the same output produced by <xsl:element> and <xsl:attribute>, as long as we specify the disable-output-escaping="yes" attribute to output the angle-brackets correctly.

Understanding XSLT Functions, Variables, and Parameters

The XSLT language supports a number of functions to provide, among other things, extended support for node-set operations. We will not be able to cover every XSLT function in this section, so we will instead highlight just those functions that can be very useful in a web environment.

Uniquely Identifying Nodes with generate-id()

We often need a way to uniquely identify nodes in the output document. We may need a unique value for an ID attribute, or to differentiate two or more nodes with the same name and value. The generate-id() function gives us this ability.

Save transform-three.xslt as transform-four.xslt in our Transforms web application. In transform-four.xslt, we'll add another column to our table, which will contain a button to display the generated ID for each <item> node.

In the <tr> tag holding table heading information, add a column named ID:

```
<tr style="background-color:#000000;color:#FFFFFF">
  <th>Line Number</th>
  <th>ID</th>
  <th>Item Number</th>
  <th>Description</th>
  <th>Quantity</th>
  <th>List Price</th>
  <th>Notes</th>
</tr>
```

Then, in the `<for-each>` element, add the code highlighted below:

```
<xsl:for-each select="//item">
  <xsl:sort  select="list-price"
    data-type="number"
    order="descending"
  />
  <xsl:element name="tr">
    <xsl:attribute name="style">
      <xsl:choose>
        <xsl:when test="position() mod 2">
          background-color:#DDDDFF;
        </xsl:when>
        <xsl:otherwise>
          background-color:#BBBBBB;
        </xsl:otherwise>
      </xsl:choose>
    </xsl:attribute>

    <td><xsl:value-of select="position()" /></td>
    <td>
      <input  type="button"
          id="{generate-id()}"
          onclick="alert(this.id);"
          value="Click!" />
    </td>
    <td><xsl:value-of select="@id" /></td>
    <td><xsl:value-of select="description" /></td>
    <td align="right"><xsl:value-of select="quantity" /></td>
    <td align="right"><xsl:value-of select="list-price" /></td>
    <td>
      <xsl:if test="@productLine='2'" >
        Call for details!
      </xsl:if>
    </td>
  </xsl:element>
</xsl:for-each>
```

Here, we have added an HTML `<input>` tag of type `button`. Notice the syntax for the `id` attribute. enclosing the function in curly braces (`{}`) produces the same effect as calling an `<xsl:value-of>` statement right inside the quotes. The function returns a string that uniquely identifies the context node, which in this case is the current `<item>` element. The `onclick` attribute calls the Javascript `alert` function to open a message box with the value of the unique ID.

Save the changes to `transform-four.xslt`, and specify it in the query string for the `TransformXML.aspx` page. The results look like this:

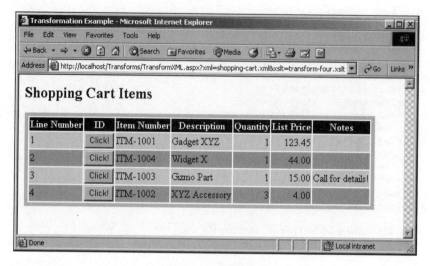

If we click the first button, we get a message box something like this:

Each button will of course return a different value. The method used to generate the ID is dependent on the implementation, and cannot be relied upon to always produce the same value for the same document, even with the same transform engine.

We will use this function again in the next example to compare nodes with each other.

Accessing Nodes using <key> and key()

A common situation I have faced when using XSLT style sheets is the need to transform data items according to the categories they are classed under in that particular XML dialect. The real challenge is to do so dynamically, without hard-coding template rules for each category. By using the XSLT <key> element and key() function, we can retrieve such "category" nodes in a document prior to processing the template rules, and then use the acquired node-set for access later.

Understanding the <key> Element

The <key> element is a top-level element, which means it must be a child of the <stylesheet> element. There are three attributes of <key>:

❑ name – Used as an identifier in the XSLT style sheet. Typically referenced by the key() function.

❏ match – An XPath expression that identifies the nodes in the source XML document to be gathered into the node-set. This search is done throughout the document, so it is not necessary to use the // operator to find all nodes.

❏ use – A relative location path identifying how to access the matched node. To access the node by its own value, supply the " . " self expression. To access the matched node by a relative node (such as an attribute of the element), provide the respective location path. This is also referenced by the key() function. This will become clearer once we've looked at an example.

Understanding the key() Function

The key() function allows us to access the matched nodes identified by the XSLT <key> element. The function accepts two arguments:

❏ name – This should match the name attribute of the corresponding <key> element.

❏ key – The value by which to access the node-set. This corresponds to the use attribute of the <key> element.

To demonstrate, we'll use the following XML document, distinct.xml:

```
<?xml version="1.0"?>
<doc>
  <parent category="E">
    <child>1</child>
  </parent>
  <parent category="D">
    <child>2</child>
  </parent>
  <parent category="E">
    <child>3</child>
  </parent>
  <parent category="A">
    <child>4</child>
  </parent>
  <parent category="B">
    <child>5</child>
  </parent>
  <parent category="B">
    <child>6</child>
  </parent>
  <parent category="C">
    <child>7</child>
  </parent>
  <parent category="A">
    <child>8</child>
  </parent>
  <parent category="A">
    <child>9</child>
  </parent>
  <parent category="B">
    <child>10</child>
  </parent>
</doc>
```

Now, say that we want to display the value of each child listed according to its parent's category. If we know all the possible category values, we could create a separate template rule for each one. But there is a more dynamic and robust way which uses the XSLT <key> element and key() function.

Create a new XSLT style sheet in our Transforms project, and name it transform-five.xslt. This style sheet will be used to transform the distinct.xml document listed above.

Begin the style sheet with the following markup:

```
<xsl:stylesheet xmlns:xsl="http://www.w3.org/1999/XSL/Transform"
 version="1.0">

  <xsl:key name="category_key" match="parent" use="@category" />
```

We have defined an XSLT <key> element, and named it category_key. The match attribute contains the single value of parent. By supplying this value, the XSLT processor will search the entire source document node by node for all occurrences of <parent> elements, and build a node-set accordingly. The use attribute informs the processor that the node-set is to be accessed by providing the value of the category attribute.

We now create a template match for the root node:

```
<xsl:template match="/">
  <html>
    <head>
      <title>Transformation Example</title>
    </head>
    <body>
      <xsl:apply-templates select="doc"/>
    </body>
  </html>
</xsl:template>
```

The above template formats the output as an HTML document. The content of the <body> tag is provided by the template matching the <doc> document element.

Now it gets interesting. This is the template matching <doc>:

```
<xsl:template match="doc">
  <xsl:for-each select="parent[generate-id(.)=
   generate-id(key('category_key', @category)[1])]">
    <xsl:sort select="@category" />
    <div style="font-weight:bold">
      Category=<xsl:value-of select="@category" />
    </div>
    <xsl:for-each select="key('category_key', @category)">
      <xsl:sort select="child"
                order="descending"
                data-type="number" />
      Child=<xsl:value-of select="child" /><br />
    </xsl:for-each>
```

```
      <br />
    </xsl:for-each>
  </xsl:template>
```

The magic really happens in the first `<for-each>` element. The XPath expression looks a little tricky, and I'll explain it as best I can. The first location step searches for `<parent>` elements that are children of the `<doc>` element (as this is the context node in this template). The predicate then selects only the `<parent>` element whose uniquely generated ID matches the first node returned from the `category_key` node-set containing the same generated ID.

The result is that this `<for-each>` neatly collects together `<parent>` nodes with distinct values in their category attribute.

The inner `<for-each>` statement then iterates through each child of each `<parent>` element, listing them in descending order.

The last thing to do is close the style sheet:

```
  </xsl:stylesheet>
```

Save the `transform-five.xslt` sheet, and feed it and the `distinct.xml` file into the `TransformXML.aspx` page in your browser. The results are shown in the following screenshot:

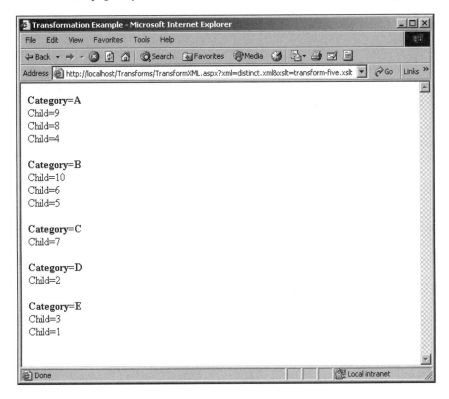

In this way, we have dynamically categorized our output. Experiment by adding or removing categories in the `distinct.xml` document – the style sheet will react accordingly.

Assigning Values with <variable>

We can assign values to use in XPath expressions with the XSLT `<variable>` element. An XSLT variable's scope is limited to the element that it is a child of, so if declared as a top-level element, it can be accessed throughout the style sheet. The element has just two attributes:

- ❑ `name` – Supplies the identifier for the variable, within the scope of its declaration
- ❑ `select` – An optional XPath expression returning the value to be assigned to the variable

Alternatively, we can specify the value of the variable by placing content directly in the element. If `select` is not provided, and the element is empty, the variable equals an empty string.

Here is a simple demonstration of how to use a variable. In the `transform-five.xslt` style sheet, locate the template match for `<doc>`, and make the changes highlighted below:

```
<xsl:template match="doc">
  <xsl:for-each select="parent[generate-id(.)=
  generate-id(key('category_key', @category)[1])]">
    <xsl:sort select="@category" />
    <xsl:variable name="CategoryName" select="@category" />
    <div style="font-weight:bold">
      Category=<xsl:value-of select="$CategoryName" />
    </div>
    <xsl:for-each select="key('category_key', @category)">
      <xsl:sort    select="child"
            order="descending"
            data-type="number" />
      Child=<xsl:value-of select="child" /><br />
    </xsl:for-each>
    <br />
  </xsl:for-each>
</xsl:template>
```

In this example, we have assigned the `category` attribute to the `CategoryName` variable. For each iteration, the variable value changes. Note the syntax to access the variable in the line that follows shortly after the variable declaration:

```
Category=<xsl:value-of select="$CategoryName" />
```

The $ character denotes a variable identifier.

This example does not change the behavior of our transformation, and may seem a little pointless. Variables can really save us a lot of trouble when used to hold complex XPath expressions that are employed several times in the same template. In following examples though, we will see another practical use of this feature: to hold a complete XML document.

Processing Multiple XML Documents with document()

There are times when data in one XML document directly relates to data in another, and in order to create meaningful output, we must take values from one XML document and relate them to the other. Linking such documents together is made possible with the document() function, which could be thought of as a SQL JOIN between the two documents.

Although there are other uses for document(), the following example focuses on how to use it to link data between XML documents during a transformation.

We will link the distinct.xml document to the following document, called categories.xml:

```xml
<?xml version="1.0"?>
<categories>
  <category id="A">ASP.NET</category>
  <category id="B">VB.NET</category>
  <category id="C">C#</category>
  <category id="D">ADO.NET</category>
</categories>
```

Open the transform-five.xslt style sheet, and add the following variable declaration as a top-level element:

```xml
<xsl:variable name="categories_doc" select="document('categories.xml')" />
```

This associates the entire categories.xml document with the variable categories_doc. Now make these changes to the template for <doc>:

```xml
<xsl:template match="doc">
  <xsl:for-each select="parent[generate-id(.)=
   generate-id(key('category_key', @category)[1])]">
    <xsl:sort select="@category" />
    <xsl:variable name="CategoryName" select="@category" />
    <div style="font-weight:bold">
      Category=<xsl:value-of select="$CategoryName" />,
        <xsl:choose>
          <xsl:when test="$categories_doc//category[@id=$CategoryName]">
            <xsl:value-of select="$categories_doc//category[@id=
                                   $CategoryName]" />
          </xsl:when>
          <xsl:otherwise>
            Unknown
          </xsl:otherwise>
        </xsl:choose>
    </div>
    <xsl:for-each select="key('category_key', @category)">
      <xsl:sort    select="child"
            order="descending"
            data-type="number" />
      Child=<xsl:value-of select="child" /><br />
    </xsl:for-each>
```

```
        <br />
      </xsl:for-each>
  </xsl:template>
```

This new XSLT `<choose>` element contains a `<when>` element that tests for the existence of a `<category>` element in the `categories.xml` document matching the value currently in our `CategoryName` variable. If the test returns `true`, we select the text value of the matching `<category>` element. Otherwise, we output Unknown to indicate there was no match in the other XML document.

Save the changes to `transform-five.xslt`, and view the results in your browser. It should look like the following screenshot:

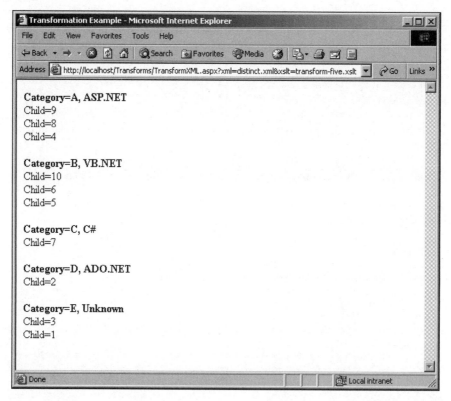

As we can see, the values from the `categories.xml` document are included in the output of the transformation. When there was no match for "E", the conditional logic output Unknown as we expect.

Creating Dynamic Output with <param>

Very similar to `<variable>` is the `<param>` element, as both can store information that we can access in our style sheet. One of the key differences is that it allows *external* data to be passed in when the transformation is invoked. Again, there are multiple uses for `<param>`, but in the following example we are going to focus on how to pass external data into the transformation to filter the results.

First, I'll just briefly mention the other important use for <param> elements: defining parameters for named templates, like so:

```
<xsl:template name="templateName">
  <xsl:param name="firstParameter" />
  <!-- Other parameters here -->
</xsl:template>
```

We then pass in parameters by setting values with <with-param> child elements of the <call-templates> element:

```
<xsl:call-template name="templateName">
  <xsl:with-param name="firstParameter" select "XPathExpression" />
  <!-- Other parameters defined here -->
</xsl:call-template>
```

These aren't something we would normally change programmatically, so we'll pay more attention to the use of parameters for style sheets.

Similarly to named templates, parameters are declared as immediate children of the <stylesheet> element (in fact, named templates can be thought of as localized inline style sheets), so add the following as a top level element of the transform-five.xslt sheet:

```
<xsl:param name="CategoryParam" />
```

Then in the template match for <doc>, incorporate an <xsl:if> element as shown below:

```
<xsl:template match="doc">
  <xsl:for-each select="parent[generate-id(.)=
  generate-id(key('category_key', @category)[1])]">
   <xsl:sort select="@category" />
   <xsl:variable name="CategoryName" select="@category" />

   <xsl:if test="not($CategoryParam) or $CategoryName=$CategoryParam">

     <div style="font-weight:bold">
       Category=<xsl:value-of select="$CategoryName" />,
         <xsl:choose>
           <xsl:when test="$categories_doc//category[@id=$CategoryName]">
             <xsl:value-of select="$categories_doc//category[@id=$CategoryName]"
             />
           </xsl:when>
           <xsl:otherwise>
             Unknown
           </xsl:otherwise>
         </xsl:choose>
     </div>
     <xsl:for-each select="key('category_key', @category)">
       <xsl:sort    select="child"
             order="descending"
             data-type="number" />
       Child=<xsl:value-of select="child" />
       <br />
     </xsl:for-each>
```

```
        <br />
      </xsl:if>

    </xsl:for-each>
  </xsl:template>
```

The `<if>` element does a clever trick here. It tests two conditions using the parameter (which is identified with $ just like a variable). The first condition determines if $CategoryParam has no value, and the second determines if the $CategoryParam value is equal to $CategoryName. If either is true, the contents of the `<if>` element are processed.

So now we just need to know how to provide a value for the $CategoryParam parameter from an ASPX page.

Using XsltArgumentList to Add Parameters

We have to return to Visual Studio .NET, and modify our `TransformXML.aspx.cs` code to provide support for parameters. We will use the `XsltArgumentList` object, which we then pass to the `Transform` method of the `XslTransform` object. Make the following changes to our `Page_Load` event handler:

```
private void Page_Load(object sender, System.EventArgs e)
{
  // Put user code to initialize the page here
  try
  {
    string _XMLPath = Request.QueryString["xml"];
    string _XSLTPath = Request.QueryString["xslt"];

    string _Param = Request.QueryString["category"];

    // Instantiate and Load the XPathDocument
    XPathDocument _SourceXml =
      new XPathDocument( Server.MapPath(_XMLPath) );

    // Instantiate and load the XslTransform object
    XslTransform _Transform = new XslTransform();
    _Transform.Load( Server.MapPath(_XSLTPath));

    // Create the XsltArgumentList object
    XsltArgumentList _Args = null;
    if (_Param != null && _Param != String.Empty)
    {
      _Args = new XsltArgumentList();
      _Args.AddParam("CategoryParam", "", _Param);
    }

    // Send result of transformation to Response.Output stream
    _Transform.Transform(_SourceXml, _Args, Response.Output );
  }
  catch (Exception handledException)
  {
    Response.Write(handledException.Message);
  }
}
```

The first change above captures a possible value named `category` from the query-string. Our next change is the declaration of a new `XsltArgumentList` object. We initialize it to `null`, and only instantiate it if there is a value in the `_Param` string. If there is a value, we instantiate the object and call the `AddParam` method to set the value of the `_Param` string as the `CategoryParam` named parameter in the XSLT style sheet. (The middle argument in `AddParam` is for namespace support.)

If we now save and rebuild the project, we can call the `TransformXML.aspx` page with the `distinct.xml` and `transform-five.xslt` files in the query-string. This gives the same results as before. Now append the query-string with the following:

&category=B

This will pass the value of "B" to our style sheet, to deliver the following results:

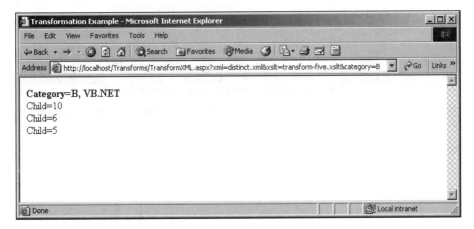

Try setting `category` to different values in the query string, and you'll see that the parameter filters the output to display only the matching category.

Summary

In this chapter, we learned how to utilize XSLT style sheets in our web applications. We covered the various reasons why and when we would use XSLT. We looked at language syntax, template rules, and saw how XPath is used throughout. We also explored how it allows us to transform data dynamically using conditional statements and XSLT functions. We looked at some typical situations we may confront during our development careers, and how XSLT provides a neat solution.

However, the examples in this chapter have used static XML documents as source data. In many cases, the XML we use may either be generated from another component, or derived from a data source such as SQL Server or MS Access. In our next chapter, we will see how to use ADO.NET and its XML features to provide a dynamic data source for our application. Along the way, we'll see an example or two of how to use XSLT against such data sources.

6

ADO.NET

Getting data onto our web pages effectively is the key to providing dynamic, useful information for users of our web applications. Our focus in this chapter takes data access to a different level, to capture the benefits of the XML features of ADO.NET in ASP.NET applications.

This chapter will focus on the following areas as they relate to developing web applications:

❑   A basic introduction to ADO.NET

❑   Accessing data with ADO.NET

❑   Understanding Security when using ADO.NET in ASP.NET

❑   Using `DataSets` with XML documents.

❑   Synchronizing an `XmlDataDocument` with a `DataSet`

❑   Transforming XML data

What is ADO.NET?

Microsoft's new solution for handling data access and manipulation in the managed environment of the Framework is called ADO.NET – but what is it? Is it a namespace? Is it simply the ADO object model exposed in the .NET Framework?

In fact, it is neither of these. Rather, it is a term which covers the many namespaces, classes, interfaces, and enumerations that provide us as developers with an awesome new way to handle data in our web-enabled applications. ADO.NET was designed expressly to meet the challenges thrown up by ASP.NET. It offers many advantages over its predecessor: it is lightweight and fast, plus it is extensible, allowing us to add data relations and constraints in addition to data itself.

The design goals for ADO.NET were primarily to leverage the power of ADO, support a disconnected environment, and, you guessed it, integrate well with XML. Looking at how it relates with XML will be a major element (no pun intended) of our explorations in this chapter.

For the moment, let's turn our attention to the support that ADO.NET offers for a disconnected environment. This is important to us as web developers, because the environment in which we work is highly disconnected. Disconnected means that we do not maintain an open connection to the data source across round trips to a web page. Rather, the data used in our web applications is retrieved as and when needed.

Data Access using Managed Data Providers

Accessing information from disparate data systems is made possible with managed data providers. Managed data providers are the link between our applications and the data source. The .NET Framework supports two providers "out of the box":

Managed Data Provider	Description
OLE DB .NET Data Provider	Used to access data exposed through the general-purpose OLE DB interface. Examples of OLE DB providers and the data source they expose include: `Microsoft.JET.OLEDB.4.0:` Access, Excel `MSDAORA:` Oracle `SQLOLEDB:` SQL Server 6.5 (or lower)
SQL Server .NET Data Provider	For SQL Server version 7.0 and higher.

Additionally, Microsoft has provided another managed data provider for ODBC support, available from the download site at http://msdn.microsoft.com/downloads. This add-on component provides access to native ODBC drivers, and is intended to work with all compliant ODBC drivers. Note however that the ODBC .NET Data Provider has only been tested with the Microsoft SQL ODBC driver, the Microsoft ODBC driver for Oracle, and the Microsoft Jet ODBC driver.

Core Components of the Managed Data Providers

Every .NET data provider has four objects at its core, which implement interfaces to enable consistent behavior across all managed data providers. These common-ground interfaces and objects exist in either the `System.Data` or `System.Data.Common` namespace. The following table displays each core interface, and the classes which implement it for each respective provider:

Core Interface(s) or Class(es)	OLE DB Implementation	SQL Server Implementation
`IDbConnection`	`OleDbConnection`	`SqlConnection`
`IDbCommand`	`OleDbCommand`	`SqlCommand`
`IdataReader` `IDataRecord`	`OleDbDataReader`	`SqlDataReader`

`IdbDataAdapter`
`DBDataAdapter`
`DataAdapter`
`IDataAdapter`
	`OleDbDataAdapter`	`SqlDataAdapter`

The role that each object plays in the data access mechanism is determined by the last part of the class name, and is either `Connection`, `Command`, `DataReader`, or `DataAdapter`. Let's now summarize what each of these roles entails.

Connection Objects

Connection objects provide the means of opening a connection to a data source, and we supply a connection string to the object to specify the nature of the connection. The most common parameters of a connection string are listed below. Note that where a default value is supplied, that parameter need not be included in the string.

- ❏ **Connection Timeout** (or `Connect Timeout`)
  Represents the length of time to wait for a successful connection before returning an error. The default value is 15 seconds.

- ❏ **Data Source** (or `Server`, `Address`, `Addr`, or `Network Address`)
  The name or network address of the database server or the path to a data file.

- ❏ **Initial Catalog** (or `Database`)
  The name of the database.

- ❏ **Integrated Security** (or `Trusted_Connection`)
  If set to `true` or `SSPI` (for Security Support Provider Interface), the connection is secured using Windows authentication, and SQL Server will authenticate the Windows identity of the process that is attempting to connect. The default is `false`.

- ❏ **User ID**
  If not using integrated security, this is the login name of the user.

- ❏ **Password** (or `PWD`)
  The password used in conjunction with `User ID` if not using Integrated Security.

Each managed provider may also have certain special attributes in the connection string. For instance, OLE DB uses the `Provider` keyword to identify the underlying data source. Here is an example of a connection string used by an `OleDbConnection` object to connect to an Access database:

```
Provider=Microsoft.Jet.OLEDB.4.0;Data Source=c:\AccessDB.mdb;
```

For SQL Server, specific feature support can be configured such as enabling or disabling connection pooling. The connection string below shows how to connect to a database called `pubs` hosted on the SQL Server instance running on the local machine:

```
Data Source=(local);Initial Catalog=pubs;Integrated Security=true;
```

Command Objects

Command objects embody actions we wish to make to the data source. We use their properties to execute a SQL statement, update data, or call on a stored procedure. Objects which implement the `IDbCommand` interface can execute commands using one of the following methods:

❑ **ExecuteNonQuery**
This typically executes DML (Data Manipulation Language) statements which don't retrieve data, such as INSERTs, UPDATEs, or DELETEs. It can also be used to call stored procedures that return no values. ExecuteNonQuery returns a value representing the number of rows affected. For statements that do not affect rows, the return value is –1.

❑ **ExecuteScalar**
This type of execution returns a singleton value, representing the value found in the first column in the first row of the result, and ignoring everything else. We would typically use this when returning an aggregate value such as SELECT Count(*) FROM Employees.

❑ **ExecuteReader**
This execution type is used when the command will yield a stream of data – such as a SELECT statement returning a set of records. The result is an object which implements the IDataReader interface (discussed in the following section).

Managed data providers may extend this behavior by defining methods specific to that provider's feature set. For example, the `SqlCommand` object supports the `ExecuteXmlReader` method, for SELECT statements which return XML markup. See Chapter 7 for more information on ExecuteXmlReader.

DataReader Objects

As we have just learned, the `ExecuteReader` method returns an object which implements the `IDataReader` interface. This is a read-only, forward-only stream of data. The two primary methods of this interface are:

❑ **Read**
This method advances the reader to the next record. The reader starts prior to the first record, so calling this method at least once is necessary to access any data. This function returns true if it successfully advanced to another record, otherwise false.

❑ **Close**
When we are finished using the reader, calling the Close method is important, as it frees up the associated object implementing the IDbConnection interface, which we can then use as the database connection for other activities.

To access column values in each row, we use the `OleDbDataReader` and `SqlDataReader` objects, which implements the `IDataRecord` interface to provide methods for accessing column values. These methods all begin with Get and are followed by the data type in question, for example GetString and GetInt32. The methods accept a number representing the ordinal value of the column.

DataAdapter Objects

`DataAdapter` objects are a link between the data source and cached tables in the application. We cache data in a `DataSet` object (discussed in more detail later this chapter) for client-side processing. Objects derived from `DBDataAdapter` contain methods to get the data from the source to the specified `DataSet` object. Two of the noteworthy methods are:

❑ **Fill**
This method is called once the `DataAdapter` object has been associated with a command object that returns data. We provide the `DataSet` object that is to be 'filled' as a parameter, and an optional name for the table generated. Subsequent calls to the `Fill` method will restore the data to the underlying values in the data source. This has the effect of losing any updated information, but any new records added will still be present in the `DataSet`.

❑ **Update**
This method is called when updates to the data cached in the `DataSet` are to be propagated to the underlying data source. There are several options when using `Update`, which we will explore later the chapter.

Populating a `DataSet` object with relational data and synchronizing changes with the data source is accomplished with `DataAdapter` objects.

Creating the ADONET Web Application

To illustrate the concepts introduced in this chapter, let's create a new web application. Open Visual Studio .NET and select File | New | Project. Select Visual C# Projects in the Project Types pane, and in the Templates pane, choose ASP.NET Web Application:

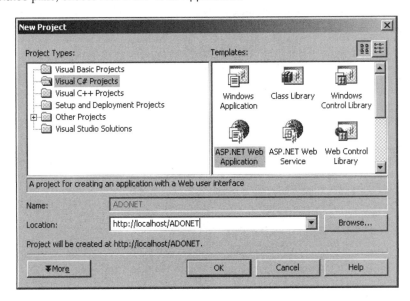

Name the application **ADONET** and click **OK**. This will build the solution and project. Before we continue, we need to address a very important issue for modern web applications: security.

Security and ADO.NET in ASP.NET Applications

Secure access to our data is an important requirement for almost every application, and understanding how to provide data access security in ASP.NET demands special attention. Choosing between integrated security or supplying specific user credentials should be weighed against the level of authentication required for a web application.

Accessing Data with User ID and Password

One way to authenticate with a data source was touched on in the discussion of connection strings, that is to provide user credentials – a user ID and password. Depending on its needs, an application can either use a single user ID and password for all data access, or it could use credentials bound to the particular user currently using the application. Let's discuss best practices in either scenario.

The following demonstrations use the Northwind sample database in SQL Server. In this chapter, I'll assume you've created a SQL Server login account with the name of DBUser, with a password of password, and with database owner access granted for the Northwind database.

Application-Level Access

When all data access is handled through a single user ID and password, the credentials are usually kept somewhere safe for the application to retrieve and use when it needs to establish a connection. *Where* the credentials are maintained is something we'll discuss next. Hopefully, for many reasons, these values are not hard-coded in our Web Forms or components, as that can constitute a bit of a maintenance headache should we need to change the details of the connection.

So what are suitable places? One available avenue is to store the credentials in the Web.config XML configuration file for the project, by defining an <appSettings> element as a child of <configuration>. This element can be used to store general application settings by setting the key and value attributes of <add> child nodes of <appSettings>, which we can then access from any Web Form that requires them. Here is an example of storing a connection string in Web.config:

```
<appSettings>
  <add key="CS1" value="Provider=SQLOLEDB; Data Source=(local);
      Initial Catalog=Northwind; User ID=DBUser; Password=password" />
</appSettings>
```

Add a similar <appSettings> element to the Web.config file in the ADONET project to associate the value of CS1 with a connection string, but using a user ID and password valid for the Northwind database on your machine.

To get hold of <appSettings> values from code, we use the NameValueCollection returned by the AppSettings property of the ConfigurationSettings class in the System.Configuration namespace. The Item indexer property of this collection takes an argument that names the key attribute of an <add> element, and returns the corresponding value.

Add a new Web Form to the ADONET web application project, and call it AppLevel.aspx. In the Properties window, select DOCUMENT in the top dropdown, and find the title property. Change it to AppLevel Example. Next, drag a Label control from the Web Forms tab of the Toolbox, and place it on the page. Set its ID property to MessageLabel, and clear its Text property. Now open the code-behind file, and make the changes highlighted:

```csharp
using System;
using System.Collections;
using System.ComponentModel;
using System.Data;
using System.Drawing;
using System.Web;
using System.Web.SessionState;
using System.Web.UI;
using System.Web.UI.WebControls;
using System.Web.UI.HtmlControls;
using System.Configuration;
using System.Data.OleDb;

namespace Wrox.ASPNET.ADONET
{
    /// <summary>
    /// Summary description for AppLevel
    /// </summary>
    public class AppLevel : System.Web.UI.Page
    {
        protected System.Web.UI.WebControls.Label MessageLabel;

        private void Page_Load(object sender, System.EventArgs e)
        {
            // Retrieve connection string from Web.config
            string _ConnectionString = ConfigurationSettings.AppSettings[
                                "CS1"].ToString();

            // Use it to open a connection
            OleDbConnection _Connection=new OleDbConnection(_ConnectionString);

            try
            {
                _Connection.Open();
                MessageLabel.Text =
                    "Connection opened successfully...";
            }

            catch (Exception handledException)
            {
                MessageLabel.Text = handledException.Message;
            }

            finally
            {
                if (_Connection!=null)
                {
                    _Connection.Close();
                }
            }
        }

        [Web Form Designer generated code]

    }
}
```

The code in the `Page_Load` event above uses the connection string value from `Web.config` to open a connection to the database. We need to include the `System.Configuration` namespace in order to get the `ConfigurationSettings` object that exposes the values stored in `Web.config`. Now compile and run the application by pressing *F5*. If the connection is successful, the following message appears in the browser:

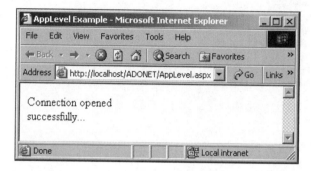

Now change the `password` attribute set for the connection string located in `Web.config` to something else, and save the changes. Refresh the page and the message label will read **Login failed for user 'DBUser'**.

As we have demonstrated, placing user credentials in the `Web.config` file allows easy access without making the credentials public, because ASP.NET prevents access to the `Web.config` file.

To further secure the user details, we could employ encryption when persisting connection information.

This way of storing and accessing connection strings could also work for behavior-specific or role-based access, where we define multiple connection strings for each role.

User-Level Access

If we need to access the data differently for each user, and the mechanism for gaining authentication is by passing in a user ID and password, we first need to establish how to obtain the user credentials. Often, a Web Form will capture the user's login and password. If this is the case, security such as Secure Sockets Layer (SSL) or Internet Protocol Security (IPSec) should be implemented to ensure the privacy of the data.

If the actual database user ID and password are not passed into a Web Form, then we would need to link users to their credentials through a table or config file, which we can query to retrieve their details. However, this approach raises issues about having all the users' credentials available to the application.

Using encryption certainly provides another layer of security. For instance, the user's password may be stored at the data source with a one-way hash. Prior to encryption, the DBA can concatenate the password with a secret key so that when the user provides the actual password to the application, our code concatenates the secret key, encrypts the merged value, and compares it to the value in the underlying data source. This approach, combined with other security measures such as SSL and web application authentication (either Passport, Windows, or Forms), provides very secure access to the data source.

Accessing Data with Integrated Security

Access to SQL Server can be controlled by the Windows NT or Windows 2000 account or group, as authenticated when the user logs on to the Windows operating system on the client. We can use these credentials to control access to SQL Server, and we'll look at the options in this section.

Application-Level Access

To use integrated security, we need to understand how the web application attempts to authenticate itself. This is configurable in the `Web.config` file, as we will now explore.

Anytime we use integrated security to access the database, we need to be aware of which account ASP.NET will use to authenticate itself. The default `Web.config` file generated by Visual Studio .NET is configured to request access to SQL Server using the `aspnet_wp` service, which runs as a local user named ASPNET. One way to grant application-level access to our web application therefore is to grant the ASPNET account access to SQL Server. However, this is not ideal, as any web application on the same web server will now have equal access to that database.

Configuring Impersonation with <identity>

We do have an alternative. In the `Web.config` XML file, we can define the context in which the application runs by providing an `<identity>` node as a child of `<system.web>`. This `<identity>` element can contain up to three attributes, as described below:

- **impersonate**
  When set to `true`, the web application runs in the context of either the client or the user account defined in the `userName` attribute. When set to `false` (the default), impersonation is disabled, and the application runs in the context of the account associated with the `aspnet_wp` service (ASPNET by default).

- **userName**
  This is the user account that our web application runs under when `impersonate` is enabled.

- **password**
  The password for the account provided in the `userName` attribute.

Thus, to enable impersonation for an account named `[MachineName]\LocalUser`, the following element should be added to the application's `Web.config` file:

```
<identity impersonate="true"
          userName="GRAYAREA\LocalUser"
          password="password"
/>
```

Where GRAYAREA in the `userName` value is the local machine name.

It's not quite this simple, as by default, the ASPNET account does not have the privilege to impersonate another account. We have two options here: either allow the ASPNET account to 'Act as part of the operating system' in the local security settings for the web server, or reassign an account which has that privilege (such as SYSTEM) to the `aspnet_wp` service in the `machine.config` XML file.

For our purposes, let us grant the privilege to the ASPNET account to 'Act as part of the operating system'. Select Start | Programs | Administrative Tools | Local Security Policy to bring up the following screen:

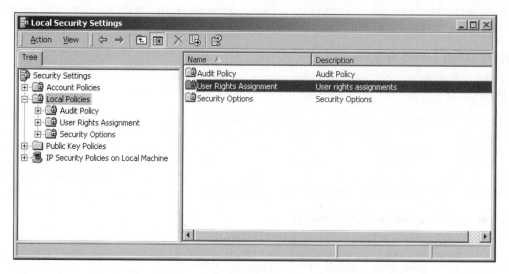

Double-click User Rights Assignment as highlighted above, and then locate and double-click the policy Act as part of the operating system. Add the ASPNET local account:

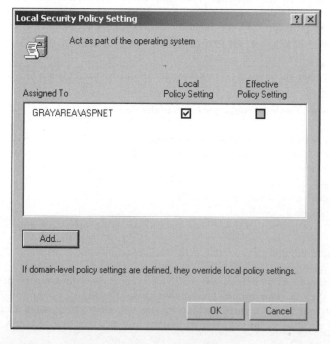

Again, GRAYAREA is the name of the local machine. Click OK.

Now make the following changes in `Web.config`:

```
<configuration>
  <appSettings>
    <add key="CS1" value="Provider=SQLOLEDB; Data Source=(local);
         Initial Catalog=Northwind; User ID=DBUser; Password=password" />
    <add key="CS2" value="Data Source=(local); Initial Catalog=Northwind;
         Integrated Security=true" />
  </appSettings>

  <system.web>
    <identity impersonate="true"
              userName="GRAYAREA\LocalUser"
              password="password"
    />

    <authentication mode="None" />

    <!-- other settings -->

  </system.web>
</configuration>
```

We're creating a new child entry of `<appSettings>` for a connection string using integrated security that we can retrieve in our code using the key value `CS2`. We've also enabled impersonation, requesting the `aspnet_wp` service to run under the local account named `LocalUser`.

Now, copy and paste `AppLevel.aspx` in Solution Explorer, and rename it `AppLevel2.aspx`. Make the highlighted changes in the code-behind file, `AppLevel2.aspx.cs`:

```
using System;
using System.Collections;
using System.ComponentModel;
using System.Data;
using System.Drawing;
using System.Web;
using System.Web.SessionState;
using System.Web.UI;
using System.Web.UI.WebControls;
using System.Web.UI.HtmlControls;
using System.Configuration;
using System.Data.SqlClient;

namespace Wrox.ASPNET.ADONET
{
  /// <summary>
  /// Summary description for AppLevel2
  /// </summary>
  public class AppLevel2 : System.Web.UI.Page
  {
    protected System.Web.UI.WebControls.Label MessageLabel;
```

```
private void Page_Load(object sender, System.EventArgs e)
{
  // Put user code to initialize the page here

  string _ConnectionString = ConfigurationSettings.AppSettings["CS2"]
                             .ToString();

  SqlConnection _Connection = new SqlConnection(_ConnectionString);

  try
  {
    _Connection.Open();

    MessageLabel.Text = "Connection opened successfully...";
  }
  catch (Exception handledException)
  {
    MessageLabel.Text = handledException.Message;
  }
  finally
  {
    if (_Connection!=null)
    {
      _Connection.Close();
    }
  }
}// Page_Load

[ Web Form Designer generated code ]

}
}
```

First, because we are using integrated security with SQL Server, we can optimize access by using the SQL Server managed data provider. We create a connection using the value of the connection string associated with the key CS2, and attempt to open it within the try block.

Set AppLevel2.aspx as the start page, and compile and run the project with *F5*. However, we'll receive the 'login failed' message, because we haven't granted the LocalUser account access to our SQL Server. The message should name the user we specified in the identity element, which at least informs us that the impersonation succeeded. Let's experiment a little now. In the Web.config file, comment out the <identity> element:

```
<!--
<identity
  impersonate="true"
  userName="GRAYAREA\LocalUser"
  password="password"
/>
-->
```

Refresh the AppLevel2.aspx page, and this time you should receive a login failure message for the ASPNET account.

Now grant the `LocalUser` account access to SQL Server, putting the account in the `db_owner` role for the Northwind database. Remove the opening and closing comment XML tags surrounding the `<identity>` element, and refresh the `AppLevel2.aspx` page again. This time we should receive a message indicating the connection was opened successfully.

With this configuration, when our web application makes requests for external resources, it is doing so using the account designated for impersonation. Because we have granted the account access to our database server, the connection was successful.

Configuring Impersonation Programmatically

Another possibility with impersonation is to programmatically apply it only when needed, as opposed to having the entire application run under an impersonated account as happens when we set it through the configuration file. Although this option provides the most control, it is also more complex to implement.

To demonstrate, we'll create a component that can be called from our web application and which will impersonate a user for a particular action. We will then create a Web Form to use the component, and use impersonation only when accessing the database.

First we must create the component. Right-click the ADONET project in Solution Explorer and select Add | New Folder, and name it Source. Right-click this folder when it appears, and choose Add | Add Class from the context menu, and name it `Impersonate.cs`. Here is the code for this class:

```csharp
using System;
using System.Security.Principal;
using System.Runtime.InteropServices;

namespace Wrox.ASPNET.ADONET
{
  // Delegate for impersonation action
  public delegate void ImpersonationAction();

  // Impersonate class
  public class Impersonate
  {
    // Unmanaged functions for account token management
    [DllImport("advapi32.dll", CharSet=CharSet.Auto)]
    public static extern int LogonUser(string lpszUserName,
      string lpszDomain,
      string lpszPassword,
      int dwLogonType,
      int dwLogonProvider,
      ref IntPtr phToken);

    [DllImport("advapi32.dll", CharSet= System.Runtime.InteropServices
            .CharSet.Auto, SetLastError=true)]
    public extern static int DuplicateToken(IntPtr hToken,
      int impersonationLevel, ref IntPtr hNewToken);

    // Private property
    private WindowsImpersonationContext _WindowsImpersonationContext;
```

```
    // Public method
    public bool DoImpersonationAction(string userName, string domain,
                string password, ImpersonationAction actionToImpersonate)
    {
      WindowsIdentity _WindowsIdentity;
      IntPtr _Token = IntPtr.Zero;
      IntPtr _DuplicateToken = IntPtr.Zero;

      if (LogonUser(userName, domain, password, 2, 0, ref _Token) != 0)
      {
        if(DuplicateToken(_Token, 2, ref _DuplicateToken) != 0)
        {
          _WindowsIdentity = new WindowsIdentity(_DuplicateToken);
          _WindowsImpersonationContext = _WindowsIdentity.Impersonate();

          if (_WindowsImpersonationContext != null)
          {

            // Invoke the delegate
            actionToImpersonate();
            _WindowsImpersonationContext.Undo();
            return true;
          }
          else
            return false;
        }
        else
          return false;
      }
      else
        return false;
    }
  }
}
```

This code defines a delegate and a class. The delegate, `ImpersonationAction`, is a placeholder for the code to execute under the credentials of the impersonated user. The `DoImpersonationAction` method in the `Impersonate` class invokes this delegate. `DoImpersonationAction` accepts user credentials and a delegate to invoke as arguments.

Next, add the following application settings to `Web.config`, and comment out the `<identity>` element again:

```xml
<configuration>
  <appSettings>
    <add key="CS1" value="Provider=SQLOLEDB; Data Source=(local); Initial
    Catalog=Northwind; User ID=DBUser; Password=password" />
    <add key="CS2" value="Data Source=(local); Initial Catalog=Northwind;
    Integrated Security=true" />
    <add key="UserName" value="LocalUser" />
    <add key="Domain" value="GRAYAREA" />
    <add key="Password" value="password" />
  </appSettings>
```

```
<system.web>

    <!--
 <identity
   impersonate="true"
   username="GRAYAREA\LocalUser"
   password="password"
 />
-->

    <authentication mode="None" />

  <!-- other settings -->

 </system.web>
</configuration>
```

The above changes to Web.config will disable impersonation for the ASPNET account. Be sure to use your machine name in place of GRAYAREA for the Domain value. Now let's create a page to try out this programmatic method for impersonation. Copy and paste AppLevel2.aspx in Solution Explorer, and rename it AppLevel3.aspx. Change the code behind like so:

```
using System;
using System.Collections;
using System.ComponentModel;
using System.Data;
using System.Drawing;
using System.Web;
using System.Web.SessionState;
using System.Web.UI;
using System.Web.UI.WebControls;
using System.Web.UI.HtmlControls;
using System.Configuration;
using System.Data.SqlClient;
using Wrox.ASPNET.ADONET;

namespace Wrox.ASPNET.ADONET
{

  public class AppLevel3 : System.Web.UI.Page
  {
    protected System.Web.UI.WebControls.Label MessageLabel;
    private SqlConnection _Connection = null;

    private void ConnectToSQLServer()
    {
      string _ConnectionString = ConfigurationSettings.AppSettings["CS2"]
                                    .ToString();
      SqlConnection _Connection=new SqlConnection(_ConnectionString);

      try
      {
        _Connection.Open();
        MessageLabel.Text = "Connection opened successfully...";
```

```
      }
      catch (Exception handledException)
      {
        MessageLabel.Text=handledException.Message;
      }

  }

  private void Page_Load(object sender, System.EventArgs e)
  {
      string _UserName = ConfigurationSettings.AppSettings["UserName"]
                    .ToString();
      string _Domain = ConfigurationSettings.AppSettings["Domain"]
                    .ToString();
      string _Password = ConfigurationSettings.AppSettings["Password"]
                    .ToString();

      Impersonate _Impersonate = new Impersonate();

      ImpersonationAction _ImpersonationAction =
                    new ImpersonationAction(this.ConnectToSQLServer);

      if (!_Impersonate.DoImpersonationAction(_UserName, _Domain,
                          _Password, _ImpersonationAction ))
      {
        MessageLabel.Text= "Impersonation Failed!";
      }

  if (_Connection!=null) _Connection.Close();

  }

      [ Web Form Designer generated code ]

  }
}
```

We declare a method named ConnectToSQLServer to use with our ImpersonationAction delegate. In the Page_Load event handler, we create an instance of the Impersonate class, and call the DoImpersonationAction method – passing in data retrieved from the Web.config file and the delegate. If the method call returns false, the impersonation failed.

Set this page as the start up, and compile and run the project. The resulting screen should show that the impersonation successfully opens the connection. If you change Web.config, say to use an incorrect password, we'll receive the message **Impersonation Failed!** in the browser.

User-Level Access

To enable user- or role-level access to SQL Server from our web applications, we are typically in an intranet environment. To impersonate the identity of a web client for SQL Server access, we need to make the following change to the <identity> element in the Web.config file:

```
<identity impersonate="true" />
```

When we don't specify a user name and password, the impersonation is performed based on the credentials of the requesting client. With this option, the `<authentication>` element in the configuration file should be set like so:

```
<authentication mode="Windows" />
```

Depending on the needs of the application, we might also disable anonymous logins through IIS. Now that we've covered the options for connecting to the database, we can turn our attention to the subject of data retrieval and manipulation.

Using DataSets in ASP.NET

In this section we'll see how to employ the XML features of `DataSets` in ASP.NET.

Filling a DataSet using DataAdapter

Our first focus will be how to go about the fundamental task of getting data from the data source into a `DataSet` object. Here are the steps needed to fill a `DataSet` object using a `DataAdapter`:

1. Create a `Connection` object.

2. Create a `SELECT Command` to retrieve the data, and associate it with the `Connection`.

3. Create a `DataAdapter` object, and associate it with the `SELECT Command`.

4. Call the `Fill` method of the `DataAdapter`, passing in the `DataSet` to be populated.

The data placed in the `DataSet` is cached – that is, it is disconnected from the underlying data source.

Binding a DataSet to a DataGrid

Let's create a Web Form to demonstrate the process. First, let's add another application setting to our `Web.config` XML file, as highlighted:

```
<appSettings>
  <add key="CS1" value="Provider=SQLOLEDB; Data Source=(local); Initial
   Catalog=Northwind; User ID=DBUser; Password=password" />
  <add key="CS2" value="Data Source=(local); Initial Catalog=Northwind;
   Integrated Security=true" />
  <add key="UserName" value="LocalUser" />
  <add key="Domain" value="GRAYAREA" />
  <add key="Password" value="password" />
  <add key="ShipperQuery" value="SELECT * FROM Shippers" />
</appSettings>
```

Add a new Web Form to our ADONET web application named ShipperData.aspx. Drag a Label and a DataGrid control from the Toolbox onto the form. The DataGrid will display the shipper data from the Northwind database and the Label will be used to display any error messages should we fail to connect. Set the ID property for the DataGrid to ShipperDataGrid, and to MessageLabel for the Label. Also clear the Text property of the Label:

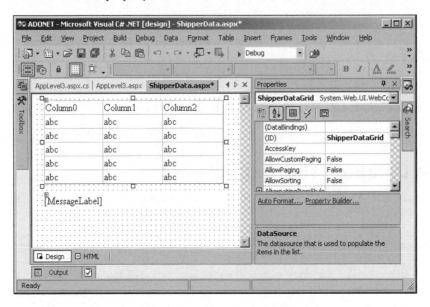

Now let's look at the code behind the page. We will impersonate a user in order to connect to SQL Server, so you'll recognize a lot of this from what we've learned so far:

```csharp
using System;
using System.Collections;
using System.ComponentModel;
using System.Data;
using System.Data.SqlClient;
using System.Drawing;
using System.Web;
using System.Web.SessionState;
using System.Web.UI;
using System.Web.UI.WebControls;
using System.Web.UI.HtmlControls;
using System.Configuration;
using Wrox.ASPNET.ADONET;

namespace Wrox.ASPNET.ADONET
{
  /// <summary>
  /// Summary description for ShipperData
  /// </summary>
  public class ShipperData : System.Web.UI.Page
  {
    // Web Controls
```

```csharp
protected System.Web.UI.WebControls.DataGrid ShipperDataGrid;
protected System.Web.UI.WebControls.Label MessageLabel;

// Private level instance variables
private SqlConnection _Connect = null;
private SqlDataAdapter _DataAdapter = null;
private SqlCommand _Command = null;
private DataSet _ShipperDataSet = null;

private void FillDataSet()
{
  try
  {
    // Get values from Web.config
    string _ConnectionString = ConfigurationSettings.AppSettings["CS2"]
                          .ToString();
    string _ShipperQuery = ConfigurationSettings.AppSettings[
                      "ShipperQuery"].ToString();

    // Instantiate the SqlConnection object
    _Connect = new SqlConnection( _ConnectionString );

    // Create the SqlCommand object
    _Command = _Connect.CreateCommand();
    _Command.CommandText = _ShipperQuery;

    // Instantiate the SqlDataAdapter object
    _DataAdapter = new SqlDataAdapter(_Command);

    // Instantiate the DataSet object
    _ShipperDataSet = new DataSet("ShipperDataSet");

    // Fill the DataSet object with data
    _DataAdapter.Fill(_ShipperDataSet, "Shippers");
  }

  catch (Exception handledException)
  {
    MessageLabel.Text = handledException.Message;
  }
}

private void Page_Load(object sender, System.EventArgs e)
{

  try
  {
    string _UserName = ConfigurationSettings.AppSettings["UserName"]
                    .ToString();
    string _Domain = ConfigurationSettings.AppSettings["Domain"]
                  .ToString();
    string _Password = ConfigurationSettings.AppSettings["Password"]
                    .ToString();
```

233

```
        ImpersonationAction _ImpersonationAction =
          new ImpersonationAction(this.FillDataSet);
        Impersonate _Impersonate = new Impersonate();
        if (! _Impersonate.DoImpersonationAction(_UserName, _Domain,
             _Password, _ImpersonationAction))
        {
          MessageLabel.Text="Impersonation Failed!";
        }
        if (_ShipperDataSet!=null)
        {
          // Set the data source to DataSet object
          ShipperDataGrid.DataSource = _ShipperDataSet;

          // Bind the DataGrid to the DataSet
          ShipperDataGrid.DataBind();
        }
      }
      catch (Exception handledException)
      {
        MessageLabel.Text=handledException.Message;
      }
    }

    [ Web Form Designer generated code ]


  }
}
```

The interesting areas above have been emboldened to highlight how we establish a connection to the database, retrieve data using the query stored in `Web.config`, and finally populate the `DataSet` with the results. To display the results, we bind the `DataGrid` to the `DataSet` object. Set `ShipperData.aspx` as the start page, and compile and run. The resulting screen should be something like this:

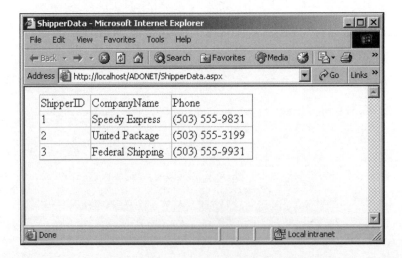

As we'd expect, data has been taken from the `Shippers` table of the Northwind database and displayed in our `DataGrid`.

Filling a DataSet with XML Content

Our data source need not be a relational database, and we can retrieve data from an XML document into a `DataSet` object as well, and then use it just as in the previous example.

There are several ways to load XML data into a `DataSet`: we can fill it from a relational database, we can build it in memory, and we can load it from an XML file, to name but a few. In the following code, we will use the `ReadXml` method to load XML data from the `shopping-cart.xml` document (introduced in Chapter 4). Add `shopping-cart.xml` to the root directory of the ADONET web application, and create a new Web Form called `ShoppingCart.aspx`.

Add a `DataGrid` and `Label` to the new form from the Toolbox, naming them **CartDataGrid** and **MessageLabel**. Clear the `Text` property of the `Label` as before, but make the `DataGrid` a little wider than it was:

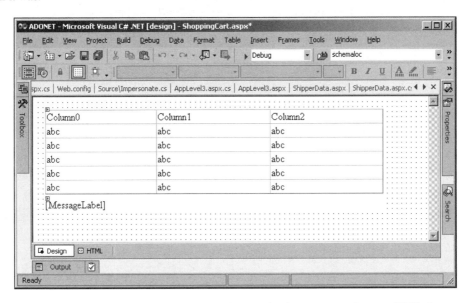

Now let's turn to the code-behind page, and see how to load a `DataSet` from an XML document:

```
using System;
using System.Collections;
using System.ComponentModel;
using System.Data;
using System.Drawing;
using System.Web;
using System.Web.SessionState;
using System.Web.UI;
using System.Web.UI.WebControls;
using System.Web.UI.HtmlControls;
```

```
namespace Wrox.ASPNET.ADONET
{
  /// <summary>
  /// Summary description for ShoppingCart
  /// </summary>
  public class ShoppingCart : System.Web.UI.Page
  {
    // Web Controls
    protected System.Web.UI.WebControls.DataGrid CartDataGrid;
    protected System.Web.UI.WebControls.Label MessageLabel;

    // Declare and initialize DataSet object
    private DataSet _CartDataSet = null;

    private void Page_Load(object sender, System.EventArgs e)
    {
      try
      {
        _CartDataSet = new DataSet("CartDataSet");
        _CartDataSet.ReadXml(Server.MapPath("/ADONET/shopping-cart.xml"),
                        XmlReadMode.InferSchema);

        // Set the DataGrid data source to DataSet object
        CartDataGrid.DataSource=_CartDataSet;

        // Set the member to <item> elements
        CartDataGrid.DataMember = "item";

        // Bind the DataGrid to the DataSet
        CartDataGrid.DataBind();

      }
      catch (Exception handledException)
      {
        MessageLabel.Text=handledException.Message;
      }
    }

    [ Web Form Designer generated code ]

  }
}
```

Within the try block, the DataSet object called _CartDataSet attempts to load the shopping-cart.xml file from the path provided. By specifying XmlReadMode.InferSchema in the call, Visual Studio will build a schema for its own internal use when dealing with the XML file based on the structure of the XML document. In production environments, it is preferable to supply an external schema, which will be used to validate the XML that we load.

Our DataSet object is more complex in form than it was in the previous example, because the shopping-cart.xml file has a hierarchical structure that must be represented in the DataSet. We need to specify exactly what part of the XML document we want the DataGrid object to bind to using the DataMember property of the DataGrid. Here we are binding to <item> elements in the document.

Now set this as the start page, and compile and run the project. We see the following results:

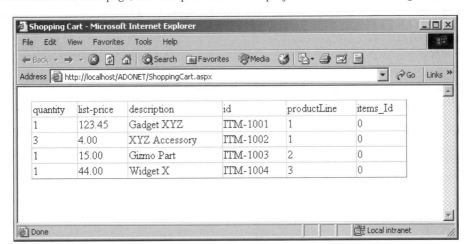

This demonstrates how simple it can be to bind XML data to a `DataGrid` in ASP.NET. We can get more control over what is displayed from the XML source by defining the schema definition for the `DataSet` prior to loading it.

Synchronizing a DataSet with XmlDataDocument

One of the exciting features of ADO.NET is the ability to use data either hierarchically or relationally according to what best meets our objectives, whether our data comes from an XML document, or SQL Server. The `DataSet` exposes our data in a relational manner, and `XmlDocument` presents it hierarchically. `XmlDataDocument`, which inherits from `XmlDocument`, can be synchronized with a `DataSet` so that both objects point to the *same* data to provide both types of access simultaneously.

Transformations using XmlDataDocument

We can exploit this `DataSet` – `XmlDataDocument` relationship to access relational data, extract its XML representation, and transform that data as we see fit. Let's try this in our `ADONET` web application, by creating a new Web Form which will query the `Employees` table in the Northwind sample database in SQL Server. The results of the query will be stored in a `DataSet` object, which we then synchronize with an `XmlDataDocument` object. After synchronization, we will perform a transformation on the data, and present the result on the Web Form.

First, let's add a new entry to `Web.config` to house the query that will be used by our Web Form:

```
<appSettings>
  <add key="CS1" value="Provider=SQLOLEDB; Data Source = (local); Initial
   Catalog = Northwind; User ID = DBUser; Password=password" />
  <add key="CS2" value="Data Source=(local); Initial Catalog=Northwind;
   Integrated Security = true" />
  <add key="UserName" value="LocalUser" />
  <add key="Domain" value="GRAYAREA" />
  <add key="Password" value="password" />
```

```
      <add key="ShipperQuery" value="SELECT * FROM Shippers" />
      <add key="EmployeeQuery" value="SELECT EmployeeID, LastName, FirstName
       FROM Employees" />
      </appSettings>
```

The EmployeeTransform.xslt Style Sheet

Add a new XSLT style sheet to our web application named `EmployeeTransform.xslt`. It will take the XML representation of our query and transform it to an HTML table. Here is what the style sheet should look like:

```xml
<?xml version="1.0" encoding="UTF-8" ?>
<xsl:stylesheet version="1.0"
 xmlns:xsl="http://www.w3.org/1999/XSL/Transform">

<xsl:output method="html" />

<xsl:template match="/" >
  <table style="border: thin solid">
  <tr>
    <th style="width:150px;background-color: #60E0C0">ID</th>
    <th style="width:150px;background-color: #60D0C0">Last Name</th>
    <th style="width:150px;background-color: #60C0C0">First Name</th>
  </tr>
    <xsl:apply-templates select="/*/Employees" />
  </table>
</xsl:template>

<xsl:template match="Employees">
  <tr>
    <td><xsl:value-of select="EmployeeID" /></td>
    <td><xsl:value-of select="LastName" /></td>
    <td><xsl:value-of select="FirstName" /></td>
  </tr>
</xsl:template>

</xsl:stylesheet>
```

Notice that we've added the `xsl` prefix to the XSLT namespace declaration on the top-level `<stylesheet>` element.

The EmployeeTransform.aspx Web Form

Add a Web Form to the ADONET web application and call it `EmployeeTransform.aspx`. Add a `Literal` control to the page from the Toolbox, and set its ID property to `TransformLiteral`. This control will be the placeholder for the transformation results.

```
<%@ Page language="c#" Codebehind="EmployeeTransform.aspx.cs"
  AutoEventWireup="false" Inherits="Wrox.ASPNET.ADONET.EmployeeTransform" %>
<!DOCTYPE HTML PUBLIC "-//W3C//DTD HTML 4.0 Transitional//EN" >
<HTML>
  <HEAD>
    <title>EmployeeTransform</title>
```

```
    <meta name="GENERATOR" Content="Microsoft Visual Studio 7.0">
    <meta name="CODE_LANGUAGE" Content="C#">
    <meta name="vs_defaultClientScript" content="JavaScript">
    <meta name="vs_targetSchema"
content="http://schemas.microsoft.com/intellisense/ie5">
  </HEAD>
  <body MS_POSITIONING="GridLayout">
    <form id="EmployeeTransform" method="post" runat="server">
      <asp:Literal id="TransformLiteral" runat="server">
      </asp:Literal>
    </form>
  </body>
</HTML>
```

In the code-behind page, we will employ many of the concepts learned so far. First, add the following five namespaces:

```
using System;
using System.Collections;
using System.ComponentModel;
using System.Data;
using System.Drawing;
using System.Web;
using System.Web.SessionState;
using System.Web.UI;
using System.Web.UI.WebControls;
using System.Web.UI.HtmlControls;
using System.Data.SqlClient;
using System.Configuration;
using System.Xml;
using System.Xml.Xsl;
using System.IO;
```

Next, set the namespace for our class:

```
namespace Wrox.ASPNET.ADONET
{
  /// <summary>
  /// Summary description for EmployeeTransform.
  /// </summary>
  public class EmployeeTransform : System.Web.UI.Page
  {
```

Our next step is to declare the class-level variables:

```
    // Maps to TransformLiteral
    protected System.Web.UI.WebControls.Literal TransformLiteral;

    // Class instance level variables
    private SqlConnection _Connect = null;
    private SqlDataAdapter _DataAdapter = null;
    private SqlCommand _Command = null;
    private DataSet _EmployeeDataSet = null;
```

The following method matches the delegate signature that will be used to provide the data connection action in a later step:

```
private void FillDataSet()
  {
    try
    {
      // Get values from Web.config
      string _ConnectionString = ConfigurationSettings.AppSettings["CS2"]
                              .ToString();
      string _EmployeeQuery = ConfigurationSettings.AppSettings[
                              "EmployeeQuery"].ToString();

      // Instantiate the SqlConnection object
      _Connect = new SqlConnection(_ConnectionString);

      // Create the SqlCommand object
      _Command = _Connect.CreateCommand();
      _Command.CommandText = _EmployeeQuery;

      // Instantiate the SqlDataAdapter object
      _DataAdapter = new SqlDataAdapter(_Command);

      // Instantiate the DataSet object
      _EmployeeDataSet = new DataSet("EmployeeDataSet");

      // Fill the DataSet object with data
      _DataAdapter.Fill(_EmployeeDataSet, "Employees");
    }
    catch (Exception handledException)
    {
      TransformLiteral.Text = handledException.Message;
    }
  }
```

The above method fills the _EmployeeDataSet DataSet property with the result of the query taken from Web.config.

We'll use the Page_Load event handler to bring all this together:

```
private void Page_Load(object sender, System.EventArgs e)
  {

    try
    {
      string _UserName = ConfigurationSettings.AppSettings["UserName"]
                        .ToString();
      string _Domain = ConfigurationSettings.AppSettings["Domain"]
                        .ToString();
      string _Password = ConfigurationSettings.AppSettings["Password"]
                        .ToString();
```

```
ImpersonationAction _ImpersonationAction =
                        new ImpersonationAction(this.FillDataSet);
Impersonate _Impersonate = new Impersonate();
if (! _Impersonate.DoImpersonationAction(_UserName, _Domain,
                            _Password, _ImpersonationAction))
{
  TransformLiteral.Text="Impersonation Failed!";
}
if (_EmployeeDataSet!=null)
{
  StringWriter x = new StringWriter();
```

This next line is where the synchronizing magic occurs:

```
XmlDataDocument _EmployeesXml =
                        new XmlDataDocument(_EmployeeDataSet);
```

Now that the _EmployeesXml object contains the same values as the _EmployeeDataSet object, we can use it as the source of our transform as seen below:

```
XslTransform _Transform = new XslTransform();
_Transform.Load(Server.MapPath("/ADONET/EmployeeTransform.xslt"));

_Transform.Transform(_EmployeesXml, null, x);

TransformLiteral.Text = x.ToString();

    }
  }
catch (Exception handledException)
{
  TransformLiteral.Text=handledException.Message;
}
  }
```

And that's all we need to add for this Web Form. Set the page as the start up, and compile and run the project. The resulting screen shows the data from the Employees table transformed into an HTML table:

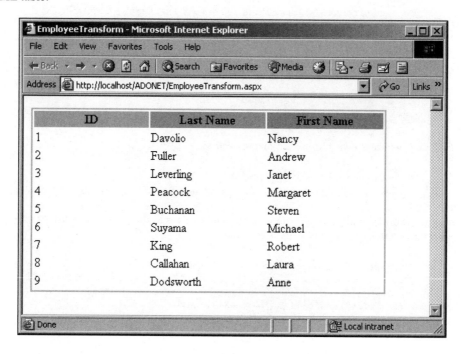

Summary

In this chapter, we've seen how ADO.NET lets us quickly get hold of data from SQL databases or XML files. Whenever we access databases from a web application, a high priority is security, whether the application is available to the wider public over the Internet, or to employees over a company intranet. We looked at storing settings in the Web.config file, as a secure central storage area which is only accessible internally to our code. We saw how we can set up our application to impersonate a given user account, by either enabling it in Web.config, or programmatically.

Once we'd covered those important issues, we explored some typical uses of a DataSet object in an ASP.NET environment, and demonstrated the ability to synchronize a DataSet with an XmlDataDocument to allow us to apply XSLT transforms to data taken from a relational source such as SQL Server.

What we haven't covered here, despite using a SQL Server database throughout the chapter, was the XML support it offers through classes associated with the SQL Server managed data provider. In the next chapter, we move on to look at some of the neat tricks that SQL's XML support enables for our applications.

7

SQL Server 2000 and SqlXml
Managed Classes

In the previous chapter, we explored the world of data access using ADO.NET. The examples generally used the .NET OLE data provider to retrieve or update data, but we had a little taste of using the SQL provider at the end. In this chapter, we will take a more detailed look at the SQL Server .NET data provider, as well as some new tools that provide even stronger support for XML when working with SQL.

We will address the following areas of interest in this chapter:

❑ Advantages of the SQL Server .NET data provider

❑ Understanding queries that return XML

❑ SqlXml 3.0 Managed Classes

    ❑ SqlXmlCommand

    ❑ SqlXmlParameter

    ❑ SqlXmlAdapter

We will explore some examples of these topics, and discuss when and why we can employ the techniques introduced to our advantage.

SQL Server .NET Data Provider

The last chapter briefly introduced the managed data providers available in the .NET Framework for accessing specific types of data sources. The `System.Data.OleDb` namespace contains classes to access OLE data. The `System.Data.SqlClient` namespace provides classes that are used to access data directly from SQL Server version 7.0 and higher. SQL Server can still be accessed through the `OleDb` classes, but connecting to SQL Server through its own managed provider provides certain advantages that we'll look at here. We'll also see how the differences of the SQL Server .NET data provider to the OLE DB .NET data provider can be beneficial in our XML-aware web applications.

Advantages of the SQL Server .NET Data Provider

Whenever we know that we will be connecting to SQL Server for our web application data, there are two overriding reasons to choose the SQL Server-specific .NET data provider.

Performance

The SQL Server .NET data provider was written to communicate directly with SQL Server version 7.0 and higher; it does not go through any other layer such as OLE DB or ODBC. It uses SQL Server's own Tabular Data Stream (TDS) protocol – thereby achieving significantly improved performance.

XML Support

In the last chapter we learned that `DataSets` are capable of exposing underlying data as XML. However, a `DataSet` may not be the best solution if we want the XML representation of the data, particularly if all we need is fast, read-only data in XML format. As we will see, the SQL Server .NET data provider has additional features for retrieving data with SQL Server 2000 XML queries.

Creating the SQL2000 Web Application

In order to examine specific features of SQL Server 2000 in ASP.NET, let's create a web application to showcase some key techniques. Open Visual Studio .NET and select **File | New | Project** to bring up the following dialog:

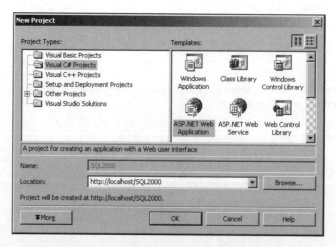

With Visual C# Projects selected, choose the ASP.NET Web Application template and name the project SQL2000 as seen in the screenshot. Press OK.

After the web application has been created, right-click the project name in Solution Explorer, and select Properties. Change the default namespace as shown below:

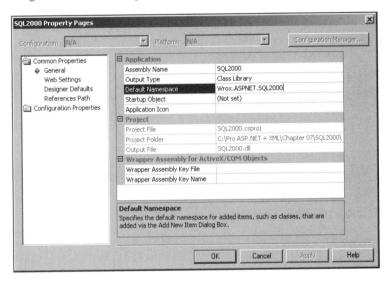

After changing the default namespace as above to conform to the recommended guidelines on naming namespaces, press OK.

Adding a Connection String to Web.config

The connection string *could* be hard-coded in our code, but this has the disadvantage of requiring recompilation should any changes be made. Also, hard-coding the connection string usually means that it is located in multiple code files in an application. For ease of maintenance, it is preferable to place the connection string in a central location accessible to the entire application. If we use Web.config for this purpose, should we change the connection string at a later date, we will not need to recompile the project, or even stop it running on the web server.

Open Web.config, and add the following XML as a child of <configuration>, which defines two connection strings that all the examples in this chapter will be able to use:

```
<appSettings>
  <add  key="SQLConnection"
    value="Data Source=(local);Initial Catalog=Northwind;
    User ID=SQLLoginAccount;Password=password"
  />
  <add  key="OLEDBConnection"
    value="Provider=SQLOLEDB;
    Data Source=(local);Initial Catalog=Northwind;
    User ID=SQLLoginAccount;Password=password"
  />
</appSettings>
```

Note the values for User ID and Password need to be changed to a SQL Server login account with access to the Northwind database on your system.

Understanding XML Queries

SQL Server 2000 allows developers to obtain the results of a SELECT statement as XML by using the FOR XML clause in the query. Once we've covered the basic usage of this clause, we'll create a page in our web application that makes use of it.

When using FOR XML, the following three modes are available:

❏   FOR XML RAW

❏   FOR XML AUTO

❏   FOR XML EXPLICIT

What primarily differentiates one mode from another is the level of control we need in the XML output.

Writing XML Queries using FOR XML

Let's look at how to write XML queries by examining the three modes mentioned above.

Using RAW Mode

When executing a query using FOR XML RAW, each row of the result is given a <row> XML element, and all non-null column values are represented by attributes of that <row> element. For example, if you execute the following SELECT statement in the SQL Server Query Analyzer:

```
SELECT [CategoryID], [CategoryName], [Description]
FROM Categories
FOR XML RAW
```

then each returned row will have the format demonstrated by this partial result:

```
<row CategoryID="1" CategoryName="Beverages" Description="Soft drinks,
 coffees, teas, beers, and ales" />
```

Note what happens if we make the following changes to our SELECT statement:

```
SELECT [CategoryID] AS [ID], [CategoryName] AS [Name], [Description]
FROM Categories
FOR XML RAW
```

We now provide aliases for the first two column names, with the result that the attributes for those columns take the new names when we run the query:

```
<row ID="1" Name="Beverages" Description="Soft drinks, coffees, teas, beers,
 and ales" />
```

Using AUTO Mode

If we use FOR XML AUTO, the resultant XML not only maps column names to attributes (as in RAW mode), but it also maps the table names to the XML element names. This is handy when we want to see the hierarchical nature of a JOIN in a SELECT statement. Consider the following SQL statement, which joins the Categories table to the Products table:

```
SELECT [Category].[CategoryID], [Category].[CategoryName],
       [Product].[ProductID], [Product].[ProductName]
FROM [Categories] AS [Category]
INNER JOIN   [Products] AS [Product]
ON [Category].[CategoryID]=[Product].[CategoryID]
FOR XML AUTO
```

The resulting XML nests the products under each category:

```
<Category CategoryID="1" CategoryName="Beverages">
  <Product ProductID="1" ProductName="Chai"/>
  <Product ProductID="2" ProductName="Chang"/>
</Category>
```

It's quite easy to have our results structured with a full XML hierarchy with the ELEMENTS clause, which returns XML devoid of attributes. Make the following change to the last line of the previous SELECT statement:

```
FOR XML AUTO, ELEMENTS
```

The result is now has this form:

```
<Category>
  <CategoryID>1</CategoryID>
  <CategoryName>Beverages</CategoryName>
  <Product>
    <ProductID>1</ProductID>
    <ProductName>Chai</ProductName>
  </Product>
  <Product>
    <ProductID>2</ProductID>
    <ProductName>Chang</ProductName>
  </Product>
</Category>
```

Notice that these XML elements contain no attributes, and that the <Product> elements are nested underneath the <Category> elements.

Using EXPLICIT Mode

When strong control of the output is required, EXPLICIT mode enables the developer to precisely define the structure of the XML in the SELECT statement, with a small tradeoff in the complexity of the query. Try this example:

```
SELECT 1 AS [Tag], NULL AS [Parent],
    [c].[CategoryID] AS [Category!1!ID],
    [c].[CategoryName] AS [Category!1!name],
    [c].[Description] AS [Category!1!!Element]
FROM [Categories] AS [c]
FOR XML EXPLICIT
```

As this shows, the FOR XML EXPLICIT clause requires more than simply adding the clause at the end, but such queries can give us invaluable control over the output. When the above SELECT statement is executed, CategoryID and CategoryName values are created as attributes, and Description is the element text:

<Category ID="1" name="Beverages">Soft drinks, coffees, teas, beers, and ales</Category>

For more information on how to write FOR XML EXPLICIT queries, consult the *SQL Server Books Online* documentation that ships with SQL Server.

Retrieving Schema Information with XMLDATA

If desired, we can request an inline schema for the resultant XML by the XMLDATA clause. This is useful if for instance we are writing SELECT statements using FOR XML EXPLICIT, and we want to define certain columns with ID, IDREF, and IDREFS for validation. The inline schema returned in SQL Server 2000, however, uses Microsoft's XML-Data Reduced (XDR) language, not the XML Schema Definition (XSD) language, which is a W3C Recommendation.

Retrieving XML in a .NET Client

Now that we have a brief background on how to write XML queries, let's see how to capture the results of such queries in a .NET client. The best approach is to use the SQL Server .NET data provider, which provides support for executing XML queries.

Executing XML Queries with ExecuteXmlReader

The SqlCommand class offers a method called ExecuteXmlReader for retrieving XML by executing SELECT statements with FOR XML clauses. The method returns an XmlReader object that we can use to navigate the resulting nodes.

To demonstrate, let's add a web form to our SQL2000 web application. Right-click the project in Solution Explorer and select Add | Add Web Form. Name the page Categories.aspx:

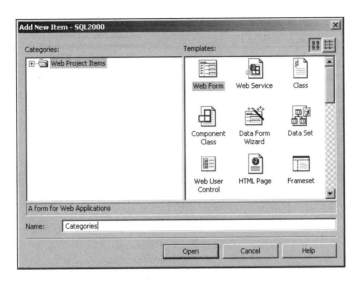

Click **Open**. When the new page appears in the VS.NET designer, drag a `DropDownList` control from the **Web Forms** tab of the Toolbox, and place it somewhere in the upper left corner. Change its ID property to **CategoriesListBox**, and its `Height` property to 150 px. We will populate this control later by running a query against the Northwind database.

Adding the XML Query to Web.config

In the `Web.config` file, insert another `<add>` element underneath `<appSettings>`, to contain the query that we will call from our code:

```
<add  key="CategoriesQuery"
  value="SELECT CategoryID, CategoryName FROM Categories FOR XML RAW"
/>
```

The Code Behind Categories.aspx

In the code behind our web form, add the lines highlighted below:

```
using System;
using System.Collections;
using System.ComponentModel;
using System.Data;
using System.Drawing;
using System.Web;
using System.Web.SessionState;
using System.Web.UI;
using System.Web.UI.WebControls;
using System.Web.UI.HtmlControls;
using System.Configuration;
using System.Xml;
using System.Data.SqlClient;
```

```
namespace Wrox.ASPNET.SQL2000
{
  /// <summary>
  /// Summary description for Categories.
  /// </summary>
  public class Categories : System.Web.UI.Page
  {
    protected System.Web.UI.WebControls.ListBox CategoriesListBox;

    private void Page_Load(object sender, System.EventArgs e)
    {
      // Get values from <appSettings> in web.config
      string ConnectionString = ConfigurationSettings.AppSettings[
                            "SQLConnection"].ToString();
      string XmlQuery = ConfigurationSettings.AppSettings[
                      "CategoriesQuery"].ToString();

      // Declare and instantiate SqlConnection object
      SqlConnection _Connection = new SqlConnection(_ConnectionString);

      // Declare and instantiate SqlCommand object
      SqlCommand _Command = new SqlCommand(_XmlQuery, _Connection);

      // Open session to SQL Server
      _Connection.Open();

      // Declare and instantiate XmlReader object
      XmlReader _XmlReader=_Command.ExecuteXmlReader();

      // Loop through XmlNodes and fill ListBox control
      while (_XmlReader.Read())
      {
        string _ID=_XmlReader.GetAttribute("CategoryID");
        string _Name=_XmlReader.GetAttribute("CategoryName");
        ListItem _ListItem = new ListItem(_Name, _ID);
        CategoriesListBox.Items.Add(_ListItem);
      }

      // Close XmlReader object
      _XmlReader.Close();

      // Close SqlConnection object
      _Connection.Close();
    }

    [ Web Form Designer generated code ]

  }
}
```

Here, we connect to SQL Server using a `SqlConnection` object. We then execute a SELECT statement with a FOR XML RAW clause using the `ExecuteXmlReader` method of the `SqlCommand` object, resulting in an `XmlReader` object, which we loop through to populate the `ListBox` control.

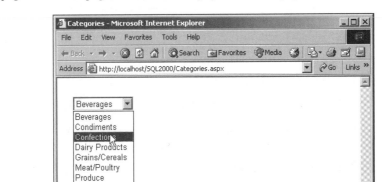

If we now view the HTML source of the page in our browser, we'll see that the dropdown contains both the category name and the ID:

```
<select name="CategoriesListBox" id="CategoriesListBox"
style="height:175px;width:100px;Z-INDEX: 101;LEFT:30px;POSITION:absolute;TOP:30px">
  <option value="1">Beverages</option>
  <option value="2">Condiments</option>
  <option value="3">Confections</option>
  <option value="4">Dairy Products</option>
  <option value="5">Grains/Cereals</option>
  <option value="6">Meat/Poultry</option>
  <option value="7">Produce</option>
  <option value="8">Seafood</option>
</select>
```

We will add more features to this web form as we progress through this chapter.

SQLXML 3.0

In February of 2002, Microsoft made SQLXML 3.0 available for download, as part of Microsoft's commitment to maintain XML support for SQL Server 2000. It provides developers even more power for bridging the gap between hierarchical and relational data. The remainder of this chapter focuses on the managed classes that ship with this version.

SQLXML 3.0 RTM is available at http://msdn.microsoft.com/sqlxml.

Benefits of SQLXML 3.0

So what does the SQLXML 3.0 release give the developer community? Below are a few of the possibilities:

❑   Querying a relational database with SQL statements and returning XML

- ❑ Querying a relational database using XPath

- ❑ Updating relational data via XML

- ❑ Applying an XSLT style sheet at query execution

- ❑ Bulk-loading of huge XML documents into SQL Server 2000

- ❑ Querying SQL Server 2000 via Internet browser

- ❑ Exploiting SQL Server 2000's XML features using .NET managed classes

Our focus in this chapter is on the new .NET classes that target the XML features of SQL Server 2000.

The SQLXML Managed Classes

All the managed classes we are interested in fall under the `Microsoft.Data.SqlXml` namespace. Once SQLXML 3.0 is installed, our next step is to set a reference to it for our Visual Studio .NET project, by following these steps:

1. Right-click References in Solution Explorer, and select Add Reference.

2. On the .NET tab, double-click Microsoft.Data.SqlXml, as in the following screenshot:

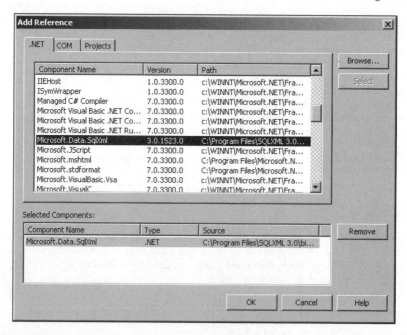

3. Click OK. The assembly is now referenced in our project, and we can use any of the classes that it contains.

Using SqlXmlCommand

The primary class in SQLXML 3.0 is `SqlXmlCommand`, which is designed to retrieve data from SQL Server 2000 in XML format. There are many options for executing the queries, such as through T-SQL, stored procedures, XPath, annotated schemas, and templates. The class also supports sending XML to SQL Server for updating data a database.

Establishing a Connection

When using the `SqlXmlCommand` class, we cannot use the SQL Server .NET data provider, and instead we need to pass in the OLEDB connection string from `Web.config` to the `SqlXmlCommand` constructor.

Choosing the Command Type

As mentioned earlier, there are many options for accessing data with `SqlXmlCommand`. The following table lists the enumerated values that can be assigned to the `CommandType` property of `SqlXmlCommand`:

CommandType	Description
DiffGram	Executes a `DiffGram` to modify data in the database.
UpdateGram	Executes an `UpdateGram` to modify data in the database.
Sql	Executes a SQL command provided in the `CommandText` property. This is the default value for this property. Example: `SELECT * FROM Customers FOR XML AUTO`
XPath	Executes an XPath expression provided in the `CommandText` property. Example: `Customer[@ID='ALFKI']`
Template	Executes an XML template specified in the `CommandStream` property.
TemplateFile	Executes an XML template from the file path specified in `CommandText` property.

Choosing an Execute Method

The `SqlXmlCommand` class supports several methods for executing a command, as described in the following table:

Method	Description
void ExecuteNonQuery()	Executes a database operation that has no return value. A typical application is when the `CommandType` property is set to either `DiffGram`, `UpdateGram`, `Template`, or `TemplateFile` (when the templates contain action statements returning no XML).

Table continued on following page

Method	Description
Stream ExecuteStream()	Returns a Stream object containing the XML response. Use this option when you want to work with the returned data as a stream of bytes.
void ExecuteToStream(Stream)	Sends the XML result of the query directly to the specified Stream object. In an ASP.NET application, the output stream can be set to the OutputStream property of the HTTP Response object.
XmlReader ExecuteXmlReader()	Returns an XmlReader object containing the XML response of the query.

Setting Other Properties

Let's now consider other key properties of the SqlXmlCommand class that we should be aware of.

BasePath

This property of type string is used to resolve relative location paths specified in the SchemaPath property, the XslPath property, or even external XML references in an XML template. As the name suggests, it is the base file path for other properties set using relative paths. If BasePath is not set, relative paths will be based on the current directory of the executing code.

ClientSideXml

Set this Boolean property to true if you wish to accomplish one or both of the following tasks:

❑ Use an existing stored procedure which is not set to return XML (with a FOR XML clause), but have the results in XML format.

❑ Move the XML conversion to the client side (which could be the middle tier). This can reduce the load on the data server.

The default is false.

CommandStream

If the CommandType is Template, Diffgram, or UpdateGram, this property can be set to contain the respective Command as a stream. Thus, if the CommandType is set to an UpdateGram, we can set the CommandStream to a stream containing the UpdateGram to execute.

CommandText

This is a string property containing the query to execute. Depending on the CommandType, this could be an ad hoc T-SQL statement, the name of a stored procedure, or an XPath expression.

RootTag

Very few XML queries result in a well-formed XML document, because results are typically a set of sibling elements, so a single document element is not present. By setting the RootTag property, we are in effect enclosing the XML fragment in a top-level element with a name of our choice.

SchemaPath

This property is set to the path of a mapping schema if one is available. An example of this property in use is provided in the `ProductsTotal.aspx` example later in the chapter.

XslPath

This property is set to the path of an XSLT style sheet. If specified, the transformation is processed on the resultset at the time of query execution.

Hopefully, we are now fairly familiar with the syntax of the `SqlXmlCommand` class, so let's see it in action!

The DisplayEmployees.aspx Web Form

Add a new Web Form to our SQL2000 web application, and name it `DisplayEmployees.aspx`. Using HTML view, remove all markup so that *only* the Page directive remains:

```
<%@ Page language="c#" Codebehind="DisplayEmployees.aspx.cs"
  AutoEventWireup="false" Inherits="Wrox.ASPNET.SQL2000.DisplayEmployees" %>
```

In the previous chapter, we used an XSLT style sheet named `EmployeeTransform.xslt` in one of our examples, and will come in useful in this project too. Add it as an existing item, placing it in the project folder.

In the code file, `DisplayEmployees.aspx.cs`, add the code highlighted below:

```
using System.Collections;
using System.ComponentModel;
using System.Data;
using System.Drawing;
using System.Web;
using System.Web.SessionState;
using System.Web.UI;
using System.Web.UI.WebControls;
using System.Web.UI.HtmlControls;
using System.Configuration;
using Microsoft.Data.SqlXml;

namespace Wrox.ASPNET.SQL2000
{
  /// <summary>
  /// Summary description for DisplayEmployees.
  /// </summary>
  public class DisplayEmployees : System.Web.UI.Page
  {
    private void Page_Load(object sender, System.EventArgs e)
    {
      // Get connection string from Web.config
      string _ConnectionString = ConfigurationSettings.AppSettings[
                              "OLEDBConnection"].ToString();

      // Declare and instantiate SqlXmlCommand object
      SqlXmlCommand _Command = new SqlXmlCommand(_ConnectionString);
```

```
    // Set SqlXmlCommand properties
    _Command.BasePath = Server.MapPath("/SQL2000/");
    _Command.XslPath = "EmployeeTransform.xslt";
    _Command.RootTag = "Root";
    _Command.CommandText = "SELECT EmployeeID, LastName, FirstName FROM "
                         + "Employees FOR XML AUTO, ELEMENTS";

    // Generate HTML output
    Response.Write("<html>");
    Response.Write("<head>");
    Response.Write("<title>Northwind Employees</title>");
    Response.Write("</head>");
    Response.Write("<body>");

    // Execute query and send result to Response stream
    _Command.ExecuteToStream( Response.OutputStream );

    // Finish HTML output
    Response.Write("</body>");
    Response.Write("</html>");
}

[ Web Form Designer generated code ]
    }
}
```

In this code, we create a `SqlXmlCommand` object and set it to use a `SELECT` statement with a `FOR XML` `AUTO, ELEMENTS` clause. We also indicate that the XML is to be transformed, by specifying `EmployeeTable.xslt` in the `XslPath` property. Finally, we execute the command, placing the *transformed* results directly into `Response.OutputStream`.

Set the new page as start up, and hit *F5*. The result is an HTML table containing values from the `Employees` table of the Northwind database:

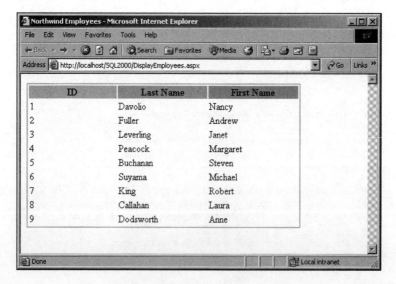

A particularly interesting point here is that we did not need to declare any XML objects (such as XmlDocument) in our code. We are able to perform the transformation without using the XslTransform class thanks to the SqlXmlCommand object.

Using SqlXmlParameter

In many cases, we are interested in dynamic resultsets based on parameters in the query. The SqlXmlParameter class is for providing parameter information for queries, be they T-SQL statements, stored procedures, XPath expressions, or templates.

SqlXmlParameter Properties

The SqlXmlParameter class is easy to learn. It only has two properties as shown below:

- ❑ **Name** – This property is only used when dealing with XPath or template queries. The name must begin with the @ character. For other query types, this property does not need to be set.
- ❑ **Value** – This is the value of the parameter passed in.

Creating SqlXmlParameter Objects

We do not instantiate SqlXmlParameter objects directly. Rather we obtain a reference to an instance of the object generated by the CreateParameter method of the SqlXmlCommand class.

The next sample demonstrates how to use SqlXmlParameter when calling a stored procedure.

The ProductTotals.aspx Web Form

Add a new Web Form to our SQL2000 web application named ProductTotals.aspx. Drag a Label, a Button, a DropDownList, and a Panel from the Toolbox onto the page. Name them CustomerLabel, ViewProductTotalsButton, CustomerDropDownList, and ResultPanel respectively, and set the Text property for the Label to Customer, to View Product Totals for the Button, and clear this property for the panel (by placing the cursor in the panel and deleting). Size and position the controls as shown below:

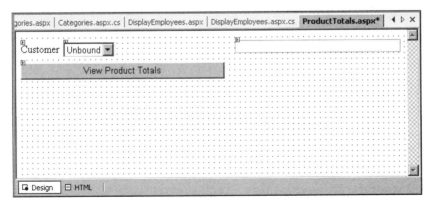

Querying SQL Server using Annotated Schemas

To explore how to query SQL Server using an annotated schema, add a new schema by opening the **Add New Item** dialog, and choosing XML Schema in the **Templates** pane. Give it the name `AnnotatedSchema.xsd`, and enter the following for that file:

```
<?xml version="1.0" encoding="utf-8" ?>
<xs:schema id="AnnotatedSchema" elementFormDefault="qualified"
 xmlns:xs="http://www.w3.org/2001/XMLSchema"
 xmlns:sqlxml="urn:schemas-microsoft-com:mapping-schema">
  <xs:element name="Customer" sqlxml:relation="Customers">
    <xs:complexType>
      <xs:sequence>
        <xs:element name="CompanyName" type="xs:string" />
      </xs:sequence>
      <xs:attribute name="CustomerID" type="xs:string" />
    </xs:complexType>
  </xs:element>
</xs:schema>
```

The above schema is a mapping schema that we will use to query the `Customers` table in SQL Server. It is a an XSD schema, with an annotation on the following element:

```
<xs:element name="Customer" sqlxml:relation="Customers">
```

The relation annotation maps the resulting `<Customer>` element to the `Customers` table. The other nodes defined in the schema will map by default to the column names they bear.

Creating the ProductTotalsTable.xslt Style Sheet

We will create a new XSLT style sheet for our project that sorts the products a customer has ordered in descending order by product total. Call it `ProductTotalsTable.xslt`, and add the following code:

```
<?xml version="1.0" encoding="UTF-8" ?>
<xsl:stylesheet version="1.0"
 xmlns:xsl="http://www.w3.org/1999/XSL/Transform">

<xsl:output method="html" />

<xsl:template match="/" >
  <table style="border: thin solid">
    <tr>
      <th style="width:100px;background-color: #DDDDDD">Product</th>
      <th style="width:100px;background-color: #DDDDDD">Total Quantity</th>
    </tr>
    <xsl:apply-templates select="/*/row">
      <xsl:sort  select="@Total" data-type="number" order="descending" />
    </xsl:apply-templates>
  </table>
</xsl:template>
```

```
<xsl:template match="row">
  <tr>
    <td><xsl:value-of select="@ProductName" /></td>
    <td><xsl:value-of select="@Total" /></td>
  </tr>
</xsl:template>

</xsl:stylesheet>
```

We will use the above style sheet in our code to handle button click events.

Loading the CustomerDropDownList Control

In the code behind the `ProductTotals.aspx` page, add the highlighted code below:

```
using System;
using System.Collections;
using System.ComponentModel;
using System.Data;
using System.Drawing;
using System.Web;
using System.Web.SessionState;
using System.Web.UI;
using System.Web.UI.WebControls;
using System.Web.UI.HtmlControls;
using System.IO;
using System.Configuration;
using System.Xml;
using Microsoft.Data.SqlXml;

namespace Wrox.ASPNET.SQL2000
{
  /// <summary>
  /// Summary description for SalesByCategory.
  /// </summary>
  public class ProductTotals : System.Web.UI.Page
  {
    protected System.Web.UI.WebControls.Button ViewProductTotalsButton;
    protected System.Web.UI.WebControls.DropDownList CustomerDropDownList;
    protected System.Web.UI.WebControls.Label CustomerLabel;
    protected System.Web.UI.WebControls.Panel ResultPanel;

    private string _ConnectionString = null;
    private string _BasePath = null;


    private void Page_Load(object sender, System.EventArgs e)
    {
      _ConnectionString = ConfigurationSettings.AppSettings[
                      "OLEDBConnection"];
      _BasePath = Server.MapPath("/SQL2000/");
```

```
    if (!IsPostBack)
    {
      // Declare and instantiate SqlXmlCommand
      SqlXmlCommand _Command = new SqlXmlCommand(_ConnectionString);

      // Set SqlXmlCommand object properties
      _Command.RootTag = "Customers";
      _Command.BasePath = _BasePath;
      _Command.SchemaPath = "AnnotatedSchema.xsd";
      _Command.CommandType = SqlXmlCommandType.XPath;
      _Command.CommandText = "Customer";

      XmlReader _XmlReader = _Command.ExecuteXmlReader();

      while (_XmlReader.Read())
      {
        if (_XmlReader.Name=="Customer")
        {
          string _CustomerID =
          _XmlReader.GetAttribute("CustomerID");

          CustomerDropDownList.Items.Add(new ListItem(XmlReader
                          .ReadElementString(), CustomerID));
        }
      }

      // Close the XmlReader object
      _XmlReader.Close();
    }
}
```

The `Page_Load` code above uses an XPath expression to query the schema specified, and populates the `CustomerDropDownList` control with customer names and values, ready for selection on our Web Form.

The next step then is to display this list of products in descending order of quantity purchased when the user clicks the `ViewProductTotalsButton` button:

```
private void ViewProductTotalsButton_Click(object sender,
                                           System.EventArgs e)
{
  // Declare and instantiate SqlXmlCommand object
  SqlXmlCommand _Command = new SqlXmlCommand(_ConnectionString);

  // Set SqlXmlCommand properties
  _Command.BasePath = Server.MapPath("/SQL2000/");
  _Command.XslPath = "ProductTotalsTable.xslt";
  _Command.RootTag = "Products";
```

In the next section of code, we set the `ClientSideXml` property to `true`, moving the process of converting the relational data into XML onto the client. This allows us to call a stored procedure which was *not* designed to return an XML response. Rather, we execute the stored procedure, and add the FOR XML RAW clause to indicate the result should be in XML:

```
_Command.ClientSideXml = true;

// Create parameratized call to stored procedure
_Command.CommandText = "EXEC CustOrderHist ? FOR XML RAW";
```

The `CustOrderHist` stored procedure (which already forms part of the `Northwind` sample database) accepts one parameter for input. We set a placeholder for the parameter by using the '?' character after the stored procedure name. The following lines provide a value for this parameter through a `SqlXmlParameter` object:

```
// Create parameter for CustomerID
SqlXmlParameter _CustomerID = Command.CreateParameter();
_CustomerID.Value=CustomerDropDownList.SelectedItem.Value;
```

Once we've set a value for the parameter, we are ready to execute the command. In this situation, we opted for the `ExecuteStream` method, which we will place in a `StreamReader` object for processing:

```
// Create StreamReader object to hold data
StreamReader _StreamReader = new StreamReader(
                            _Command.ExecuteStream());

// Place results in Panel object
ResultPanel.Controls.Add(new LiteralControl(
                        _StreamReader.ReadToEnd()));

    }

  }
}
```

Displaying the ProductTotals.aspx Web Form

Set the new page as a start up, and hit *F5*. When the screen appears, choose a customer from the dropdown, and click the button:

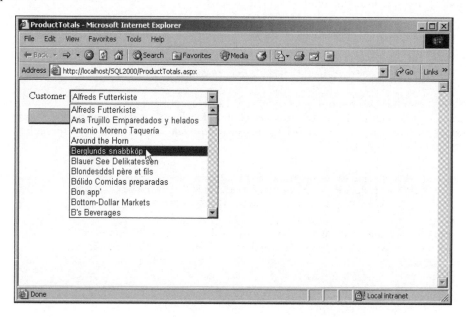

This produces a list of products sorted in descending order based on total units purchased:

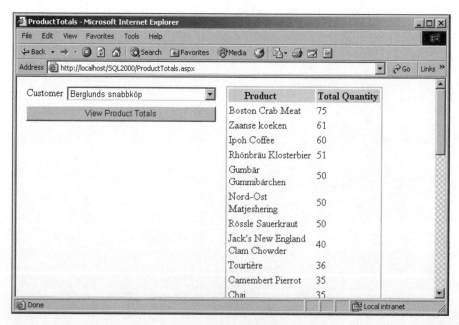

Using SqlXmlAdapter

We have been demonstrating various ways up to this point for the retrieval and display of data. In most real world applications, we also wish to update our SQL Server 2000 databases based on user input, and this is a task that we can achieve quite simply thanks to the `SqlXmlAdapter` class.

SqlXmlAdapter Methods

The two key methods of the `SqlXmlAdapter` class are:

❑ **Fill** – Used to initially fill a provided `DataSet` object.

❑ **Update** – Used to update data in SQL Server.

Much like the `DataAdapter` object seen in the other data providers, the `SqlXmlAdapter` can fill a `DataSet` object with data. It is tailored for interacting with SQL databases using XML, and its `Update` method synchronizes any changes with the underlying data source.

Summary

In this chapter, we had an opportunity to look at the exciting XML features of SQL Server 2000, and how we can interact with them using the new managed classes that ship with SQLXML 3.0. We learned that we can optimize our access to SQL Server 2000 by using the SQL Server .NET data provider classes of the `System.Data.SqlClient` namespace. We also saw how this provider can assist in the retrieval of XML data from SQL Server 2000.

We moved on to explore some of the possibilities for using two of the most important of the new .NET classes that come with the SQLXML 3.0 package, namely:

❑ `SqlXmlCommand`

❑ `SqlXmlParameter`

We also had a quick look at `SqlXmlAdapter`, which can be used for making changes to a database using XML. These three classes allow us to author .NET code that takes advantage of the XML features provided by SQLXML 3.0, and provide a useful starting point for any ASP.NET applications that mix XML functionality with relational data.

8

E-Business and XML

Exchanging data electronically is nothing new. Electronic Data Interchange (EDI) has been around for over 20 years and has enabled many organizations to greatly streamline their processes and thus reduce costs. Due to the complexity and substantial implementation costs involved however, the take-up of EDI has been restricted to large organizations where the sheer volume of transactions justifies the expenditure.

In conjunction with the recent success of the Internet, XML, as a universal data format, has changed all that. It is now a straightforward matter for even the smallest of enterprises to make their data available for sharing, with almost every new application having some sort of support for XML.

Of course, it's not just a matter of having your data formatted in XML, you still have to move it about, and the recent explosion in XML Web Services represents a suitably platform-independent mechanism for this.

In this chapter, we will take a closer look at the open standards on which the XML Web Services programming model is built, namely SOAP, WSDL, and UDDI. (We'll define and explain these acronyms below.) This is not intended to be a tutorial on how to build XML Web Services, as that is a book in itself – well, several actually, such as Wrox Press's *Professional ASP.NET Web Services* (ISBN 1-86100-545-8) and *Professional C# Web Services* (ISBN 1-86100-439-7).

We will also take a look at the Global XML Web Services Architecture and see how Microsoft, with IBM and VeriSign, are extending the XML Web Services specifications to make it more flexible, reliable, and secure, through the new specifications of WS-Routing, WS-Referral, WS-Inspection, WS-Security, and WS-License.

Finally, we will take a short tour of ebXML, the open global e-business framework sponsored by the UN and OASIS, that builds on EDI to provide an extensive and integrated approach to electronic business transactions and which, according to some analysts, is destined to become the dominant e-business standard.

Transacting with XML Web Services

Fundamentally, XML Web Services are centered on the sending and receiving of XML-based messages. Sure, they expose programming logic, they do provide distributed computing capabilities, and yes they can help integrate disparate legacy systems, but outwardly, a Web Service does little more than receive and/or send out XML documents.

This all sounds rather simple and you might be wondering just why we need to complicate matters with the alphabet soup that is SOAP, WSDL, and UDDI? Let's consider an example to see just what is involved in a business transaction.

Suppose that you are applying for a loan for a new car and the finance company wishes to run a credit check on you. With a suitable Web Service, they can send your name and other salient details over the wire to a credit check company that carries out the check and returns your rating in a matter of seconds. This is good for the credit check company because they can dramatically reduce the number of call-center staff. It's also good for the finance company because they have reduced their own telephone, faxing, and staffing bills and now they can offer loan applications and instant approvals via their web-site; and it's good for the customer because they get to know pretty much instantly if they've got the loan.

So, to perform the credit check via Web Service, the finance company needs to know:

- That the credit check company's Web Service exists in the first place.

- The details for invoking the Web Service – what transport protocol to use (HTTP, HTTPS, FTP, SMTP) and the address where the Web Service lives. Most often, transactions take place using HTTP or HTTPS to send the request and receive the response, and so this address would be in the form of a URL.

- The information the service needs to process the request, such as the name and social security number of their prospective client, and how this information is formatted (we do know that it will be an XML document).

- Any additional information to send and where to put it in the request. For instance, the credit check application may also require additional information to verify that the originator of any request is authorized to use the facility.

- The information the response will contain and how it is formatted.

- How errors are reported, so that any problems encountered in the transaction can be handled appropriately.

Transactions such as the one described here, while simple in terms of basic requirements, do in fact carry a hefty infrastructure requirement. Were the two parties that wished to exchange data to build this infrastructure from scratch, then they would be facing the same problems that have held back EDI.

Enter the Baseline Specifications of **SOAP**, **WSDL**, and **UDDI**. Together, they provide a framework for transacting online that is platform-neutral, software-neutral, and vendor-neutral, so it doesn't matter that the finance company is Windows-based and the credit check company runs Unix. These standards define message formats including the format of any data passed between sender and receiver, fault reporting procedures, and a method for finding organizations and the services they provide. Together they form the foundation for XML Web Services and an understanding of each specification will greatly aid your Web Services development.

So, let's take a closer look at each of the specifications.

SOAP – The Backbone of Electronic Messaging

SOAP is a protocol for the exchange of XML messages using common transport protocols such as SMTP, FTP, and most notably HTTP. The latest version of SOAP is 1.2, which at the time of writing is a Working Draft and can be viewed at http://www.w3c.org/2002/ws. If you look at that URL closely, you'll see that the W3C has now placed SOAP specification development under the Web Services Activity. This is a good indication of how SOAP is inextricably linked with XML Web Services.

The .NET Framework is SOAP 1.1 compliant and so we will concentrate on this version. However, you will find a list of the differences between 1.1 and 1.2 at the end of this chapter and I will point out the significant changes as we move through our discussion of SOAP.

Basic SOAP communication is essentially one-way, but as the SOAP specification points out, applications are expected to, and of course do, combine these one-way communications to provide request-response and more elaborate conversational communication mechanisms. SOAP also distinguishes between remote procedure call (RPC) messages and document-style messages.

Remote Procedure Call (RPC) Messages

RPC is the most prevalent message type, as it has been designed to mimic the model of object methods and parameters, and so is readily understood by developers. In RPC, the method name, its parameters, and their values are serialized into an XML document and sent down the line to the remote procedure. It de-serializes the message, executes the method, serializes the result, and sends it back to the client. In .NET, with its use of proxy clients that actually handle all the SOAP message building, invoking a remote procedure is virtually identical to calling a method on a local object.

The serialization and de-serialization of the method and its parameters is performed according to SOAP encoding rules (often simply referred to as Section 5) described in Section 5 of the SOAP specification. The theory goes that as the encoding rules are standard, then every standards-compliant SOAP client will serialize and de-serialize any RPC message with exactly the same result enabling any client, be it UNIX, Linux, AS/400 or mainframe to invoke, for example, a .NET-based Web Service.

Document-style Messages

In an RPC call we cared little about the actual message, as it was just an XML representation of our object method call. With document-style messages we are not invoking any remote procedures but simply sending an XML document, the format of which we are totally responsible for, to a remote location where it will be processed and we may receive an XML message in response.

The encoding style in document-style messages is said to be literal: in effect, there is none, messages are passed as is to the remote location. This style of messaging is most suited to situations where we are dealing with the movement of documents, such as being able to place a purchase order directly with a supplier.

SOAP Messaging Exchange Model

The SOAP specification extends the one-way communication model by introducing the concept of a message path. The path starts at the initial sender and ends at the ultimate receiver; it may include none or any number of Intermediaries (which are by implication also receivers and senders). The simplest, and most common, message path contains only one sender and one receiver. Each stop on the path is known as a SOAP Node and it must process the message.

The SOAP Message

A SOAP message follows a hierarchical structure, as appropriate for encoding as XML. Look at the diagram below of a typical SOAP Message:

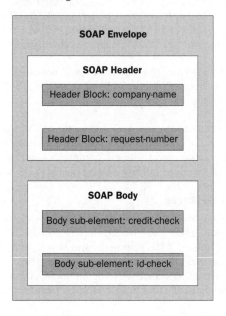

The Envelope

The outermost element of a SOAP message is the SOAP Envelope, and is the top-level XML SOAP element. As the name implies, it represents the message container and is mandatory. It always carries the namespace attribute defining the version of SOAP being used. The Envelope element may contain a single Header element (in which case it must be the first child) and must contain a single Body element.

The Header

The <Header> element is optional and consists of one or more header blocks. The header blocks are designed to extend SOAP's functionality by containing information that is not part of a document or function call, but may be required for the additional processing of a message. For example, in our credit check example, the header may contain the name and user ID of the finance company, so that the credit check company can log the checks made by each of its clients.

Header Block Attributes

Header blocks can have the attributes actor or mustUnderstand. The actor attribute determines which SOAP node is to process the header block information and allows header block information to be targeted at different nodes.

The `actor` attribute takes a URI as its value. There are four possibilities, as indicated below:

URI of `actor` Attribute	Description
`http://www.w3.org/2001/09/soap-envelope/actor/next`	This special URI indicates that the header must be processed only by the very first receiver node
specific URI, for example: `http://acmecredit.com/actor/accountMgr`	Must only be processed by node acting in this role
blank	Must only be processed by node assuming role of ultimate receiver

The `mustUnderstand` attribute is a simple switch (0 is false, 1 is true) to specify whether the node processing the header block must recognize it and is able to process it. If this attribute is 1, and any node doesn't recognize it's meaning, then that node must raise a SOAP `MustUnderstand` fault (see following section) and return processing immediately to the initial SOAP sender.

The Body

The body part of the message is known as the payload and is mandatory. It carries either a document or the RPC call information and is constructed in the same way as the header, consisting of one or more body blocks.

SOAP Faults

Fault blocks are the only predefined SOAP body block and, as their name suggests, are designed to pass back error messages to the initial SOAP sender. Only one fault block can appear in a SOAP body and it must contain a `<faultcode>` (see list below) and a `<faultstring>` – a descriptive error message – as child elements. It can optionally include the elements `<faultactor>`, to identify the node that raised the fault, and `<detail>`, a general-purpose element to contain application specific data. The `<detail>` element may only be present if the fault occurred during the processing of the body and therefore an application can determine whether the fault relates to the header or body by checking for the existence of the `<detail>` element.

Fault Code Values

The `<faultcode>` element must contain one of the following values:

Value	Meaning
`VersionMismatch`	The namespace on the envelope is invalid. This could occur if the SOAP node is expecting a 1.1 namespace and the envelope has a namespace that is not `http://www.w3.org/2001/09/soap-envelope`.
`MustUnderstand`	A SOAP header block had the `mustUnderstand` attribute set to `true`, but could not be processed by a SOAP Node.

Value	Meaning
`Client` (Sender in SOAP 1.2)	The message was incorrectly formed (not valid XML), or it did not contain the appropriate information. This indicates a problem with the initial SOAP sender and will most likely require an application change.
`Server` (Receiver in SOAP 1.2)	The message could not be processed even though it is properly formed and contains all the appropriate information. This may indicate a problem such as an intermediary SOAP node that is not responding.

Using SOAP for RPC

SOAP has been designed to cater for both document-style message exchange, where the SOAP sender and the SOAP receiver exchange XML documents, and RPC, where we are participating in a more familiar function-call scenario.

There do not appear to be any hard and fast rules as to when to use document style and when to use RPC and it will pretty much be up to you as to which you wish to implement. However, the RPC style is most like the programming models we are used to and so we will discuss RPC a little further.

First, let's look at an example:

```xml
<?xml version='1.0' ?>
<env:Envelope xmlns:env="http://schemas.xmlsoap.org/soap/envelope/">
  <env:Header>
    <auth:authentication xmlns:auth="http://www.creditcheck.com/auth">
      <userid>1234567890</userid>
    </auth:authentication>
  </env:Header>
  <env:Body>
    <m:checkIndividual
        env:encodingStyle="http://www.w3.org/2001/12/soap-encoding"
                xmlns:m="http://www.creditcheck.com/checkIndividual" >
      <firstName>John</firstName>
      <lastName>Smith</lastName>
      <ssn>123-456-789-012</ssn>
    </m:checkIndividual>
  </env:Body>
</env:Envelope>
```

This is what a SOAP message invoking the credit check service that we mentioned earlier could look like. We translate the interface into XML: the method name is `checkIndividual` and three parameters provide name and social security number details. We also need to pass a `userid` to enable the service to perform basic authentication but because this is not part of the function call, this information is coded in a header block.

The service returns `checkResult`, a flag indicating whether the check was OK or not. The service also returns `requestID` in a header block, so that requests can be logged and tracked by the finance company.

The response from the credit check service would be something like this:

```
<?xml version='1.0' ?>
<env:Envelope xmlns:env=" http://schemas.xmlsoap.org/soap/envelope">
  <env:Header>
    <req:requestID xmlns:req="http://www.creditcheck.com/requestID">
      1234-39090-0
    </req:requestID>
  </env:Header>
  <env:Body>
    <m:checkIndividualResponse
        env:encodingStyle="http://www.w3.org/2001/12/soap-encoding"
                xmlns:m="http://www.creditcheck.com/checkIndividual" >
      <checkResult>1</checkResult>
    </m:checkIndividualResponse>
  </env:Body>
</env:Envelope>
```

As you can see, in the body block, the literal `Response` has been added to the method name.

Using SOAP over HTTP

HTTP is the dominant transport protocol for SOAP messages simply because it is so prevalent with virtually every organization and application being able to make use of HTTP, especially as port 80 is often the only port left open on a firewall. The request and response pattern of HTTP POST makes it ideally suited for RPC calls.

The URI in the HTTP request identifies the location of the service. SOAP makes no requirements on the syntax of the URI other than it must be a valid URI. The HTTP `Content-Type` header must be set to `text/xml` (or `application/soap` for SOAP 1.2).

Here is an example of an HTTP POST for the check credit service:

```
POST /Charging HTTP/1.1
Host: www.checkCredit.com
Content-Type: application/soap; charset="utf-8"
Content-Length: 1234
<?xml version='1.0' ?>
<env:Envelope xmlns:env=" http://schemas.xmlsoap.org/soap/envelope ">
  <env:Header>
    .
    .
    .
  </env:Header>
  <env:Body>
    <m:checkIndividual>
      .
      .
      .
    </m:checkIndividual>
  </env:Body>
</env:Envelope>
```

Using SOAP over E-Mail

As previously mentioned, SOAP is not tied exclusively to HTTP but is designed to work with any transport protocol. One obvious alternative to HTTP is the mail protocol SMTP. Sending our credit check request over SMTP may look something like this (although SOAP does not actually specify any bindings, that is what needs to appear in an e-mail header and body, for SMTP):

```
From: online.application@theloancompany.com
To: creditcheck@checkcredit.com
Subject: Individual Credit Check
Date: Fri, 1 Dec 2002 10:30:00 GMT
Message-Id: <JHELJLBBOJDGMPNDPFINIEIBCAAA@theloancompany.com>
<?xml version='1.0' ?>
<env:Envelope xmlns:env=" http://schemas.xmlsoap.org/soap/envelope">
  <env:Header>
    .
    .
    .
  </env:Header>
  <env:Body>
    <m:checkIndividual>
      .
      .
      .
    </m:checkIndividual>
  </env:Body>
</env:Envelope>
```

SOAP Security

There are going to be times when the data we are exchanging is sensitive and needs some level of protection. As a messaging format, the SOAP specification deliberately avoids issues related to security, and leaves those details entirely in our hands.

The general approach to securing SOAP data exchange has been to secure the transmission, rather than the message itself, which usually means utilizing a combination of certificates, SSL, and Basic Authentication. As most of your SOAP messages will pass over HTTP, this is far from disastrous and uses technologies that we are all familiar with. Therefore, the only real disadvantage, apart from the increased time in processing an HTTPS request, is that the technique has to be replicated for each sender/receiver node pairing. How big a problem this presents will depend on how you set up your service.

For the purists among you, though, there is a shimmering light on the horizon. In fact, there are two shimmering lights: **XML Signature** and **XML Encryption**. These specifications are currently only in Working Draft, so I won't spend too much time on them, other to say that they provide a standard way to digitally sign and encrypt XML messages. This allows the receiver to authenticate the sender of the message, to ensure that the message has not been tampered with during transport, and to encrypt the response message for the entire message path.

Encoding, Serialization, and Proxies

Firstly, let's get some definitions out of the way:

❑   **Serialization** is the translation of an object to, in this case, an XML representation.

❑   **Encoding** is the set of rules for performing the serialization.

❑ **Proxies** are classes that reside on the client that mimic the properties and methods of a class on a remote machine

Your use of encoding, serialization, and proxies will vary depending on the type of SOAP message you are sending. In a document-style message it is likely, although not definite, that you won't make use of them at all. As you are simply sending an XML document to a service, the chances are that no serialization will be required: the encoding is said to be **literal** and the service will treat the message simply as an XML document.

An RPC message is very different. In ASP.NET, we use a proxy on the client to mirror the methods of the service, thus by calling a method on our local proxy we in fact invoke the remote method on the service. To invoke the method on the service, the proxy converts the method and its parameters to XML (in this case a SOAP message) and sends the message to the Service.

For example, in our proxy, the credit check service method would be invoked as:

```
CheckIndividual(string firstName, string lastName, string ssn) As String
```

When serialized into a SOAP RPC call, it would look like this:

```
<env:Body>
  <m:CheckIndividual
    env:encodingStyle="http://www.w3.org/2001/12/soap-encoding"
            xmlns:m="http://www.creditcheck.com/checkIndividual" >
    <firstName>John</firstName>
    <lastName>Smith</lastName>
    <ssn>123-456-789-012</ssn>
  </m:CheckIndividual>
</env:Body>
```

The Web Service follows the reverse procedure, receiving the SOAP message, de-serializing the XML, and making the appropriate call. The results are packaged up and sent as the SOAP response in a similar fashion.

Encoding defines a set of rules for Serialization and so long as the same rules are used to serialize and de-serialize, then not only can we make these remote calls but the platform on which the client and the service resides is largely irrelevant. In this case, as in most cases, we are using SOAP-encoding as defined by the URI in the encodingStyle attribute.

In order to correctly serialize the parameters for RPC calls, we are going to have to specify the data type. SOAP-encoding includes all the primitive and simple types defined in the XML Schemas definition (for more on schemas see http://www.w3.org/XML/Schema) as well as multiple references and compound types.

Multiple References

When the same piece of information appears more than once, references allow the information to be coded once but referenced multiple times by using an id attribute. For example, Wrox Books are often multi-authored so a snippet of an XML document listing some books could look like this:

```
<e:Books xmlns:e="http://www.wrox.com/books">
  <e:Book xmlns:e="http://www.wrox.com/books" >
    <title>Professional SOAP</title>
```

275

```
      <author href="#a1"/>
      <author href="#a2"/>
      <author href="#a3"/>
   </e:Book>
   <e:Book xmlns:e="http://www.wrox.com/books" >
     <title>Professional XML</title>
     <author href="#a1"/>
   </e:Book>
   <e:Book xmlns:e="http://www.wrox.com/books" >
     <title>Professional XML Web Services</title>
     <author href="#a2"/>
     <author href="#a3"/>
   </e:Book>
   <e:Person xmlns:e="http://www.wrox.com/books" id="a1" >
     <name>Author One</name>
     <email>a1@wrox.com</email>
   </e:Person>
   <e:Person xmlns:e="http://www.wrox.com/books" id="a2" >
     <name>Author Two</name>
     <email>a2@wrox.com</email>
   </e:Person>
   <e:Person xmlns:e="http://www.wrox.com/books" id="a3" >
     <name>Author Three</name>
     <email>a3@wrox.com</email>
   </e:Person>
 </e:Books>
```

The `href` attribute can also point to an external reference by providing a URL.

Multiple references can dramatically reduce the size of a message that may be desirable if performance considerations are paramount.

SOAP's Compound Types

SOAP encoding has two compound types: `struct` and `array`. The SOAP specification defines these types as follows:

Type Name	SOAP Specification
struct	A `struct` is a compound value in which the accessor name is the only distinction between member values, and no accessor has the same name as any other.
array	An `array` is a compound value in which ordinal position serves as the only distinction among member values.

Arrays

Arrays appear as an ordered sequence of elements that usually have a name that indicates their data type, although this is not necessary. The type of the elements is determined by the `enc:arrayType` attribute on the accessor, an `xsi:type` attribute on the actual element, or by the element name. As a result it is perfectly legitimate to have arrays where the members are of different types. Here the `arrayType` is set to `anyType` to allow for multiple data types for the members of the array:

```
<enc:Array xmlns:enc="http://www.w3.org/2001/12/soap-encoding"
           xmlns:xs="http://www.w3.org/2001/XMLSchema"
           xmlns:xsi="http://www.w3.org/2001/XMLSchema-instance"
        enc:arrayType="xs:anyType[3]">
  <thing xsi:type="xs:string">Chris</thing>
  <thing xsi:type="xs:date">9/15/1968</thing>
  <thing xsi:type="xs:anyURI">http://www.wrox.com/authors/chrisk/</thing>
</enc:Array>
```

Or without the XML Schema namespace:

```
<enc:Array xmlns:xs="http://www.w3.org/2001/XMLSchema"
           xmlns:enc="http://www.w3.org/2001/12/soap-encoding"
        enc:arrayType="xs:anyType[3]" >
  <enc:string>Chris</enc:string>
  <enc:date>9/15/1968</enc:date>
  <enc:anyURI>http://www.wrox.com/authors/chrisk/</enc:anyURI>
</enc:Array>
```

The enc:arrayType attribute defines the type of the elements as well as the dimension of the array.

An array can be an array of structs, for example:

```
<enc:Array xmlns:enc="http://www.w3.org/2001/12/soap-encoding"
           xmlns:xyz="http://example.org/2001/06/Orders"
        enc:arrayType="xyz:Order[2]">
  <Order>
    <Product>Apple</Product>
    <Price>1.56</Price>
  </Order>
  <Order>
    <Product>Peach</Product>
    <Price>1.48</Price>
  </Order>
</enc:Array>
```

It can also be a multi-dimensional array:

```
<enc:Array xmlns:xs="http://www.w3.org/2001/XMLSchema"
           xmlns:enc="http://www.w3.org/2001/12/soap-encoding"
        enc:arrayType="xs:string[2,3]" >
  <item>row1col1</item>
  <item>row1col2</item>
  <item>row1col3</item>
  <item>row2col1</item>
  <item>row2col2</item>
  <item>row2col3</item>
</enc:Array>
```

Here the enc:arrayType attribute specifies the dimensions of the array.

Partially Transmitted and Sparsely Transmitted Arrays

As the multiple references feature illustrates, a high priority of the designers of SOAP was increasing performance, in particular by reducing the size of messages wherever possible. Partially transmitted and sparsely transmitted arrays are further examples of this emphasis. Both allow portions of an array to be serialized: partially transmitted arrays allow you start at an offset whilst sparsely transmitted arrays allow you to explicitly specify which elements you are sending.

In this example, we use a partially transmitted array to send the fourth and fifth elements of a six-element array:

```
<enc:Array xmlns:enc="http://www.w3.org/2001/12/soap-encoding"
           xmlns:xs="http://www.w3.org/2001/XMLSchema"
       enc:arrayType="xs:string[6]"
           enc:offset="[3]" >
  <item>The fourth element</item>
  <item>The fifth element</item>
</enc:Array>
```

The `enc:offset` attribute indicates how far from 0 we are in the array.

Here we use a sparsely transmitted array to send just the second and fourth elements of an array of strings:

```
<enc:Array xmlns:enc="http://www.w3.org/2001/12/soap-encoding"
           xmlns:xs="http://www.w3.org/2001/XMLSchema"
           enc:arrayType="xs:string[6]">
  <item enc:position="[1]">The second element</item>
  <item enc:position="[3]">The fourth element</item>
</enc:Array>
```

The `enc:position` attribute is added to the member elements to signify their position within the array. Don't forget that arrays are zero-based so the fourth element is at position 3!

Differences between SOAP 1.1 and SOAP 1.2

At the time of writing, SOAP 1.2 is in Working Draft. ASP.NET's Web Service support is 1.1 compliant and WSDL binds to 1.1 but for completeness we will have a look the current major differences between SOAP 1.1 and SOAP 1.2 (in addition to the different namespace of course):

- ❑ SOAP 1.2 does not permit any element after the body.

- ❑ SOAP 1.2 defines the new `<Misunderstood>` header element for conveying information on a mandatory header block that could not be processed.

- ❑ SOAP 1.2 provides two new fault codes `MustUnderstand` and `DTDNotSupported`.

- ❑ SOAP 1.2 defines two new actor roles, `none` and `anonymous`, together with a more detailed processing model on how these behave.

- ❑ In the SOAP 1.2 HTTP binding, the `SOAPAction` header is not required, and a new HTTP status code 427 has been sought from IANA for indicating cases where it is needed.

❑   In the SOAP 1.2 HTTP binding, the `Content-type` header is `application/soap` rather than `text/xml` as required by SOAP 1.1.

❑   SOAP 1.2 provides a finer grained description of the use of the various 2xx, 3xx, 4xx HTTP status codes.

❑   SOAP 1.2 has removed the 'dot' notation for fault codes, which are now simply of the form `env:name`, where `env` is the SOAP envelope namespace.

❑   SOAP 1.2 replaces `client` and `server` fault codes with `Sender` and `Receiver`

❑   SOAP 1.2 provides a `<response>` element for RPCs.

❑   SOAP 1.2 provides several additional fault codes in the RPC namespace.

Of immediate impact to ASP.NET users are two HTTP binding changes. As ASP.NET is 1.1 compliant it will not accept a request unless the `SOAPAction` header is present, and the `Content-type` HTTP header is `text/xml`.

Describing Web Services with WSDL

Imagine going into a fast food restaurant, walking up to the counter, looking up and there's nothing there. No pictures and no menu listing the tasty snacks available. So you start guessing and each time you guess the person serving you just chirps cheerfully, "We don't do that, sorry!"

It might sound like some surreal comedy sketch, but it illustrates an important point about Web Services. Only knowing the URI for a Web Service is like being in this situation; you know where the restaurant is, but you have no idea what functions are available or what the input and output parameters are. What we need is a *menu* – a way of describing a Web Service, telling us all we need to know in order to use it; and we want it in XML so that it can easily be integrated into other applications such as automated proxy builders.

Web Services Description Language, WSDL (often pronounced "whizz-dull", which seems like an oxymoron to me!), is an XML grammar that does all this and more. It is a joint initiative of IBM and Microsoft, and although it is currently at the lowly status of a W3C Note, it is rapidly gaining recognition as the de facto standard.

The W3C Note describes WSDL as follows:

> *"WSDL is an XML format for describing network services as a set of endpoints operating on messages containing either document-oriented or procedure-oriented information. The operations and messages are described abstractly, and then bound to a concrete network protocol and message format to define an endpoint. Related concrete endpoints are combined into abstract endpoints (services). WSDL is extensible to allow description of endpoints and their messages regardless of what message formats or network protocols are used to communicate, however, the only bindings described in this document describe how to use WSDL in conjunction with SOAP 1.1, HTTP GET/POST, and MIME."*

Abstract and Concrete

The most important concept in WSDL is that of **abstract definitions** and **concrete descriptions**.

The **abstract definitions** describe the functions or methods, their parameters, document descriptions (if this is a document-style exchange rather than RPC), and data type definitions for the Web Service. They are considered abstract because everything they describe is platform-neutral.

The **concrete descriptions** detail the physical implementation, generally specifying that such and such function call maps to such and such URI.

The separation of the abstract and the concrete provides tremendous flexibility. It is entirely feasible that an abstract definition can be shared between multiple service providers, each with their own concrete descriptions. In fact, what may well happen is that we get a Web Services equivalent of the BizTalk initiative (let's call it WebSTalk and you read it here first!). The WebSTalk initiative could be a grouping of organizations that offer the same type of Web Service, getting together to agree a standard abstract definition that consumers can confidently integrate into their applications because it is independent of the service provider.

For example, say all the online brokerage companies agree an abstract definition for a stock quote service. We use this to integrate the service into our application and we initially implement with the concrete descriptions provided by 'The PayAsYouGoQuotes Company'. This seems like a good idea because we aren't sure how many quote enquiries we will be making. Down the track, we find that we are making so many quote enquiries that it would be better to use 'The YearlySubscriptionQuote Company'. All we would need to do is change the concrete descriptions to use the new service provider. There's no need to worry about how to call the functions with the new provider, or the format of the response because they are the same.

WSDL Structure

Let's consider the elements that make up a WSDL document, the function they perform and how they relate to each other. We will use the WSDL document from one of the services described in the Web Services Case Study as an example, but first let's take a look at a diagram that illustrates the key relationships within a WSDL document

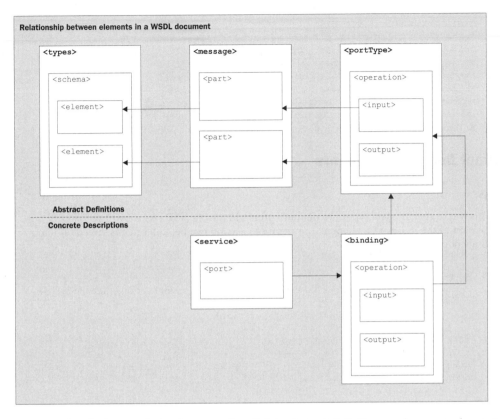

Relationship between elements in a WSDL document

As we have already discussed, the document is split into abstract definitions and concrete descriptions. In the concrete descriptions, we have a `<service>` element that represents a Web Service. It contains a `<port>` for each implementation of the service (SOAP, HTTP-GET, HTTP-POST) and is linked to a `<binding>` element. The `<binding>` element provides information specific to the implementation (for example for a SOAP implementation it has the SOAPAction) and it is linked to a `<portType>` in the abstract definitions. The `<operation>` in the `<binding>` is also linked to an `<operation>` in the `<portType>`.

In the abstract definitions, the `<portType>` element contains `<operation>` elements that, in turn, contain two child elements, `<input>` and `<output>`. Each of these is linked to a `<message>` element and defines the format of the input and output to the operation, or service. The `<message>` element consists of one or more `<part>` elements that are linked to `<element>`s in the `<schema>` element, which can be found in the `<types>` element.

Let's take a closer look at the elements. We will split them into the root element, abstract definition elements, and concrete description elements.

Root Element

The root element of a WSDL document is the `<definitions>` element. As you can see, it specifies certain global namespace declarations. It may also have a `name` attribute (a recurring theme in WSDL elements), although Visual Studio WSDL files are not generated with one:

```
<?xml version="1.0" encoding="utf-8"?>
<definitions xmlns:s="http://www.w3.org/2001/XMLSchema"
 xmlns:http="http://schemas.xmlsoap.org/wsdl/http/"
 xmlns:mime="http://schemas.xmlsoap.org/wsdl/mime/"
 xmlns:tm="http://microsoft.com/wsdl/mime/textMatching/"
 xmlns:soap="http://schemas.xmlsoap.org/wsdl/soap/"
 xmlns:soapenc="http://schemas.xmlsoap.org/soap/encoding/"
 xmlns:s0="http://tempuri.org/" targetNamespace="http://tempuri.org/"
 xmlns="http://schemas.xmlsoap.org/wsdl/">
```

Abstract Definition Elements

<types>

This is where specific data types are defined, preferably using XSD. As we will see later in our discussion of the <import> element, the <types> section can be, and often is, hived-off into a separate document.

```
<types>
   <s:schema attributeFormDefault="qualified" elementFormDefault="qualified"
targetNamespace="http://tempuri.org/">
      <s:element name="p_iItemID" type="s:int" />
      <s:element name="getItemResult" nillable="true">
        <s:complexType mixed="true">
          <s:sequence>
            <s:any />
          </s:sequence>
        </s:complexType>
      </s:element>
    </s:schema>
  </types>
```

<message>

The <message> element provides a definition for the data being sent to or received from a Web Service. It consists of one or more <part> elements. <message> elements are uniquely identified through the use of a name attribute.

```
<message name="getItemSoapIn">
   <part name="p_iItemID" element="s0:p_iItemID" />
</message>
<message name="getItemSoapOut">
   <part name="getItemResult" element="s0:getItemResult" />
</message>
```

<part>

The <part> element describes the datatype for a message. It consists of a name attribute, so that it can be uniquely identified, and an element attribute that will generally contain a reference to an <element> defined in our schema in the <types> element.

`<portType>`

A `<portType>` defines a set of operations and their messages and again uses a `name` attribute as a unique identifier. WSDL considers there to be four types of operation (see table below) with the type determining the operation's messaging requirements. There can be multiple `<operation>`s in a `<portType>` but each `<operation>` must be one of the four types. An `<operation>` consists of a combination of `<input>`, `<output>`, and `<fault>` elements: the type of operation as detailed in the following table determines the inclusion and ordering of these elements:

Type	Description	Required Child Elements
One-way	Web Service receives a message	`<input>`
Request-response	Web Service receives a message and sends a reply	`<input>`, `<output>`, `<fault>` (optional)
Solicit-response	Web Service sends a message and expects a reply	`<output>`, `<input>`, `<fault>` (optional)
Notification	Web Service sends a message without a request	`<output>`

The `<input>` and `<output>` elements have a `message` attribute that directly relates to the name attribute of a previously defined `<message>` element. So, from the above table, a request-response operation type will consist of an `<input>` element, an `<output>` element, and an optional `<fault>` element, in that order:

```
<portType name="CatalogueServiceSoap">
  <operation name="getItem">
    <input message="s0:getItemSoapIn" />
    <output message="s0:getItemSoapOut" />
  </operation>
</portType>
```

The `<operation>` element has a `name` attribute and an optional `parameterOrder` attribute. The latter contains a whitespace-delimited list of message names indicating the order of the parameters. This attribute is really aimed at imitating methods in RPC situations.

Concrete Description Elements

The concrete descriptions describe the physical implementation of the service. As you will see, the descriptions are a mix of WSDL elements and extensibility elements specific to the protocol that is used to invoke the service, generally SOAP. We will be discussing SOAP Binding in the next section, so here we will just concentrate on the WSDL elements.

`<binding>`

A `<binding>` element defines the message formats and protocol details for a particular `<portType>` child of the `<portTypes>` element of the abstract definitions. A `<portType>` can have multiple bindings if, for example, the service is to be made available on a number of different protocols. A `<binding>` element can only relate to one protocol. Here's an example:

```
<binding name="CatalogueServiceSoap" type="s0:CatalogueServiceSoap">
  <soap:binding transport="http://schemas.xmlsoap.org/soap/http"
   style="document" />
  <operation name="getItem">
    <soap:operation soapAction="http://tempuri.org/getItem" style="document"/>
    <input>
      <soap:body use="literal" />
    </input>
    <output>
      <soap:body use="literal" />
    </output>
  </operation>
</binding>
```

Although we are concentrating on SOAP in this chapter, for comparison here is a `<binding>` element which describes invoking the service with HTTP GET:

```
<binding name="CatalogueServiceHttpGet" type="s0:CatalogueServiceHttpGet">
  <http:binding verb="GET" />
  <operation name="getItem">
    <http:operation location="/getItem" />
    <input>
      <http:urlEncoded />
    </input>
    <output>
      <mime:content part="Body" type="text/xml" />
    </output>
  </operation>
</binding>
```

The `type` attribute on the `<binding>` element contains the name of the `<portType>` and a `name` attribute to uniquely identify the `<binding>`. The example above includes the protocol in the binding name, which is generally good practice. Each `<binding>` element has an `<operation>` child element that directly relates to an `<operation>` element in the `<portType>`. An `<operation>` element contains an `<input>` and `<output>` element that use the protocol's extensibility elements to describe the physical format of ingoing and outgoing messages for that binding.

<service>

A `<service>` element groups together `<port>`s and, in keeping with all other elements, uses a `name` attribute as a unique identifier. In example, there this is a service for invocation via SOAP and HTTP GET:

```
<service name="CatalogueService">
  <port name="CatalogueServiceSoap" binding="s0:CatalogueServiceSoap">
<soap:address location=
 "http://localhost/E-commerceEngine/CatalogueService.asmx" />
  </port>
  <port name="CatalogueServiceHttpGet" binding="s0:CatalogueServiceHttpGet">
    <http:address location=
      "http://localhost/E-commerceEngine/CatalogueService.asmx" />
  </port>
</service>
```

We can add `<documentation>` elements as children of `<service>` elements, as with any other WSDL element, to provide some limited form of documentation within the WSDL document. The `<port>` element specifies a single endpoint address, such as a URI, for the `<binding>` element named by the binding attribute. There can be multiple `<port>` elements for a `<service>` and the address is defined by a protocol extensibility element.

SOAP Binding

WSDL has been specifically designed to allow it to describe the consumption of a Web Service over any protocol, hence the frequent occurrence of extensibility elements in the concrete descriptions. We are primarily interested in services that use SOAP, so we will now focus on how WSDL binds with that protocol.

First though, what exactly do mean by binding? We know that in order to send a SOAP message we need certain information: the location (URI or e-mail address) of the endpoint or recipient, a value for the SOAPAction HTTP header (don't forget, in SOAP 1.1 this is mandatory, in SOAP 1.2. it is not), and definition of the SOAP headers to be included in the Envelope. Binding allows us to specify this information in the WSDL file and so enables applications to automatically generate valid SOAP messages from a WSDL document.

Let's go back to our example and look again at the concrete descriptions:

```
<binding name="CatalogueServiceSoap" type="s0:CatalogueServiceSoap">
  <soap:binding transport="http://schemas.xmlsoap.org/soap/http"
   style="document" />
  <operation name="getItem">
    <soap:operation soapAction="http://tempuri.org/getItem" style="document"/>
    <input>
      <soap:body use="literal" />
    </input>
    <output>
      <soap:body use="literal" />
    </output>
  </operation>
</binding>
<service name="CatalogueService">
  <port name="CatalogueServiceSoap" binding="s0:CatalogueServiceSoap">
  <soap:address location=
   "http://localhost/E-commerceEngine/CatalogueService.asmx" />
  </port>
</service>
```

<soap:binding>

The `<soap:binding>` element is an immediate child of `<binding>` and identifies which version of SOAP we are using and the style of messaging. The element has two attributes, style which indicates whether the binding is document-style or RPC (if it is not present then document is assumed) and, transport to hold the namespace of the SOAP version. As you can see we are using SOAP 1.1.

<soap:operation>

The <soap:operation> element is an immediate child of <operation> and provides information specific to this <operation>. The style attribute here is the same as on the <soap:binding> element defaulting to document style if not present. The soapAction attribute specifies an absolute URL to be placed in the SOAPAction HTTP header and should only be absent if the HTTP protocol is being used. (Remember in SOAP 1.2. the SOAPAction is not required, although it is not an error to specify it.)

<soap:body>

The <soap:body> element appears as a child of the input and output elements. It determines how the message parts appear in the SOAP body. If the call is document-style then the message appears directly under the body element. If the call is RPC, then each message part appears under a wrapper that has the same name as the method. Which message parts appear in the body is determined by a whitespace-delimited list of names in the optional parts attribute. Each name either references an <element> in the abstract definitions <types> element or an <element> in a concrete description schema.

If the attribute is not coded then it is assumed that all parts appear in the body. Encoding of the message body is determined by the use and encodingStyle attributes. The use attribute can be either literal or encoded. If it is encoded, then the encodingStyle attribute must be present and contain a reference to the encoding rules that have been used to serialize the call.

<soap:address>

The <soap:address> element sits inside the <service> <port> element and specifies an address for an endpoint (URI). It must be valid for the transport protocol declared in the <soap:binding>, for example a URL for HTTP, or an e-mail address for SMTP. Only one <soap:address> element can appear as a child of the <port> element and it must specify only one address.

Two other extensibility elements not related to <binding> and <service> can also be specified, as described next.

<soap:fault>

The <soap:fault> element defines the format of a SOAP Fault Details element, using the name attribute to relate the <soap:fault> to the <wsdl:fault> defined for the operation. The use, encodingStyle, and namespace attributes are all as for the <soap:body> element, except that, as headers do not contain parameters, a style attribute value of document is assumed.

<soap:header>

The <soap:header> element defines the header blocks that may be transmitted in the header element of the SOAP Envelope. The use, encodingStyle, and namespace attributes are all the same as for the <soap:body> element with the exception that, as headers do not contain parameters, a style attribute value of document is assumed.

The header type is related to the relevant message part via the message and part attributes. If the use is set to literal then the part may also include definitions for the <soap:actor> and the <soap:mustUnderstand> attributes.

The SOAP specification dictates that all header errors must be returned as faults inside the header element. The <soap:headerfault> element allows the format of a header fault to be defined.

Using the <import> Element

The <import> element allows the WSDL for a particular Web Service to be split over several documents, which improves readability, but more importantly allows various parts of a document to be included in other documents. As we have already seen, this could enable a single abstract definition to be included in multiple WSDL documents, each having a different concrete description.

For our example, the abstract definition WSDL file could look like this:

```xml
<?xml version="1.0" encoding="utf-8"?>
<definitions xmlns:s=http://www.w3.org/2001/XMLSchema
 xmlns:http="http://schemas.xmlsoap.org/wsdl/http/"
 xmlns:mime="http://schemas.xmlsoap.org/wsdl/mime/"
 xmlns:tm="http://microsoft.com/wsdl/mime/textMatching/"
 xmlns:soap="http://schemas.xmlsoap.org/wsdl/soap/"
 xmlns:soapenc="http://schemas.xmlsoap.org/soap/encoding/"
 xmlns:s0="http://tempuri.org/" targetNamespace="http://tempuri.org/"
 xmlns="http://schemas.xmlsoap.org/wsdl/">
  <types>
    <s:schema attributeFormDefault="qualified" elementFormDefault="qualified"
     targetNamespace="http://tempuri.org/">
      <s:element name="p_iItemID" type="s:int" />
      <s:element name="getItemResult" nillable="true">
        <s:complexType mixed="true">
          <s:sequence>
            <s:any />
          </s:sequence>
        </s:complexType>
      </s:element>
    </s:schema>
  </types>
  <message name="getItemSoapIn">
    <part name="p_iItemID" element="s0:p_iItemID" />
  </message>
  <message name="getItemSoapOut">
    <part name="getItemResult" element="s0:getItemResult" />
  </message>
  <portType name="CatalogueServiceSoap">
    <operation name="getItem">
      <input message="s0:getItemSoapIn" />
      <output message="s0:getItemSoapOut" />
    </operation>
  </portType>
</definitions>
```

This would be saved and made available at the URL http://tempuri.org/catalogueservice.wsdl. A service provider could then produce their own WSDL for this service by importing the above abstract definition and appending their own specific concrete descriptions:

```xml
<?xml version="1.0"?>
<definitions xmlns:s="http://www.w3.org/2001/XMLSchema"
 xmlns:http="http://schemas.xmlsoap.org/wsdl/http/"
 xmlns:mime="http://schemas.xmlsoap.org/wsdl/mime/"
```

```
 xmlns:tm="http://microsoft.com/wsdl/mime/textMatching/"
 xmlns:soap="http://schemas.xmlsoap.org/wsdl/soap/"
 xmlns:soapenc="http://schemas.xmlsoap.org/soap/encoding"/
 xmlns:defs="http://tempuri.org/catalogueservice/definitions"/>
   <import namespace="http://tempuri.org/catalogueservice/definitions"
    location="http://tempuri.org/catalogueservice.wsdl"/>
   <binding name="CatalogueServiceSoap" type="defs:CatalogueServiceSoap">
      <soap:binding transport="http://schemas.xmlsoap.org/soap/http"
       style="document" />
      <operation name="getItem">
         <soap:operation soapAction="http://tempuri.org/getItem"
          style="document" />
         <input>
           <soap:body use="literal" />
         </input>
         <output>
           <soap:body use="literal" />
         </output>
      </operation>
   </binding>
   <service name="CatalogueService">
      <port name="CatalogueServiceSoap" binding="s0:CatalogueServiceSoap">
        <soap:address location=
         "http://localhost/E- commerceEngine/CatalogueService.asmx" />
      </port>
   </service>
</definitions>
```

You'll notice that the namespaces are distinct in both files so that we won't have any clashes. Notice also how a new namespace of defs has been added. The URI for the defs namespace matches the namespace attribute on the <import> element that has the location of the definition document. The only other change is that the <binding> element's type attribute is now qualified using the new defs namespace.

Discovering Organizations and Services using UDDI

In all our discussions so far, we have assumed that we already know of the existence of a particular Web Service. When dealing with trading partners, this will generally be the case, although there is a school of thought that envisages that when Organization A is looking to expand its business, it hops onto the Internet looking for Organization B in the appropriate field. When Organization B is found, Organization A checks what services it provides, builds applications to interact with the Web Services which provide the desired functionality, and the two then start interacting.

The discovery of Web Services seems to be most relevant for software providers: those organizations that provide Web Services that can be integrated into your own applications just as you probably have done in the past with third-party COM objects. Whatever are the motives for the initiative, Microsoft, IBM, and Ariba have gotten together to produce UDDI, for Universal Description, Discovery, and Integration. Today the UDDI community is definitely gaining momentum and boasts over 300 member companies.

UDDI is in essence a registry containing pertinent information about organizations and the services they provide. The registry is often described as the "phone book of Web Services" with "white pages" giving organization location and contact details; "yellow pages" classifying the organization using a number of different classifications and taxonomies; and "green pages" containing all the necessary technical information to start using a service (usually a WSDL file).

You can interact with the UDDI registry in two ways, either by going to one of its administration sites (such as http://uddi.microsoft.com) or by using one of the 30 functions exposed by UDDI Web Services. You might want to use the UDDI Web Service to automatically register your organization, for example, rather than going through the online process manually.

You can find out more about UDDI, including detailed references on its data structures and API, at http://uddi.org.

How Microsoft and IBM are extending Web Services

XML Web Services may be the golden child on the block right now, and new Web Services are springing up daily, but they do have drawbacks, particularly when it comes to security, routing (configuring paths for messages to travel down), message reliability (that is guaranteeing delivery), and transactions.

If companies were to try to produce solutions to these limitations as and when required, then not only would the cost of implementing Web Services be greatly increased, but the goal of creating a standard platform and approach for exposing functionality would become much harder to achieve. In a bid to try to provide a standard approach to resolving these limitations, Microsoft and IBM have come up with what they call the Global XML Web Services Architecture that builds on the baseline specifications of SOAP, WSDL, and UDDI to provide a far more robust and reliable framework.

The new Architecture has been designed to be modular, general purpose, distributed, (that is, without a need for a central location) and, most importantly, standards-based. It consists of five new specifications that are described next.

WS-Security and WS-License

The purpose of this specification is to provide a set of SOAP extensions that can be used separately or together to build secure Web Services by enabling the passing of security information (credentials), the use of **XML-Signature** to ensure message integrity, and the use of **XML-Encryption** for message confidentiality.

Credentials

Organizations use **credentials** to positively identify each other before they start transacting. WS-Security can be used to exchange many different types of credentials, providing a standard mechanism to pass credentials from one organization to another. WS-Security does not rely on any particular technology.

Here is an example of a credential header in a SOAP message, taken from the WS-Security draft specification:

```
<S:Header>
    <m:path xmlns:m="http://schemas.xmlsoap.org/rp">
        <m:action>http://fabrikam.org/getQuote</m:action>
```

289

```
            <m:to>soap://fabrikam.org/stocks</m:to>
            <m:from>mailto:johnsmith@fabrikam.com</m:from>
            <m:id>uuid:84b9f5d0-33fb-4a81-b02b-5b760641c1d6</m:id>
        </m:path>
        <wsse:credentials
            xmlns:wsse="http://schemas.xmlsoap.org/ws/2002/01/secext">
            <wsse:binaryLicense wsse:valueType="wsse:x509v3"
                        wsse:encodingType="xsd:base64Binary"
                                xsi:type="wsse:BASE64_BINARY_LICENSE">
            MIIEZzCCA9CgAwIBAgIQEmtJZc0rqrKh5i
                .
                .
                .
            RnSNBe8DQveqD6a3gUACyZ6XVe3u
        </wsse:binaryLicense>
        </wsse:credentials>
    </S:Header>
```

WS-License is very closely related to WS-Security and describes license types and how they can be placed within the <credentials> tag. Specifically, WS-License describes how to encode X.509 certificates and Kerberos tickets.

Message Integrity

Message integrity is about ensuring that a message has not been tampered with en route to the receiver. WS-Security uses **XML-Signature** to sign an envelope with the specification permitting messages to contain multiple signatures. Multiple signatures could be crucial in a scenario that involves a message passing through many intermediate nodes where each node may be making changes to the message and resigning the message with its own key. Now the final recipient of the message can check the signatures to ensure that the not only has the message maintained its integrity but that it has traveled the correct path and be seen by all the necessary nodes.

Message Confidentiality

It is more than likely that the information contained in an electronic transaction is sensitive. For that reason, encryption of the message so that unauthorized eyes can't view it is almost a pre-requisite. WS-Security uses **XML-Encryption** to ensure that confidential parts of a message remain so.

For more about the WS-Security specification, go to:

http://msdn.microsoft.com/library/en-us/dnglobspec/html/ws-security.asp.

WS-Inspection

WS-Inspection is an XML grammar that provides the locations of descriptive documents for a Web Service at the point of service – such as WSDL documents. Therefore, if you knew the address of a Web Service, you could access the WS-Inspection document on the server to find out all you need to know about it and any other available Web Services.

WS-Inspection is little more than a collection of pointers to files in other locations, and supports the referencing of existing repositories, such as UDDI, so as to eliminate the duplication of information. The WS-Inspection specification gives the following example of an inspection document for two services:

```xml
<?xml version="1.0"?>
<inspection xmlns="http://schemas.xmlsoap.org/ws/2001/10/inspection/"
 xmlns:wsiluddi="http://schemas.xmlsoap.org/ws/2001/10/inspection/uddi/">
  <service>
    <abstract>A stock quote service with two descriptions</abstract>
    <description referencedNamespace="http://schemas.xmlsoap.org/wsdl/"
                location="http://example.com/stockquote.wsdl"/>
    <description referencedNamespace="urn:uddi-org:api">
       <wsiluddi:serviceDescription
         location="http://www.example.com/uddi/inquiryapi">
         <wsiluddi:serviceKey>4FA28580-5C39-11D5-9FCF-BB3200333F79
         </wsiluddi:serviceKey>
       </wsiluddi:serviceDescription>
    </description>
  </service>
  <service>
    <description referencedNamespace="http://schemas.xmlsoap.org/wsdl/"
                location="ftp://anotherexample.com/tools/calculator.wsdl"/>
  </service>
  <link
    referencedNamespace="http://schemas.xmlsoap.org/ws/2001/10/inspection/"
    location="http://example.com/moreservices.wsil"/>
</inspection>
```

Let's have a look at the document in more detail. We start off with the `<inspection>` document-element:

```xml
<?xml version="1.0"?>
<inspection xmlns="http://schemas.xmlsoap.org/ws/2001/10/inspection/"
 xmlns:wsiluddi="http://schemas.xmlsoap.org/ws/2001/10/inspection/uddi/">
```

An `<inspection>` element must contain at least one `<service>` element or at least one `<link>` element. In this example we have one of each. First, the `<service>` contains an optional `<abstract>` element, providing a location for some descriptive text about the service:

```xml
<abstract>A stock quote service with two descriptions</abstract>
```

This is followed by the `<description>` elements. A `<description>` gives us details of where further details about the service can be found. The `referencedNamespace` attribute identifies the type of document or service being described and the `location` attribute gives us, not surprisingly, a URI for the details. In this first `<description>`, we are describing the location of a WSDL document:

```xml
<description referencedNamespace="http://schemas.xmlsoap.org/wsdl/"
            location="http://example.com/stockquote.wsdl"/>
```

In the second description element, the `referencedNamespace` attribute indicates that we are making a reference to a UDDI entry. You'll notice that the description element no longer has a location attribute but instead has a `<serviceDescription>` child. This is an example of UDDI binding and basically provides us with a `<serviceKey>` with which we can query UDDI, either manually or via its Web Service API, to retrieve a service description.

```
<description referencedNamespace="urn:uddi-org:api">
    <wsiluddi:serviceDescription
     location="http://www.example.com/uddi/inquiryapi">
    <wsiluddi:serviceKey>4FA28580-5C39-11D5-9FCF-BB3200333F79
    </wsiluddi:serviceKey>
    </wsiluddi:serviceDescription>
</description>

</service>
```

Finally, we have a `<link>` element. This element simply points us in the direction of another Inspection document that contains information on similar or related services:

```
<link referencedNamespace=
        "http://schemas.xmlsoap.org/ws/2001/10/inspection/"
        location="http://example.com/moreservices.wsil"/>
</inspection>
```

This is only a very simple example of Inspection and UDDI binding: for more details, you should consult the WS-Inspection specification at http://msdn.microsoft.com/library/en-us/dnglobspec/html/ws-inspection.asp.

WS-Routing

The path a SOAP message takes on its way from sender to receiver is not defined by SOAP but by the transport protocol (such as HTTP). In a message path that contains intermediary nodes, SOAP can only define which parts of the message are for which nodes; it cannot define in which order those nodes are to be accessed. WS-Routing has been created to allow us to specify the messaging routes from the sender to the receiver, including intermediaries, and optionally specify a return path, all within the SOAP message structure.

For example, let's say that we had a purchase order that needed to go to accounts, inventory, and finally delivery. The SOAP message complete with WS-Routing might look like this:

```
<env:Envelope xmlns:env="http://schemas.xmlsoap.org/soap/envelope/">
    <env:Header>
        <m:path xmlns:m="http://schemas.xmlsoap.org/rp/">
            <m:action>http://www.example.org/PostOrder</m:action>
            <m:to>soap://www.example.org/Delivery</m:to>
            <m:fwd>
                <m:via>soap://www.example.org/Accounts</m:via>
                <m:via> soap://www.example.org/Inventory</m:via>
            </m:fwd>
            <m:from>mailto:henrikn@microsoft.com</m:from>
            <m:id>uuid:84b9f5d0-33fb-4a81-b02b-5b760641c1d6</m:id>
        </m:path>
    </S:Header>
    <S:Body>
        .
        .
        .
    </S:Body>
</S:Envelope>
```

The `<action>` element is very similar to the `SOAPAction` found in HTTP Headers and defines the 'intent' of the message. The `<to>` element identifies the final recipient of the message, and the `<via>` element identifies the intermediate nodes. The `<from>` element identifies who or what is responsible for the message and although it can be any valid **URI**, it is generally an e-mail address. The `<id>` element uniquely identifies the message.

By freeing SOAP from the need to use transport protocols such as HTTP that generate their own message paths, a SOAP message that uses WS-Routing can use transport protocols such as TCP and UDP and have total control of the intermediate nodes and their order in the message path. Find out more about WS-Routing at http://msdn.microsoft.com/library/en-us/dnglobspec/html/ws-routing.asp.

WS-Referral

If we cast our minds back to our discussion of SOAP, we will recall that a message passes between SOAP nodes that assume a specific role, and process the SOAP message header according to the `actor` attributes. We have also seen that WS-Routing gives us the opportunity to specify in which order the SOAP Nodes will process the message. WS-Referral takes message paths a step further by providing a means by which the SOAP Nodes – and therefore the message path – can be dynamically manipulated by adding, deleting, or querying the Nodes.

The WS-Referral Specification provides the following example:

```
<r:ref xmlns:r="http://schemas.xmlsoap.org/ws/2001/10/referral">
  <r:for>
    <r:exact>soap://example.org/example1</r:exact>
    <r:prefix>soap://example.org/example/example1</r:prefix>
  </r:for>
  <r:if>
    <r:ttl>43200000</r:ttl>
  </r:if>
  <r:go>
    <r:via>soap://example.com/mirror</r:via>
  </r:go>
  <r:refId>uuid:09233523-345b-4351-b623-5dsf35sgs5d6</r:refId>
  <r:desc>
    <r:refAddr>http://example.com/references/2001/10/1234.xml</r:refAddr>
  </r:desc>
</r:ref>
```

This WS-Referral file is specifying that if the SOAP node currently processing the message has the role of `"soap://example.org/example1"` or a role name starting with the string `"soap://example.org/example/example1"` then, if the referral is less than 12 hours old, go via the SOAP node `"soap://example.com/mirror"`. Note that the time given in the `<ttl>` element (for 'time to live') is in milliseconds.

More information on WS-Referral can be found at http://msdn.microsoft.com/library/en-us/dnglobspec/html/ws-referral.asp.

Collaborative Electronic Business with ebXML

We have just seen how Microsoft and IBM propose to extend the basic XML Web Services architecture to provide a more flexible, robust, and secure environment for business transactions. As you can imagine, Microsoft and IBM are not the only players in this particular field and we will end this chapter with a brief look at what many predict will be the dominant business communication standard, ebXML.

What is ebXML?

As you have may have guessed, ebXML, takes its name from the phrase "electronic business XML". With its roots in EDI, ebXML is jointly sponsored by **UN/CEFACT** (United Nations Center for Trade Facilitation and Electronic Business) and **OASIS** (the Organization for the Advancement of Structural Information Standards), and provides an extensive XML-based framework for conducting business electronically. To quote the ebXML homepage (http://www.ebxml.org):

> *"ebXML is a set of specifications that together enable a modular electronic business framework. The vision of ebXML is to enable a global electronic marketplace where enterprises of any size and in any geographical location can meet and conduct business with each other through the exchange of XML-based messages."*

ebXML provides a standard by which organizations:

- ❑ Identify common business transactions

- ❑ Define message schemas to represent these business transactions

- ❑ Publish information about themselves and the services they offer

- ❑ Discover information about other organizations and their services

- ❑ Facilitate the negotiation of terms between organizations before engaging in business

- ❑ Define the method for transporting massages

- ❑ Define security and reliability mechanisms

As you can see, while ebXML shares much in common with XML Web Services, service discovery, service description, message formats, and message transmission (ebXML has adopted SOAP as its messaging protocol), it attempts to encompass a whole lot more. While XML Web Services concentrate more on the implementation, ebXML delves straight into actually describing an organization's functions to provide a framework for electronic – and therefore automatic – negotiation and contract brokering.

Most of the top companies are involved in ebXML, with the notable exception, it seems, of Microsoft.

It is also interesting to note that IBM is keeping a foot in both camps, being a major sponsor of UDDI as well as an ebXML participant. Industry pundits and experts alike are expecting big things for ebXML and many seem to think that it will be the dominant protocol for business interaction within five years. In this chapter, we can barely brush the surface of what is a highly involved subject.

If you wish to learn more about ebXML, go to the ebXML web site at
http://www.ebXML.org, or get hold of a copy of *Professional ebXML Foundations*
(Wrox Press, ISBN 1-86100-590-3).

The ebXML Model

In order to make ebXML as flexible as possible, the model used for describing transactions is split into two separate views: the **Business Operation View (BOV)** and the **Functional Services View (FSV)**.

The BOV provides details on the business aspects of a transaction, while the FSV specifies, in the words of the ebXML Technical Architecture Specification, the "mechanistic needs of ebXML": that is, how it can be physically implemented.

The FSV is viewed as a reference for software vendors to help them build ebXML compliant software and it is pretty much a given that organizations wishing to implement ebXML-based transactions are more likely to use 3rd-party ebXML solutions rather than custom building their own solution.

Key ebXML Components

Organizations need a method for discovering each other and accessing information about an organization and the services that it provides or can engage in. The **ebXML Registry** allows the discovery of other organizations, while the **ebXML Repository** holds data (in XML form) including:

- ❑ Business Processes – generally an XML document (although it can be UML) that formally describes an organization's activities
- ❑ The Core Library
- ❑ Collaboration Protocol Profiles
- ❑ The Business Library

This is a very similar setup to UDDI and it is likely that there will soon be a push to allow ebXML registries to talk to UDDI registries and vice versa.

Core Library

The Core Library consists of a collection of components provided by the ebXML initiative that may be used to create bigger components. For example, an organization's business process may be built using one or more components from the Core Library. Core components represent business information that is common across departments and industries and are stored in the registry as XML documents. A bank account identification consisting of a account name and an account number is one example of a core component.

Collaboration Protocol Profile (CPP)

This document contains all the salient details about an organization and the business processes and transactions it supports. It provides general details such as contact information and industry classification as well as information specific to the business processes such as interface requirements and Messaging Service requirements.

Collaboration Protocol Agreement (CPA)

A CPA defines the Business Processes that two or more organizations have agreed to engage in and the Interface and Messaging Service requirements for those processes (such as transport protocol, message formats, security). This information is derived from each organization's CPP document. The Messaging Service will then use the CPA to ensure that all exchanges adhere to what the parties involved agreed.

The ebXML Functional Phases

The ebXML initiative defines three Functional Phases in the creation and implementation of an ebXML application, as described here. First a diagram to illustrate the phases and their steps:

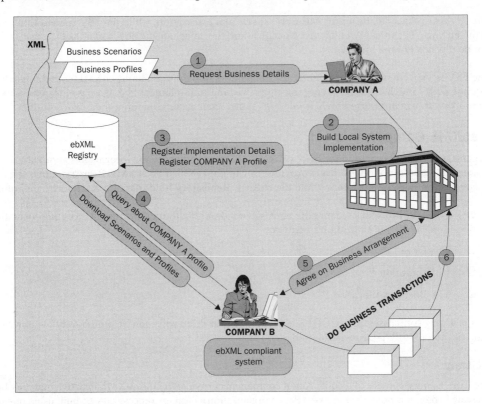

Implementation Phase

The first phase deals with the creation of an ebXML compliant application:

1. Organization A downloads copies of ebXML specifications and the Core Library.

2. Organization A deploys an ebXML compliant application either by custom building, or by buying an off-the-shelf solution.

3. Organization A publishes its own Collaboration Protocol Profile to the ebXML registry. This allows other organizations to review Organization A's ebXML capabilities and supported business transactions.

Discovery and Retrieval Phase

This phase involves the discovery of ebXML related resources:

4. Organization B searches the Registry and finds Organization A's entry.

5. Organization B sends a request to Organization A, to start using one or more of Organization A's published transactions (Organization B will also need to have an ebXML application). Organization B submits a Collaboration Protocol Agreement to Organization A, outlining the transactions they will engage in, the messaging requirements, contingency plans, and security requirements.

Run-time Phase

This is the final step in the process:

6. Organization A accepts the CPA. The two organizations start exchanging ebXML messages using the ebXML Messaging Service.

The ebXML Messaging Service

Trading partners exchange ebXML messages using the ebXML Messaging Service. The service is transport protocol independent, and supports one-way and request/response (either synchronous or asynchronous) messaging. While the messaging service defines the format for all messages, it does not restrict the content of the payload, and for situations where multiple messages are exchanged, it can sequence the payloads.

Rules for how Messaging takes place are contained in the **Collaboration Protocol Agreement** and the Messaging Service ensures that these rules are followed. Security, for example, may be defined in the CPA. If any of the rules are violated then the Messaging Service will raise the error and deliver it appropriately.

An ebXML Example Scenario

This example, taken from the ebXML Technical Architecture Specification, shows the steps that two trading partners take to enable them to start transacting using ebXML:

❑ Each partner creates a **Collaborative Protocol Profile** (CPP). The CPP references at least one business process from the ebXML registry and at least one message definition. The CPP defines which transactions the partner wishes to engage in, the transport protocol that the partner supports and any other requirements the transaction has such as the use of encryption, validation, and authentication.

❑ The partners acknowledge each other's CPP and use them to create a **Collaborative Protocol Agreement** (CPA).

❑ The partners implement the respective part of the CPP by either exposing a business service interface, or upgrading a legacy system so that it can engage in the agreed transactions and create messages that conform to the agreed definitions, such that the exchange may occur on the agreed technical platform (with the specified transport protocol, security considerations, and so on).

❑ The partners start exchanging messages in accordance with the rules laid down in the CPA.

Summary

This has been a long and theory-heavy chapter and I wouldn't be surprised if it took a couple of coffees to get through it (I'm not going to tell you how many it took to write it!) but you should now have at least a basic understanding of the standards that drive XML Web Services.

While you are unlikely to ever need to code a SOAP message or a WSDL document by hand, thanks to the proliferation of tools and the excellent support for XML Web Services in ASP.NET, this basic understanding will be invaluable in designing, building, and debugging your applications.

You will also have some idea of what the future holds for XML Web Services, as Microsoft and its partners evolve the Global Architecture, plugging the gaps in the current architecture, particularly security, and extending XML Web Services to become an indispensable business tool.

We also looked at ebXML, the global initiative for electronic business; and herein lies a problem. Although not a direct competitor to XML Web Services, as it approaches electronic business from a different and more encompassing angle, there is enough crossover, particularly with repositories and messaging, to create a dilemma for organizations wishing to develop electronic business applications.

It seems likely that both technologies will develop side by side. Organizations, particularly those that have already utilized EDI, will probably use ebXML for their inter-organization communication, where the modeling of processes and the ability to manage a relationship through electronic agreements will quickly offset the initial implementation costs. XML Web Services look likely to flourish in the distributed computing and application integration arena. Using third-party Web Services in much the same way as we have used COM and enabling disparate applications to communicate by exposing functionality as a Web Service potentially offers tremendous capabilities.

How long, I wonder, before the average e-commerce site is nothing more than a presentation layer on top of a Web Service e-commerce engine situated somewhere? With no extensive programming, no need for a database and no need to worry about the infrastructure, you could quite happily host your site on any $10-a-month, 50MB hosting plan.

Lastly, it used to be said that the only two certainties in life are death and taxes. Perhaps we should add one more to that list: just when you think you have a web technology licked, they go and change it, or release something completely different. The pace of change is staggering (and, for us old mainframe programmers, this is what makes web development almost exciting!); so promise me that you will add at least one Web Services and one ebXML web site to your browser favorites because what we've covered in this chapter is merely the tip of a very, very big iceberg.

In the next chapter, we will be taking a look at some emerging XML-Related technologies; enjoy!

9

XQuery

In this chapter, we're going to take a look at an emerging XML technology that's likely to become relevant to ASP.NET developers in the near future: XQuery. We're not going to take a heavy, theoretical approach, but more of a practical one: after taking a taking a quick look at its development and how it's intended to work, we'll download a set of demonstration classes from the Microsoft web site, and put together a small ASP.NET web application to get a feel for how it may be used.

XQuery 1.0

W3C status at the time of writing: W3C Working Draft, www.w3.org/XML/Query

XQuery is an XML querying language devised by the W3C to provide flexible, SQL-like query facilities for extracting data from virtual (dynamically generated) and real (existing) XML documents or document collections. Among its main aims are that it should be easily readable, and easy to use.

XQuery is not an entirely new technology. Rather, it has grown from a mix of earlier query languages, including a specification called **Quilt**. In turn, Quilt itself was built using concepts from other existing languages:

- ❑ From XPath 1.0 and XML Querying Language (XQL), it took a path expression syntax suitable for hierarchical documents.

- ❑ From XML-Querying Language (XML-QL) it borrowed the notion of binding variables and then using the bound variables to create new structures.

- ❑ From SQL came the idea of clauses based on keywords to provide a pattern for restructuring data (the SELECT-FROM-WHERE pattern).

❑ From the Object Querying Language (OQL), it took the notion of a functional language composed of several different kinds of expressions that can be nested with full generality.

❑ Quilt was also influenced by other XML query languages such as Lorel and YATL.

In December 1998, the Query Language Workshop (QL'98) was hosted by the W3C in Boston, Mass. This led to the formation of a new working group (WG) called the *XML Query Language Working Group*, and shortly after that Quilt was proposed to the WG. This proposal was adopted as the basis for development of XQuery 1.0. So far, the list of specifications published by the XML Query Language WG includes the following:

XQuery 1.0: An XML Query Language	This is the entry document, and reading its introduction will give you a general idea of what XQuery is. It goes on to describe in detail all of the expression types that you can use in your XQuery queries.
XQuery 1.0 Formal Semantics	This document contains the formal semantics for XQuery.
XML Query Requirements	Contains all of the requirements that form the basis for the development of XQuery.
XML Query Use Cases	Contains a set of practical query examples, and their solutions in XQuery. The set is classified into use cases. Each use case addresses a specific application area.
XML Syntax for XQuery 1.0 (XQueryX)	This document describes the XML-based version of XQuery, XQueryX.

XQuery is closely related to XPath. As you may know, XPath was originally a part of XSL, but is now considered to be a separate technology in its own right. It's used in other W3C language standards, such as XSLT 1.0 and XPointer 1.0, and it was the subject of Chapter 4 of this book. XQuery is also closely related to XSLT 1.0 – the working groups behind both are now collaborating on the development of XPath 2.0 and XSLT 2.0. In the near future, XPath 2.0 will be an integral part of both XQuery 1.0 and XSLT 2.0.

XQuery has two defined syntaxes. The first is the so-called "human-readable" syntax called XQuery; the second is entirely based on the XML standard, and is called XQueryX. The latter is tailored for XML-aware automated processes, while the former is to be used by you, the developer.

XQuery (Human-Readable) Syntax

XQuery is not an XML 1.0 application, because the queries do not adhere to the XML rules, as we'll see in some examples later on. Depending on the input query and the given XML source document, the queries you write will produce XML fragments, or well-formed documents.

The following list details some of the principal and extended forms of XQuery syntax, taken from the example that comes later in the chapter.

Expressions	The expressions used in XQuery include primary, path, sequence, arithmetic, comparison, and logical expressions. They contain language-specific keywords, symbols, and operands.
	An example of a path expression is:
| | ```
document("Orders")/root/Orders[CustomerID = $a/CustomerID]
``` |
	Here, the variable $a contains a customer node, which means that this expression will evaluate to a list of the orders that have been placed by that customer.
Constructors	In XQuery, constructors are used to generate XML structures. There are constructors for elements, attributes, CDATA sections, processing instructions, and comments.
	An example of a constructor for an XML element is:
| | ```
<orderdetails>
  <d1>
    <customer> { $a/* } </customer>
  </d1>
</orderdetails>
``` |
| | This will place the <orderdetails> element into the output of the query; the use of braces "{" and "}" is necessary here to be able to insert the result of an expression between the elements. If this is not done, the expression will be treated as text, and will not be executed against the XML source. |

Table continued on following page

FLWR Expressions	This probably XQuery's most powerful expression type. FLWR (pronounced "flower") expressions are capable of performing iterations and binding variables to intermediate result values. Its name stands for its four clauses: the FOR, LET, WHERE, and RETURN clauses. A FLWR construct can contain multiple FOR clauses, which is extremely useful when joining multiple documents.
	An example query that features a FLWR expression is:

	<pre><code><orderdetails>
	{
	  FOR $c IN document("OrderDetails")
	    /root/Order_x0020_Details[OrderID = $b/OrderID]
	  RETURN
	  <d3>
	    <OD> { $c/OrderID, $c/ProductID, $c/Quantity } </OD>
	    {
	      FOR $d IN document("Products")
	        /root/Products[ProductID = $c/ProductID]
	      RETURN <P> { $d/ProductID, $d/UnitPrice, _
	        $d/ProductName } </P>
	    }
	  </d3>
	}
	</orderdetails></code></pre>

	Note that this query contains two nested FLWR expressions. Note also that a space in a SQL table name, like "Order Details", is represented as "Order_x0020_Details" in the code. This is done to conform to the XML rule that an element name cannot contain spaces.
Sorting Expressions	Sorting expressions are used to control the order of a sequence of elements. In XQuery, the order in which a set of elements that's been returned from a FLWR construct appears in the document can be specified through a SORTBY clause.
	An example of a sorted query is:

	<pre><code><orderdetails>
	{
	  FOR $d IN document("Products") _
	    /root/Products[ProductID = $c/ProductID]
	  RETURN <P> { $d/ProductID, $d/UnitPrice, $d/ProductName }
	        <P/>
	  SORTBY(ProductName DESCENDING)
	}
	</orderdetails></code></pre>

	The SORTBY clause accepts an ASCENDING or DESCENDING keyword, where ASCENDING is the default. There are other keywords that can be used as well.

Conditional Expressions	XQuery's conditional expressions, IF, THEN, and ELSE, make it possible to execute parts of a query depending on the results of a test. The test expression evaluates to a Boolean TRUE or FALSE value.
	An example query is:

	<pre><orderdetails>
	{
	  FOR $a IN document("Customers")/root/Customers
	    WHERE $a/CompanyName="Alfreds Futterkiste"
	  RETURN
	    IF ($a/CustomerID)
	    THEN
	      <d1>
	        <customer> { $a/* } </customer>
	      </d1>
	    ELSE
	      <d1>
	        <customer>There is no customer named "Alfreds
	          Futterkiste" in the database.</customer>
	      </d1>
	}
	</orderdetails></pre>

Later on, we'll create an application that makes use of all of the expression types mentioned above. It is, however, beyond the scope of this chapter to explain every form of the XQuery syntax in detail. For that purpose, the W3C site (www.w3c.org/TR/XQuery) is highly recommended.

Implementations of XQuery

The XML Query Language working group maintains a list of early XQuery implementations, of which the most interesting, stable, and specification-compliant ones are listed below. (To see the complete list, see www.w3c.org/XML/Query#products.)

IPSI-XQ: http://ipsi.fhg.de/oasys/ projects/ipsi-xq/index_e.html	IPSI-XQ features an online demonstration, and a download that you can try out for yourself. It's implemented using Java.
Microsoft: http://xqueryservices.com	Microsoft's XQuery demonstration has an online component where you can try your own queries or run the given examples. You can also download a set of managed classes for use in the .NET Framework. This gives you the ability to create your own .NET applications that use XQuery.
Oracle: http://otn.oracle.com/tech/xml/ xmldb/htdocs/querying_xml.html	This implementation doesn't have an online demonstration, but you can download and install a Java-based XQuery prototype for use with the Oracle9i database.

Table continued on following page

Software AG: http://developer.softwareag.com/ tamino/quip	Software AG has developed an XQuery implementation called Quip, available for download from the site. Quip is developed using a highly functional language called Haskell. Quip can be used to query the company's XML database, called Tamino.
X-Hive: http://217.77.130.189:8080/ demos/xquery/index.html	X-Hive features a good online demonstration: you can browse the XML documents used for testing, and you can specify your own queries or use the given examples. Sadly, there's no downloadable demo.

Of these, the only one with direct relevance to the subject of this book is Microsoft's demonstration, which comprises two components:

❑   A downloadable class library (get it at http://xqueryservices.com/setup/xquery.msi) consisting of a set of managed classes that can be programmed against using the .NET Framework SDK. These classes allow us to apply XQuery expressions (called **XQueries** from this point on) to selected arbitrary documents from within your web applications.

❑   The demonstration page, which is built on top of Microsoft's existing XQuery class library, at http://xqueryservices.com.

Microsoft's .NET Classes for XQuery

In order to execute queries over an arbitrary collection of XML documents from within your ASP.NET web application, you must first download and install the XQuery Demo class library from the location above. Make sure you have a clean .NET development server – that is, a machine that doesn't have a beta installed, as this blocks installation of the XQuery Demo.

The XQuery Demo class library consists of the four classes shown in the following diagram:

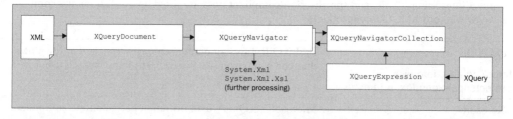

In this scheme, the XML document that you want to run XQueries against is loaded into an instance of XQueryDocument. With this object, it is possible to create an instance of XQueryNavigator, which is similar to XPathNavigator – it enables navigation through one or more XML source documents.

The XQueries that you want to run against XML documents are first placed in XQueryExpression objects, during which process a run-time check on their syntax is made. After that, the queries can be run against objects of type XQueryNavigatorCollection, which are collections of XQueryNavigators. In this way, it's possible to run queries over several XML documents at the same time. The output generated by an XQueryNavigator object is pure XML.

It is possible to have more than one `XQueryNavigatorCollection` *object, which is useful when (for example) you have more than one database, or you want to split one database up into separate virtual XML databases.*

A Sample ASP.NET Project using XQuery

Let's see how XQuery could be used in an ASP.NET project by creating an application to retrieve the current orders of any customer in the SQL Server Northwind sample database, and display the customer's details together with some order details.

This project uses SQLXML and SQL Server 2000 to set up a virtual XML database, and then runs XQueries over the selected customer. The results are in XML format, so we'll use XSLT to present them on the user's screen. Note that although XQuery will *eventually* support updates (to databases and documents), this is still in development, and therefore not something that we can play with right now.

First of all, we'll need a way to create a virtual XML database. If you have SQL Server 2000, a good option is to use SQLXML 3.0, which dramatically extends the XML capabilities of that product.

Setting up the Project in VS.NET

Setting up the new project is easy. Open Visual Studio .NET, create a new C# ASP.NET Web Application named `XQuerySearchEngine`, and delete `WebForm1.aspx`. Then, right-click on the project in Solution Explorer, and add the `OrderSearch.aspx`, and `OrderSearch2.aspx` files from the downloaded chapter code with the **Add Existing Item...** option.

As stated earlier, the application also makes use of SQLXML 3.0 – specifically, its ability to extract SQL data over HTTP in XML format. This makes it possible to convert a relational database into an XML database. Before going any further, make sure that you've installed SQLXML 3.0 from http://msdn.microsoft.com/downloads/default.asp?URL=/downloads/sample.asp?url=/msdn-files/027/001/824/msdncompositedoc.xml.

After installing SQLXML, but before configuring it for the project, create a new project subdirectory called `xml\templates` using Solution Explorer, and add the following files. These will be used to execute stored procedures in the Northwind database, creating XML documents for us to run XQueries against.

- ❑ `GetAllCustomers.xml`
- ❑ `GetAllData.xml`
- ❑ `GetAllOrderDetails.xml`
- ❑ `GetAllOrders.xml`
- ❑ `GetAllProducts.xml`
- ❑ `GetCustomers.xml`

Next, we need to configure SQLXML. Run SQLXML's Configure IIS Support and open the computer folder. There, right click on Default Web Site, and choose the New | Virtual Directory option to open the New Virtual Directory Properties dialog, which has six tabs:

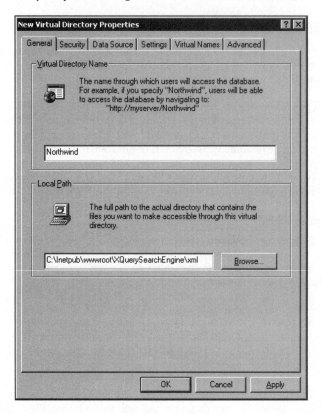

1. In the General tab, enter the name Northwind, and set the path to the xml project subdirectory that you just created (probably C:\Inetpub\wwwroot\XQuerySearchEngine\xml).

2. Switch to the Security tab, and type in the required credentials for your SQL Server installation.

3. On the Data Source tab, specify the server, and choose the Northwind database.

4. On the Settings tab, leave the default options as they are (so that only Allow template queries is checked).

5. Then, in the Virtual Names tab, add a new name called templates (of type template) point it to the project's xml\templates subdirectory, and save it.

6. Leave the options in the Advanced tab at their default settings.

7. Click Apply, and OK.

Now, create another project subdirectory, and call it xsl. This will contain the XSL stylesheets for the presentation of the XML results returned by the XQueries, so copy `orderdetails.xsl` and `orderdetails2.xsl` into it.

The next step is to add a reference to the `Microsoft.Xml.XQuery.dll` to your project using the **Add Reference** dialog, as shown in the figure below:

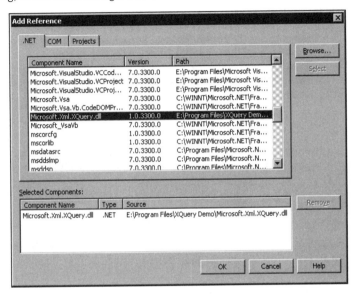

Creating the XQueryNavigatorCollection Object

Everything's now ready for us to begin writing some C# code, starting with the code-behind page, `Global.asax.cs`. Add the following namespace declarations at the top of the file, just before the `namespace XQuerySearchEngine` line:

```
// Added namespaces
using System.Xml;
using Microsoft.Xml.XQuery;
```

Then, add the following variable declarations just after the `public class Global` declaration:

```
// Declare variables
string strUrlXmlTemplateCustomers;
string strUrlXmlTemplateOrders;
string strUrlXmlTemplateOrderDetails;
string strUrlXmlTemplateProducts;

string strNavNameCustomers;
string strNavNameOrders;
string strNavNameOrderDetails;
string strNavNameProducts;

string strUrlXmlTemplateAllData;
string strNavNameAllData;
```

The first four string variables will be used to store the URLs that point to the stored-procedure-running XML templates. These variables, like the others in this list, will be hard-coded to keep the demonstration simple.

The second group of four strings will be assigned with the names of the four corresponding XQueryNavigator objects that will be created later, when the corresponding URL is requested and the XML formatted data is returned.

The last two strings will be used for the creation of one big XQueryNavigator object, which will contain data in XML format from all the tables together.

Still in Global.asax.cs, add the following code to the Application_Start event handler:

```
protected void Application_Start(Object sender, EventArgs e)
{
    // Define the SQL Template URLs and their related collection names
    strUrlXmlTemplateCustomers =
            "http://localhost/northwind/templates/GetAllCustomers.xml";
    strUrlXmlTemplateOrders =
            "http://localhost/northwind/templates/GetAllOrders.xml";
    strUrlXmlTemplateOrderDetails =
            "http://localhost/northwind/templates/GetAllOrderDetails.xml";
    strUrlXmlTemplateProducts =
            "http://localhost/northwind/templates/GetAllProducts.xml";

    strNavNameCustomers = "Customers";
    strNavNameOrders = "Orders";
    strNavNameOrderDetails = "OrderDetails";
    strNavNameProducts = "Products";

    strUrlXmlTemplateAllData =
            "http://localhost/northwind/templates/GetAllData.xml";
    strNavNameAllData = "AllData";

    // Create an XQueryNavigatorCollection object and fill it with four
    //  Northwind tables: Customers, Orders, Order Details, and Products
    XQueryNavigatorCollection navCol = new XQueryNavigatorCollection();

    // Add the Customers navigator to the collection
    XQueryDocument doc1 = new XQueryDocument(strUrlXmlTemplateCustomers,
                                        strNavNameCustomers);
    navCol.AddNavigator(doc1.CreateNavigator());

    // Add the Orders navigator
    XQueryDocument doc2 = new XQueryDocument(strUrlXmlTemplateOrders,
                                        strNavNameOrders);
    navCol.AddNavigator(doc2.CreateNavigator());

    // Add the Order Details navigator
    XQueryDocument doc3 = new XQueryDocument(strUrlXmlTemplateOrderDetails,
                                        strNavNameOrderDetails);
    navCol.AddNavigator(doc3.CreateNavigator());
```

```
    // Add the Products navigator
    XQueryDocument doc4 = new XQueryDocument(strUrlXmlTemplateProducts,
                                            strNavNameProducts);
    navCol.AddNavigator(doc4.CreateNavigator());

    // Try it another way and create one big navigator with all the data
    XQueryNavigatorCollection navColAD = new XQueryNavigatorCollection();

    // Add the Customers, Orders, Order Details, and Products tables in one go
    XQueryDocument doc5 = new XQueryDocument(strUrlXmlTemplateAllData,
                                            strNavNameAllData);
    navColAD.AddNavigator(doc5.CreateNavigator());

    // Create and store the doc object for filling the drop-down list box
    XmlDocument doc = new XmlDocument();
    doc.Load(strUrlXmlTemplateCustomers);
    Application["doc"] = doc;

    // Store the navCol XQueryNavigatorCollection object in the Application
    Application["navCol"] = navCol;

    // Store the navColAD XQueryNavigatorCollection object in the Application
    Application["navColAD"] = navColAD;
}
```

What's going on in this code? Well, first of all, the strings are assigned with URLs and navigator names, as described above. Then, each XML template is loaded into an XQueryDocument object in turn, and the CreateNavigator method of the latter is called to create an XQueryNavigator object.

```
    ...

    XQueryNavigatorCollection navCol = new XQueryNavigatorCollection();

    // Add the Customers navigator to the collection
    XQueryDocument doc1 = new XQueryDocument(strUrlXmlTemplateCustomers,
                                            strNavNameCustomers);
    navCol.AddNavigator(doc1.CreateNavigator());

    ...
```

In this way, *two* XQueryNavigatorCollection objects are created and filled with XML data. The first collection consists of four navigators, each containing all of the available data from one of the four Northwind tables: Customers, Orders, OrderDetails, and Products. The second collection contains one big navigator that contains all of the data from all four tables:

```
    XQueryNavigatorCollection navColAD = new XQueryNavigatorCollection();

    // Add the Customers, Orders, Order Details, and Products tables in one go
    XQueryDocument doc5 = new XQueryDocument(strUrlXmlTemplateAllData,
                                            strNavNameAllData);
    navColAD.AddNavigator(doc5.CreateNavigator());
```

Finally, we store the two collections in the ASP.NET `Application` object, so that we can get to them later. We also load the "customers" template into an ordinary XML document object, so that we can use it to populate a drop-down listbox in our application's user interface, and store that too.

```
// Create and store the doc object for filling the drop-down list box
XmlDocument doc = new XmlDocument();
doc.Load(strUrlXmlTemplateCustomers);
Application["doc"] = doc;

// Store the navCol XQueryNavigatorCollection object in the Application
Application["navCol"] = navCol;

// Store the navColAD XQueryNavigatorCollection object in the Application
Application["navColAD"] = navColAD;
```

In a moment, we'll see how these navigator collections are accessed at page level, and how the returned XML data is transformed and displayed. Before that, you need to copy the image files `minus.gif` and `plus.gif` to a new project subdirectory called `images`. Finally, the web pages include a small JavaScript function for opening each order's details. Create a last new project subdirectory called `inc`, and copy the `orderdetails.js` file into it using Solution Explorer.

This file is embedded into the HTML on the page by using the following `<script>` element, which you can see if you open the HTML view of `OrderSearch2.aspx`:

```
<script language=JavaScript src="inc/orderdetails.js" type=text/jscript>
</script>
```

In Solution Explorer, the project should now look like this:

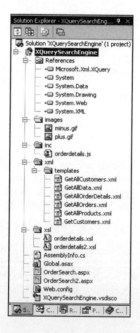

It ought not be necessary to modify Web.config, as extra permissions for the ASPNET account are not needed in this case. But if you want to (say) save and view the result of an XQuery, you'll need to add the following lines to your Web.config file:

```
<?xml version="1.0" encoding="utf-8" ?>
<configuration>

  <system.web>

    ...

    <!--   SECURITY SETTINGS
           Setting impersonate="true" allows for application execution with
           the same account with which the thread created by IIS runs,
           therefore not applying .NET Security rules. NOTE: You need this
           ONLY when (for example) saving the XQuery result tree to a disk
           file!
    -->
    <identity impersonate="true" />

    ...

  </system.web>

</configuration>
```

The code that requires this account impersonation is included but commented out in the OrderSearch.aspx and OrderSearch2.aspx pages. It looks like this:

```
XmlTextWriter writer1 = new XmlTextWriter(
                  Server.MapPath("/XQuerySearchEngine/XQuery_output.xml"),
                  System.Text.Encoding.UTF8);
writer1.Formatting = Formatting.Indented;
writer1.Indentation = 2;
doc.Save(writer1);
writer1.Close();
```

Getting back to the code that we *will* be using in this demonstration, run the SQL script that's included in the download material. The file is called SP_XQuerySearchEngine.sql, and it creates five new stored procedures in the Northwind database. It will come as little surprise that these are named GetAllCustomers, GetAllData, GetAllOrderDetails, GetAllOrders, and GetAllProducts.

We're finished! Set the start page to OrderSearch.aspx, and compile and run the project. The browser should show the following – once all of the initial compilation has been completed, of course:

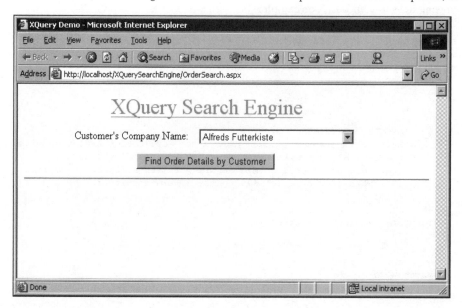

Pressing the Find Order Details by Customer button will then result in the following:

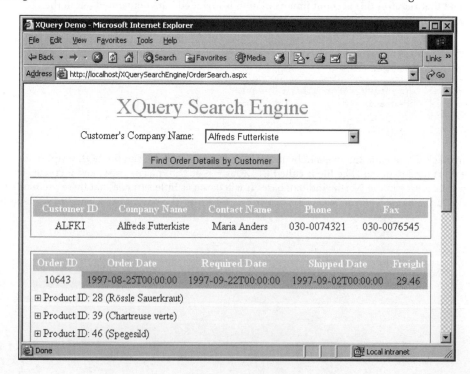

Analyzing the XQuery

Let's have a closer look at the code that produces this web page. You'll find the handler for the Find Order Details by Customer button on the code-behind page OrderSearch.aspx.cs. It looks like this:

```
private void Button1_Click(object sender, System.EventArgs e)
{
  // Executes the XQuery Search on the XQueryNavigatorCollection
  //  using an XML Web Server Control
  if(lstCustomer.SelectedItem != null)
  {
      selectedCustomer = lstCustomer.SelectedItem;
  }

  if("" != selectedCustomer.Value)
  {
    string strXQuery1 = "<orderdetails> { FOR $a IN
document(\"Customers\")/root/Customers WHERE $a/CompanyName=\"" +
selectedCustomer.Value + "\" RETURN <d1> <customer> { $a/CustomerID,
$a/CompanyName, $a/ContactName, $a/Phone, $a/Fax } </customer> { FOR $b IN
document(\"Orders\")/root/Orders[CustomerID = $a/CustomerID] RETURN <d2> <O> {
$b/OrderID, $b/OrderDate, $b/RequiredDate, $b/ShippedDate, $b/Freight } </O> { FOR
$c IN document(\"OrderDetails\")/root/Order_x0020_Details[OrderID = $b/OrderID]
RETURN <d3> <OD> { $c/OrderID, $c/ProductID, $c/Quantity } </OD> { FOR $d IN
document(\"Products\")/root/Products[ProductID = $c/ProductID] RETURN <P> {
$d/ProductID, $d/UnitPrice, $d/ProductName } </P> } </d3> } </d2> } </d1> }
</orderdetails>";

    // Compile the XQuery (this checks for any errors)
    XQueryExpression expr1 = new XQueryExpression(strXQuery1);

    // Run the XQuery
    XQueryNavigator nav1 = expr1.Execute(navCol);

    if(true == nav1.HasChildren)
    {
      // Port the XML result for saving and display
      XmlDocument doc = new XmlDocument();
      doc.LoadXml(nav1.ToXml());

      // View the result as HTML in the XML Web Server Control, XmlOD
      XmlOD.Document = doc;
      XmlOD.TransformSource = "xsl\\orderdetails.xsl";
    }
    else
    {
      // Customer does not have any current order
      XmlDocument docn = new XmlDocument();
      docn.LoadXml("<root><noOrder>This Customer currently " +
                "does not have any order.</noOrder></root>");

      XmlOD.Document = docn;
      XmlOD.TransformSource = "xsl\\noOrder.xsl";
    }
  }
}
```

It might look messy, but because the XQuery in `strXQuery1` is a one-line string, no concatenation is required, resulting in superior performance. It's a well-structured XQuery that can be rewritten rather more legibly as:

```
<orderdetails>
{
  FOR $a IN document(\"Customers\")/root/Customers
  WHERE $a/CompanyName=\"" + selectedCustomer.Value + "\"
  RETURN
  <d1>
    <customer>
      { $a/CustomerID, $a/CompanyName, $a/ContactName, $a/Phone, $a/Fax }
    </customer>
    {
      FOR $b IN document(\"Orders\")/root/Orders[CustomerID = $a/CustomerID]
      RETURN
      <d2>
        <O> { $b/OrderID, $b/OrderDate, $b/RequiredDate,
                          $b/ShippedDate, $b/Freight } </O>
        {
          FOR $c IN document(\"OrderDetails\")/root/
                          Order_x0020_Details[OrderID = $b/OrderID]
          RETURN
          <d3>
            <OD> { $c/OrderID, $c/ProductID, $c/Quantity } </OD>
            {
              FOR $d IN document(\"Products\")/root/
                              Products[ProductID = $c/ProductID]
              RETURN <P> { $d/ProductID, $d/UnitPrice, $d/ProductName } </P>
            }
          </d3>
        }
      </d2>
    }
  </d1>
}
</orderdetails>
```

The approach being used here is based on querying the first navigator, which represents the `Customers` table. Then with the resulting data, the second table, `Orders`, is queried, and so on.

Running the Query and Styling the Output

The XQuery is compiled and run over the collection of navigators as follows:

```
// Compile the XQuery (this checks for any errors)
XQueryExpression expr1 = new XQueryExpression(strXQuery1);

// Run the XQuery
XQueryNavigator nav1 = expr1.Execute(navCol);
```

Then, the data in XML format that's returned is passed on to an XSL stylesheet:

```
if(true == nav1.HasChildren)
{
  // Port the XML result for saving and display
  XmlDocument doc = new XmlDocument();
  doc.LoadXml(nav1.ToXml());

  // View the result as HTML using the XML Web Server Control
  XmlOD.Document = doc;
  XmlOD.TransformSource = "xsl\\orderdetails.xsl";
}
else
{
  // Customer does not have any current order
  XmlDocument docn = new XmlDocument();
  docn.LoadXml("<root><noOrder>This Customer currently does not have any
order.</noOrder></root>");

  XmlOD.Document = docn;
  XmlOD.TransformSource = "xsl\\noOrder.xsl";
}
```

Here, the `if` construct determines whether the XML returned contains any orders by checking whether the XML result tree has any child elements: `nav1.HasChildren`. If so, the XML result tree is assigned to the XML web server control on our ASPX page. A typical XML result tree starts like this:

```
<?xml version="1.0" encoding="utf-8"?>
<orderdetails>
  <d1>
    <customer>
      <CustomerID>ALFKI</CustomerID>
      <CompanyName>Alfreds Futterkiste</CompanyName>
      <ContactName>Maria Anders</ContactName>
      <Phone>030-0074321</Phone>
      <Fax>030-0076545</Fax>
    </customer>
    <d2>
      <O>
        <OrderID>10643</OrderID>
        <OrderDate>1997-08-25T00:00:00</OrderDate>
        <RequiredDate>1997-09-22T00:00:00</RequiredDate>
        <ShippedDate>1997-09-02T00:00:00</ShippedDate>
        <Freight>29.46</Freight>
      </O>
      <d3>
        <OD>
          <OrderID>10643</OrderID>
          <ProductID>28</ProductID>
          <Quantity>15</Quantity>
        </OD>
        <P>
          <ProductID>28</ProductID>
```

```
          <UnitPrice>45.6</UnitPrice>
          <ProductName>Rössle Sauerkraut</ProductName>
        </P>
      </d3>

      ...

    </d2>
  </d1>
</orderdetails>
```

Then, the OrderDetails.xsl XSL stylesheet is assigned to the control, and invoked before returning the result to the client. The XSL stylesheet looks like this:

```
<?xml version='1.0' ?>
<xsl:stylesheet xmlns:xsl="http://www.w3.org/1999/XSL/Transform"
                xmlns:ms="urn:schemas-microsoft-com:xslt" version="1.0">

  <xsl:output method="html" indent="yes" />

  <xsl:template match="/">
    <xsl:apply-templates select="orderdetails/d1" />
  </xsl:template>

  <xsl:template name="d1" match="d1">
    <table cellpadding="3" cellspacing="0" border="1" width="600">
      <tr>
        <td>
          <table cellpadding="3" cellspacing="0" border="0" width="600">
            <tr>
              <th align="center" bgcolor="Lightblue">
                <font color="white">Customer ID</font></th>
              <th align="center" bgcolor="Lightblue">
                <font color="white">Company Name</font></th>
              <th align="center" bgcolor="Lightblue">
                <font color="white">Contact Name</font></th>
              <th align="center" bgcolor="Lightblue">
                <font color="white">Phone</font></th>
              <th align="center" bgcolor="Lightblue">
                <font color="white">Fax</font></th>
            </tr>
            <tr>
              <td align="center">
                <xsl:value-of select="customer/CustomerID" />
              </td>
              <td align="center">
                <xsl:value-of select="customer/CompanyName" />
              </td>
              <td align="center">
                <xsl:value-of select="customer/ContactName" />
              </td>
              <td align="center">
                <xsl:value-of select="customer/Phone" />
              </td>
```

```
                  <td align="center">
                    <xsl:value-of select="customer/Fax" />
                  </td>
                </tr>
              </table>
            </td>
          </tr>
        </table>
        <br />
        <table cellpadding="3" cellspacing="0" border="1" width="600">
          <tr>
            <td>
              <table cellpadding="3" cellspacing="0" border="0" width="600">
                <tr>
                  <th align="center" bgcolor="Lightgreen">
                    <font color="white">Order ID</font></th>
                  <th align="center" bgcolor="Lightgreen">
                    <font color="white">Order Date</font></th>
                  <th align="center" bgcolor="Lightgreen">
                    <font color="white">Required Date</font></th>
                  <th align="center" bgcolor="Lightgreen">
                    <font color="white">Shipped Date</font></th>
                  <th align="center" bgcolor="Lightgreen">
                    <font color="white">Freight</font></th>
                </tr>
                <xsl:apply-templates select="d2">
                  <xsl:sort select="O/OrderID" />
                </xsl:apply-templates>
              </table>
            </td>
          </tr>
        </table>
</xsl:template>

<xsl:template name="d2" match="d2">
  <tr>
    <td align="center" bgcolor="cornsilk">
      <xsl:value-of select="O/OrderID" />
    </td>
    <td align="center" bgcolor="silver">
      <xsl:value-of select="O/OrderDate" />
    </td>
    <td align="center" bgcolor="silver">
      <xsl:value-of select="O/RequiredDate" />
    </td>
    <td align="center" bgcolor="silver">
      <xsl:value-of select="O/ShippedDate" />
    </td>
    <td align="center" bgcolor="silver">
      <xsl:value-of select="O/Freight" />
    </td>
  </tr>
  <tr>
    <td colspan="5">
```

319

```
        <xsl:apply-templates select="d3">
          <xsl:sort select="OD/ProductID" />
        </xsl:apply-templates>
      </td>
    </tr>
  </xsl:template>

  <xsl:template name="d3" match="d3">
    <xsl:param name="OrderID-ProductID"
            select="concat(OD/OrderID,'-',OD/ProductID)" />
    <tr>
      <td colspan="5" onmouseover="this.style.cursor='hand'"
          onclick="ToggleOrder('{$OrderID-ProductID}')">
        <img SRC="images/plus.gif" />
         Product ID: 
        <xsl:value-of select="OD/ProductID" />
         (<xsl:value-of select="P/ProductName" />)
      </td>
    </tr>
    <tr>
      <td colspan="5">
        <table cellpadding="3" cellspacing="0" width="100%"
              id="{$OrderID-ProductID}" style="display:none" border="1">
          <tr>
            <td bgcolor="cornsilk" width="15%">
              <b>Quantity</b>
            </td>
            <td bgcolor="cornsilk" width="15%">
              <b>Unit Price</b>
            </td>
            <td bgcolor="cornsilk" width="70%">
              <b>Product Name</b>
            </td>
          </tr>
          <tr>
            <td>
              <xsl:value-of select="OD/Quantity" />
            </td>
            <td>
              <xsl:value-of select="P/UnitPrice" />
            </td>
            <td>
              <xsl:value-of select="P/ProductName" />
            </td>
          </tr>
        </table>
      </td>
    </tr>
  </xsl:template>
</xsl:stylesheet>
```

Here, the XML is processed using a few XSL templates, but the approach is again quite straightforward. The first template matches the root element of the XML source, and then control is passed on to the next template:

```
<xsl:template match="/">
  <xsl:apply-templates select="orderdetails/d1" />
</xsl:template>
```

Upon entering the second template, the current node is set to orderdetails/d1. In this template, the upper and lower <table> are built, each using a combination of an outer and an inner table. The outer tables have a border set to "1", and the inner ones to "0". Thus, the thin gray lines drawn around the two tables shown on the screen come from the outer table, giving the page a nicer look.

Inside the inner table, after inserting the header row (which is simply hard-coded), the <td> tags are filled in sequence by selecting values from our XML source, using XPath expressions. Here's an example of that process (the XPath expressions are shown in bold):

```
<tr>
  <td align="center">
    <xsl:value-of select="customer/CustomerID" />
  </td>
  <td align="center">
    <xsl:value-of select="customer/CompanyName" />
  </td>
      .
      .
      .
</tr>
```

The JavaScript function ToggleOrder, which is used to 'open' each order to show more details, needs its argument to be a unique value. In this case, the XSLT function concat is used to form that unique value by first selecting the OrderID, and then adding the value of the ProductID to it. This procedure is necessary because a product can appear twice in a given customer's orders, so the ProductID alone is not a sufficient differentiator. If you don't also specify the OrderID, a conflict in the script may occur. The unique argument value is created as follows:

```
<xsl:param name="OrderID-ProductID"
           select="concat(OD/OrderID,'-',OD/ProductID)" />
<tr>
  <td colspan="5" onmouseover="this.style.cursor='hand'"
      onclick="ToggleOrder('{$OrderID-ProductID}')">
    <img SRC="images/plus.gif" />
     Product ID: 
    <xsl:value-of select="OD/ProductID" />
     (<xsl:value-of select="P/ProductName" />)
```

An <xsl:param> element is used here to concatenate the OrderID with each ProductID, making the compound ID unique. The <td> tag is wired to the onClick event that triggers the ToggleOrder function. The outcome is that clicking on the '+' and '-' icons has the effect that we've all come to expect.

Summary

That concludes our quick tour of XQuery 1.0. You've seen what XQuery is, and we looked at its background, and at its intended purpose. Furthermore, we've explored some of the syntax used in XQuery expressions, and taken a closer look at the class library that Microsoft has developed for its demonstration of XQuery. Finally, we saw how XQuery can be used with ASP.NET and its rich XML support.

The XQuery specification is still a working draft, and there are many issues still to be resolved – it is to be hoped, for example, that support for updating databases and documents will indeed be added. However, it is likely to be some time before XQuery 1.0 reaches W3C recommendation status, and the current development of XPath 2.0 and XSLT 2.0 will only add to this delay.

What *is* clear is that Microsoft is committed to integrating XQuery in one or more of its future products. A good guess is that XQuery will likely be supported in SQLXML (as another option to turn SQL Server into a XML database), MSXML (to give another option for querying and transforming XML besides the XPath-XSLT combination), and VS.NET (for example, an XQuery Query Builder with IntelliSense support) once (or perhaps even before) it has reached W3C recommendation status.

10

Performance

As the Internet continues to improve in appeal and accessibility, there is an increasing need to extract the maximum output from our hardware and software. Improving performance not only allows us to support ever more complex web applications, but those applications can themselves support greater numbers of users. Designing an application with performance in mind from the start is essential, and performance analysis needs to form an integral part of each and every development iteration cycle. This will help ensure that, when an application finally sees the light of day, we avoid comments such as, "Well, it looks great, but it's a bit slow" – a sure sign that the application isn't (yet) worth a cent in a production environment.

Although *scalability* is closely related to application performance, it should be noted that first you need to improve application performance as much as you can; then, you can check if any scaling is necessary of your current hardware. You can either decide to *scale up* (by adding processors or memory) or *scale out* (by adding servers). This is however outside the scope of this chapter.

Since ASP.NET is a brand-new programming environment, our trusty old ASP 3.0 performance tips and tricks don't apply anymore. Hopefully though, this chapter will provide a good head start in this area. Naturally, given the remit of the book, we'll be concentrating on applications that involve XML (and related technologies), but many of the points will apply equally to other areas of ASP.NET development.

We'll be doing this by:

- ❏ Looking at general approaches to performance improvement in ASP.NET applications
- ❏ Investigating specific tools in ASP.NET that can improve the response of our applications
- ❏ Demonstrating the performance testing tool that forms part of the Enterprise edition of Visual Studio .NET: **Application Center Test**

To illustrate the topics covered, we'll use, and extend, the XQuery example from the previous chapter. Thus we'll be working with an application that involves XML, XPath, XSL, XSLT, and XQuery – it will use related namespace classes at different levels (page, session, and application level), and a Web Service will be added to the mix (which we'll run both locally and remotely). These applications will then be subject to a load-test using Application Center Test (ACT) and the results compared.

Before we get stuck into the example, let's begin by looking at some general tactics for developing efficient ASP.NET applications.

Improving ASP.NET Application Performance

There are a few important things to keep in mind when designing any application in ASP.NET. Specifically, the following subjects deserve special attention:

❑   Caching

❑   Data Access

❑   Working with strings

There are many other factors which can impact performance and are worthy of attention during the development phase, namely: buffering, language independence, Interop Services, garbage collection, pre-compilation, Web Controls, viewstate, session state, process model, and threading. Since these do not directly involve XML and are merely system-dependent factors however, we won't look at them in this chapter.

Caching

ASP.NET has some really neat caching capabilities for optimizing application performance. They are:

❑   Output Caching

❑   Fragment Caching

❑   Cache API

❑   Document Caching

By default, page caching is turned off in an ASP.NET web page, due to its disconnected nature. Each page request results in the Page object being instantiated, processing the request, and then when the result is sent back to the client, the object is destroyed. When caching is turned on however, the page (or items on page) is kept on the server. These cached items can then be used for subsequent requests, either from the originating, or from another user.

Output caching is the caching of the static (X)HTML document corresponding to an ASP.NET web page, and it can give significant (if not massive) performance boosts. This type of caching is like serving up static web pages; the only difference is that caching uses machine resources. If the pages only contain static data, it would be better to generate them on a stage server and then copy them onto the web server. This way you get the best performance the web server can give you. If the pages do change, but if the change frequency is low, you can always opt for updating them using a batch web page generation process, running it every once in a while.

Fragment caching is used when you can't cache the whole page. Here caching can be applied to user controls, data objects, and even page fragments. This approach can help a lot in optimizing your web application, but it requires setting up a performance measuring and registration service with the capability to compare accurately new test results with older results. In .NET, you can cache page fragments using the @OutputCache directive.

Finally, custom caching can be performed using the **Cache API**. This API supports caching any object, along with any dependencies, expiration, and user callbacks on expiration. Caching an object temporarily is possible using an expiration time, say 5 seconds. This cached item lives then for 5 seconds on the server. Any request made during these 5 seconds is responded to with the cached data. After that, the cache is updated with the next request.

Document caching is useful when, for example, performing XSLT transforms. ASP.NET can cache static XSL style sheets with a significant resultant performance boost. Note that this option cannot be applied when generating XSL style sheets dynamically. Of course, document caching is not limited to stylesheets; in principle any document would qualify if caching would result in better performance.

The downside is that caching consumes resources (memory), so it is generally not a good idea to cache every page or user control, but only those that are most frequently used, or provide the biggest benefit. Guidance here should come from classifying what resources each control or page needs, and then only caching items where a large amount of resources is needed for concurrent requests. Performance testing for each development cycle iteration provides an overall guideline here. In general, it is best to use the appropriate user control or data object for its intended purpose. The more functionality a control or object has, the more overhead it causes on the web server, thus resulting in lower performance.

Another general rule is to make use of the ASP.NET Page.IsPostback property whenever possible, as in this example taken from the XQuerySearchEngine project from the download material for this chapter:

```
private void Page_Load(object sender, System.EventArgs e)
{

  // Get the doc1 Application object
  XmlDocument doc1 = (XmlDocument)(Application["doc1"]);

  if (!Page.IsPostBack)
  {
    // Fill the DropDownBox - create a Node list and then loop through it
    XmlNodeList oNodeList = doc1.SelectNodes("//CompanyName");

    foreach(XmlNode ond in oNodeList)
      lstCustomer.Items.Add(ond.InnerXml);
  }

  // Get the navCol Application object
  navCol = (XQueryNavigatorCollection)(Application["navCol"]);
}
```

The `Page.IsPostBack` property avoids unnecessary processing on a round trip, as it is set to `true` when a previously opened page is posted back to the server, for instance in response to a button click. The code above uses it to ensure the `lstCustomer` dropdown is only filled with data the first time the page is requested. If we were not to check this property, the dropdown would be appended with the same list every time the page is requested, which of course is not what we want. The `ViewState` property will maintain the contents of the dropdown during server roundtrips. Note that the `XQueryNavigatorCollection` object (assigned to `navCol`) is created every time the page is processed, but its value is held in an application variable, and all we do here is set a new object instance. The actual work, like accessing the database and creating the collection navigator object, occurs in the `Global.asax` file, when a user requests a page in the web application for the first (and only the first) time.

We'll be looking at this topic later in this chapter, when we come to discuss the demo web application. Specifically, we'll look at a case where an XSL style sheet is cached with a resultant improvement in overall application performance. This is especially useful where multiple users request the same web page and XSL stylesheet, but supply different data for presentation.

Data Access

Accessing data stores from a web page can involve a significant performance hit, as it requires one or more server roundtrips. This generally means external network access (as in practice the web server and database server will be separate), sometimes over long distances over a private company's network, or even over the Internet.

When getting data in XML format, there are several good options to choose from. One good fast option is to use SQLXML 3.0's SQL Template Query functionality. Basically a virtual directory is set up which contains the query templates. The templates themselves are XML files that contain one or more SQL queries or stored procedures.

These queries or stored procedures produce conventional recordsets, but when the clause FOR XML AUTO, ELEMENTS (or in any other FOR XML form) is used in the query, SQL Server generates and returns an XML document corresponding to the recordset. You run the templates by requesting a template URL on the Web Server. This request is then translated to a database call by SQL Server, which returns the XML to the caller over HTTP. The default encoding used by SQLXML is UTF-8.

If our database server is heavily loaded (for example, this can happen when the database is heavily queried by various clients, or web servers), we can opt for processing the XML on the client – which in this case, is the Web Server. This can be done programmatically, as the following example illustrates. The following Template Query formats the XML on the *server side*:

```
<ROOT xmlns:sql="urn:schemas-microsoft-com:xml-sql">
  <sql:query client-side-xml="0">
    SELECT *
    FROM Employees
    FOR XML AUTO
  </sql:query>
</ROOT>
```

and this one carries out the XML formatting on the *client side*:

```
<ROOT xmlns:sql="urn:schemas-microsoft-com:xml-sql">

    <sql:query client-side-xml="1">

    SELECT *
    FROM Employees
    FOR XML AUTO
    </sql:query>
</ROOT>
```

The `client-side-xml` attribute tells SQL where to make the final transformation – on the server (`"0"`), or on the client (`"1"`).

There are a few things to be aware of when using either client-side or server-side XML formatting. The most important are:

❑ Queries that generate multiple row sets are not supported in client-side XML formatting, and they require server-side formatting.

❑ GROUP BY and aggregate functions are only supported by client-side XML formatting. If the formatting is on the server-side, an error is generated because SQL Server 2000 does not support GROUP BY or aggregate functions for queries with FOR XML.

The downside of this approach is that, despite creating a separate layer for data extraction, the structural database information is still kept inside the stored procedures. More specific, although stored procedures hide database information from the user, and are compiled objects, they do contain information that relates to the structure of the database. If the database structure changes, the stored procedure may need to be updated also. This, in turn, can affect the way the XML recordset is created, which finally can affect the output generated by an XSL Transformation. So, in the end, you may need to update the whole chain of documents, including your XSL Stylesheet.

To address this, a second option is to use XDR or XSD Schemas. Using XPath, we can extract the XML from the database via a mapping schema, and then easily perform an XSLT transform on it. This allows us to keep the application code independent of the database design, because design details are held inside the mapping schema, including relational information. The drawback of this approach is that creating the mapping schema can be a laborious task. Another reason that it is not being used here is that XPath is in some ways limited in power compared to SQL. The limitations include recursion queries, and related to recursion, static variable assignment. A SQL query is also much more readable than an XPath expression.

A third method is to use ADO.NET and the .NET System.Data namespace. This namespace contains classes for querying and updating databases, as discussed in Chapter 6. The data obtained can be passed to an XmlDataDocument, which then can be used for XSL transformations.

A good article for you to read and be able to compare the above mentioned three methods, both in performance and development time, is *SQL Server 2000 and XML – Developing XML-Enabled Data Solutions for the Web* by Scott Howlett and Darryl Jennings, *MSDN Magazine*, January 2002. It can be found at http://msdn.microsoft.com/msdnmag/issues/02/01/SQLXML/SQLXML.asp.

Working with Strings

When working with strings, such as when performing concatenation, it is recommended that the StringBuilder class be used (the .NET namespace is System.Text). This class is much more efficient in its use of resources, when compared to the String class (from the System namespace). This is because the String class creates new objects every time an operation is performed (that is, every time when one of its methods is used), while StringBuilder does not.

Concatenating many strings in a loop for instance, can have a real hit on the performance of an application, and using StringBuilder in such a case would consume much less resources and be far more efficient, mitigating the performance penalty. An example of where StringBuilder would be of real benefit would be an XML processor module; where textual input such as the XML source and the XSL style sheet is manipulated to produce the output result tree.

Performance Monitoring in ASP.NET

Now we've looked at some general approaches to efficient ASP.NET application development, let's now have a look at some specific tools that ASP.NET gives us to improve and monitor performance.

Before we can collect reliable and useful performance data, we must of course be sure that the application is bug free and functionally correct, and to this end the trace facility implemented in the System.Web class library can be a great help. Tracing code paths within an application may not only highlight errors, but it can help identify potential improvements in command execution – so enhancing the responsiveness of our code.

In this part of the chapter we'll be looking at:

❑   Using the trace facility

❑   Measuring performance in ASP.NET with profiling services, performance counters, sampling, and the Application Center Test tool

Our first task, however, is to define some measures of performance.

An Aside – What is Application Performance?

Basically, there are two ways to measure application performance. The first is **Machine Throughput**, measured in requests per second. The other is **Response Time**, which has two measures: **Time To First Byte** (TTFB), which is the time between sending the request and receiving the first byte of the response, and **Time To Last Byte** (TTLB), the time between sending the request and receiving the last byte of the response. These times are measured in milliseconds.

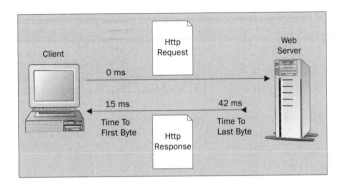

TTFB provides a measure of the *processing time* on the server, when page buffering is turned on (in IIS 5.0, this is the default), and it also includes *transmission time*. Page buffering must be turned on to force the web server to process the complete response, and therefore be able to measure the real TTFB time. Note here that the server is most probably already processing another request by the time the client receives the first byte. This influences the time period between the TTFB and TTLB.

TTLB indicates the time it took the server to process the complete request, including returning the complete result to the client. Therefore, TTLB represents the overall response time and can be used to determine any latency problems on the server. Latency problems in this case represent wasted time on the server, in other words, the server takes too long to completely process requests.

Trace Facility

To assist in the process of functional for testing our web applications, ASP.NET offers a tracing facility that traces coding paths through the application. Note that turning the Trace facility on means adding some overhead, and is only meant as an aiding method in the process of optimizing your web application.

In ASP prior to .NET, developers are accustomed to making frequent use of Response.Write in a page in order to aid debugging. The developer would remove them all when the page has been determined error-free. There are many obvious problems with such an approach, such as the time consumed by going through the code searching for all occurrences, and the need to reinstate them, should an error surface once the application is in production.

ASP.NET's solution is Trace.Write, which we can simply use in place of Response.Write, and which can be set to write output to the client by the following page directive at the top of an ASP.NET page:

```
<%@ Page Trace="false|true" .. .. %>
```

Setting the above attribute to false results in all Trace.Write statements being completely ignored. The trace facility is implemented in the namespace System.Web, by the TraceContext class, and its two methods called Warn and Write. Both generally accept two parameters, but have an overloaded method that takes a third parameter. The two first parameters are category and message, where category defines the category name to write to, and message sets the text to write. The additional parameter of the overloaded method is errorInfo, which contains information about the exception that occurred. This is very useful if we need more details at run time on what exactly is going wrong when tracing a faulty code path.

The `TraceTest` ASP.NET C# project from the chapter download material demonstrates how we can use the trace facility at page level. Set up the folder containing this project on your hard drive as a virtual directory in IIS, and open it by double-clicking the `csproj` file.

The project contains just one Web Form, called `Trace.aspx`. This is a very simple page, as we can see in the code-behind file. All the code there is contained in the event handler for clicks on `Button1`:

```
private void Button1_Click(object sender, System.EventArgs e)
{
  Trace.Warn("Entering Button1_Click()","This is red text (Warning)");

  int a = 4;
  int b = 3;
  Trace.Write("Inside Button1_Click() a: ", a.ToString());
  Trace.Write("Inside Button1_Click() b: ", b.ToString());

  Label1.Text = (a + b).ToString();

  Trace.Warn("Leaving Button1_Click()","This is also red text (Warning)");
}
```

If we look at the HTML view for the page, we'll see the `Trace` attribute on the `Page` directive at the top of the page. If we set this attribute to `false` (the default value), we disable tracing, and when we run the project we'll just see the intended output:

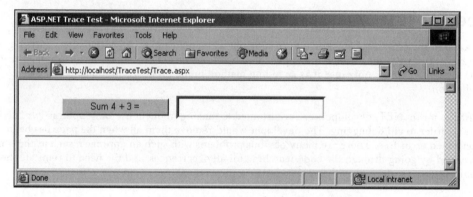

Now enable tracing by setting the `Trace` attribute to `true`, and restart the project:

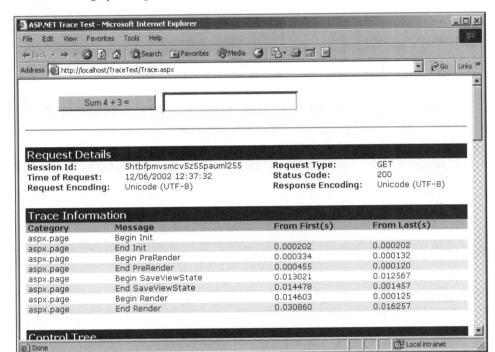

The information that we see here is arranged into the following categories:

- ❑ Request Details
- ❑ Trace Information
- ❑ Control Tree
- ❑ Cookies Collection
- ❑ Headers Collection
- ❑ Server Variables

These are all fairly self-explanatory. The Trace Information section details the processes that have been traced through up to the current point of processing. Now click the button labeled Sum 4 + 3 =, and this section will be appended with the details of the steps that are invoked, including the `Trace.Warn` and `Trace.Write` method calls that we added to the code inside the click event handler:

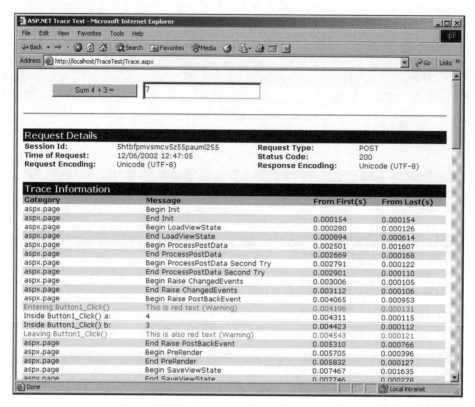

Note that the trace information is always added to the end of the page. The column **From First(s)** indicates the total time elapsed in seconds, while the column **From Last(s)** indicates the time elapsed relative to the last time measuring event.

ASP.NET's trace facility opens up a whole range of possibilities for tracing code paths through an application. The information it provides can be invaluable for streamlining applications, and it is very simple to turn on and off.

We can also turn on tracing at application level, in the Web.config file:

```
<configuration>
  <system.web>
    <trace enabled="true" requestLimit="40" localOnly="false"/>
  </system.web>
</configuration>
```

The attribute requestLimit sets the maximum number of requests on a per-application basis that should include tracing information, and localOnly determines if the trace output should only appear on the web server. If tracing is enabled at application level, setting the Page directive's attribute Trace to false will override it for that page

Now we've got the functional tests and debugging phases out of the way, it's time to move on to look at ways to measure performance.

Measuring Performance in ASP.NET

So when our application, functionally speaking, fulfills its design brief and achieves its stated aims, we can concentrate on tuning it up so that it works as fast as possible, under the given circumstances. Remember that the final performance should always be kept in mind during development, and analyzed at the end of each development iteration.

Before gathering performance information, we must first think carefully about what information will be useful, and how to administrate it.

We'll need to compile our performance testing history, so that we can compare new tests with old ones. We also need to record details of the test configuration, so that we can check that tests are comparable with the previous ones.

So, to make our application run faster, we first need to gather information about its run-time behavior under ASP.NET. For this, there are a few advanced ways in which we can measure performance and profile our application in ASP.NET. In short, they are:

❑   Profiling Services

❑   Performance Counters

❑   Analyzing performance with Sampling

❑   Application Center Test (ACT)

Application Center Test, a feature of VS.NET Enterprise Architect, is the most valuable of these, and so will be subject to a closer investigation than the others.

Profiling Services

ASP.NET Profiling Services provide a means for gathering performance data for an application at run time, which can be used to streamline it and improve performance.

Profiling Services are implemented using a classic COM server, which implements a profiling service. The COM server consists of two interfaces: `ICorProfilerCallBack`, and `ICorProfilerInfo`. You might ask why plain old COM is being used here in the brave new world of the .NET Framework. Well, the main reason is probably because it will not interfere with the .NET Framework, and instead works in an unmanaged space, allowing it to peep inside an application, and get the data it needs, whenever the programmer needs it. Also, as a COM component, the Profiler application is quite independent of the Framework, and any problems there will not affect it, and vice versa.

Take a look at the following simple diagram showing how the Profiling Services work:

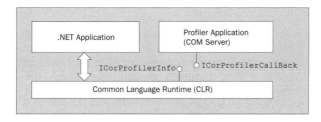

The COM Interface `ICorProfilerCallBack` has methods for all the event types (listed below) that can be fired inside the CLR during run time. When an event happens, the CLR calls the appropriate method of the COM Interface `ICorProfilerCallBack`.

For example, if you would like to know how long a function takes to execute and return its result, simply invoke the Profiler, and measure the time between the function load and leave events (formally called `FunctionEnter` and `FunctionLeave`).

Invoking the Profiler is remarkably easy: we simply set the values of two environment variables. The first, `Cor_Enable_Profiling`, indicates that the CLR should connect to a profiler by a non-zero value. The second, `Cor_Profiler`, is a string specifying either the CLSID or the ProgID of the profiler to use. For instance, we could set it on the command line like so:

By CLSID:
>**set Cor_Profiler={32E2F4DA-1BEA-47ea-88F9-C5DAF691C94A}**

By ProgID:
>**set Cor_Profiler="MyProfiler"**

The Profiling Services can do many things for us, much more in fact than merely profiling an application. `ICorProfilerCallBack` methods can be grouped into the following categories:

❑ CLR startup and shutdown events

❑ Application domain creation and shutdown events

❑ Assembly loading and unloading events

❑ Module load/unload events

❑ COM `VTable` (which is a structure in the header of every class object that contains the memory addresses of the actual code associated with the properties and methods implemented in the interface) creation and destruction events

❑ JIT compiles, and code pitching events

❑ Class load/unload events

❑ Thread birth/death/synchronization

❑ Routine entry/exit events

❑ Exceptions

❑ Transitions between managed and unmanaged execution

❑ Transitions between different Runtime contexts

❑ Information about Runtime suspensions

❑ Information about the Runtime memory heap and garbage collection activity

It would be too exhaustive to explain the methods contained in each category, but every method is detailed in the `Profiling.doc` Word document, along with additional related information. It should be located in the `C:\Program Files\Microsoft Visual Studio .NET\FrameworkSDK\Tool Developers Guide\docs` directory by default.

Matt Prietek's MSDN article at
http://msdn.microsoft.com/msdnmag/issues/01/12/hood/hood0112.asp has more
information on getting started with the .NET Profiling API and the DNProfiler Tool.

Profiling Services is a very powerful way of obtaining specific information about an application's
performance, highlighting bottlenecks, wrong code routes, and more. In the next section, we look at a
different way of gathering performance information, .NET Performance Counters.

Performance Counters

Performance counters are objects that give another way of profiling a program by supplying
performance data provided by applications, services, and drivers during execution. Windows 2000
provides a host of performance objects, counters, and instances.

We can add counters to a program using the Performance utility in Admin Tools. With the System
Monitor selected in the left hand tree view, click the plus button on the toolbar that appears along the
top of the right-hand pane to bring up the Add Counters dialog:

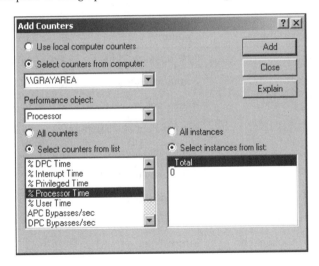

ASP.NET offers a wide range of performance counters. Some provide information about a specific piece
of hardware, others about what is happening during code execution.

There are two basic categories of ASP.NET performance objects available: ASP.NET and ASP.NET
Applications. The first is a set of counters that give information about the global ASP.NET installation.
The second provides counters that give application-specific information. This lets us easily separate
performance data for each application running on the server, to see which is causing the headache.

In addition, each ASP.NET installation has a set of performance counters specific to the installed
version, which have names similar to two categories already mentioned, but with the version number
tacked on at the end. For example, my computer has these four ASP.NET categories:

There are quite a few counters and instances available as the above list shows, and thus we need a clear idea of what information we would like monitored in order to satisfy our performance test, and then add relevant counters to our profiling or performance tool.

In our case, measuring the performance of a web application, the following counters are most useful for determining overall performance:

Performance Object	Counter	Instance
Processor	% Processor Time	_Total
Memory	Available Bytes	*N/A*
Memory	Pages/sec	*N/A*
ASP.NET	Worker Process Restarts	*N/A*
ASP.NET	Requests Queued	*N/A*
ASP.NET	Requests Rejected	*N/A*
ASP.NET Application	Requests/Sec	_Total
ASP.NET Application	Requests Executing	_Total
ASP.NET Application	Errors Total	_Total
ASP.NET Application	Sessions Active	_Total

We'll look at each of these now.

The % Processor Time Counter

The **% Processor Time Counter** indicates the percentage of time that the processor spends executing non-idle threads. A level of 0% indicates the processor is not occupied with useful tasks, and a level of 100% means that the processor is dedicating its full processing power to requesting threads. At this level, processor queuing may occur.

When there are multiple processors installed, you can select an instance for each. If you test on the local machine, then CPU usage reflects all current activities, including database access and other activities that might not form part of the processing of a request.

Typical optimal values of this counter should be about 70-90% when running a web application at its maximum demand, meaning that the processor still has some processing power left when the amount of requests go up when in production. A web application that is continuously above 90% is considered too loaded and should be either scaled up (by adding processors or memory) or scaled out (adding servers).

The Available Bytes Counter

The **Available Bytes Counter** indicates the amount of physical memory, in bytes, currently free on the computer – it is not an average. It is the sum of the space detailed on the **Zeroed**, **Free**, and **Stand By** memory lists. Only Free memory is ready for use. Zeroed memory has been overwritten with zeroes to prevent other processes reading data from a previous process. Finally, Stand By memory is in the process of being freed from a process's allocated set, but can still be recalled for use.

The amount of memory available indicates how much resources are consumed by an application. High memory usage can indicate that an application is not scalable perhaps, or that the amount of available RAM is insufficient.

The Pages/sec Counter

The **Pages/sec Counter** shows a count of the memory pages that must be read from or written to disk in order to supply the application with the data it needs (these are known as 'hard page faults'). If this number is too high, it indicates that the system is too busy reading and writing to disk, with consequent response delays. The displayed value is a mean, obtained by evaluating the difference between the values of the last two samples, and dividing it by the sample interval.

As said, high values indicate a high level of disk access, which in turn could mean that virtual memory is set too low, or that the application is poorly designed, such that, for example, it allocates too little memory for concurrent operations. In such cases, caching pages or objects could help alleviate the problem.

The Worker Process Restarts Counter

The **Worker Process Restarts Counter** measures the number of times the ASP.NET worker process, `aspnet_wp.exe`, has had to restart on the machine. .NET supports automatic restarts of working processes. If a worker process restarts, it indicates that there was a problem during its execution. It is costly in terms of performance, and should therefore be fully investigated if it occurs.

In .NET, you can configure the way automatic worker process restarts are handled by looking at the `<processModel>` element in the `machine.config` file.

The Requests Queued Counter

The **Requests Queued Counter** gives the number of requests currently waiting to be processed. When requests are being queued it means either that the CPU has reached maximum capacity, or that all available threads are being used. If, however, CPU usage is low, you can increment the maximum number of threads available to ASP.NET – this is part of the process of tuning your web server.

In .NET, the maximum number of threads can be increased by setting the `maxWorkerThreads` and `maxIoThreads` attributes of the `<processModel>` element in the `machine.config` file.

The Requests Rejected Counter

The **Requests Rejected Counter** simply tells us the number of requests that have been rejected because the request queue was full. This generally means that the capacity to process them is at its upper limit. Generally, scaling up (increasing hardware on the server) or scaling out (spreading load over more servers) will help alleviate this problem.

The Requests/Sec Counter

The **Requests/Sec Counter** is concerned with the number of requests executed per second. It is the main indicator for overall performance of the application or web server. The higher it is, the better. In Application Center Test, this counter is the most important of all, as we'll see later on.

The Requests Executing Counter

The **Requests Executing Counter** simply counts the number of requests currently executing. This counter tells us the level of activity currently on the web server.

The Errors Total Counter

As its name implies, the **Errors Total Counter** quantifies the total number of errors that have occurred and if not zero, indicates that the application is not functioning correctly. This counter should always be zero at all times, and any error should be investigated right away, as it will slow down performance and may well indicate a flaw in the application's functionality.

The Sessions Active Counter

The **Sessions Active Counter** indicates the current number of sessions currently active. Sessions normally represent resource usage. A high level of active sessions means a high amount of resources in use, thus reducing the scalability of your application.

Using Counters

We can programmatically access these performance counters through the `PerformanceCounter` class of the `System.Diagnostics` namespace, and it is easy to add a performance counter object to a VS.NET project with Server Explorer. Each computer listed under the Servers node has a Performance Counter node, which expands to list all available categories, which in turn expand to display the counters in that category:

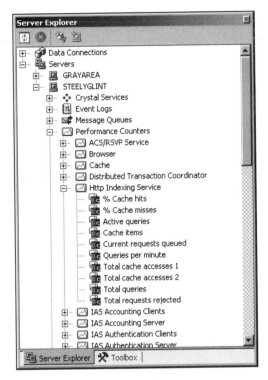

We add an object for one of these counters by simply dragging it (or an instance if applicable) onto a page. The performance counter object does not have a user interface so it will be placed in the component tray at the bottom of the page:

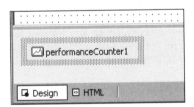

Another way to add a performance counter object to a project is to choose the `PerformanceCounter` object from the **Components** tab of the Toolbox. A third method is to programmatically declare a Performance Counter Object.

The last two methods do not define exactly which counter is used, and we need to set that afterwards. Hence, the first method can be the simplest, as we can look at each category and see the counters available together with their instances.

Analyzing Performance with Sampling

Sampling gives the ability to analyze performance in a more specialized way. It involves measuring certain performance counters at certain defined intervals. The results obtained can be presented in certain ways, for instance as an average.

A profiling tool can make extensive use of sampling performance counters. These tools allow us to look right inside an application and watch each block or even each instruction code line execute. A very detailed report can be generated from the information obtained, to help identify and eliminate bottlenecks in an application.

Application Center Test

Application Center Test (ACT) is a testing tool originally developed and shipped with Microsoft's Application Center. A cut-down version of the tool is shipped with Enterprise editions of Visual Studio .NET, for functional, performance, and load testing during development.

ACT's predecessor is the well-known **Web Application Stress** (WAS) tool, which allows us to stress a web application to a certain load, as expressed in number of threads or concurrent requests.

It can be freely downloaded from http://webtool.rte.microsoft.com/. The site also provides a lot of information about its usage, and how to interpret the obtained results. Note though, that WAS is designed to test performance in a three-tier traditional ASP web environment, running on Windows NT4 or 2000. WAS is not meant to be used with ASP.NET – ACT is.

ACT has more functionality than WAS (as we'll see later on), such as the ability to pass parameter values to newly requested pages. It is also integrated into the VS.NET IDE, although not yet as integrated as it could be. You cannot, for example, add performance counters to a script in an ACT project loaded in VS.NET, nor can you see the graphical displays of ACT's results. For both these things, you have to open the project in the standalone version of ACT.

In the remainder of the chapter, we'll use the standalone version of ACT to generate test scripts, adding performance counters to each, and run some performance tests with different concurrent client connections.

Testing ASP.NET Web Applications with ACT

To demonstrate ACT, we'll use two ASP.NET web applications that demonstrate a variety of code techniques that we can compare and contrast with ACT. The project folders for each application need to be set as a Virtual Directory in IIS, as does the Northwind folder, which contains the SQL templates.

The northwind virtual directory needs to be set up with SQLXML 3.0's "Configure IIS Support", as described in Chapter 9, under the section *Setting up the project using VS.NET*. All the other project directories are activated using Internet Service Manager (ISM), once they have been copied. Note also that the local server localhost has been used when running the templates. You can run them on another SQL 2000 Server with SQLXML 3.0 installed, if you wish.

Lastly, run the SP_XquerySearchEngine.sql script on the Northwind database, to create the stored procedures that our XQueries invoke.

The Applications

❑ The first application (XQuerySearchEngine) is the same that we looked at in detail in the previous chapter. It contains two Web Forms that each use one application-level variable defined in Global.asax. The first variable is of type XQueryNavigatorCollection, and contains four independent navigators. The second variable contains a single big navigator. Both variables hold the four Northwind tables Customers, Orders, OrderDetails, and Products.

❑ The second application (XQuerySearchEngineWS) consumes the XML Web Service created in the WS_XQuerySearchEngine project (see Chapter 8 for more information on Web Services) to run queries. The application uses two Web Forms to call into one of two web methods of the XML Web Service, to run XQueries on the data that the Web Service stores in two navigator collections which contain all data from all four Northwind tables.

Let's have a look at some of the application code. Basically, each application creates the navigator collections in the same way, although the Web Service does this slightly differently compared to XQuerySearchEngine. XQuerySearchEngine uses application-level variables set in Global.asax as shown below:

```
protected void Application_Start(Object sender, EventArgs e)
{
  // Define the SQL Template URLs and their related collection names
  strUrlXmlTemplateCustomers =
    "http://localhost/northwind/templates/GetAllCustomers.xml";
  strUrlXmlTemplateOrders =
    "http://localhost/northwind/templates/GetAllOrders.xml";
  strUrlXmlTemplateOrderDetails =
    "http://localhost/northwind/templates/GetAllOrderDetails.xml";
  strUrlXmlTemplateProducts =
    "http://localhost/northwind/templates/GetAllProducts.xml";
  strNavNameCustomers = "Customers";
  strNavNameOrders = "Orders";
  strNavNameOrderDetails = "OrderDetails";
  strNavNameProducts = "Products";

  strUrlXmlTemplateAllData =
    "http://localhost/northwind/templates/GetAllData.xml";
  strNavNameAllData = "AllData";

  // Create an XQueryNavigatorCollection object and fill it with four
  //  Northwind tables: Customers, Orders, Order Details, and Products
  XQueryNavigatorCollection navCol = new XQueryNavigatorCollection();

  // Add the Customers navigator to the collection
  XQueryDocument doc1 = new XQueryDocument(strUrlXmlTemplateCustomers,
                                           strNavNameCustomers);
  navCol.AddNavigator(doc1.CreateNavigator());

  // Add the Orders navigator
  XQueryDocument doc2 = new XQueryDocument(strUrlXmlTemplateOrders,
                                           strNavNameOrders);
  navCol.AddNavigator(doc2.CreateNavigator());
```

```
// Add the Order Details navigator
XQueryDocument doc3 = new XQueryDocument(strUrlXmlTemplateOrderDetails,
                                         strNavNameOrderDetails);
navCol.AddNavigator(doc3.CreateNavigator());

// Add the Products navigator
XQueryDocument doc4 = new XQueryDocument(strUrlXmlTemplateProducts,
                                         strNavNameProducts);
navCol.AddNavigator(doc4.CreateNavigator());

// Try it another way and create one big navigator with all the data
XQueryNavigatorCollection navColAD = new XQueryNavigatorCollection();

// Add the Customers, Orders, Order Details, and Products tables in one go
XQueryDocument doc5 = new XQueryDocument(strUrlXmlTemplateAllData,
                                         strNavNameAllData);
navColAD.AddNavigator(doc5.CreateNavigator());

// Create and store the doc object for filling the drop-down list box
XmlDocument doc = new XmlDocument();
doc.Load(strUrlXmlTemplateCustomers);
Application["doc"] = doc;

// Store the navCol XQueryNavigatorCollection object in the Application
Application["navCol"] = navCol;

// Store the navColAD XQueryNavigatorCollection object in the Application
Application["navColAD"] = navColAD;
}
```

First, the URLs for the query templates are set up, together with their corresponding Navigator Collection names. Next, have a closer look at the following code sample:

```
// Add the Customers navigator to the collection
XQueryDocument doc1 = new XQueryDocument(strUrlXmlTemplateCustomers,
                                         strNavNameCustomers);
navCol.AddNavigator(doc1.CreateNavigator());
```

Here, the first highlighted line loads the document pointed by the URL. This document contains a SQL template. But this template is not returned – instead, SQL handles the HTTP request, and starts processing the template. Since this template contains a SQL query, it is run against the database, which if you recall was specified in the northwind virtual directory, set up with SQLXML 3.0's "Configure IIS Support". The result of the query, in this case an XML result tree, is then returned to the XQueryDocument class. If an error were encountered during the execution of the query, SQL would return them also in XML format, so that the application can gracefully handle them rather than simply crashing.

The second highlighted line shows how the Navigator collection item is created using the CreateNavigator method of the XQueryDocument class.

This process of creating navigators within the collection objects is then continued, and finally, when this is done, two application objects are created, one for filling the Customers dropdown listbox, and the other for the first Navigator Collection, which then contains four navigators.

After that, one more big navigator is created, containing all the data from four database tables retrieved in one template query. From this navigator collection object, another application object is created.

Both application objects created in `Global.asax` are now ready for use and are accessible by any user who makes a page request from the web application.

The Web Service (`WS_XQuerySearchEngine`) also creates an XML virtual database in `Global.asax` using exactly the same code, so we won't look at that again. The only difference is that the first application variable, used to fill the `Customers` dropdown listbox is not implemented in the Web Service project, but in the consuming project, `XquerySearchEngineWS`. The Web Service exposes two methods: the first, `SearchNavCol1`, queries the four independent navigators, and the other, `SearchNavCol4`, queries the single navigator containing all XML data. The code for both of them is as follows:

```
[WebMethod(Description="Searches an XQueryNavigatorCollection object with one big
Navigator containing all data from the Northwind tables Customers, Orders,
OrderDetails, and Products.")]
public string SearchNavCol1 (string strXQuery)
{
  try
  {
    XQueryExpression expr = new XQueryExpression(strXQuery);

    // Get the navColAD Application object
    navColAD = (XQueryNavigatorCollection)(Application["navColAD"]);

    // Run the XQuery
    XQueryNavigator nav;
    nav = expr.Execute(navColAD);

    if ("" != nav.Value)
    {
      return nav.ToXml();
    }
    else
    {
      // Customer does not have any orders...
      return "<orderdetails>This Customer does not have any orders.
              </orderdetails>";
    }
  }
  catch (Exception e)
  {
    // Return error message
    return "Error occurred in: " + e.Source + "; " + e.Message;
  }
}

[WebMethod(Description="Searches an XQueryNavigatorCollection object with four
Navigators, each containing all data from the Northwind tables Customers, Orders,
OrderDetails, and Products.")]
public string SearchNavCol4 (string strXQuery)
```

```
{
  try
  {
    XQueryExpression expr = new XQueryExpression(strXQuery);

    // Get the navCol Application object
    navCol = (XQueryNavigatorCollection)(Application["navCol"]);

    // Run the XQuery
    XQueryNavigator nav;
    nav = expr.Execute(navCol);

    if ("" != nav.Value)
    {
      return nav.ToXml();
    }
    else
    {
      // Customer does not have any orders
      return "<orderdetails>This Customer does not have any orders.
              </orderdetails>";
    }
  }
  catch (Exception e)
  {
    // Return error message
    return "Error occurred in: " + e.Source + "; " + e.Message;
  }
}
```

Both methods parse and build an XQuery expression, as the following line shows:

```
XQueryExpression expr = new XQueryExpression(strXQuery);
```

This is then run over the requested navigator collection, obtaining a result in XML format. This result is returned to the calling application as a string. During the expression build, the query string is checked for any syntax errors. For example, if you test this method in VS.NET pressing *F5*, and try to execute the following query:

```
<orderdetails>
{
  FOR $a IN document('Customers')/root/Customers
  WHERE $a/CompanyName='Alfreds Futterkiste'
  RETURN <customer> { $a/CustomerID, $a/CompanyName, $a/ContactName,
                      $a/Phone, $a/Fax } </customer>
</orderdetails>
```

where the last closing brace between the closing XML tags </customer> and </orderdetails> has been forgotten, the output shown by VS.NET is:

```
<?xml version="1.0" encoding="utf-8" ?>
  <string xmlns="http://tempuri.org/">Error occurred in: Microsoft.Xml.XQuery; '}'
expected.</string>
```

Note also that when testing a Web Service in VS.NET, the input string does have a limit. For example, if you try to execute the query that is used to query the four-navigator collection object in our demo application, it will generate a syntax error because the string is being cut off at a certain length.

Now, let's have a look at how the XQueries are run, and how the result is transformed and displayed. The first application does it like this:

```
private void Button1_Click(object sender, System.EventArgs e)
{
    // Executes the XQuery Search on the XQueryNavigatorCollection
    //  using an XML Web Server Control
    if (lstCustomer.SelectedItem != null)
    {
        selectedCustomer = lstCustomer.SelectedItem;
    }

    if ("" != selectedCustomer.Value)
    {
        string strXQuery1;

        strXQuery1 = "<orderdetails> { FOR $a IN
        document(\"Customers\")/root/Customers WHERE $a/CompanyName=\"" +
        selectedCustomer.Value + "\" RETURN <d1> <customer> { $a/CustomerID,
        $a/CompanyName, $a/ContactName, $a/Phone, $a/Fax } </customer> { FOR
        $b IN document(\"Orders\")/root/Orders[CustomerID = $a/CustomerID]
        RETURN <d2> <O> { $b/OrderID, $b/OrderDate, $b/RequiredDate,
        $b/ShippedDate, $b/Freight } </O> { FOR $c IN
        document(\"OrderDetails\")/root/Order_x0020_Details[OrderID =
        $b/OrderID] RETURN <d3> <OD> { $c/OrderID, $c/ProductID, $c/Quantity }
        </OD> { FOR $d IN document(\"Products\")/root/Products[ProductID =
        $c/ProductID] RETURN <P> { $d/ProductID, $d/UnitPrice, $d/ProductName
        } </P> } </d3> } </d2> } </d1> } </orderdetails>";

        // Compile the XQuery
        // This checks for any errors
        XQueryExpression expr1 = new XQueryExpression(strXQuery1);

        // Run the XQuery
        XQueryNavigator nav1;
        nav1 = expr1.Execute(navCol);

        if (true == nav1.HasChildren)
        {
            // Port the XML result for saving and display
            XmlDocument doc = new XmlDocument();
            doc.LoadXml(nav1.ToXml());

            // To save the XQuery result for viewing, uncomment these lines:
            // XmlTextWriter writer1 = new XmlTextWriter(Server.MapPath(
            //                    "/XQuerySearchEngine/XQuery_output.xml"),
            //                    System.Text.Encoding.UTF8);
            // writer1.Formatting = Formatting.Indented;
            // writer1.Indentation = 2;
            // doc.Save(writer1);
            // writer1.Close();
```

```
        // View the result as HTML using the XML Web Server Control
        XmlOD.Document = doc;
        XmlOD.TransformSource = "xsl\\orderdetails.xsl";
    }
    else
    {
        // Customer does not have any current orders
        XmlDocument docn = new XmlDocument();
        docn.LoadXml("<root><noOrder>This Customer does not have any orders.
                </noOrder></root>");

        XmlOD.Document = docn;
        XmlOD.TransformSource = "xsl\\noOrder.xsl";
    }
    }
}
```

The query expression is quite unreadable, so I'll repeat it here in a more human-readable form:

```
<orderdetails>
{
  FOR $a IN document(\"Customers\")/root/Customers
  WHERE $a/CompanyName=\"" + selectedCustomer.Value + "\"
  RETURN
  <d1>
      <customer> { $a/CustomerID, $a/CompanyName, $a/ContactName, $a/Phone,
                  $a/Fax } </customer>
    {
      FOR $b IN document(\"Orders\")/root/Orders[CustomerID = $a/CustomerID]
      RETURN
      <d2>
        <O> { $b/OrderID, $b/OrderDate, $b/RequiredDate, $b/ShippedDate,
            $b/Freight } </O>
        {
          FOR $c IN document(\"OrderDetails\")/root/Order_x0020_Details[
                  OrderID = $b/OrderID]
          RETURN
          <d3>
            <OD> { $c/OrderID, $c/ProductID, $c/Quantity } </OD>
            {
              FOR $d IN document(\"Products\")/root/Products[
                      ProductID = $c/ProductID]
              RETURN <P> { $d/ProductID, $d/UnitPrice, $d/ProductName } </P>
            }
          </d3>
        }
      </d2>
    }
  </d1>
}
</orderdetails>
```

When the button is clicked, the XQuery is compiled and run over the requested navigator collection, and the XML result returned is transformed and displayed using an XSL style sheet. There is also some code added to write the XML result to a file for checking, but this code is commented here – if you want to use it just uncomment those lines. Check if the path is correct and if the account used to run the application has write permission (by default, the ASP.NET account does not have it, and must be changed by setting `<identity impersonate="true" />` in the file `web.config`, after the `<system.web>` element. Do take care with this as this affects application security), and with each button click, the XML result is persisted to disk.

Let's compare this with the `XQuerySearchEngineWS` application; this gets the data through the Web Service's web methods, but from then on the code is the same:

```
private void Button1_Click(object sender, System.EventArgs e)
{
    // Executes the XQuery Search on the XQueryNavigatorCollection Web Service
    //  using an XML Web Server Control
    if (lstCustomer.SelectedItem != null)
    {
        selectedCustomer = lstCustomer.SelectedItem;
    }

    if ("" != selectedCustomer.Value)
    {
        string strXQuery;

        strXQuery = "<orderdetails> { FOR $a IN
            document(\"Customers\")/root/Customers WHERE $a/CompanyName=\"" +
            selectedCustomer.Value + "\" RETURN <d1> <customer> { $a/CustomerID,
            $a/CompanyName, $a/ContactName, $a/Phone, $a/Fax } </customer> { FOR
            $b IN document(\"Orders\")/root/Orders[CustomerID = $a/CustomerID]
            RETURN <d2> <O> { $b/OrderID, $b/OrderDate, $b/RequiredDate,
            $b/ShippedDate, $b/Freight } </O> { FOR $c IN
            document(\"OrderDetails\")/root/Order_x0020_Details[OrderID =
            $b/OrderID] RETURN <d3> <OD> { $c/OrderID, $c/ProductID, $c/Quantity }
            </OD> { FOR $d IN document(\"Products\")/root/Products[ProductID =
            $c/ProductID] RETURN <P> { $d/ProductID, $d/UnitPrice,
            $d/ProductName } </P> } </d3> } </d2> } </d1> } </orderdetails>";

        localhost.WS_XQuerySearchEngine ws = new
            localhost.WS_XQuerySearchEngine();


        // Port the XML result for saving and display
        XmlDocument doc = new XmlDocument();
        doc.LoadXml(ws.SearchNavCol4(strXQuery));

        // View the result as HTML using the XML Web Server Control
        XmlOD.Document = doc;
        XmlOD.TransformSource = "xsl\\orderdetails.xsl";
    }
}
```

When the button is clicked, the Web Service is accessed to obtain the XML resulting from the XQuery expression passed in as a string parameter to one of the two web methods, in this case `SearchNavCol4`.

Now that we know how the applications work, we can start to set up a test machine, and get to work with ACT. I have used a desktop PC, a Dell GX240 with a single Intel Pentium 4 CPU running at 1.5 GHz, and equipped with 256 MB of RAM, and a 20 GB HD. To set up the machine, I applied the following software installation procedure – note that the order in which the software is installed is important, because some components depend on others already being installed:

- Windows 2000 Server SP2, without any change
- SQL 2000 Server with SP1
- Windows Installer Service 2.0
- MSXML 4.0 RTM SP1
- SOAP Toolkit 2.0 SP2
- SQLXML 3.0 RTM
- MDAC 2.7
- .NET Framework SDK 1.0 RTM with SP1 applied
- MS XQuery Demo 1.0
- If you test through a firewall, install MS Proxy Client 2.0 or the ISAServer Client (if you install this, check the Bypass proxy server for local addresses option in Internet options to ensure that the proxy will not interfere the tests in any way)
- Set up the directories containing the `XquerySearchEngine`, `XquerySearchEngineWS`, and `WS_XQuerySearchEngine` applications as Virtual Directories using Internet Services Manager. ASP.NET will compile when the first HTTP Request is received. Also, as said before, don't forget to first set up and test the virtual directory northwind for the SQL Query templates, using SQLXML 3.0's "Configure IIS Support" program. Then, test the Web Service before using it in VS.NET by pressing F5, and making use of the example queries.

The first two and the proxy client for the final point are commercial products, but the rest is freely downloadable from the Microsoft MSDN site (apart from the XQuery demo which can be found at http://xqueryservices.com/Setup/xquery.msi).

When copying or moving project directories for use in VS.NET, it can happen that the virtual directory that was originally used to run the project is not correct anymore. When VS.NET shows you the next screen, even after you have created the virtual application using the Internet Service Manager (ISM), check the first option, as shown here:

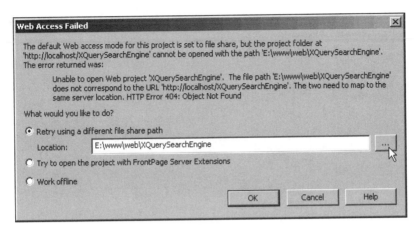

After choosing the first option, use the browse button to navigate to the correct location path of the project, and click OK.

Creating Tests

ACT was used to run various tests on the applications. My system does *not* represent a production testing environment because the machine houses all three tiers locally – the database, the Web Server (IIS and ASP.NET), and the ACT testing tool. Depending on the production environment envisaged, these would normally be set up on different machines, with ACT running on a separate machine to prevent its own resource demands adding 'noise' to the test results.

New test scripts are easy to set up in ACT. We create new test scripts with the New Test Wizard, which records a web session, or sets up skeleton test scripts to which we can add to create custom tests.

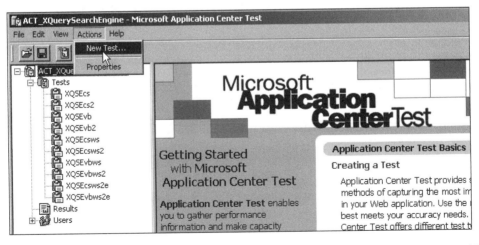

When recording a web session, it generates a corresponding script in VBScript. It is quite possible to modify generated scripts afterwards for particular needs.

Once we've completed the web session that we want to record, we stop the recording, and name the test script, which then appears in the right-hand windowpane. Note that in the previous screenshot, the test scripts were already present. Before we run each test script though, we need to make sure that it is set up correctly. To do this, open the property page by right-clicking the test and choosing **Properties**:

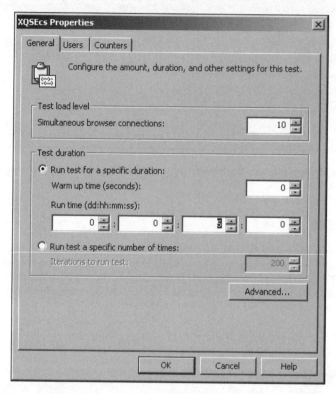

The **General** tab lets us set the load level for the test in terms of concurrent browser connections (to simulate multiple users requesting the page at once), and the duration of the test, as a time or by specifying the iterations to run. Also, we can specify a warming up time (used to gradually increase server load, thereby simulating a more realistic test), to damp the effect of the sudden load change as the web server starts up, which would otherwise skew the results.

The **Users** tab lets us choose between automatically generating users or specifying particular ones in the left pane. In this case, we can use the default behavior and have ACT automatically generate users. We can also manually generate users by selecting **Actions | Generate Users**, or even import users by selecting **Actions | Import Users**, and then opening a comma delimited file (.txt or .csv).

The **Counters** tab lets us define the interval between collecting the counter values. I set this to 5 seconds, and added the following counters in the counter area:

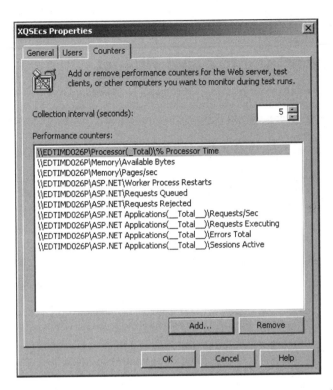

In fact, counters added to a test are recorded in an XML document, like this one (perfCounters-XQSEcs.xml):

```xml
<?xml version="1.0" encoding="UTF-8" ?>
<!DOCTYPE PerfCounters>
<PerfCounters>
  <Counter name="\\localhost\Processor(_Total)\% Processor Time"/>
  <Counter name="\\localhost\Memory\Available Bytes"/>
  <Counter name="\\localhost\Memory\Pages/sec"/>
  <Counter name="\\localhost\ASP.NET\Worker Process Restarts"/>
  <Counter name="\\localhost\ASP.NET\Requests Queued"/>
  <Counter name="\\localhost\ASP.NET\Requests Rejected"/>
  <Counter name=
            "\\localhost\ASP.NET Applications(__Total__)\Requests/Sec"/>
  <Counter name=
        "\\localhost\ASP.NET Applications(__Total__)\Requests Executing"/>
  <Counter name=
            "\\localhost\ASP.NET Applications(__Total__)\Errors Total"/>
  <Counter name=
          "\\localhost\ASP.NET Applications(__Total__)\Sessions Active"/>
</PerfCounters>
```

This document is another example of the widespread use of XML in new software products. ACT also uses XML for the test result reports, and for the test properties. Just open the ACT_XQuerySearchEngine project, where you can examine each of the listed files.

Now, let's see what ACT can do for us when trying to optimize our Web Application.

The ACT_XQuerySearchEngine Project

The ACT_XQuerySearchEngine project from the chapter download material aims to demonstrate the use of ACT, and to demonstrate that different implementations of the same application can affect overall performance in different ways. If you open it now, you'll find that it contains the following prerecorded tests:

Test Name	Description
XQSEcs	This test comprises four HTTP Requests to the XQuerySearchEngine project, using the navigator collection with four separate navigators: ❑ requests the /XQuerySearchEngine/OrderSearch.aspx file with the GET method ❑ gets the /XQuerySearchEngine/inc/orderdetails.js script file ❑ this is the request when the button " Find Order Details by Customer" is pressed; it gets the /XQuerySearchEngine/OrderSearch.aspx page again, passing the viewstate in oRequest.Body ❑ when the results are returned, this request gets the gif file at /XQuerySearchEngine/images/plus.GIF
XQSEvb	This is the same test, but run on the VB.NET version of the above project, XQuerySearchEngineVB. It calls the corresponding files, adding the name suffix ".vb".
XQSEcs2	This test is similar to the first project, XQuerySearchEngine, but the four requests are done at the project files with the name suffix "2", thereby addressing the navigator collection with one big navigator.
XQSEvb2	Same test as XQSEvb, but addressing the project files with suffix "2", thus using the singular big navigator collection.
XQSEcsws	Same as the XQSEcs script, but it uses a "WS" suffix, thereby using the Web Service client, which in turn accesses the Web Service to query the 4-navigator collection.
XQSEvbws	Same as the XQSEvb script, but it uses the "VBWS" suffix, and thus uses the VB version of the Web Service client, which in turn accesses the Web Service to query the 4-navigator collection.
XQSEcsws2	Same as the XQSEcsws script, but is makes requests to the OrderSearch2WS.aspx page; therefore it uses the Web Service to query the singular big navigator collection.
XQSEvbws2	Same as the XQSEvbws script, but making a request to the OrderSearch2VBWS.aspx page, thus using the Web Service to query the singular big navigator collection.

Test Name	Description
XQSEcsws2e	Same as XQSEcsws2, but this time the Web Service is installed on another server, thereby demonstrating the possibility of remote access.
XQSEvbws2e	Same as XQSEvbws2, but also accessing the Web Service on a remote machine.

When you open this project, the above tests will appear in the left-hand tree view. As you click on each test in the tree view, the right pane shows the VBScript that will be executed when that test is run:

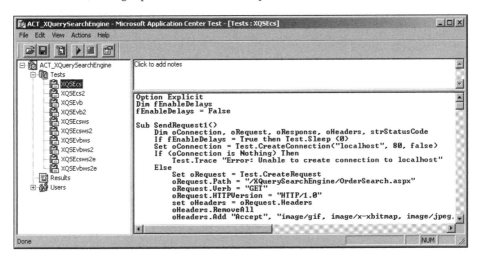

The scripts specify localhost as the target machine, so you'll need to change that to the target server name if you're running the tests remotely.

The test scripts are regular VBScript files, such as XQSEcs.vbs shown above, containing a number of subroutines, each one representing an HTTP Request. There is also a Main subroutine that calls each Request subroutine in turn:

```
Sub Main()
    call SendRequest1()
    call SendRequest2()
    call SendRequest3()
    call SendRequest4()
End Sub

Main
```

The command Main, appearing right at the end of the script, starts the test run. Let's take a look at the code of the SendRequest1 subroutine (of the file XQSEcs.vbs) in a little more detail:

```
Sub SendRequest1()
    Dim oConnection, oRequest, oResponse, oHeaders, strStatusCode
    If fEnableDelays = True then Test.Sleep (0)
```

```
      Set oConnection = Test.CreateConnection("localhost", 80, false)
   If (oConnection is Nothing) Then
       Test.Trace "Error: Unable to create connection to localhost"
   Else
       Set oRequest = Test.CreateRequest
       oRequest.Path = "/XQuerySearchEngine/OrderSearch.aspx"
       oRequest.Verb = "GET"
       oRequest.HTTPVersion = "HTTP/1.0"
       set oHeaders = oRequest.Headers
       oHeaders.RemoveAll
       oHeaders.Add "Accept", "image/gif, image/x-xbitmap, image/jpeg," _
                  + "image/pjpeg, application/vnd.ms-powerpoint," _
                  + "application/vnd.ms-excel, application/msword, */*"
       oHeaders.Add "Accept-Language", "en-us"
       oHeaders.Add "User-Agent", "Mozilla/4.0 (compatible; MSIE 6.0;" _
                  + "Windows NT 5.0; .NET CLR 1.0.3705)"
       'oHeaders.Add "Host", "localhost"
       oHeaders.Add "Host", "(automatic)"
       oHeaders.Add "Cookie", "(automatic)"
       Set oResponse = oConnection.Send(oRequest)
       If (oResponse is Nothing) Then
           Test.Trace "Error: Failed to receive response for URL to " _
                  + "/XQuerySearchEngine/OrderSearch.aspx"
       Else
           strStatusCode = oResponse.ResultCode
       End If
       oConnection.Close
   End If
End Sub
```

The first line determines if the process has to pause (sleep) for a specified amount of milliseconds (in this case, the test always results in `false` as the test variable is set to `false` at the beginning of the test script):

```
If fEnableDelays = True then Test.Sleep (0)
```

Then, the connection to the web server is opened, and the request is created by setting various properties:

```
Set oConnection = Test.CreateConnection("localhost", 80, false)
If (oConnection is Nothing) Then
    Test.Trace "Error: Unable to create connection to localhost"
Else
    Set oRequest = Test.CreateRequest
    oRequest.Path = "/XQuerySearchEngine/OrderSearch.aspx"
    oRequest.Verb = "GET"
    oRequest.HTTPVersion = "HTTP/1.0"
    set oHeaders = oRequest.Headers
    oHeaders.RemoveAll
    oHeaders.Add "Accept", "image/gif, image/x-xbitmap, image/jpeg," _
               + "image/pjpeg, application/vnd.ms-powerpoint," _
               + "application/vnd.ms-excel, application/msword, */*"
    oHeaders.Add "Accept-Language", "en-us"
    oHeaders.Add "User-Agent", "Mozilla/4.0 (compatible; MSIE 6.0;" _
               + "Windows NT 5.0; .NET CLR 1.0.3705)"
```

```
'oHeaders.Add "Host", "localhost"
oHeaders.Add "Host", "(automatic)"
oHeaders.Add "Cookie", "(automatic)"
```

Then, the request is sent by executing the following line of code:

```
Set oResponse = oConnection.Send(oRequest)
```

The web server processes the request, and finally returns the result in the oResponse object:

```
If (oResponse is Nothing) Then
    Test.Trace "Error: Failed to receive response for URL to " _
            + "/XQuerySearchEngine/OrderSearch.aspx"
Else
    strStatusCode = oResponse.ResultCode
End If
```

Finally, the connection object is closed, and the request subroutine is ended:

```
    oConnection.Close
End If
```

The next request, SendRequest2, is a request for the client JavaScript file, orderdetails.js, which runs on the client when the plus sign is clicked on one of the orders.

Any parameters needed for a subsequent request can be passed along in ACT, as the following example of SendRequest3 shows – note that not all code is shown, for readability:

```
Sub SendRequest3()
    Dim oConnection, oRequest, oResponse, oHeaders, strStatusCode
    If fEnableDelays = True then Test.Sleep (5219)
    Set oConnection = Test.CreateConnection("localhost", 80, false)
    If (oConnection is Nothing) Then
        Test.Trace "Error: Unable to create connection to localhost"
    Else
        Set oRequest = Test.CreateRequest
        oRequest.Path = "/XQuerySearchEngine/OrderSearch.aspx"
        oRequest.Verb = "POST"
        oRequest.HTTPVersion = "HTTP/1.0"
        oRequest.EncodeBody = False
        set oHeaders = oRequest.Headers
        oHeaders.RemoveAll
        oHeaders.Add "Accept", "image/gif, image/x-xbitmap, image/jpeg," _
                + "image/pjpeg, application/vnd.ms-powerpoint," _
                + "application/vnd.ms-excel, application/msword, */*"
        oHeaders.Add "Referer", _
                    "http://localhost/XQuerySearchEngine/OrderSearch.aspx"
        oHeaders.Add "Accept-Language", "en-us"
        oHeaders.Add "Content-Type", "application/x-www-form-urlencoded"
        oHeaders.Add "User-Agent", _
    "Mozilla/4.0 (compatible; MSIE 6.0; Windows NT 5.0; .NET CLR 1.0.3705)"
```

```
'oHeaders.Add "Host", "localhost"
oHeaders.Add "Host", "(automatic)"
oHeaders.Add "Pragma", "no-cache"
'oHeaders.Add "Cookie", "ASP.NET_SessionId=xizuom55qgfd5y55n1g0rp45"
oHeaders.Add "Cookie", "(automatic)"
oHeaders.Add "Content-Length", "(automatic)"
oRequest.Body = "__VIEWSTATE=dDwtMTY0ODE3MDk1O3Q8O2w8aTwxPjs%2BO2w8"
oRequest.Body = oRequest.Body _
            + "dDw7bDxpPDM%2BOz47bDx0PHQ8O3A8bDxpPDA%2BO2k8MT47aT"
oRequest.Body = oRequest.Body _
            + "YXpkPjs%2BPjs%2BOzs%2BOz4%2BOz4%2BOz6EG5n5jATKuVSw"

oRequest.Body = oRequest.Body _
            + "qLETuoAcmabYMQ%3D%3D&lstCustomer=Alfreds+Futterkis"
oRequest.Body = oRequest.Body _
            + "te&Button1=Find+Order+Details+by+Customer"
Set oResponse = oConnection.Send(oRequest)
If (oResponse is Nothing) Then
    Test.Trace "Error: Failed to receive response for URL to " _
            + "/XQuerySearchEngine/OrderSearch.aspx"
Else
    strStatusCode = oResponse.ResultCode
End If
oConnection.Close
    End If
End Sub
```

The first line;

```
If fEnableDelays = True then Test.Sleep (5219)
```

lets the process sleep for 5,219 milliseconds if the test variable would resolve to true, but as said, this feature has not been used here.

Then, as with the other requests, a new connection to the web server is attempted, and when successful, the request's properties are set:

```
Set oConnection = Test.CreateConnection("localhost", 80, false)
If (oConnection is Nothing) Then
    Test.Trace "Error: Unable to create connection to localhost"
Else
    Set oRequest = Test.CreateRequest
    oRequest.Path = "/XQuerySearchEngine/OrderSearch.aspx"
    oRequest.Verb = "POST"
    oRequest.HTTPVersion = "HTTP/1.0"
    oRequest.EncodeBody = False
    set oHeaders = oRequest.Headers
    oHeaders.RemoveAll
    oHeaders.Add "Accept", "image/gif, image/x-xbitmap, image/jpeg," _
            + "image/pjpeg, application/vnd.ms-powerpoint," _
            + "application/vnd.ms-excel, application/msword, */*"
    oHeaders.Add "Referer", _
            "http://localhost/XQuerySearchEngine/OrderSearch.aspx"
```

```
         oHeaders.Add "Accept-Language", "en-us"
         oHeaders.Add "Content-Type", "application/x-www-form-urlencoded"
         oHeaders.Add "User-Agent", _
 "Mozilla/4.0 (compatible; MSIE 6.0; Windows NT 5.0; .NET CLR 1.0.3705)"
         'oHeaders.Add "Host", "localhost"
         oHeaders.Add "Host", "(automatic)"
         oHeaders.Add "Pragma", "no-cache"
```

For example, here the header is assigned a cookie, containing the ASP.NET SessionId:

```
         'oHeaders.Add "Cookie", "ASP.NET_SessionId=xizuom55qgfd5y55n1g0rp45"
```

and then another cookie, containing the viewstate information:

```
         oHeaders.Add "Cookie", "(automatic)"
         oHeaders.Add "Content-Length", "(automatic)"
         oRequest.Body = "__VIEWSTATE=dDwtMTY0ODE3MDk1O3Q8O2w8aTwxPjs%2BO2w8"
         oRequest.Body = oRequest.Body _
                 + "dDw7bDxpPDM%2BOz47bDx0PHQ8O3A8bDxpPDA%2BO2k8MT47aT"
         oRequest.Body = oRequest.Body _
                 + "YXpkPjs%2BPjs%2BOzs%2BOz4%2BOz4%2BOz6EG5n5jATKuVSw"
```

Note that next the parameter passed is resolved to the value of the Customer dropdown listbox, which was selected before the button **Find Order Details by Customer** was clicked:

```
         oRequest.Body = oRequest.Body _
                 + "qLETuoAcmabYMQ%3D%3D&lstCustomer=Alfreds+Futterkis"
         oRequest.Body = oRequest.Body _
                 + "te&Button1=Find+Order+Details+by+Customer"
```

Then, the request is sent to the web server:

```
         Set oResponse = oConnection.Send(oRequest)
```

Then, the web server's response is processed:

```
         If (oResponse is Nothing) Then
             Test.Trace "Error: Failed to receive response for URL to " _
                     + "/XQuerySearchEngine/OrderSearch.aspx"
         Else
             strStatusCode = oResponse.ResultCode
         End If
```

Then, the connection is closed, and the request subroutine ends:

```
         oConnection.Close
     End If
```

This explanation is representative to all the tests run with ACT with regard to this demo.

The Test Results

ACT records reports in XML format. The project properties are also saved in XML format.

Now run the test, by clicking the Start Test button in the horizontal toolbar. A test screen will show up, and after a while the test starts to run. Click the Show Details button to see the results graph being created in real time while the test continues, as the screenshot of the XQSEcs test shows below:

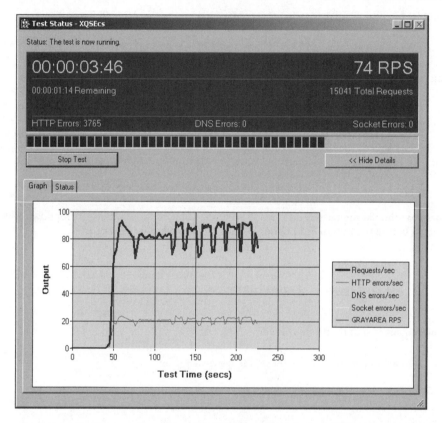

For example, this graph shows us that after an initial delay (which is caused by system start up, and really should be ignored as has been mentioned before in this chapter), the graph is dynamically created and the X- and Y-axis are adjusted automatically when the test progresses. This is a really cool feature of ACT, and a big improvement compared to the old WAS Tool, as this tool lacked graphical output completely.

Another thing to note in this graph is that various test items are shown, like Requests/sec, HTTP errors/sec, DNS errors/sec, Socket errors/sec, and in this case GRAYAREA RPS. The first, Requests/sec, indicates the throughput of the web server and is considered a principal indicator of general web application performance. The other parameters are important also and are self-explanatory. In this case, the HTTP errors/sec (red line) indicates there were quite a few errors during the HTTP requests made, possibly indicating a web server's incapacity to respond adequately and within time limits.

Once all the tests have been run with different concurrent browser connections, for example 1, 2, 4, 8, 16, 32, and 64, we can start to browse the results and see what graphs ACT can generate to help us compare them.

With ACT, it is possible to create many different types of graphs. Many of them are of little relevance to what is actually needed. In general, you as the tester are the one who has to (and can) make the decision as of which types are relevant to the purposes of the performance test being done.

For example, an interesting graph is displayed if we click the Results node in the left-hand pane and choose Graphs from the Report listbox in the upper right corner. You'll see something like this:

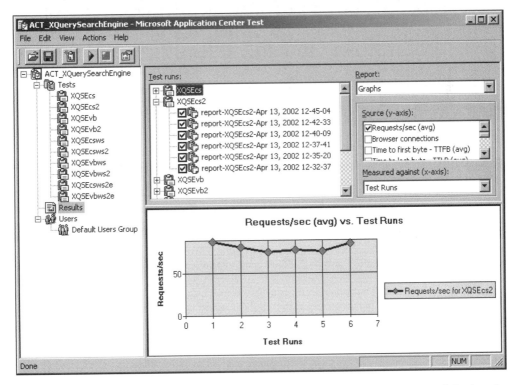

In the above graph, only the reports for the XQSEcs2 test run have been selected and displayed.

Now deselect all the test runs, and then open all the tests in turn from top to bottom, selecting only the ones that have the suffix "2" (either C# or VB), and see how the new graph is created. The final result should resemble the following figure:

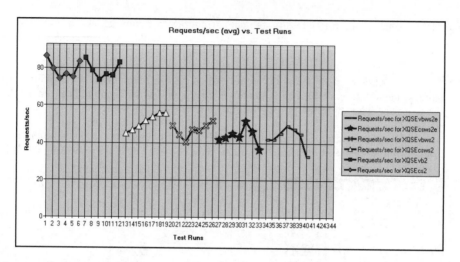

The above graph shows us the following. On the Y-axis, the requests per second are shown in the range from 0 to 100. On the X-axis, the Test Runs are shown, in the order that you select them in the Test Run windowpane.

From the graph we can observe how the various tests ran using different implementations and languages. For example, there's not much difference in using C# and VB, which is of course predictable when you know that .NET run-time code does not depend heavily on the language used.

What is more interesting here to note is that the throughput in the first two test runs is much higher than the rest of the four test runs. Remember that the first two used the singular navigator collection, created in the `Global.asax` of the project, and that the other four tests used the Web Service to access the singular navigator collection and run the query expression. This means that the Web Service does add some overhead to the application and bogs down general application performance.

Another thing to note is that with increasing concurrent users, the general throughput is not affected very much, and is variable; in some cases it first decreases and then increases as the load increases, but in other cases it is vice versa, or only increases.

Last thing to note here is that accessing the Web Service locally or remotely has very little effect on the general performance, but as can be seen, it does have a small negative effect.

What to learn from this? Well, in general, do not use Web Services if not absolutely necessary, as they add overhead to the application and therefore can decrease significantly general application performance (RPS).

Another useful graph can be created by combining all the C# tests into a single graph of requests per second versus test runs:

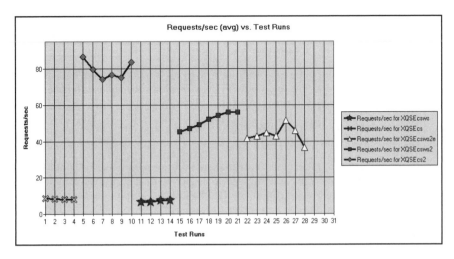

The first test run shows the results of the **XQSEcs** script, which used the four-navigator collection to execute the query expression and display the results. It has a very low throughput, a little below 10.

Then, the next test shows the results of the **XQSEcs2** script, which queried the singular navigator collection, and as you can see it has a much higher throughput, which lies around 80. Then, the next test shows us the results of the **XQSEcsws** script, showing a low throughput again, which resembles the first test, **XQSEcs**. It uses the Web Service, and obviously the overhead added by the Web Service is (in this case) not of importance since the results are almost the same.

The fourth test shows us the results of the **XQSEcsws2** script, which should be compared with the second test, **XQSEcs2**. Here, the only new factor is that the script is using the Web Service locally to query the navigator collection. The last test, **XQSEcsws2**, shows a similar graph to the **XQSEcsws2**, but with a slightly lower throughput, because of the Web Service being accessed remotely.

Another worthwhile chart plots TTFB and TTLB results against test runs. The following screenshot shows the sort of thing we'll see if we select all test runs performed:

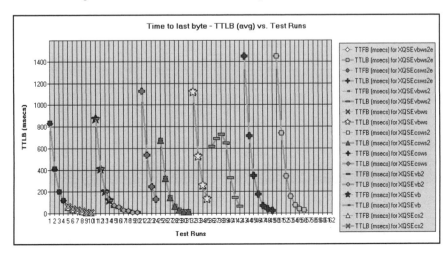

363

You may recall that the TTFB is the time it takes the web server to process the request with page buffering turned on. You also may remember that the TTLB is the time that takes the web server to complete a request, including having returned the response back to the client.

With this in mind, the first thing to be noticed from this graph is that the lower the outcomes, the better the result is. So, in general, the scripts that used the singular navigator collection have the lowest response time, therefore allowing a higher throughput (RPS).

Furthermore, although it is maybe a bit difficult to see in this graph, the TTFB is almost equal to the TTLB time, indicating that returning the response to the client takes almost no time.

Then, comparing each test run, it becomes clear that, as we have seen in earlier graphs, the introduction of the Web Service, locally, does have a considerable negative effect on the maximum throughput. Also, remotely accessing the Web Service as can be seen in the last two graph lines on the right side increases even more the time that it takes for the web server to respond.

Finally, the performance counters data can be displayed, but there is no graph generated. If you want graphs displayed, use the Performance monitor program, add the counters, run it on the web server, and take screenshots from it while running the load tests. You can also log the monitor session, and then use the resulting text file to produce the graphs you need. ACT does generate a useful report though, as can be seen in the following figure:

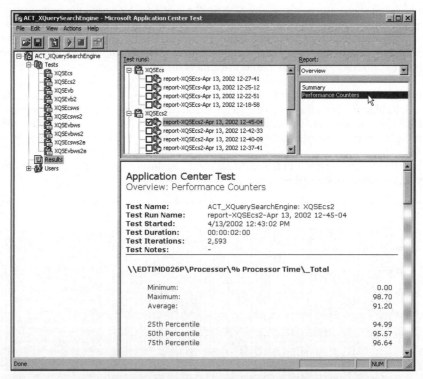

In this screenshot, you can see some interesting results from the performance counters. The minimum, maximum, and average are displayed for each counter, together with three Percentiles. There is no graph displayed here though.

If you have installed the ACT project directory from the chapter's download material, you can have a look for yourself at the graphs that are shown when you click on the Summary option of the Report Overview. For example, interesting graphs show up where the requests are plotted against time and when including different test runs.

Finally, I installed the XML Web Service on another machine (Dell GX110, Intel PIII CPU 800MHz, 128 MB RAM, and a 20 GB HD) with exactly the same software configuration indicated earlier in this chapter. The results were, compared with the other two tests with the Web Service running locally, as follows:

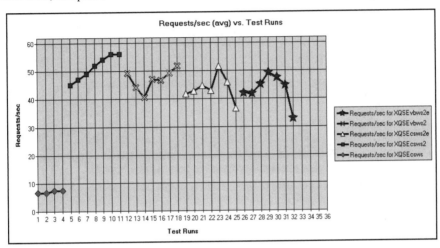

You can clearly see here that performance is best (read the highest Requests Per Second, or RPS) when using C#, and when running XQueries over the single big navigator collection. The test runs where the XML Web Service was remotely accessed performed a bit less well, because this introduces network access.

For contrast, the results of the test where the four-navigator collection was used were also included (XQSEcsws, the first one shown), the change to using one big navigator improved application performance dramatically. This shows again how ACT can really help decide between alternative techniques when we are faced with a choice.

Summary

The chapter started off with a general discussion of the factors that affect application performance, and looked at some key ways to improve performance in XML ASP.NET applications. These included caching, data access, and working with strings. We moved on to look at ASP.NET's very powerful and effective trace facility, which provides a view right into the heart of the ASP.NET processing engine, and can be very useful for pinpointing areas of an application that require streamlining.

After this, we briefly summed up the other avenues that are available for measuring performance in ASP.NET, namely profiling services, performance counters, and analyzing performance with sampling. Lastly, we took a detailed look at Application Center Test (ACT), from setting up the test machine, creating and running the test scripts, through to interpreting the ACT test results.

I hope the chapter has given a useful overview of how the performance of an application can be measured and improved. I also hope that it's underlined the importance of this issue: it's one which should never be overlooked if we are to make professional production-standard web applications that we can be proud of.

11

A Web Services Case Study – An E-Commerce Business Engine

In Chapter 8 we looked at e-business and XML, and developed an appreciation of the standards that underpin XML Web Services. In this chapter we're going to build on that foundation and examine a simplified e-commerce business engine, which is exposed as a Web Service. Over the course of the case study we'll be pulling together a number of previously encountered topics – we'll use a wide variety of the .NET XML classes, including transformations and serialization, as well as performing a fair amount of manipulation of the XmlDocument. Additionally we'll be making great use of the Xml interface provided by the DataSet class.

> *Since this case study makes use of a number of classes and style sheets, we won't be exhaustively listing every line of code; what we will be doing is explaining the design of the engine, highlighting interesting aspects of its implementation, and illustrating how it can be used. Full working code, including database scripts, is available from www.wrox.com.*

Over the course of this study we'll:

❑ Describe the design of the e-commerce engine

❑ Set up a small trial database

❑ Highlight and discuss the most important sections of code in the engine itself

❑ Implement a simple front-end (an online shop) to demonstrate use of the engine

Before we dive into the practical details though, let's just pause and briefly consider why we should care about XML Web Services.

Web Services – For All?

XML Web Services are a cornerstone of the .NET Framework and they come into their own their own in two main areas:

- ❏ Distributed computing
- ❏ Application integration

The former allows us to access common functionality no matter where it is located, be it internal or external to our organization; the latter allows us to provide interfaces to different systems, (in particular legacy systems), providing them with an efficient and relatively easy method to communicate with each other.

XML Web Services represents a mechanism that takes Microsoft's DNA architecture to a new level. Not only can we easily split our presentation, business logic, and data layers, but we can distribute them as well. There is no longer any need to have all our application's components running in the same environment: they could be on different servers within our organization, or provided by an organization on the other side of the world. We can now build our applications by simply consuming any amount of third-party functionality exposed as XML Web Services without any need to download and install a COM package.

Let's make a bold prediction: we are about to witness the age of business engine applications that have all the business logic and data access but none of the presentation layer. Their functionality will be delivered as a collection of Web Services to be consumed as the purchaser sees fit, be it via browser, cell phone, PDA, or whatever.

We may choose to install the engine on our own servers or we may prefer to simply access the engine on an Application Service Provider's servers. That way we don't have to worry about software updates, the infrastructure, or availability. And with all our major applications, our accounting package, our CRM software, our document management system, all running as Web Service based engines, we can provide a common custom interface to them all via the organization's intranet, extranet, and Internet. Did I forget to mention we could easily offer global access to internal applications?

Although this may make it sound like the benefits are all for the big end of town, the economies of scale offered by this approach offer benefits for us all. Now that the application service provider can employ totally new business models (for example pay-per-use), software that has previously been beyond the means of smaller organizations, due to initial costs and the infrastructure requirements, can now be utilized. Furthermore, it can all be accessed through that small organization's very own presentation layer. Thus, the software accessed may be highly personalized and yet consistent with that organization's other applications.

An E-Commerce Illustration

To show how this future may be implemented, we're going to investigate how to build a simple e-commerce business engine. Essentially, the engine will provide the functionality required to support an online shopping application. However, unlike traditional approaches, we, as service providers, are not going to provide a front-end presentation layer and nor will our hypothetical small business customers, the online storeowners, install our code on their servers. They, or their trusty web developer, will simply build the presentation layer that calls up whatever functionality they require.

In this scenario the small business is freed from detailed concerns about servers, databases, or the development language of the engine. The functions are accessed by Web Services, so, as long as their chosen platform can make a valid XML Web Services request, then they can run on whatever platform takes their fancy.

Of course, if they have a server with the .NET platform installed then we could just sell them the engine and they could install it on their own infrastructure. This may be the preferred approach for B2B scenarios where trading partner's applications are doing most of the talking, but for now we are going to assume that the engine will run on our servers.

So, let's turn our attention to the design of the e-commerce engine.

The E-Commerce Engine

The e-commerce engine is going to provide centralized functionality associated with a standard e-commerce site and has been split into three distinct services:

❑   Catalogue service

❑   Basket service

❑   Order service

Each one of these services provides the basic methods you would expect of a simple online store. For example, the catalogue service allows you to retrieve the catalogue hierarchy for building menus, return a list of products for a category, and get the details for a product.

The client accesses these basic methods by invoking the method of the appropriate service through SOAP. Since there are over 70 implementations of SOAP, as well as the obvious support for Web Services in .NET, the client has a wide choice of platforms. They can also use Internet Explorer 6.0 (via its Web Service behavior) and as Office XP products also offer the ability to consume Web Services, implementation does not *have* to involve the traditional web site.

We can visualize a system using the e-commerce engine as follows:

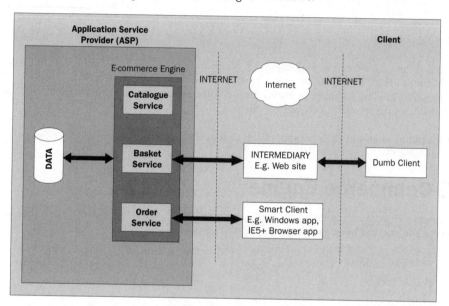

As you can see, the customer of the service really doesn't have to build too much. The functionality is all provided by the Web Services and the data is housed in the engine's databases. No matter what the platform, the client is really building an enhanced presentation layer: the data layer and almost all the business logic layer are being housed in the e-commerce engine.

For example, to show a list of products for a category, the client makes a SOAP call to the catalogue service, passing it the category name. The Web Service queries the database, retrieves the list of products as an XML document, and returns this document to the client. The client can then either use an XSLT stylesheet to render the HTML page, or programmatically pull the product information out of the XML document and format it to HTML. All the while the data is stored centrally, as is the functionality, and with most SOAP toolkits the process is virtually the same as, say, calling the methods of a COM component.

The customer (or service consumer) has a dramatically reduced infrastructure requirement because the application they are running is very simple. In fact, the client only needs to have access to an ISP that can provide a hosting package that allows scripting (with no database required, IIS hosting that allows ASP pages is available at the moment for under $10 a month), and they can build an e-commerce application that is as complicated as the e-commerce functionality will allow.

Of course the engine could be used in a number of different scenarios, three of which are:

Business to Customer

The most likely scenario, as already alluded to, is that it will be used by third parties who create their own presentation layer, be this in ColdFusion, or via a VB6 application, an ASP.NET web application, or a traditional ASP web site. Here the traditional COM-based development is just being replacing with a Web Service development, although we now have the distinct advantage of not having to worry about storing the data.

Business to Business – Portal

A business could use the engine to provide catalogue information to a retail portal. Rather than constantly having to send catalogue details, the portal could display a list of the business's products by consuming the catalogue service to generate the category pages.

Business to Business – Supply Chain

Where a business has customers of varying sizes, the engine could help in providing a means to delivering order processing to a wide variety of platforms and applications. The business's larger trading partners may want to use their own applications to perform the generation of an order, and thus can consume the catalogue service to get catalogue details, and the order service to post an order.

For smaller customers, the business may create a web site for ordering, in which case it can make full use of all the services, or produce a simple Excel spreadsheet that could automatically update itself with catalog information and could even post an order.

Demonstrating the Concept

Our main aim in this study is to investigate how XML and XML Web Services can be used to meet practical needs. Obviously real world e-commerce applications are quite complex in order to meet the demands of error handling, high functionality, scalability, and so forth – here we are just going to concentrate on the overall approach to show how the concept may be realized. Even this simple study generated a substantial amount of code so, within the body of the chapter, we'll concentrate on the most interesting code from the application, which is included in full in the book's download material.

The case-study code consists of three main parts:

❑ Description of a very simple database (here described for Access, but the download also contains SQL Server set-up scripts)

❑ A description of the most interesting parts of the implementation of the Web Services – the ECommerceEngine project

❑ A brief discussion of a web application that can consume the Web Services provided by the engine – the EComConsumer project

As we may expect from previous discussions, the engine's functionality is delivered via three services:

❑ The CatalogueService

❑ The BasketService

❑ The OrderService

To give a taste of what lies ahead, let's look at the functionality that those services will provide.

CatalogueService

Method	Description
getHierarchy	Returns an XML document containing the menu hierarchy
getCategory	Returns an XML document containing category details, parent and child categories, and items for the category
getItem	Returns an XML document containing item details and parent category details for the specified item
searchItems	Returns an XML document containing the results of searching categories and items for the search string

BasketService

Method	Description
getBasket	Returns an XML document containing the specified basket's details
createBasket	Returns an integer containing the basket ID of the new basket
listBaskets	Returns an XML document containing a list of baskets (uses an age check
addItem	Adds an item to a basket (if the item already in basket then quantity is updated).
removeItem	Removes an item from the basket
updateItem	Updates the quantity on an item (if 0 then item is removed)

OrderService

Method	Description
createOrder	Creates a new order from an existing basket – returns the order ID
addCustomerInfo	Adds customer information such as billing address to order
addShippingInfo	Adds shipping information to order
listOrdersByDays	Returns an XML document containing all the orders placed in the last n days
listOrdersByCustomer	Returns an XML document containing all the orders for a customer ID
getOrder	Returns an XML document containing the details for the specified order

Obviously, these are far from exhaustive lists for the functionality required for a commercial application (for example we haven't provided any methods for back-end administration of the application), but there should be more than enough to get us through and demonstrate the principle of distributed business engines.

So the first task is to set up the database backend.

The Database

Which database we use for the engine is a matter of personal preference. The example described here uses Microsoft Access 2000 (e-commerce.mdb is provided in the code download), simply because it is widely available but, as the calls to the data all generate their own SQL, it's a simple matter of changing the connection string to change the database.

We obviously wouldn't go 'public' with an Access backend, we'd probably want to use SQL Server 2000 and exploit SQLXML (as described earlier in this book) but we don't want to get too bogged down in database specifics.

The database is very simple and has the following form:

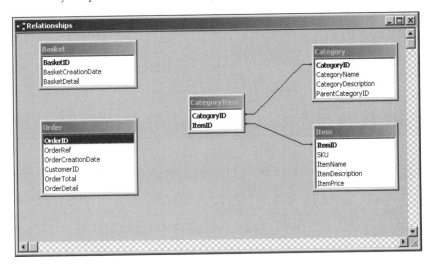

The tables are set up as described below:

Basket

Field	Type	Indexed
BasketID	autonumber	yes – unique
BasketCreationDate	datetime	yes
BasketDetails	memo	

Category

Field	Type	Indexed
CategoryID	autonumber	yes – unique
CategoryName	text(50)	yes
CategoryDescription	memo	yes
ParentCategoryID	number	yes

CategoryItem

Field	Type	Indexed
CategoryID	number	yes
ItemID	number	yes

Item

Field	Type	Indexed
ItemID	autonumber	yes – unique
SKU	text(20)	yes
ItemName	text(50)	yes
ItemDescription	memo	yes
ItemPrice	currency	

Order

Field	Type	Indexed
OrderID	autonumber	yes – unique
OrderRef	text(20)	yes
OrderCreationDate	datetime	yes
CustomerID	number	yes
OrderTotal	currency	
OrderDetail	memo	

The CategoryItem table enables a 'many-to-many' relationship with the Category and Item tables. Also notice that the Category table has a ParentCategoryID column that allows a 'one-to-many' relationship with the categories. Apart from these, the database is clearly simplified and quite deliberately doesn't include all the relationships one might require for a fully functional service.

Now we're ready for the main event – implementing the Web Services.

Building the Services

Before we start on the services contained in the `ECommerceEngine` project it's appropriate to comment on the development environment you may wish to use. While Visual Studio .NET is wonderful for building Web Services, you might also want to have a few dedicated XML tools handy for creating and testing stylesheets, as Visual Studio.NET seems a bit light in that department.

The XMLSpy IDE (www.xmlspy.com) provides an excellent environment for working on any XML-based document (the Schema creation graphical interface is particularly useful for fast schema development), and the Xslerator product (www.marrowsoft.com) provides excellent tools for creating and testing XSLT documents.

The main purpose of this section is to examine the code in the `ECommerceEngine` project, and to achieve that we'll be:

❑ Examining the `CatalogueService` class – the methods, highlights of the code, and some of the XSLT stylesheets

❑ Testing the `CatalogueService`

❑ Looking at the methods and interesting code in the `BasketService` and `OrderService` classes

We will cover the `CatalogueService` in some detail, so that you can see how the service fits together, how we can test it, and how we can consume it – this will mean we can move through the other two services a little faster.

The CatalogueService

As we saw in our summary table, the `CatalogueService` provides some basic methods for working with a catalogue providing methods to retrieve its category hierarchy, a category and its associated items, an item, and the result of a search.

The Methods

The various methods always return an `XmlDocument` and all make use of XSLT transformations in order to make the results a bit more presentable and, in the case of the hierarchy, useful.

Method	Input	Output	Comments
`getHierarchy`	*none*	`XmlDocument` containing the menu hierarchy	Retrieves a list of categories from the `Category` table and then uses an XSLT style sheet to nest them according to their `ParentCategoryID`.

Table continued on following page

Method	Input	Output	Comments
getCategory	CategoryID (int)	XmlDocument containing category details, parent, and items for the category	Builds a `DataSet` containing the results of four queries. Uses the `GetXml` method to load the data into an `XmlDocument`. This document is then transformed to a more logical format using an XSLT stylesheet.
getItem	ItemID (int)	XmlDocument containing item details and parent category details for the specified item	Builds a `DataSet` containing the results of two queries. Uses the `GetXml` method to load the data into an `XmlDocument`. Transforms the document to a more logical format using an XSLT stylesheet.
searchItems	SearchString (string)	XmlDocument containing the categories and items whose name, or description, contain the search string	Builds a `DataSet` containing the results of two queries. Uses the `GetXml` method to load the data into an `XmlDocument`. A new element is created to hold the search information before the document is transformed using an XSLT stylesheet.

Apart from looking at all four methods, here we'll also cover the XSLT stylesheets used by the getCategory and getHierarchy methods.

Implementing the Methods of the CatalogueService

Let's step through the code in CatalogueService.asmx.cs and pick out the more interesting bits.

Firstly we have our namespace references, including those related to Web Services and XML:

```
using System;
using System.Collections;
using System.ComponentModel;
using System.Data;
using System.Data.OleDb;
using System.Diagnostics;
using System.IO;
using System.Text;
using System.Web;
using System.Web.Services;
using System.Web.Services.Description;
using System.Web.Services.Protocols;
```

```
using System.Xml;
using System.Xml.XPath;
using System.Xml.Xsl;
```

Next we have the initial declaration and the connection string to the database (here the Access database):

```
namespace ECommerceEngine
{
  /// <summary>
  /// Provides access to the catalogue
  /// Method  Description
  /// getCategory  Retrieves the category, it's child and parent categories
  /// and it's Items
  /// getItem      Retrieves the item and its parent categories
  /// getHierarchy    Retrieves the category hierarchy
  /// search       Retrieves a list of categories and items that match search
  /// string
  /// </summary>
  [SoapDocumentService(Use=SoapBindingUse.Literal,
                                ParameterStyle=SoapParameterStyle.Bare)]
  public class CatalogueService : System.Web.Services.WebService
  {
    string sSource = "Provider=Microsoft.Jet.OLEDB.4.0;Data
                            Source=G:/Databases/e-commerce.mdb;";
```

Our aim is to deal with as clean XML as possible, so we are going to use document style SOAP calls, and the parameters should have the minimum of extra elements wrapped around them.

The first method we're going to look at is the getCategory method.

The getCategory Method

The getCategory method returns an XML document containing the category details, details of any parent and child categories, and a list of items that are in this category:

```
[WebMethod]
public XmlDocument getCategory(int p_iCategoryID)
{
string sSQL = "SELECT Category.* FROM Category WHERE CategoryID = " +
            p_iCategoryID.ToString();

XmlDocument objXmlDocument = new XmlDocument();
DataSet objDataSet = new DataSet();

OleDbConnection objConnection = new OleDbConnection(sSource);
objConnection.Open();

// get the category information
OleDbDataAdapter objAdapter = new OleDbDataAdapter(sSQL,objConnection);
```

The `DataSet` is first filled with the category details:

```
objAdapter.Fill (objDataSet,"Category");
```

Then we add the list of items in this category (using a join on the `CategoryItem` table):

```
// get the items for obj category
sSQL = "SELECT Item.* FROM CategoryItem INNER JOIN Item ON
        CategoryItem.ItemID = Item.ItemID WHERE CategoryItem.CategoryID
        = " + p_iCategoryID.ToString();
OleDbDataAdapter objAdapter2 = new OleDbDataAdapter(sSQL,objConnection);
objAdapter2.Fill (objDataSet,"Item");
```

Next, we get the list of parent categories (this time we join the `category` table to itself):

```
// get the parent category for obj category
sSQL = "SELECT ParentCategory.* FROM Category INNER JOIN Category AS
        ParentCategory ON Category.ParentCategoryID =
        ParentCategory.CategoryID WHERE Category.CategoryID = " +
        p_iCategoryID.ToString();
OleDbDataAdapter objAdapter3 = new OleDbDataAdapter(sSQL,objConnection);
objAdapter3.Fill (objDataSet,"ParentCategory");
```

Finally the list of child categories is added:

```
// get the parent category for obj category
sSQL = "SELECT Category.* FROM Category WHERE ParentCategoryID = " +
        p_iCategoryID.ToString();
OleDbDataAdapter objAdapter4 = new OleDbDataAdapter(sSQL,objConnection);
objAdapter4.Fill (objDataSet,"ChildCategory");
```

The `DataSet` XML is then loaded into an `XmlDocument` using the `GetXml` method. This allows us to load *only* the data XML, dropping the Schema XML that is also held in a `DataSet`:

```
objXmlDocument.LoadXml (objDataSet.GetXml());
```

The resultant XML is not in the format that we want, so we transform it to a new format using an XSLT stylesheet:

```
XslTransform objXslTransform = new XslTransform();
XPathNavigator objXPathNavigator = objXmlDocument.CreateNavigator();

objXslTransform.Load (Server.MapPath("createCategoryInfo.xslt"));
XmlReader objXmlReader = objXslTransform.Transform
                        (objXPathNavigator,null);
```

The `XmlReader` now has the result of the transformation. We'll create a new `XmlDocument`, load in the contents of the `XmlReader`, and then return the document to the consumer:

```
XmlDocument objXmlDocument2 = new XmlDocument();
objXmlDocument2.Load (objXmlReader);
return objXmlDocument2;


}
```

The XSLT transformation is a straightforward re-organization of the document so that it is in a more logical format – we'll look at the createCategoryInfo.xslt stylesheet at the end of this section.

The getItem Method

The second method we'll look at is getItem – this method performs a very similar function to getCategory. Here an XmlDocument containing item details and a list of parent categories is returned:

```
[WebMethod]
public XmlDocument getItem(int p_iItemID)
{
    string sSQL = "SELECT Item.* FROM Item WHERE ItemID = " +
                    p_iItemID.ToString();

XmlDocument objXmlDocument = new XmlDocument();
DataSet objDataSet = new DataSet();

OleDbConnection objConnection = new OleDbConnection(sSource);
objConnection.Open();

// get the item information
OleDbDataAdapter objAdapter = new OleDbDataAdapter(sSQL,objConnection);
objAdapter.Fill (objDataSet,"Item");

// get the categories for obj item
sSQL = "SELECT Category.* FROM CategoryItem " +
        "INNER JOIN Category ON CategoryItem.CategoryID =
        Category.CategoryID " + " WHERE CategoryItem.ItemID = " +
        p_iItemID.ToString();

OleDbDataAdapter objAdapter2 = new OleDbDataAdapter(sSQL,objConnection);
objAdapter2.Fill (objDataSet,"Category");

objXmlDocument.LoadXml (objDataSet.GetXml());
XslTransform objXslTransform = new XslTransform();
XPathNavigator objXPathNavigator = objXmlDocument.CreateNavigator();

objXslTransform.Load (Server.MapPath("createItemInfo.xslt"));
XmlReader objXmlReader = objXslTransform.Transform
                            (objXPathNavigator,null);

XmlDocument objXmlDocument2 = new XmlDocument();
objXmlDocument2.Load (objXmlReader);
return objXmlDocument2;


}
```

The searchItems Method

In the third method, searchItems, an XmlDocument is generated containing a list of items and categories whose name or description contains the passed search string:

```
[WebMethod]
public XmlDocument search(string p_sSearchString)
{

string sSQL = "SELECT Item.* FROM Item " +
              " WHERE (ItemName LIKE '%" + p_sSearchString + "%') OR
                 (ItemDescription LIKE '%" + p_sSearchString + "%')";

XmlDocument objXmlDocument = new XmlDocument();
DataSet objDataSet = new DataSet();

OleDbConnection objConnection = new OleDbConnection(sSource);
objConnection.Open();

// get the item information
OleDbDataAdapter objAdapter = new OleDbDataAdapter(sSQL,objConnection);
objAdapter.Fill (objDataSet,"Item");

// get the categories for obj item
sSQL = "SELECT Category.* FROM Category WHERE (CategoryName LIKE '%" +
        p_sSearchString + "%') OR (CategoryDescription LIKE '%" +
        p_sSearchString + "%')";
OleDbDataAdapter objAdapter2 = new OleDbDataAdapter(sSQL,objConnection);
objAdapter2.Fill (objDataSet,"Category");

objXmlDocument.LoadXml (objDataSet.GetXml());
```

Up to this point the code has been very similar to the previous methods; however, in this method, we want to add a new element to the XmlDocument before it is reformatted. This element is called <Search>, and it contains, not surprisingly, the details of the search.

Firstly, we need to use the CreateElement method to create the new element:

```
XmlElement objXmlElement = objXmlDocument.CreateElement("Search");
```

Now we can set the attributes. First the search criteria:

```
objXmlElement.SetAttribute ("criteria",p_sSearchString);
```

Next, how many matches we found. Remember that the input parameters to SetAttribute are both strings, so any other data types need to be converted to a string first!

```
objXmlElement.SetAttribute ("itemsMatched",
                            objDataSet.Tables["Item"].
                            Rows.Count.ToString());
objXmlElement.SetAttribute ("categoriesMatched",
                            objDataSet.Tables["Category"].
                            Rows.Count.ToString());
```

Now add the element as a child of the `DocumentElement`:

```
objXmlDocument.DocumentElement.AppendChild (objXmlElement);

XslTransform objXslTransform = new XslTransform();
XPathNavigator objXPathNavigator = objXmlDocument.CreateNavigator();

objXslTransform.Load (Server.MapPath("createSearchInfo.xslt"));
XmlReader objXmlReader = objXslTransform.Transform
                                       (objXPathNavigator,null);

XmlDocument objXmlDocument2 = new XmlDocument();
objXmlDocument2.Load (objXmlReader);
return objXmlDocument2;

}
```

The getHierarchy Method

Our final method is `getHierarchy`. This returns an `XmlDocument` containing the category hierarchy, that is all the categories listed as children of their parents. Such a hierarchy, may for example, have the form:

```
<Hierarchy>
  <Category>
    <CategoryID>1</CategoryID>
    <CategoryName>Childrens Clothes</CategoryName>
    <Category>
      <CategoryID>11</CategoryID>
      <CategoryName>Boys</CategoryName>
      <Category>
        <CategoryID>111</CategoryID>
        <CategoryName>Boys 0-2</CategoryName>
      </Category>
      <Category>
        <CategoryID>112</CategoryID>
        <CategoryName>Boys 3-7</CategoryName>
      </Category>
      .
      .
      .
    </Category>
    <Category>
      <CategoryID>12</CategoryID>
      <CategoryName>Girls</CategoryName>
      <Category>
        <CategoryID>121</CategoryID>
        <CategoryName>Girls 0-2</CategoryName>
      </Category>
      <Category>
        <CategoryID>122</CategoryID>
        <CategoryName>Girls 3-7</CategoryName>
```

```
        </Category>
            .
            .
            .
        </Category>
    </Category>
</Hierarchy>
```

Here we are going to generate the hierarchy by dumping the categories to an XmlDocument, and then use an XSLT stylesheet to rearrange the order for us. Again, the method is very similar to the previous three, with the action taking place in the XSLT stylesheet (discussed later). This stylesheet takes a flat list of Category elements and produces the nested hierarchy desired.

```
[WebMethod]
public XmlDocument getHierarchy()
{

    string sSQL = "SELECT Category.* FROM Category";

    XmlDocument objXmlDocument = new XmlDocument();
    DataSet objDataSet = new DataSet();

    OleDbConnection objConnection = new OleDbConnection(sSource);
    objConnection.Open();

    // get the item information
    OleDbDataAdapter objAdapter =
                        new OleDbDataAdapter(sSQL,objConnection);
    objAdapter.Fill (objDataSet,"Category");

      // load the XmlDocument with the categories
      objXmlDocument.LoadXml (objDataSet.GetXml());

    // produce the nested hierarchy by transforming
    XslTransform objXslTransform = new XslTransform();
    XPathNavigator objXPathNavigator = objXmlDocument.CreateNavigator();

    objXslTransform.Load (Server.MapPath("createCategoryHierarchy.xslt"));
    XmlReader objXmlReader = objXslTransform.Transform
                                    (objXPathNavigator,null);

    XmlDocument objXmlDocument2 = new XmlDocument();
    objXmlDocument2.Load (objXmlReader);
    return objXmlDocument2;

}
```

Now we've finished looking at the methods, let's investigate the stylesheets associated with the getCategory method (createCategoryInfo.xslt), and the getHierarchy method (createCategoryHierarchy.xslt).

createCategoryInfo.xslt

As we said previously, the XSLT transformation is just to re-organize the document into a more logical format. As we are generating an XML document, we set the xsl:output method accordingly:

```
<?xml version="1.0" encoding="UTF-8" ?>
<xsl:stylesheet version="1.0" xmlns:xsl="http://www.w3.org/1999/XSL/Transform">

   <xsl:output method="xml" />
```

The root element of the GetXml() method is NewDataSet. We want to replace that with Catalogue:

```
<xsl:template match="NewDataSet">
  <xsl:element name="Catalogue">
```

To ensure the ordering of the elements, we'll be specific about picking them out. We are going to group the ParentCategory, ChildCategory, and Item nodes under appropriate parents. The parents are only created if their respective children are in the document.

```
      <xsl:apply-templates select="Category" />
      <xsl:if test="ParentCategory">
        <xsl:element name="ParentCategories">
          <xsl:apply-templates select="ParentCategory" />
        </xsl:element>
      </xsl:if>
      <xsl:if test="ChildCategory">
        <xsl:element name="ChildCategories">
          <xsl:apply-templates select="ChildCategory" />
        </xsl:element>
      </xsl:if>
      <xsl:if test="Item">
        <xsl:element name="Items">
          <xsl:apply-templates select="Item" />
        </xsl:element>
      </xsl:if>
    </xsl:element>
</xsl:template>
```

The following two templates copy the Category, ParentCategory, ChildCategory, and Item nodes to the new document:

```
<xsl:template match="Category | ParentCategory | ChildCategory | Item">
  <xsl:copy>
    <xsl:apply-templates select="node()" />
  </xsl:copy>
</xsl:template>

<xsl:template match="Category/* | ParentCategory/* | ChildCategory/* |
                                                    Item/*">
  <xsl:copy>
    <xsl:apply-templates select="node()" />
  </xsl:copy>
```

```
    </xsl:template>

  </xsl:stylesheet>
```

Although not strictly necessary, it is a good idea to create an XML Schema for the XML result. It not only makes it easier to test the service (you can validate that your input XML and output XML are as expected) but can also help with the service's WSDL file.

createCategoryHierarchy.xslt

This stylesheet does all the hard work for the `getHierarchy` method to produce a nested hierarchy. It only contains three templates: one to match the root node and give us a starting point, one to copy nodes, and the other, a named template, that performs the work including recursively calling itself.

```
<?xml version="1.0" encoding="UTF-8" ?>
<xsl:stylesheet version="1.0" xmlns:xsl="http://www.w3.org/1999/XSL/Transform">
  <xsl:template match="/">
    <Hierarchy>
```

We've opened our new root node, now let's call our workhorse template, passing it the `Category` node with a `ParentCategoryID` of 0 as this must be our top `Category`. Note that only the first `Category` that satisfies this match will be processed; any others will be ignored.

```
      <xsl:call-template name="Category">
        <xsl:with-param name="objCategory"
                              select="//Category[ParentCategoryID=0]" />
      </xsl:call-template>
    </Hierarchy>

  </xsl:template>
```

Our workhorse template selects, and outputs, the `<Category>` elements correctly nested:

```
      <xsl:template name="Category">
```

The template expects a parameter called `thisCategory` and represents the current `<Category>` node being processed:

```
        <xsl:param name="thisCategory" />
```

An internal variable is created to store the current `CategoryID`:

```
        <xsl:variable name="objCategoryID">
          <xsl:value-of select="$objCategory/CategoryID" />
        </xsl:variable>
```

Now we create a new element called <Category>, and copy all the child nodes of the current <Category>:

```
<xsl:element name="Category">
  <xsl:apply-templates select="$objCategory/node()" />
```

To find and process the children of the current <Category>, we use a <xsl:for-each> statement and search the entire document for <Category> elements whose child element ParentCategoryID equals the CategoryID of the current <Category>:

```
<xsl:for-each select="//Category[ParentCategoryID=$objCategoryID]">
```

The workhorse template is recursively called with a parameter of the child node. This, in effect, builds each branch of the hierarchy to its conclusion as it goes:

```
        <xsl:call-template name="Category">
          <xsl:with-param name="objCategory" select="." />
        </xsl:call-template>
      </xsl:for-each>
    </xsl:element>
  </xsl:template>
```

Our simple template to perform the copy of a node is:

```
  <xsl:template match="node()">
    <xsl:copy>
      <xsl:value-of select="." />
    </xsl:copy>
  </xsl:template>

</xsl:stylesheet>
```

Recursive templates are extremely powerful and, despite the fact that they are extremely easy to get wrong, are well worth investigation (see for example, resources such as www.topxml.com/xsl/articles/recurse).

The advantages of putting this kind of logic into a stylesheet are that it makes our program code much smaller and less cluttered, and the logic itself is easy to test as a self-contained unit.

Testing the CatalogueService

Now we've covered the CatalogueService code, let's build it and navigate to CatalogueService.asmx, in a browser. We should get the following screen:

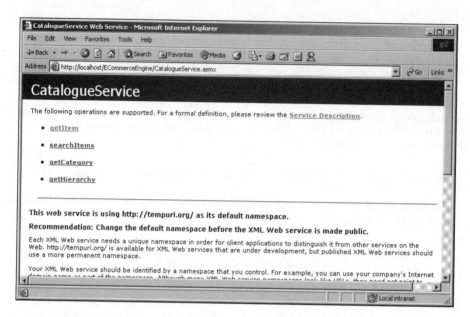

This screen presents us with a list of the methods that are available (basically any public method in the class that is preceded with the WebMethod attribute) in the service. Clicking on getItem should bring up the following screen:

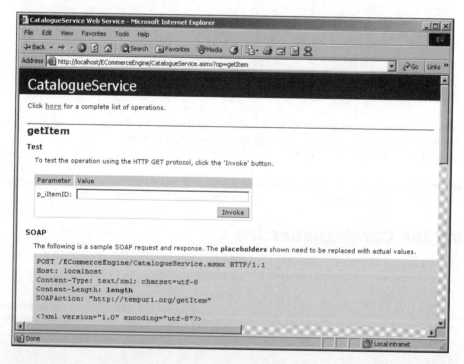

This screen gives us a simple way of testing our method, as well as details of what the SOAP request and response documents look like and what the HTTP bindings should be.

Entering a value into the p_iItemID input box (like 21), that corresponds to an ItemID in the Item database table should induce, after clicking the **Invoke** button, a new window to pop up like so:

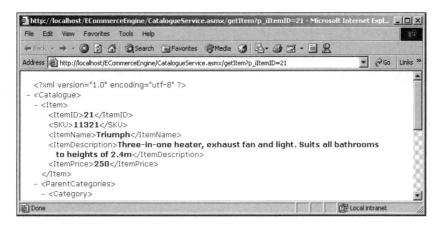

So, clicking the **Invoke** button invoked the getItem method of our CatalogueService by submitting a form to the **CatalogueService** page, with a form action of the URL of the service and a form method of GET.

For example, the HTML form to call the getItem method of the CatalogueService is:

```
<form action= http://localhost/ECommerceEngine/CatalogueService.asmx/
                  getItem method="GET">
  <input type="text" name="p_itemID" size="50">
</form>
```

While this is straightforward, the limitations of using HTTP GET or HTTP Post to test are immediately seen if a string like "bananas" is entered as a **p_iItemID**: here all we get back is a block of text containing a list of .NET-generated error messages, none of which mean very much to the client trying to access the web service. Thus we don't have any error handling in this situation.

Fortunately, SOAP gives us a much more controlled, and most importantly, standard, approach to returning errors by using the <SOAP:fault> nodes (see Chapter 8 for a more detailed look at SOAP).

Another disadvantage of using the HTTP GET and POST methods is that they cannot handle complex types, as you are restricted to name-value pairs. This means that you cannot pass structures or arrays using POST or GET, so, for example, passing an order that includes header information and item details, is impossible.

If we want to properly test our services and get more controlled error messages back, we need to use a SOAP-based test harness …

Building a SOAP Test Harness

Building a simple SOAP-based application to test our services can easily be done in an Internet Explorer HTML page. In the code download, `testHarness2.htm`, gives us a suitable test harness and has the following appearance:

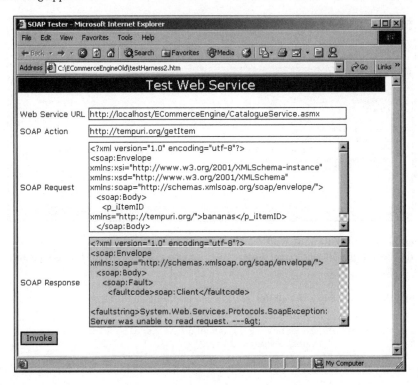

The harness uses the `MSXML2.XMLHttp` object to send a SOAP `Request` to a Web Service and display the response. Here's the function that performs the call:

```
Function testSOAP()

   Dim oHttp   ' As MSXML2.XMLHttp

   Set oHttp = CreateObject("MSXML2.XMLHttp")

   oHttp.Open "POST",frmTest.txtURL.value,false
   oHttp.SetRequestHeader "Content-type","text/xml"
   oHttp.SetRequestHeader "SOAPAction",frmTest.txtSOAPAction.value
   oHttp.Send frmTest.txtSOAPRequest.value

   frmTest.txtSOAPResponse.value = oHttp.ResponseText

   testSOAP = false

End Function
```

As we can see, it is quite straightforward – it just opens the URL, sets a couple of Http Headers and then sends the request. This is a synchronous call, meaning that the function will wait until a response is returned by the service.

To use the harness, simply enter the URL of the service and then cut and paste the **SOAP Action** and **SOAP Request** XML from the operation test page (for example the **getItem** page we saw previously) and click **Invoke**.

Invoking the Web Service with a **p_iItemID** of "bananas" will yield the following type of output:

```
<?xml version="1.0" encoding="utf-8"?>
<soap:Envelope xmlns:soap="http://schemas.xmlsoap.org/soap/envelope/">
  <soap:Body>
    <soap:Fault>
      <faultcode>soap:Client</faultcode>
      <faultstring>System.Web.Services.Protocols.SoapException: Server was
        unable to read request. ---&gt; System.Exception: There is an error
        in XML document (4, 63). ---&gt; System.FormatException: Input
        string was not in a correct format.
        at System.Number.ParseInt32(String s, NumberStyles style, NumberFormatInfo info)
        at System.Xml.XmlConvert.ToInt32(String s)
        at XmlSerializationReader1.Read5_getItem()
        at System.Xml.Serialization.XmlSerializer.Deserialize(XmlReader xmlReader)
        at System.Web.Services.Protocols.SoapServerProtocol.ReadParameters()
        at System.Web.Services.Protocols.SoapServerProtocol.ReadParameters()
        at System.Web.Services.Protocols.WebServiceHandler.Invoke()
        at System.Web.Services.Protocols.WebServiceHandler.CoreProcessRequest()
      </faultstring>
      <detail />
    </soap:Fault>
  </soap:Body>
</soap:Envelope>
```

It's pretty much the same information as we got when using the `HTTP Get`, except that this time it is wrapped in a `SOAP Fault` element. The `faultcode` is set to `soap:Client`, which tells us that it is the SOAP Request that was at fault (at least we can rest easy!). Of course, the `faultstring` is a little long winded, although embedded in all the messages that .NET has generated, is the reason for this calamity:

    Input string was not in a correct format.

In our commercial version of the engine we might pre-process the SOAP Request, check its validity, and generate our own more meaningful and less verbose messages, but that's a little beyond the scope of this case study.

So, by now we've gone through the first service, the `CatalogueService`. We've seen how we can retrieve information from the database and, using XSLT, transform it into more manageable formats, and dipped our toe ever so slightly into the more advanced techniques of XSLT such as recursive templates. We also pondered the testing of our service using the operation detail page and a very basic SOAP-based test harness that we built ourselves.

Now we will take a less-detailed look at the other services that make up our engine, before looking at how our customers might build applications to consume them.

The BasketService

The BasketService provides the functionality to select, edit, and maintain a list of items with methods that are pretty much as you would see in a traditional e-commerce web site (although, as we've said previously, in a very simplified manner). The basket details are all held in a single column, BasketDetails, as an XmlDocument, so any actions on an item are all preformed by retrieving this column, moving it to an XmlDocument, manipulating the document, and then storing it back in the table.

Method	Input	Output	Comments
getBasket	BasketID (int)	XmlDocument containing the specified basket's details	Retrieves the BasketDetail column from the appropriate row and loads this straight into an XmlDocument for returning to the client.
createBasket	*none*	(int) BasketID of the new basket	Creates a new row in the Basket table. Re-reads the table to get the new BasketID.
listBaskets	Days (int)	XmlDocument containing a list of baskets	Builds a DataSet of the baskets that are older than the passed number of days. As we only want to change the name of the DocumentElement for this list, an XmlDocument is loaded with the new name, a DocumentFragment is loaded via the GetXml() method, and then the InnerXml of the fragment is moved to the document.
addItem	ItemID (int) Qty (int)	*none*	Retrieves the BasketDetail column from the appropriate row and loads the value into an XmlDocument. A check is made to see if an Item node exists with this ItemID – if it does then the quantities are added, if not then a new Item element is created, populated, and added to the XmlDocument. The itemCount attribute is updated before the XML is stored back into the BasketDetail column.

Method	Input	Output	Comments
removeItem	ItemID (int)	*none*	Retrieves the BasketDetail column from the appropriate row and loads the value into an XmlDocument. The Item is located and the element removed. The itemCount attribute is updated before the XML is stored back into the database table.
updateItem	ItemID (int) Qty (int)	*none*	Retrieves the BasketDetail column from the appropriate row and loads the value into an XmlDocument. The Item is located – if the new quantity is 0 then the element is removed, otherwise the old quantity is overwritten with the new quantity.

We won't go through the entire code for this service – we'll just pick out some of the highlights.

The BasketService – Selected Code

Here we'll just be looking at the listBaskets method, where we use document fragments, and the addItem method, as an example of manipulating and storing the basket details as an XmlDocument. Again, the database connection string for the service is placed at the top of the class.

The listBaskets Method

In the listBaskets method we make use of document fragments and the very useful InnerXml property to create an XmlDocument with only a name change on DocumentElement. We could have done this via an XSLT stylesheet, but there was less coding to do it in the service code itself:

```
    [WebMethod]
    public XmlDocument listBaskets(int p_iAgeInDays)
{

    string sSQL  = "SELECT Basket.BasketID, Basket.BasketCreationDate " +
                "FROM Basket WHERE (BasketCreationDate <= (Date() - " +
                p_iAgeInDays.ToString() + ")) " +
                "ORDER BY BasketCreationDate, BasketID";

    XmlDocument objXmlDocument = new XmlDocument();
    DataSet objDataSet = new DataSet();

    OleDbConnection objConnection = new OleDbConnection(sSource);
    objConnection.Open();

    OleDbDataAdapter objAdapter = new
                            OleDbDataAdapter(sSQL,objConnection);
    objAdapter.Fill (objDataSet,"Basket");
```

We have populated our `DataSet` with the list of baskets. Now we load the `XmlDocument` with only a single element:

```
objXmlDocument.LoadXml ("<Baskets/>");
```

Next, we create a document fragment and use it to store the `DataSet` data XML. Document fragments have no `load()` method, so the easiest way to populate them is to set their `InnerXml` property:

```
XmlDocumentFragment objXmlFragment;
objXmlFragment = objXmlDocument.CreateDocumentFragment();
objXmlFragment.InnerXml = objDataSet.GetXml();
```

Now we need to move across all the `Basket` elements. These are held as children of the top node in the `DocumentFragment`, which means we can't simply copy the fragment across to the document. We can copy all the children in one hit, however, by setting the `InnerXml` property of the `DocumentElement` to the `InnerXml` property of the top node in the fragment. Remember, `InnerXml` contains the XML for all descendants of the node, and `OuterXml`, which is a read-only property, includes the `InnerXml` plus the XML for the node itself.

```
objXmlDocument.DocumentElement.InnerXml =
                        objXmlFragment.ChildNodes.Item(0).InnerXml;
```

Finally, we set the `basketCount` attribute on the `DocumentElement` to a count of the `Basket` nodes in the document:

```
objXmlDocument.DocumentElement.SetAttribute
                ("basketCount",objXmlFragment.SelectNodes("//Basket").
                Count.ToString());

return objXmlDocument;
}
```

The addItem Method

As we are only retrieving a single column for a single row, and because this column already contains XML, we are going to use the slimmer `DataReader` class to retrieve the basket details:

```
[WebMethod]
public XmlDocument addItem(int p_iBasketID, int p_iItemID, int p_iQty)
{
  // get the basket

  string sSQL  = "SELECT Basket.BasketDetail FROM Basket WHERE
               BasketID = " + p_iBasketID.ToString();

  OleDbDataReader objDataReader;
  OleDbConnection objConnection = new OleDbConnection(sSource);
  objConnection.Open();

  // get the basket detail
  OleDbCommand objCommand = new OleDbCommand (sSQL,objConnection);
```

```
objDataReader = objCommand.ExecuteReader();
objDataReader.Read();
```

We then create an `XmlDocument` and load it with the value of the `BasketDetails` column. We use the `ToString` method to ensure that we are providing the proper data type to the `LoadXml` method:

```
// load it into an XmlDocument
XmlDocument objXmlDocument = new XmlDocument();
objXmlDocument.LoadXml (objDataReader.GetValue(0).ToString());
objDataReader.Close();
```

Once the details are loaded, we check to see if an `Item` element already exists for the `ItemID`. If it doesn't (that is `SelectSingleNode` returned a null value), then a new `Item` element is created. If it does then the quantities are added:

```
// check to see if this item id is already in basket
XmlNode objItemNode;
objItemNode =
        objXmlDocument.DocumentElement.SelectSingleNode("Item[ItemID=" +
        p_iItemID.ToString() + "]");

if (objItemNode == null)
{
   // not there so let's create it
   XmlElement objItemElement;
   objItemElement = objXmlDocument.CreateElement("Item");
```

To retrieve the appropriate details from the `Item` table for populating the new `Item` element we use the following SQL. To make it easier, we also return two values that don't exist in the table, `Qty` and `LineValue`:

```
sSQL = "SELECT ItemID,SKU,ItemName,ItemPrice, " +
        p_iQty.ToString() + " AS Qty, " + p_iQty.ToString() +
        " * ItemPrice  AS LineValue " + "FROM Item " +
        "WHERE ItemID = " + p_iItemID.ToString();

objCommand.CommandText = sSQL;
objDataReader = objCommand.ExecuteReader();
objDataReader.Read();
XmlElement objNewElement;
```

To create an `Item` element, we create and append a new element for each object in the `DataReader` `Fields` collection. Each new element's nodename is set to the field name and its text value (the `InnerText` property) is set to the value of the field, converted to a string. This will also create elements for the two additional values we added to the SQL statement, `Qty` and `LineValue`:

```
for (int iField = 0; iField < objDataReader.FieldCount; iField++)
{
   objNewElement = objXmlDocument.CreateElement
                           (objDataReader.GetName(iField));
   objNewElement.InnerText =
```

```
                            objDataReader.GetValue(iField).ToString();
            objItemElement.AppendChild (objNewElement);
      }

      objDataReader.Close();
```

Our new `Item` element is now populated, so we'll append it to the `DocumentElement` and then reset the value of the `itemCount` attribute:

```
      objXmlDocument.DocumentElement.AppendChild (objItemElement);
      int iItemCount = objXmlDocument.DocumentElement.ChildNodes.Count;
      objXmlDocument.DocumentElement.SetAttribute
                              ("itemCount",iItemCount.ToString());
   }
   else
   {
```

If the `Item` element already exists then we are just going to update the `Qty` and `LineValue` elements:

```
      // just add the new quantity to existing quantity
      int iQty = int.Parse(objItemNode.SelectSingleNode("Qty").InnerText)
                                            + p_iQty;
      float iPrice =
         float.Parse(objItemNode.SelectSingleNode("ItemPrice").InnerText);
      float iLineValue = iPrice * p_iQty;
```

Don't forget, the `InnerText` property is a string, so we have to use the `ToString` method to convert our `Qty` and `LineValue` variables to a string type, otherwise setting the `InnerText` property will fail:

```
      objItemNode.SelectSingleNode("Qty").InnerText = iQty.ToString();
      objItemNode.SelectSingleNode("LineValue").InnerText =
                                     iLineValue.ToString();
   }

   objXmlDocument.DocumentElement.SetAttribute ("basketTotal",
                     getBasketTotal(objXmlDocument).ToString());
```

To store the basket detail XML we set up the SQL to populate the `BasketDetail` column with the `OuterXml` property value from the `DocumentElement`. We use `OuterXml` here, as we want to include all the XML for the document:

```
sSQL = "UPDATE Basket SET BasketDetail = '" +
         objXmlDocument.DocumentElement.OuterXml.ToString() +
         "' WHERE BasketID = " + p_iBasketID.ToString();

   objCommand.CommandText = sSQL;
   objCommand.ExecuteNonQuery();

   objConnection.Close();
   return objXmlDocument;
   }
```

That's it for the `BasketService`. By storing the basket details in a piece of XML (really a string or text field in our database table) and by manipulating that XML, the basket changes. Therefore we are able to keep the basket to a single table and have a very simple method of displaying the basket by returning a single column and transforming its contents with an XSLT stylesheet.

The OrderService

The `OrderService` provides some basic functionality for creating an order and then adding information to that order. Like the `BasketService`, it uses a single table to store the order information, with the order details (that is which items have been ordered) being stored as a string of XML data.

Method	Input	Output	Comments
createOrder	BasketID (int)	OrderID (int)	Uses a `DataReader` to retrieve the `BasketDetails` for the `BasketID`. An `XmlDocument` is loaded with an order skeleton; a `DocumentFragment` is loaded with the `BasketDetails` XML. The basket items are copied across to the `OrderDetails` node in the `XmlDocument` and the `OrderTotal` computed before the order is inserted into the `Order` table. The table is re-read to get the `OrderID`, which is then passed back to the client.
addCustomerInfo	OrderID (int) CustomerClass	*none*	The order details are retrieved and loaded into an `XmlDocument`. The `CustomerClass` is serialized and the resultant XML appended to the `DocumentElement` of the order `XmlDocument`. The `OuterXml` is then stored back in the database table.
			This is an overloaded `addOrderInfo` method.

Table continued on following page

Method	Input	Output	Comments
addShippingInfo	OrderID (int) Shipping Class	*none*	The order details are retrieved and loaded into an XmlDocument. The ShippingClass is serialized and the resultant XML appended to the documentElement of the order XmlDocument. The OuterXml is then stored back in the database table. This is an overloaded addOrderInfo method.
listOrdersByDays	Days (short)	XmlDocument containing all the orders placed in the last *n* days	A DataSet is created that contains all the orders that have been created in the last *n* days. By the familiar technique of moving the XML to a documentFragment the DocumentElement name is changed. This is an overloaded listOrders method.
listOrdersByCustomer	Customer ID (int)	XmlDocument containing all the orders for a CustomerID	A DataSet is created that contains all the orders that relate to a particular CustomerID. The DocumentElement name is changed by moving the DataSet data XML to a DocumentFragment and copying the child nodes over. This is an overloaded listOrders method
getOrder	OrderID (int)	XmlDocument containing the details for the specified order	The OrderDetails column of the appropriate row in the Order table is loaded into an XmlDocument, which is returned to the client.

The OrderService – Selected Code

In `OrderService`, we made use of overloading methods. Although we can overload methods in Web Service code, we cannot make them available with the same name and let .NET figure out which of the overloaded methods to invoke.

We have to provide unique method names, which is achieved by coding a `MessageName` on the [WebMethod] attribute as follows:

```
[WebMethod(MessageName="listOrdersByDays")]
public XmlDocument listOrders(short p_iAgeInDays)
```

```
[WebMethod(MessageName="listOrdersByCustomer")]
public XmlDocument listOrders(int p_iCustomerID)
```

Here we have overloaded methods for `listOrders`: one which takes an age in days, with a datatype of `short`, and one which takes a `CustomerID` as an `integer`.

However, a client invoking these methods would use the `MessageName`, not the method name. For example, to invoke the `listOrders(short p_iAgeInDays)` method a client would use:

Protocol	URL	SOAPAction
SOAP	/E-commerceEngine/OrderService.asmx	http://tempuri.org/listOrdersByDays
HTTP-GET	/E-commerceEngine/OrderService.asmx/listOrdersByDays?p_iAgeInDays=	
HTTP-POST	/E-commerceEngine/OrderService.asmx/listOrdersByDays	

The methods `addCustomerInfo` and `addShippingInfo` are also overloaded, both having the method name `addOrderInfo`. These methods also make use of the serialization class to convert a passed class into XML for appending to the `OrderDetail` XML.

We'll take a closer look at the `addOrderInfo` method to see this in action.

The addCustomerInfo Method

The `MessageName` on the [WebMethod] attribute lets us give this overloaded method a unique identity:

```
[WebMethod(MessageName="addCustomerInfo")]
public void addOrderInfo(int p_iOrderID, CustomerClass p_objCustomer)
{
  // get the order

  string sSQL  = "SELECT Order.OrderDetail " +
```

```
                    "FROM [Order] WHERE OrderID = " + p_iOrderID.ToString();

        OleDbDataReader objDataReader;

        OleDbConnection objConnection = new OleDbConnection(sSource);
        objConnection.Open();

        // get the order detail
        OleDbCommand objCommand = new OleDbCommand (sSQL,objConnection);
        objDataReader = objCommand.ExecuteReader();
        objDataReader.Read();

        // create and load XmlDocument
        XmlDocument objXmlDocument = new XmlDocument();
        objXmlDocument.LoadXml (objDataReader.GetValue(0).ToString());

        objDataReader.Close();
```

The OrderDetail XML is now loaded into an XmlDocument. Next, we create a DocumentFragment
that will hold the result of our serialization:

```
        // create an xml document fragment
        XmlDocumentFragment objXmlDocFrag =
                            objXmlDocument.CreateDocumentFragment();
```

When we create our XmlSerializer we have to tell it what class we will be serializing. In this case, it's
the CustomerClass:

```
        //Serialize the customer class
        XmlSerializer objXmlSerializer = new
                            XmlSerializer(typeof(CustomerClass));
```

We need somewhere to serialize to, so we will also create a StringBuilder and StringWriter:

```
        StringBuilder objStringBuilder = new StringBuilder();
        StringWriter objStringWriter = new StringWriter(objStringBuilder);
```

We serialize the passed customer data and put it in the StringWriter:

```
        objXmlSerializer.Serialize (objStringWriter,p_objCustomer);
```

The resultant string of XML is then moved into an XmlDocument and has its attributes removed
(mostly namespace declarations) before being copied over to the Order XmlDocument:

```
        // load serialized class into a document
        XmlDocument objXmlDocument2 = new XmlDocument();
        objXmlDocument2.LoadXml(objStringWriter.ToString());
        objXmlDocument2.DocumentElement.RemoveAllAttributes();

        // now insert the contents from document2
```

```
objXmlDocument.DocumentElement.InnerXml =
                objXmlDocument.DocumentElement.InnerXml +
                objXmlDocument2.DocumentElement.OuterXml;
```

The updated order XML is then stored back in the database table:

```
    // update the order
    sSQL = "UPDATE [Order] " +
           " SET CustomerID = " + p_objCustomer.CustomerID.ToString() +
           "," + "      OrderDetail = '" +
            objXmlDocument.DocumentElement.OuterXml + "'" +
           " WHERE OrderID = " + p_iOrderID;

    objCommand.CommandText = sSQL;
    objCommand.ExecuteNonQuery();

    objConnection.Close();
}
```

The serialization classes (namespace `System.Xml.Serialization`) are extremely useful for converting between non-XML data and XML. .NET uses the `deserialize` method in Web Services for converting the parameters in SOAP Requests to their code-friendly data-types and then the `Serialize` method to create the Response. In fact, we are actually serializing what .Net has already de-serialized to make the SOAP parameters acceptable for our method!

In our method, the serializer takes the `CustomerClass`:

```
public class CustomerClass
{
  public int CustomerID;
  public string FirstName;
  public string LastName;
  public AddressClass BillingAddress;
}

public class AddressClass
{
  public string Line1;
  public string Line2;
  public string Line3;
  public string Locality;
  public string State;
  public string Zip;
  public string Country;
}
```

and converts it to this XML:

```
    <CustomerClass>
    <CustomerID />
    <FirstName />
    <LastName />
  <BillingAddress>
      <Line1 />
      <Line2 />
      <Line3 />
      <Locality />
      <State />
      <Zip />
      <Country />
  </BillingAddress>
</CustomerClass>
```

The Online Shop – A Consuming Example

As the main drive of this case study was to build the engine, this example is going to be brief, and will just serve to indicate how to consume the services of the engine we have just considered.

We are going to build a very simple online store for the imaginary Light n Heat Online Shop implementing functions from just two of our services – the `CatalogueService` and the `BasketService`.

The application is going to be an ASP.NET Web Application involving a couple of simple ASP.NET pages that utilize transformations to render the pages from the XML returned by the service methods. We'll be looking at two ASP.NET pages:

❑   `Catalogue.aspx`, which will consume the `CatalogueService`

❑   `Basket.aspx`, which consumes the `BasketService`

Before we look at the ASP.NET pages, we firstly need to consider how the pages will reference the services we've just considered. While there are a number of ways of doing this (via `.vsdisco` files etc.), we'll leave that topic for detailed Web Services books, and use the simple method of adding the individual Web Service files manually.

To do this, right-click on the project in the Solution Explorer pane of Visual Studio .NET and select Add Web Reference. This will bring up the following screen:

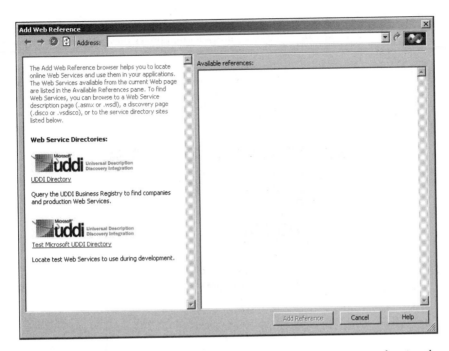

From here navigate to the appropriate .asmx file, which will bring up a screen showing the methods available to consumers of that Web Service. In this example we add the CatalogueService reference first – easily achieved by clicking the **Add Reference** button.

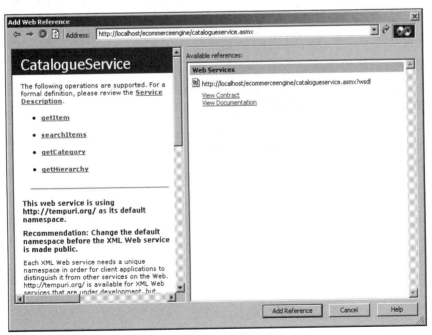

The effect of this is to add a **Web References** folder under the project, and within this folder will be a further sub-folder – **Localhost** – that contains auto-generated proxy files that will handle the calling of the appropriate service.

Since we'll also be using the `BasketService` in this section, the process for adding a web reference needs to be repeated with `BasketService.asmx` being addressed. Interestingly this will add another sub-folder under the **Web References** folder – **localhost1** – that will contain the proxy class for the `BasketService`.

Of course this discussion (quite deliberately) skates over exactly what is happening when we add these references, and what the proxy classes are doing. All we are going to concern ourselves with is that, after adding those references, we have auto-generated classes that allow us to invoke the `CatalogueService`, using the SOAP protocol as though it were just another class in our application.

So, let's build an ASP.NET page to consume the `CatalogueService` and display our products.

Consuming CatalogueService

This will be an extremely simple page, which will allow us to display the catalogue hierarchy in the left-hand column, with the catalogue details in the right. We'll call it `catalogue.aspx` and it will look something like this:

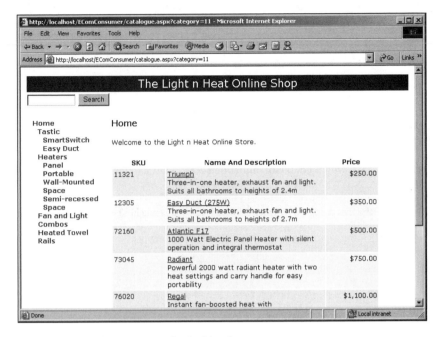

The `catalogue.aspx` ASP.NET page looks like this:

```
<%@ Page language="c#" Codebehind="catalogue.aspx.cs" AutoEventWireup="false"
Inherits="EComConsumer.catalogue" %>
<HTML>
<HEAD><link rel="stylesheet" href="style.css"></HEAD>
<BODY>
  <table width="100%">
  <tr>
    <td class="banner" colspan="2" valign="center" align="middle">
      The Light n Heat Online Shop
    </td>
  </tr>
  <tr>
    <td align="middle">
      <form action="catalogue.aspx" method="post">
        <input type="text" size="10" maxlength="30" name="txtSearch"> 
        <input type="submit" value="Search">
      </form>
    </td>
    <td align="right">
      <% if (Session["basketID"] != null) {%>
        <a class="menuLink" href="basket.aspx">Show Basket</a>
      <% } %>
    </td>
  </tr>
  <tr>
    <!-- hierarchy -->
    <td id="myHierarchy" width="150" valign="top" align="left">
```

```
        <% showHierarchy(); %>
      </td>
      <!-- details -->
      <td id="myDetails" valign="top" align="middle">
        <% showDetail(); %>
      </td>
    </tr>
  </table>
</BODY>
</HTML>
```

This is very basic HTML with a couple of embedded ASP.NET statements to output the hierarchy and the catalogue detail.

The code behind, in the `catalogue.aspx.cs` file, is shown next. First we add some standard references:

```
using System.Xml;
using System.Xml.XPath;
using System.Xml.Xsl;

namespace EComConsumer
{
  /// <summary>
  /// Summary description for catalogue.
  /// </summary>
  public class catalogue : System.Web.UI.Page
  {
    public catalogue()
    {
      Page.Init += new System.EventHandler(Page_Init);
    }

    private void Page_Load(object sender, System.EventArgs e)
    {

    }
```

Then the methods – the `showDetail` method takes the `XmlDocument` passed back from the `CatalogueService` and using an XSLT stylesheet transforms it to HTML. The first step is to instantiate the proxy class for the `CatalogueService`:

```
    public void showDetail()
    {
    localhost.CatalogueService objCatalogueService =
                                new localhost.CatalogueService();
    XmlDocument objCatalogue = new XmlDocument();

    string sStyleSheet = "";
```

We check the `QueryString` property to see if we are making an `item` request, a `category` request, or a `search` request. Then the appropriate method in the `CatalogueService` proxy is invoked, the result loaded straight into an `XmlDocument`, and the style sheet that we will use to display the results is set:

```
if (Request.QueryString["item"] != null)
{
  objCatalogue.LoadXml (objCatalogueService.getItem
      (int.Parse(Request.QueryString["item"])).OuterXml);
  sStyleSheet = "itemOutput.xslt";
}

if (Request.QueryString["category"] != null)
{
  objCatalogue.LoadXml (objCatalogueService.getCategory
      (int.Parse(Request.QueryString["category"])).OuterXml);
  sStyleSheet = "categoryOutput.xslt";
}

if (Request.Form["txtSearch"] != null)
{
  objCatalogue.LoadXml (objCatalogueService.searchItems
      (Request.Form["txtSearch"].ToString()).OuterXml);
  sStyleSheet = "searchOutput.xslt";
}
```

Next we set up the transformation (as long as a stylesheet has been selected):

```
// Check that stylesheet has been set
if (sStyleSheet =="")
{
  //It hasn't so write prompt
  Response.Write("<p>Please select a category from the menu</p>");
} else {

  // It has so transform the XML using the set stylesheet
  XPathNavigator objCatalogueNav = objCatalogue.CreateNavigator();
  XslTransform objTransform = new XslTransform();

  objTransform.Load (Server.MapPath(sStyleSheet));
```

Then we transform the XML, sending the resultant HTML straight to the Response stream (and therefore, the browser):

```
  objTransform.Transform (objCatalogueNav,null,Response.Output);
  }
}
```

The showHierarchy method is very similar, retrieving the XML for the hierarchy and sending the transformed HTML directly to the browser:

```
public void showHierarchy()
{
  // Get XML for this category or Item
  localhost.CatalogueService objCatalogueService = new
          localhost.CatalogueService();
  XmlDocument objCatalogue = new XmlDocument();
```

```
    string sStyleSheet = "";
    objCatalogue.LoadXml (objCatalogueService.getHierarchy().OuterXml);
    sStyleSheet = "showHierarchy.xslt";

    XPathNavigator objCatalogueNav = objCatalogue.CreateNavigator();
    XslTransform objTransform = new XslTransform();

    objTransform.Load (Server.MapPath(sStyleSheet));

    objTransform.Transform (objCatalogueNav,null,Response.Output);

}
```

As you will have noticed, the code accesses four XSLT style sheets to create the HTML for the page: one for the hierarchy (showHierarchy.xslt), one for the search results (searchOutput.xslt), one for the category display (categoryOutput.xslt), and one for the item display (itemOuput.xslt).

Implementing a Basket

Now that we have the catalog working and are able to navigate around the categories and the items, so we can select products to buy we'll implement a basket – basket.aspx. Its HTML is almost identical to that in catalogue.aspx except that showDetail() has been replaced with showBasket().

Let's pick out just a few parts of the code behind for discussion. In the Page_Load method, we check for an action in the QueryString and take the appropriate action:

```
private void Page_Load(object sender, System.EventArgs e)
{
  localhost1.BasketService objBasketService =
                                    new localhost1.BasketService();

  // check the action to see what we need to do
  switch (Request.QueryString["action"])
  {
```

When it is add, we check if we have a basketID in a Session object, and if we don't we'll invoke the createBasket method before invoking the addItem method:

```
case "add":
  if (Session["basketID"] == null)
  {
    Session["basketID"] = objBasketService.createBasket();
  }
  objBasketService.addItem (
        int.Parse(Session["basketID"].ToString()),
         int.Parse(Request.Form["txtItemID"]),
         int.Parse(Request.Form["txtQty"]));
  break;
```

When the action is update, we check to see if the quantity is 0. If it is then we invoke the removeItem method, otherwise we invoke the udpateItem method:

```
case "update":
  if (Session["basketID"] != null)
  {
    int iQty = int.Parse(Request.Form["txtQty"].ToString());
    if (iQty == 0)
    {
      objBasketService.removeItem (
          int.Parse(Session["basketID"].ToString()),
          int.Parse(Request.Form["txtItemID"]));
    }
    else
    {
      objBasketService.updateItem (
          int.Parse(Session["basketID"].ToString()),
          int.Parse(Request.Form["txtItemID"]),iQty);
    }
  }
  break;
}
}
```

The showBasket method invokes the getBasket method to return an XmlDocument containing the basket details and then uses a style sheet to transform the XML to HTML. Once again, the transformation output is sent straight to the browser.

Note that here when we instantiate the proxy class for the BasketService, we have to reference localhost1. Of course to avoid worrying about which localhostX folder we are referencing, we could add appropriate using statements to the page, although for simplicity we haven't here.

```
public void showBasket()
{

  // Get XML for this category or Item
  localhost1.BasketService objBasketService =
                                  new localhost1.BasketService();
  XmlDocument objBasket = new XmlDocument();

  objBasket.LoadXml (objBasketService.getBasket(
      int.Parse(Session["basketID"].ToString())).OuterXml);

  XPathNavigator objBasketNav = objBasket.CreateNavigator();
  XslTransform objTransform = new XslTransform();
  objTransform.Load (Server.MapPath("showBasket.xslt"));

  objTransform.Transform (objBasketNav,null,Response.Output);
}
```

The showBasket.xslt does a little more work than its counterparts in catalogue.aspx, so we'll take a closer look at the style sheet:

```
<?xml version="1.0" encoding="UTF-8" ?>
<xsl:stylesheet version="1.0" xmlns:xsl="http://www.w3.org/1999/XSL/Transform"
xmlns:fo="http://www.w3.org/1999/XSL/Format">
  <xsl:output method="html" />
```

Things start to happen when we match on Basket:

```
<xsl:template match="Basket">
  <p align="left" class="detailTitle">Basket Details</p>
  <p align="left">
    <table width="90%" border="0" cellpadding="2" cellspacing="2">
      <thead>
        <tr>
          <th>SKU</th>
          <th>Item</th>
          <th>Qty</th>
          <th>Price</th>
          <th>Total</th>
        </tr>
      </thead>
      <tbody>
        <xsl:apply-templates select="Item"/>
        <tr class="tblRow0">
          <td colspan="4" align="right">Total</td>
          <td align="right">$<xsl:value-of select=
            "format-number(@basketTotal,'###,##0.00')"/></td>
        </tr>
      </tbody>
    </table>
  </p>
</xsl:template>
```

In the Item template, we are going to hook up the ItemName as a link to the item detail page and create a form around each quantity, so we kick-off the adjusting of a quantity with an onchange event:

```
<xsl:template match="Item">
  <tr class="tblRow1">
    <td valign="top">
      <xsl:value-of select="SKU" />
    </td>
    <td valign="top">
      <a class="itemLink">
      <xsl:attribute name="href">
      catalogue.aspx?item=<xsl:value-of select="ItemID" />
      </xsl:attribute>
      <xsl:value-of select="ItemName" />
      </a>
    </td>
    <td valign="top" align="right">
```

A form is generated around the quantity field: a QueryString is used on the action URL so that basket.aspx knows that this is an update. The hidden field is used to relay to basket.aspx the ItemID of the item we want to update:

```
    <form method="post" action="basket.aspx?action=update">
      <input type="hidden" name="txtItemID">
        <xsl:attribute name="value">
          <xsl:value-of select="ItemID"/>
        </xsl:attribute>
      </input>
      <input type="text" name="txtQty" size="3" maxlength="3"
                                       onchange="submit()">
        <xsl:attribute name="value">
          <xsl:value-of select="Qty" />
        </xsl:attribute>
      </input>
    </form>
  </td>

  <td valign="top" align="right">
```

Use the `format-number` function to format our prices:

```
    $<xsl:value-of select="format-number(ItemPrice,'###,##0.00')" />
  </td>
  <td valign="top" align="right">
    $<xsl:value-of select="format-number(LineValue,'###,##0.00')" />
  </td>
  </tr>
 </xsl:template>
</xsl:stylesheet>
```

The above style sheet produces the following output:

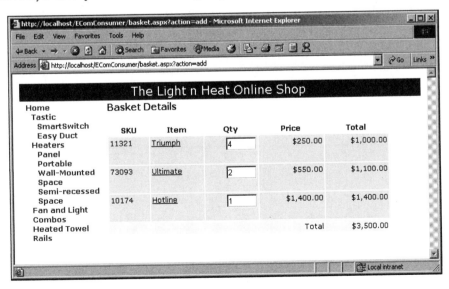

Now we have catalogue navigation with basket capabilities and, although we could go on, this should provide enough insight for further experimentation.

Summary

Web Services continue to be the major talking point in web development today and probably rightly so. If you can get beyond the stock quote (the "Hello World" of this particular area), you can see that they really do have enormous potential for distributed computing and application integration. In this case study we have looked a distributed computing approach that is only possible with Web Services: the majority of the business-logic layer and the data layer are running remotely on servers that could be located anywhere in the world with only the presentation layer, that is the user interface (in our consumer example, a web site) operating locally.

What makes this all possible is the use and adoption of XML coupled with ever increasing bandwidth. XML is now the predominant format for data exchange between organizations and all the major Web Services specifications, SOAP, WSDL, and UDDI, use XML as their grammar. .NET does its part by making the building and consuming of Web Services as straightforward as programming with regular classes and COM components.

We have tried to cover a fair amount of ground quickly in this case study to show the possibilities of this type of approach, but obviously we have really only scratched the surface. Also bear in mind that Web Services are still evolving as attempts are made to add transactional capabilities, security, and enhanced messaging such as guaranteed delivery.

There are a great many improvements that could be made to the engine if time and scope allowed. We have not attempted to restrict access to our service, provide any transaction support, or caching, and our error handling has been left to SOAP and is, therefore, extremely generic. As already mentioned, such an engine would not be implemented commercially using a database such as Microsoft Access 2000 – with its far-reaching support for XML, SQL Server 2000 would be the first choice with its ability to return XML directly from a SQL query and its updategram capabilities.

If this case study has in any way whet your appetite for Web Services, and we certainly hope that it has, then we would strongly urge you to take a look at a dedicated Web Services title such as *Professional ASP.NET 1.0 Web Services with VB.NET* (ISBN 1-86100-775-2) also from Wrox Press.

Index

A Guide to the Index

The index is arranged hierarchically, in alphabetical order, with symbols preceding the letter A. Most second-level entries and many third-level entries also occur as first-level entries. This is to ensure that users will find the information they require however they choose to search for it.

X

435

Notes

Notes

ASP Today

The daily knowledge site for professional ASP programmers

ASPToday brings the essence of the Wrox Programmer to Programmer philosophy to you through the web. Every working day, www.asptoday.com delivers a new, original article by ASP programmers for ASP programmers.

Want to know about Classic ASP, ASP.NET, Performance, Data Access, Site Design, SQL Server, and more? Then visit us. You can make sure that you don't miss a thing by subscribing to our free daily e-mail updates featuring ASPToday highlights and tips.

By bringing you daily articles written by real programmers, ASPToday is an indispensable resource for quickly finding out exactly what you need. ASPToday is THE daily knowledge site for professional ASP programmers.

In addition to our free weekly and monthly articles, ASPToday also includes a premier subscription service. You can now join the growing number of ASPToday subscribers who benefit from access to:

- Daily in-depth articles
- Code-heavy demonstrations of real applications
- Access to the ASPToday Living Book, our collection of past articles
- ASP reference material
- Fully searchable index and advanced search engine
- Tips and tricks for professionals

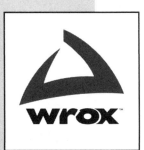

Visit ASPToday at: www.asptoday.com

p2p.wrox.com
The programmer's resource centre

A unique free service from Wrox Press
With the aim of helping programmers to help each other

Wrox Press aims to provide timely and practical information to today's programmer. P2P is a list server offering a host of targeted mailing lists where you can share knowledge with four fellow programmers and find solutions to your problems. Whatever the level of your programming knowledge, and whatever technology you use P2P can provide you with the information you need.

ASP
Support for beginners and professionals, including a resource page with hundreds of links, and a popular ASP.NET mailing list.

DATABASES
For database programmers, offering support on SQL Server, mySQL, and Oracle.

MOBILE
Software development for the mobile market is growing rapidly. We provide lists for the several current standards, including WAP, Windows CE, and Symbian.

JAVA
A complete set of Java lists, covering beginners, professionals, and server-side programmers (including JSP, servlets and EJBs)

.NET
Microsoft's new OS platform, covering topics such as ASP.NET, C#, and general .NET discussion.

VISUAL BASIC
Covers all aspects of VB programming, from programming Office macros to creating components for the .NET platform.

WEB DESIGN
As web page requirements become more complex, programmer's are taking a more important role in creating web sites. For these programmers, we offer lists covering technologies such as Flash, Coldfusion, and JavaScript.

XML
Covering all aspects of XML, including XSLT and schemas.

OPEN SOURCE
Many Open Source topics covered including PHP, Apache, Perl, Linux, Python and more.

FOREIGN LANGUAGE
Several lists dedicated to Spanish and German speaking programmers, categories include. NET, Java, XML, PHP and XML

How to subscribe:
Simply visit the P2P site, at http://p2p.wrox.com/

Got more Wrox books than you can carry around?

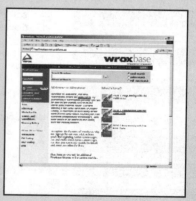

wrox

Programmer to Programmer™

Registration Code: 72485344VF9OU501

Wrox writes books for you. Any suggestions, or ideas about how you want
information given in your ideal book will be studied by our team.
Your comments are always valued at Wrox.

Free phone in USA 800-USE-WROX
Fax (312) 893 8001

UK Tel.: (0121) 687 4100   Fax: (0121) 687 4101

Professional ASP.NET 1.0 XML with C# – Registration Card

Name _____

Address _____

_____

_____

City _____ State/Region _____

Country _____ Postcode/Zip _____

E-Mail _____

Occupation _____

How did you hear about this book?

❏ Book review (name) _____

❏ Advertisement (name) _____

❏ Recommendation _____

❏ Catalog _____

❏ Other _____

Where did you buy this book?

❏ Bookstore (name) _____ City _____

❏ Computer store (name) _____

❏ Mail order _____

❏ Other _____

What influenced you in the purchase of this book?

❏ Cover Design ❏ Contents ❏ Other (please specify):

_____

How did you rate the overall content of this book?

❏ Excellent ❏ Good ❏ Average ❏ Poor

What did you find most useful about this book? _____

_____

What did you find least useful about this book? _____

_____

Please add any additional comments. _____

_____

What other subjects will you buy a computer book on soon? _____

What is the best computer book you have used this year? _____

Note: This information will only be used to keep you updated
about new Wrox Press titles and will not be used for
any other purpose or passed to any other third party.

wrox

Programmer to Programmer™

Note: If you post the bounce back card below in the UK, please send it to:

Wrox Press Limited, Arden House, 1102 Warwick Road,
Acocks Green, Birmingham B27 6HB. UK.

Computer Book Publishers